Rebels with a Cause

Laws framed by man are either just or unjust. If they be just, they have the power of binding a conscience.
—St. Thomas Aquinas,
"Treatise on Law," in *Summa Theologica* (1273)

Must the citizen even for a moment, or in the least degree, resign his conscience to the legislator? Why has every man a conscience, then?
—Henry David Thoreau,
On the Duty of Civil Disobedience (1849)

My conscience hath a thousand tongues . . .
—William Shakespeare,
Richard III, act V, scene iii (1592)

Rebels with a Cause

The Minds and Morality of Political Offenders

Nicholas N. Kittrie

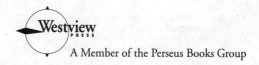

A Member of the Perseus Books Group

Published in 2000 in the United States of America by Westview Press, 5500 Central Avenue, Boulder, Colorado 80301-2877, and in the United Kingdom by Westview Press, 12 Hid's Copse Road, Cumnor Hill, Oxford OX2 9JJ.

Find us on the World Wide Web at www.westviewpress.com

Library of Congress Cataloging-in-Publication Data
Kittrie, Nicholas N., 1930–
    Rebels with a cause : the minds and morality of political
offenders / Nicholas N. Kittrie.
        p.   cm.
    Includes bibliographical references and index.
    ISBN 0-8133-6849-9
    1. Political crimes and offenses.   I. Title.
HV6254.K58   1999
364.1'3—dc21   99-32828
                                                                         CIP

The paper used in this publication meets the requirements of the American National Standard for Permanence of Paper for Printed Library Materials Z39.48-1984.

10   9   8   7   6   5   4   3   2   1

For my children
Orde Felix, Norda Nicole,
Zachary McNair, and David

Contents

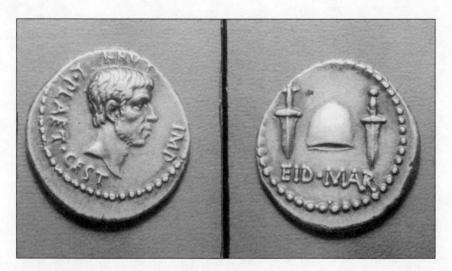

Roman coin struck in 43 B.C., during the rule of Brutus, canonizing one of history's most infamous acts, the murder of Julius Caesar in 44 B.C. The obverse of the coin depicts the head of Brutus. The reverse shows a cap known as a plieus, a Roman symbol of liberty, flanked by two daggers. Beneath these symbols are the initials EID MAR, the Ides of March. Thus the day, the means, the rationale, and the perpetrator of this act are all depicted on the coin.

Preface

Confronting the Political Offender

*In considering the insanity of power, we may look at it
in two ways, the madness of the tyrant in abusing it
and the madness of the people in submitting to it.*
—W. W. Ireland, *The Blot upon the Brain* (1870)

*It is organized violence at the top which
creates individual violence at the bottom.*
—Emma Goldman, *My Disillusionment in Russia* (1923)

*So long as the superstition that a man should
obey unjust laws exists, so long will their slavery exist.*
—Mohandas K. Gandhi,
"Satyagraha, or Passive Resistance," in *Non-Violent Resistance* (1948)

The Profusion and Confusion of Labels

Civil disobedients. Conscientious objectors. Dissidents. Fanatics. Freedom fighters. Fundamentalists. Militants. Political prisoners. Pseudopoliticals. Rebels. Regicides. Resisters. Revolutionaries. Terrorists. Garbed in coats of different colors, all are passionately driven by assertions of irreconcilable wrongs or unattainable rights. Challenging their national or local institutions of authority—political or economic, social or religious—but increasingly reaching beyond international boundaries and oceans to strike at distant adversaries, political offenders have become specters of chaos and dread.

No sooner had five of America's recent and notorious political violence trials come to a close—Timothy J. McVeigh and Terry L.
Nichols convicted for the Oklahoma City carnage, Ramzi Yousef
found guilty for masterminding the New York World Trade Center
bombing, Mir Aimal Kansi sentenced for the killings in front of the
CIA's Virginia headquarters, and Unabomber Ted Kaczynski entering a plea bargain for a national campaign of terror launched from
his Montana cabin—than new mindless murders were committed
against the security police of the U.S. Capitol. Throughout the
world—in Congo and Kenya, Rwanda and Saudi Arabia, Kashmir
and Sri Lanka, the Kurdish lands and Russia's Chechnya, Corsica
and former Yugoslavia—even more wrenching eruptions of political
unrest and bloodletting forecast the discontents of the coming millennium.

◇　　◇　　◇

After Nelson Mandela, a onetime political offender convicted of
treason, was released from prison and later assumed the presidency
of South Africa in 1994, he was besieged by pleas of amnesty from
other South Africans similarly confined for acts of political protest,
violence, and rebellion.[1] Particularly difficult for Mandela, who set
out not only to dismantle apartheid but also to heal the country's old
wounds, were the claims of two inmates sitting on Pretoria prison's
death row. The first, Robert McBride, a "colored" member of the
militant African National Front, had been convicted of planting a
bomb in a residential Durban street, killing three white women in
June 1986. The second, Barend Strydom, a white member of the
racist Afrikaner Resistance Movement, had been found guilty of
shooting to death eight blacks in Pretoria in November 1988.

Should the two—one an opponent of apartheid and the other its
advocate—be entitled to equal consideration? Who is the freedom
fighter and who is the terrorist? Could South Africa's struggling new
government, or the world community as a whole, agree upon an explicit line of demarcation between the two? Ultimately, President
Mandela freed both killers in the interest of his country's "new justice," but how satisfactory is a justice driven by political compromise and expediency?[2]

No less difficult dilemmas have been faced by the government of
Israel in its quest for accommodation and peace with its former

nemesis, the Palestine Liberation Organization. Hundreds of Palestinian inmates convicted of political crimes against Israel and its population were released from prison as a goodwill gesture toward Yassir Arafat's new regime. Following the release, Israel's government was urged to free scores of Israeli Jews convicted of anti-Palestinian vigilantism. Taking part in a heated parliamentary debate, Israel's Minister of Justice, David Libai, voiced in 1994 the growing concern that while Palestinian marauders guilty of serious acts of violence against Israelis had been released from prison, Jewish extremists convicted of like crimes against Palestinians had not benefited from such amnesty.[3]

Should both camps of South Africans, as well as the Palestinian and Israeli political offenders, be treated alike? Do some deserve continued punishment and the others exoneration? No existing code of laws, treatise, or even fragmentary jurisprudential doctrine has thus far advanced an acceptable solution to this and similar dilemmas emerging not only in Israel and South Africa but also elsewhere throughout the world.

It is to two prevailing extreme doctrinal positions, both central to understanding the questions posed above, that this volume is addressed. The first is the position that actors who claim to be motivated by ideology and conscience (often popularly referred to as "political prisoners," "prisoners of conscience," or "political offenders")[4] cannot and should not be differentiated from common criminals. The second position is expressed in the jaded aphorism, still given credence not only in the marketplace of politics but also within the ivy-covered walls of academia, that "one person's freedom fighter is another's terrorist." This pretentiously sophisticated yet in fact simplistic proposition conveys the disheartening dogma that the causes and motives that drive people into protest and militant action do not matter, and that, in any event, the righteousness or evil of a political cause or action is exclusively a matter for subjective judgment. It is this allegedly "value-free" yet in fact nihilistic conclusion—that in matters of politics no universal truths can be discerned—that this volume sets out to challenge.

Pejorative as well as laudatory labels and appellations, be they "terrorist," "tyrant," and "dictator," or, conversely, "political prisoner," "asylum seeker," and "freedom fighter," are potent instruments in the struggle between competing political camps. Often they are indiscriminately used by contesting parties to either dignify or vilify, reward or punish, both the labelers and their adversaries. Frequently, labels and appellations not only describe what people already are but further help determine what they might become.

These badges and designations carry considerable weight in the implementation of national policies and laws, whether with regard to the regulation and control, prosecution and defense, sentencing, extradition, or amnesty of political opponents. These labels often play an equally important role in international affairs and laws. The United States, as well as other nations that serve as hosts for foreign refugees and, increasingly, as participants in missions of humanitarian intervention abroad, must avoid being befuddled not only by the claims of their homegrown political offenders, but also by the pleas of hoards of alleged political asylum seekers approaching their shores or borders in quest of haven.

The United States and other nations that proclaim adherence to humanitarian commitments must learn to tell whether those knocking on their gates engage in flight from political tyranny, constitute merely poverty-ridden populations in search of economic betterment, or are made up, instead, of former tyrants, thugs, and concentration camp guards, seeking shelter from just punishment. With labels and classifications exerting such great power, cannot objective criteria be developed to distinguish the freedom fighter from the terrorist? The honest resister to abuse of power from the iniquitous pursuer of absolute and brutal power? For separating the victim of governmental abuse from the seeker of totalitarian dominance over others? The one who engages in self-defense against evil authority from the venal actor who views all society as his or her nemesis?

Conventional wisdom continues to insist that there are no sound and universal tests, founded on law, morality, or even simple common sense, for deciding whether given individuals are to be deemed common criminals or political offenders, terrorists or their victims. No objective test, the argument insists, can determine who are to be embraced as political heroes worthy of asylum, who are to be rejected as illegal immigrants, and who are to be detained and punished as international criminals. This volume advances a contrary approach to address and help remedy the prevailing uncertainty and confusion regarding the classification and treatment of political offenders. This ongoing confusion frequently continues to serve only the ideological proclivities of those in power, who by leaving the criteria of political criminality unchartered remain free to assert, like Humpty Dumpty in *Through the Looking Glass:* "When I use a word . . . it means just what I choose it to mean—neither more nor less."

Even the apparently straightforward actions of such a politically disgruntled offender as Timothy J. McVeigh, convicted in 1997 of bombing the Alfred P. Murrah Federal Building in Oklahoma City, remained unexplored and unexplained by either the prosecution or his defense team. It seemed clear from the evidence that McVeigh and his alleged co-conspirator, Terry L. Nichols, intended to blow up the building out of fanatic hatred for the U.S. governmental establishment. But where did this hatred come from and why did it take such a murderous form? The jury, judge, and attorneys did not attempt to find out. Michael Tigar, noted criminal defense lawyer and counsel to Nichols, pointed out after the McVeigh verdict that the jurors claimed never to have understood the motives and mindset of the defendant.[5] Tigar considered this lack of understanding as the McVeigh trial's greatest failure. One could readily agree that so long as lawmakers, lawyers, juries, and the public ignore the unique character, mission, and zeal of political offenders, society will never be able to prevent their offenses or respond to them effectively.

The Escalation of Domestic Strife

The labels that the media, scholars, legislatures, and law enforcement practitioners attach to political dissidents and rebels (as well as to the public policies and practices sprouting from these labels) would not be as critical in a less politically volatile world. But ours is a globe rife with political conflict and disorder. Numerous undeclared yet unceasing civil and domestic contests for political power, legitimacy, and world sympathy rage around us as the twentieth century draws to a close. Today, more countries than ever before—North and South, East and West—are being torn asunder by internal conflicts and communal violence. Nearly one-third of all independent states are experiencing wrenching and divisive domestic contests among citizens, communities, and governments.[6]

The battlegrounds are many. The struggles take place in politically and economically mature countries and in underdeveloped or developing ones, in nations with long democratic traditions and in those merely emerging from the yokes of colonialism, totalitarianism, and authoritarianism. In the United States they take place in front of embattled abortion clinics, in urban ghettoes, in schools, on roads, and in subways. They are revealed in the rising smoke of burning crosses, in desecrated houses of worship, in governmental sieges of dissident encampments, in bombed-out federal buildings.

The warriors' weapons are diverse—from nerve gas to suicide bombs, from open mass rallies to underground seditious posters, from antiquated duplicating machines to elusive well-equipped militias. At different times and in different places the combatants, whether scrabbling to retain power or aspiring to seize it, have threatened and subjected one another to imprisonment, torture, expulsion, rape, terror, mass murder, and other regrettably common types of violence. Yet the fiercest struggle is often the one for the hearts and minds of the public and the media, local and global.

Public opinion and the granting or withholding of its support have become increasingly critical to both political offenders and their oppressors as this century draws to a close. During the earlier decades of this century the campaign against foreign and colonial rule and for self-determination loomed as a generally laudable lodestar on the political agenda of the world community. But most of this global struggle against colonialism and for self-rule and autonomy has given way in recent times to internal battles within countries for the maintenance of the status quo or even for retrogression, for political, social, and economic reform and change, or for repression.

Emerging from long-festering political, religious, ethnic, social, or economic grievances, these domestic conflicts are often rekindled by new incidents and aspirations. Many of those mounting the barricades in local struggles may invoke such revolutionary slogans as America's "life, liberty, and the pursuit of happiness" or France's "liberty, equality, and fraternity." Others may be urged on by different or narrower orthodoxies: historical claims, divine rights, tribalism, ethnicism, racism, religious fundamentalism, totalitarianism, Marxism-Maoism, or some other brand of absolutism. Whatever rationale is advanced by the protagonists, the common denominator of most contemporary conflicts appears to be the eternal conflict between those in possession of political power and those who aspire to it.[7]

More of the U.N. Security Council's time is now spent addressing civil wars than addressing the international conflicts that were supposed to be the core of its business.[8] Internal strife has thoroughly contaminated contemporary politics worldwide. Political commentator Pranay Gupte attributes this epidemic of domestic unrest to an overall decline in the cohesive power of the modern state. He asserts that several of the long-established European, Latin American, and Asian states, not to mention the young postcolonial countries of Asia, Africa, and the Americas, are "confronted with the depressing reality that in countries that are multi-ethnic and multicultural, the most riveting issues" and loyalties are "often and increasingly communal and tribal, not national."[9]

There is a growing and urgent need to formalize the response of the United States and of other nations professing adherence to democratic principles, to those individuals and communities who choose to resort to proscribed means in their struggles for greater political, social, and economic rights, or even for mere survival. Should the community of nations continue to accord deference to the unbending principles of national sovereignty, leaving the fate of domestic political activists to the mercy of their governments, even when domestic laws and practices collide with the growing international call for the primacy of individual human rights? As the gap widens between the free and the oppressed, between the elites and the masses, between the economically strong and the economically hopeless, how should nations committed to stability and to orderly politics of reform respond to the worldwide unrest brought about by modern-day claimants to the mantles of William Tell and Robin Hood?

With few exceptions, the escalating global challenge to political power and authority has not received the necessary scrutiny from the academic disciplines: psychology and sociology, criminology and law, history and international relations, politics and military science. Not only scholars and communications media but also governments have proven unable or, more ominously, unwilling to formulate coherent, morally consistent, responsible, and effective responses to the turmoil posed by political offenders, who usually proclaim themselves agents of justice, equality, autonomy, historical rights, or some other ideology or divine conviction. So gross and lasting has been the past neglect of "political criminals" and their "political crimes" that not until 1979 did *Webster's New Collegiate Dictionary* define or even list "political" criminality.

Political Offenders and the Global Crisis of Legitimacy

The research for this volume began over a decade and a half ago in an effort to document and understand the unheralded role of political rebels and dissidents in America's historical quest for political and civil justice. The outcome of that initial undertaking is contained in a compilation I coedited with Eldon D. Wedlock Jr., *The Tree of Liberty: A Documentary History of Rebellion and Political Crime in America.*[10]

At the conclusion of that inquiry into the rebellious domestic history of the United States, it became clear that there existed not merely an American but a global escalation of political dissent and resistance that could no longer be ignored. Political crime and rebellion were not simply occasional or New World aberrations but endemic events worldwide. Moreover, what often commenced as domestic or local struggles against authority (whether by disgruntled and alienated loners or by ethnic, racial, or other subnational communities) were increasingly spilling over into the international arena, affecting the security and well-being of the larger community of nations.

It was the recognition of the widespread character of these domestic struggles throughout the world that led to my second volume, *The War Against Authority: From the Crisis of Legitimacy to a New Social Contract.*[11] Delving into foreign and international history and law, and resorting to political, sociological, psychological, and philosophical writings and data, *The War Against Authority* identified a currently escalating global crisis of political legitimacy. After analyzing the current crisis in light of the historical, indeed perpetual, conflict between the forces of authority (sometimes ruling benevolently but often resorting to abuses of power) and their political adversaries (whether liberators of humanity or mere destroyers of order), I advocated avenues for the renewal of the public trust in governance, including the replacement of bureaucratic and elitist structures with more decentralized and pluralistic political institutions and processes.

The most difficult assignment remained for *Rebels with a Cause*. The task is to portray and explain the puzzling complexity of political offenders—their minds, motives, morality, deeds, and standing under international and domestic law. Critical to this task is an understanding of the political offender's natural habitat: the confusing and muddy borderland territories where politics, criminality, and warfare often overlap.

Rebels with a Cause begins with an exploration of the diverse and often contradictory facets of the political offender. Next is a review of the emergence of this unique class of offender, with assessment of their societal roles and their treatment by those in power. The account of the disparate roles played by political offenders in the development of Western as well as non-Western societies, politics, and law is followed with a review of previous attempts to define political criminality and assess its history. From these historical and definitional origins, the discussion proceeds to an analytical survey of the political offender's contemporary status in national as well as international law. Finally, the volume introduces a comprehensive classification system to aid with the identification, categorization, and treatment of the diverse and complex community known as political offenders, a group that has been playing a critical role in what continues to be a less than perfect, less than just, and less than well-ordered world.

At the outset, the reader must be alerted as to what this volume is and is not. It is a multidisciplinary exploration of the historical and theoretical underpinnings of political criminality, the political offender, and societal responses to them. It is not a comprehensive historical work nor a legal treatise; although some events, cases, and offenders are examined in depth, most are referred to, if at all, in passing. This volume does not seek to document or examine state terrorism or abuse of power, a topic I addressed in *The War Against Authority*. Generally, this volume does not examine the specifics of the criminal process against political offenders: surveillance, arrests, trials, sentencing, and imprisonment. These topics are reserved for later volumes and other authors.

In no way is *Rebels with a Cause* intended to be an indiscriminate endorsement of the extralegal and sometimes violent means used to secure self-proclaimed or even internationally acknowledged rights. In evaluating the conflicting claims of those in power and their antagonists, one must always remain mindful that resort to proscribed political means is a double-edged sword, capable of serving oppression and tyranny as well as advancing liberty and justice. Individuals and communities must therefore be constantly on guard against the escalation of political rhetoric and militant action, whether by those in authority or by those defying it, since extremism can and often will deteriorate into mindless, indiscriminate, and pathological violence and terror.

Nicholas N. Kittrie
Ramsbridge Farm
Leesburg, Virginia

Acknowledgments

As with *The Tree of Liberty* and *The War Against Authority*, I wish to thank the many organizations and individuals without whose assistance this trilogy could not have been completed. The National Endowment for the Humanities provided assistance for the initiation of this work, permitting me unencumbered time to plan my research during a visiting professorship at the London School of Economics. The National Institute of Justice of the United States Department of Justice granted me a fellowship in residence, allowing me to compile much of my data and complete an early draft of this manuscript. For the next decade, my field research for this volume was carried out in the United States as well as abroad—in Egypt, Germany, Guatemala, Hungary, Israel, Italy, the Ivory Coast, Japan, Korea, Kenya, Lebanon, Mexico, the Philippines, Poland, El Salvador, the (now former) Soviet Union, Thailand, Togo, Ukraine, and the United Kingdom.

The work has benefited from the assistance and counsel of many students, colleagues, and friends, including Christina Cerna, H. H. A. Cooper, Franco Ferracuti, Robert Goldman, Matthew Lippman, Fahmy Saadi, and Stephen Schafer. Former deans Thomas Buergenthal and Elliott Milstein and presiding dean Claudio Grossman of the American University Law School generously supported the various stages of this undertaking. My sons Orde and Zachary Kittrie have been responsible for some suggestions and editing, and my daughter Norda Nicole has helped with illustrations and graphic advice. Beth Levenson participated in the earliest editorial work. Professor Eldon D. Wedlock of the University of South Carolina, coeditor of *The Tree of Liberty,* successfully undertook the task of revising several earlier drafts of *Rebels with a Cause* and contributed significantly to its advanced versions. Brad Flecke, Anthi Jones,

Robert K. Morrow, Philip Mueller, James Didden Jr., Ann-Marie Kagy, William Hurlock, and Jennifer Hentz participated in the research and updating of the work. David Trieloff, whose promising career was prematurely cut short, and John Nahajzer played important and creative roles during the early stages of the editing, and Alan Fisher was ultimately responsible for the final and most difficult stages of the rewriting and comprehensive editing.

Grateful acknowledgment is due to several members of the staff at the United States National Institute of Justice, particularly Winifred Reed and Patrick Langan. Finally, one could barely enumerate the exceptional services of Georgette J. Sobel, without whose good humored and nourishing, yet energetic and unrelenting management, neither the research nor the final volume itself could have been completed. The responsibilities of typing and supervising the early and final drafts of this manuscript were discharged patiently, cheerfully, and effectively by Martin Ernst, Katharine Lukianoff, Kriselda V. P. Valderrama, Linda Clark, Ana Granados, Bernard Stokes, Donna Bradley, Elma Gates, Michelle Chapman, Sharon Huie, Tracy Vervelde, Robert J. Kelso, and lastly, and with great distinction, Mark Williams.

Finally, I wish to thank the entire staff of Westview Press, under the direction of Leo A.W. Wiegman, executive editor, for its devotion and assistance in seeing this project to its timely fruition.

N.N.K.

Credits

Who's the Illegal Alien, Pilgrim? Yolanda M. Lopez, offset lithograph (printed in 1981).

Rebels with a Cause

Prologue

In the Eyes of the Beholders: Heroes or Rogues?

The defining mark of the state is authority, the right to rule. The primary obligation of man is autonomy, the refusal to be ruled.

—Robert Paul Wolff,
In Defense of Anarchy (1990)

The struggle between Liberty and Authority is the most conspicuous feature in . . . history.

—John Stuart Mill,
On Liberty (1859)

Woe unto them who call evil good, and good evil.

—Isaiah 5:20

The Eternal Struggle Between
Authority and Autonomy

"We want our rights and we don't know how; we want our revolution and want it NOW," sings an impetuous chorus in *The Persecution and Assassination of Jean-Paul Marat*,[12] Peter Weiss's drama of political warfare and terror in revolutionary France. To secure those rights, the infamous Bastille (long reputed as the repository of the monarchy's staunchest political enemies) was stormed on July 14, 1789, marking the beginning of the French Revolution. In confinement were found, surprisingly, only seven prisoners, including two certified lunatics, all of whom were released.[13] Within three years the fruits of this revolution were offered to the rest of the world. By November 19, 1792, even before the execution of Louis XVI and Marie Antoinette, the National Convention of France issued a proclamation offering assistance to people of all nations who wished to overthrow their unworthy governments in the pursuit of "liberty."[14]

During a three-month political purge in 1793, more than 15,000 suspected "counterrevolutionaries" were guillotined or drowned in the city of Nantes alone in the purported defense of the revolution and its French motherland.[15] More than 129,000 of France's most prominent citizens fled the country during the sectarian warfare and anarchy that ensued.[16] In the end, the revolution that proclaimed the triple goals of "liberté," "égalité," and "fraternité" provoked political fratricide of unequaled proportions, ignited an all-consuming "Reign of Terror," and forestalled true French democracy for half a century.[17]

In the more than two hundred years since revolutionary France's historic Declaration of the Rights of Man and the Citizen in 1789, and in the more than fifty years since the U.N.'s more contemporary Universal Declaration of Human Rights in 1948, new veneers of civilization and order have been applied to cover humanity's naked brutishness and to mask the continuing tyranny of power. Slavery has been universally banned and racism is today in disrepute. Autocratic monarchy has virtually disappeared, while republicanism, professing democratic and popular goals, has become the model, if not always the reality, for modern states. National self-determination has become the lodestar of world order, and the community of

3

sovereign nations has grown from fewer than 50 to more than 180 members.

The once radical doctrines of the rights of man, which sparked the American and French Revolutions, have become the solemnly intoned political beliefs of the new world. Aggressive war has purportedly been outlawed,[18] and the conduct of armed conflict has been regulated in the interest of humanitarianism.[19] Moreover, rigidly confining nationalism has been rejected in favor of international and regional cooperation, which has been not only widely proclaimed but at times actually practiced.

Despite these distinct advances, many nations, peoples, and minorities still lack fundamental rights and liberties, and more than half of the world's people continue to live under governments that persecute, imprison, and otherwise punish those suspected of political opposition or dissidence.[20] Not surprisingly, the liberating doctrines proclaimed and initially advanced in the revolutions of the past two centuries have raised still more subtle and critical questions concerning the rights of the people and the duties of governments. Defined as "life, liberty, and the pursuit of happiness" by the American Declaration of Independence and as "liberty, equality, and fraternity" by the French Declaration of the Rights of Man and the Citizen, these "natural" or "fundamental" rights may be intractably at odds with one other. Does the implementation of equality contradict the right to liberty? Can the pursuit of equality and fraternity justify dissent and rebellion against defaulting governments and underlying socioeconomic systems in the same way that the political quest for liberty can?[21] What means are permitted to those seeking to implement these rights in the face of militant opposition? How should members of minority or otherwise deprived communities, be they ethnic, religious, racial, or cultural, protect themselves individually and collectively against oppression or extinction? And when the "rights" of different groups or communities are in conflict, who is to decide between competing claims to autonomy, liberty, equality, and justice? Moreover, under what circumstances may groups or communities lay the claim to self-determination and even ultimate sovereignty through secession from a recognized nation?

Other critical questions also remain unanswered. Who is to protect the fundamental human rights and identities (ethnic, political,

religious, social, or economic) of a citizen or a group when the op-
pressor is their own government? Are there civilized rules and enforcement mechanisms (national or multinational) that can restrain
governmental abuse of state power? Are citizens who take up arms
in internal conflicts against authority entitled to foreign sanctuary or
to the safeguards historically available to lawful belligerents in international warfare?

These and other unresolved issues continue to fester in the heart of
the world community and account for the exacerbation of many of
the domestic and transnational tensions that erupt around us. Governmental abuse of power and its more virulent manifestation, state
terror, continue to plague the peoples and nations of the world. In
response, oppressed individuals and communities have not ceased
their struggles against both real and imagined wrongs, and for vary-
ing notions of life, liberty, equality, fraternity, and the pursuit of
happiness.

The vanguard of this struggle, deemed patriots or freedom fighters
by some and traitors or terrorists by others, cannot be readily classified or judged. Passionately challenging the legitimacy of the extant
political, religious, or socioeconomic orders, proclaiming the higher
morality of their own ends, and blatantly refusing to forswear either
illegal means or violence in the pursuit of their goals, political offenders are at the center of the crucible of modern politics, morality,
and justice. Viewing themselves as soldiers of just wars,[22] these men
and women have shaken conventional notions of politics, morality,
criminology, warfare, and law.

Political dissidents and rebels enjoy an ancient and often illustrious heritage that includes Greece's Socrates, the Bible's young David
(rebelling against King Saul), Rome's Brutus, Switzerland's William
Tell, England's Oliver Cromwell, France's Charlotte Corday, Latin
America's Simon Bolivar, America's John Brown, China's Sun Yat-
Sen, India's Mohandas Gandhi, and Kenya's Jomo Kenyatta. In contemporary politics and society the political offender has been similarly represented by such disparate dramatis personae as the former
Soviet Union's Andrei Sakharov,[23] Northern Ireland's Bobby Sands,
the Palestine Liberation Organization's Yasser Arafat, Germany's Ulricke Meinhof, South Africa's Nelson Mandela, and Zimbabwe's
Joshua Nkomo. In recent years America's cast of self-proclaimed rebellious characters has included figures as dramatically different as

Martin Luther King Jr., Malcolm X, Angela Davis, Sirhan Sirhan, John W. Hinckley Jr., Lt. Col. Oliver North, Timothy J. McVeigh, and Ted Kaczynski, the Unabomber.

Millions of uncelebrated "dissidents," "protesters," "resistance groups," "guerrillas," "freedom fighters," and "terrorists" throughout the world also claim the mantle of the political offender. These men and women, professing loyalty to a divine or higher law, to the call of individual conscience, or to the imperatives of some perceived public good, have challenged the legitimacy and authority of the institutions of their governments. Whether resisting objectionable laws and procedures, or struggling against the very existence of government itself, the political offender is usually pitted in a relentless war against authority and its aiders and abettors.

Gnawing at the roots of the modern state and public order, political dissidents have increasingly titillated popular interest and public concern. Yet neither the media nor the general public are certain how to respond to this unique and purposeful group of lawbreakers. Should political offenders be considered a special breed of criminal? Do their exploits justify their being accorded a folk hero–like status? Do individuals or groups indeed have the right (or duty) to take up arms against a government? Under what circumstances and with what limitations may one rise against those who oppress the community and its members or otherwise subvert divine, universal, or constitutional commandments?

The formulation of appropriate responses to the deeds or misdeeds of political offenders has been a complex task not only for philosophers and scholars worldwide, but also for the community of nations and most governments. In their domestic policies, how should governments and those in power respond to violent or otherwise legally impermissible challenges to their authority? Should the police, prosecutors, judges, and jailers recognize the political offender's assertion of "noble" motives? Should the punishments imposed on the political criminal differ in quantity or quality from those imposed on the common criminal? In dealing with domestic rebels, should governments be held, at the very least, to the civilized standards accorded to enemy citizens and soldiers in international war?

Advancing to the international arena, how should the world community respond to an oppressive and tyrannical regime? And how should it treat any country's citizens who, out of ideological convictions, disobey or resist the laws of the realm? Does the principle of sovereignty of nations prevent international intervention against countries that resort to abusive practices against their own people? Moreover, how should the law of nations treat refugees from an oppressive regime? Might political offenders be afforded international protection and asylum as "human rights activists" or "freedom fighters" within the boundaries of other nations, or should they be condemned by their hosts as offenders against both domestic and world public order?

Finally, one must consider the particular problems confronting neutral or "host" nations that result from the exportation of political criminality. Countries increasingly face the situation of their own citizens becoming victims of another nation's struggles, of their own towns and institutions becoming shelters for foreign warriors as well as battlegrounds for distant conflicts. How willing should any nation be to place the advancement of some fundamental ideology or of worldwide human rights and international morality above the protection of its own domestic tranquillity or the public order of other nations? Should the United Kingdom be praised or condemned for providing shelter to author Salman Rushdie, whom the authorities of Islamic Iran had sentenced to death for alleged heresy? Should France, in retrospect, have denied the asylum request of the Ayatollah Khomeini, who afterward imposed religious fundamentalism and oppression on his native Iran? And what is the responsibility of Afghanistan for permitting the launching from its territory of an international "Holy War" against so-called Crusaders and Jews throughout the world?

Variations on the Theme of Dissidence, Disobedience, and Rebellion

Both the means and the ends advanced by the political offender are riddled with paradoxes. Frequently, it is the political, moral, ideological, and religious predispositions of the offender's observers and judges that color their vision and judgment. Of the increasingly politicized society in America, art critic Richard Bernstein observed in a different context that "at times there seems to be no human truth anymore, only an ethnic truth or a racial truth."[24]

The perception of political dissidence has varied greatly according to period, place, society, and cultural outlook. By its supporters, political resistance has been viewed as a civic duty, as heroism, as the inevitable response to governmental corruption, as an antidote to abuse of power, as the rebellion of victims against their tormentors, as a protest against unjust law, and as obedience to the commands of higher or divine justice. It has been viewed by those in power, on the other hand, as treason, as heresy, as sacrilege, as anarchy, as individual conscience gone awry, as terrorism, and as insanity.

Much like the blind men in the ancient fable, each grasping a distinct part of the elephant and describing a different object, the viewers and judges of political criminality have addressed discrete dimensions of a broad and varied phenomenon with only partial vision of its reality. Seen in isolation, these disparate visions obscure the larger picture. Taken together, they provide a whole perspective of the proverbial animal—what John Stuart Mill described as the perpetual struggle between liberty and authority.[25]

Turning now to the consideration of several of these discrete visions of political crime, it is evident that they are not all-encompassing, nor are they meant to be. They are simply twelve examples of the unceasing struggle between the proponents and opponents of authority. They illuminate the interplay of crime and punishment, of intent and motive, of freedom and oppression, and show the disparate ways in which political crimes are perceived by their perpetrators, their victims, and the public.

Vision One: The Corruption of Power

"The sword came upon the world on account of the delay of justice and the perversion of justice," concluded Judah Hanassi, an ancient Judean sage. Lord Acton's warning that "power tends to corrupt and absolute power corrupts absolutely"[26] has known no geographic or historical boundaries.

No sooner had the American Pilgrims, themselves refugees from abuse of power, settled in Massachusetts Bay than they began to fiercely protect their newly acquired lands against "subversion" by fellow settlers. In 1658 so-called heretical Quakers were threatened with death for daring to venture north to preach their controversial version of the Gospel amongst the Pilgrims. Failing to heed previous warnings, Quaker Mary Dyer was convicted and promptly hanged.[27]

More widespread depredations, not in pursuit of religious cleansing but for the cause of national expansionism, were later visited by the colonists upon their Native American neighbors. In 1864, near the conclusion of an era of genocidal warfare against the Native Americans, members of the Colorado Militia under the command of J. M. Chivington (a Methodist minister in private life) attacked an unsuspecting camp of Cheyenne who previously had given up their arms in exchange for a promise of protection. Blatantly ignoring the Cheyenne's white flag of peace, the militia slaughtered and mutilated more than 450 men, women, and children. The dead and dying were scalped, and women's genitals were cut out and stuck on poles or worn in the soldiers' hats. A local newspaper characterized the event as "a brilliant feat of arms."[28]

Corruption and abuse of power have not been country-specific or historically constrained. They have prevailed throughout the world and through all periods of human history: from the ancient tyrants of Greece, Asia Minor, and Sicily to such later Roman dictators as Sulla, Nero, and Caligula; from the treacheries of the Middle Ages and the Renaissance to the "Reign of Terror" in revolutionary France; from the genocidal massacre of the Armenians in Turkey during and after World War I to the Japanese "Rape of Nanking" and the totalitarian and authoritarian despots and juntas of modern Europe, Africa, Asia, and Latin America; from the Nazi holocaust to the Stalinist elimination of more than 20 million Russian citizens through the regime's labor camps, forced collectivization programs, mass executions, and deliberately caused famines; from the genocide committed against the Mayan populations in the remote Cuchumatn highlands of Guatemala in the 1970s and 1980s to the extraordinary brutalities visited by Pol Pot's Khmer Rouge regime upon nearly a third of Cambodia's population of 7 million during the 1970s. Still uncounted are the victims of the recent or ongoing massacres imposed by those in power against their adversaries in Cambodia, Colombia, the Congo, Kosovo, Liberia, Rwanda, the Sudan, and elsewhere.[29]

Vision Two: Liberty as Treason

After their capture in Harper's Ferry, Virginia, on Tuesday, October 18, 1859, John Brown and six members of his "Army of Liberation" were charged with three crimes: treason, murder, and conspiring with slaves to rebel. The rebels had expected the raid to launch a widespread war against slavery in the South, but their spark failed to ignite the tinder of the hoped-for rebellion. In his last address to the Virginia court that convicted him, John Brown voiced his disdain for the law's "wicked, cruel and unjust enactments" and denied feeling any "consciousness of guilt."[30] On December 2, 1859, together with six followers, the fifty-nine-year-old abolitionist was hanged.

The U.S. Marines who crushed Brown's rebellion were led by Col. Robert E. Lee, who personally regarded slavery as evil. Less than two years later, he too chose to pursue the demands of his conscience. Refusing an offer to command the Union Army, he resigned and later assumed leadership of the Confederate Army in what he considered the War Between the States.

Vision Three: Human Rights as Crimes

In 1969, Astavacatur Unanovic Balejan, a six-time wounded Armenian veteran of the Soviet Army and a former member of the Communist Party, was convicted of writing critical articles in the underground *samizdat* press that, in the opinion of the Soviet court presiding over the case, "slandered Soviet reality."[31] About the same time, a nineteen-year-old Latvian woman was sent to a Soviet labor camp for displaying the Latvian national flag. A Moldavan beekeeper, employed by a state farm, was similarly charged with writing letters objecting to the Russification of Moldava and composing a leaflet titled "Moldava for the Moldavans, Russia for the Russians." Sentenced to seven years in a labor camp, he died after going on a hunger strike.[32]

In 1974 a Ukrainian priest, Daniel Romanovic Bakhtalovskij, was sentenced to a labor camp and to five years' exile for contravening the Soviet law prohibiting religious instruction of minors. In Lithuania, Birute Poskene, a woman janitor who joined the Seventh Day Adventist Church and became a vegetarian, was likewise punished for refusing to feed her children meat and for celebrating Saturday as the day of rest. In addition to being divested of her parental rights, she was committed to a mental hospital. Until its very collapse, the Soviet Union continued to totally disregard the glorious promises given the Soviet comrades in the postrevolutionary constitutions.

Despite the demise of Stalinism, the dark chambers of human rights oppression in many other countries remain filled. Christians continue to be persecuted in Egypt and Pakistan and enslaved in the Sudan.[33] In the People's Republic of China, which insists that no political offenders are held in its prisons,[34] student leaders and other democracy activists are convicted of "counterrevolutionary propaganda and incitement" and sedition, and are sentenced to long imprisonment for engaging in such subversive conduct as the defacing of the large Mao Zedong portrait hanging in Tiananmen Square,[35] or for publicly appealing for human rights reforms.[36] Tibetan nationalists are imprisoned for unfurling their country's national flag in Tibet's capital of Lhasa,[37] and Kurdish civil rights activists who dare speak out about the plight of their community are convicted of treason and sentenced to long terms in Turkish prisons.[38]

Vision Four: Pregnancy as Political Offense

In 1989, Wang Saizhen, a thirty-four-year-old married mother of one child, fled the People's Republic of China. Having become pregnant for a second time, and fearing that she would be compelled to undergo an abortion or have to pay the heavy fines imposed upon couples giving birth to more than one child without government authorization, she sought refuge in Canada. After a brief stay, she and her husband, Li Jinlin, attempted, with the aid of smugglers, to illegally enter the United States but then applied for asylum when they were captured by U.S. immigration officers near Albany, New York. Early in 1990 the U.S. Department of State acknowledged that Mr. Li and Ms. Wang, both then working in New York City restaurants, had left their homeland to escape China's family-planning policies. The couple thereby qualified for refugee status and for an eventual grant of political asylum in the United States.[39]

Vision Five: Environmental Protection as Folly

Chaining himself to the top of a lamppost in front of London's Westminster Abbey during a 1991 international economic summit conference, Swiss naturalist Bruno Manser was immediately catapulted to the position of Europe's leading environmental activist. After sitting at his perch for ninety minutes, Manser was cut loose by the police, arrested, and taken to a nearby police station.

"They sat me down at a table and asked me what I was protesting against," Manser reported the next morning. "I pointed to the table and said: This is what I am protesting against. I am protesting against the fact that you have this table made out of wood from the rain forest."

A Swiss artist and naturalist, Manser had decided in 1984 to find a place as remote from modern civilization as possible. Making his way to Borneo, a province of Malaysia, he penetrated the ancient rain forest and established contact with a small aboriginal tribe, the Penan. He immersed himself in their culture and lived among them for six and a half years.

"I didn't know about the logging problems when I went there," he said in an interview. But he soon realized that "if these people do not get help from outside, they will become extinct as a culture. They will lose their economy, and with it their freedom."[40]

While Bruno Manser was protesting in front of Westminster Abbey, some five hundred Penan tribesmen in distant Borneo chained themselves to loading cranes, constructed blockades, and stood in the way of trucks bringing logs out of the Sarawak forests. Fifty-five protesters were arrested by the Malaysian police, who also ordered the expulsion of two foreign journalists who had described the natives' plight in dispatches to the world press. The offenders were charged under Malaysia's Internal Security Act, which allows detention without trial. Lashing out at critics who accused him of oppressing the native tribes, Malaysian prime minister Mahathir Mohamad urged that "romantic" notions about preserving the environment and tribal ways of life had to be dispelled.[41]

Vision Six: Choosing Between Rebellion and Unjust Law

"Rebellion against tyranny is obedience to God," asserted Thomas Jefferson. Abraham Lincoln, a symbol of national unity, also spoke of the people's right "to rise up and shake off the existing government and form a new one that suits them better."[42] Upon being charged with burning Selective Service records in protest against the Vietnam War, Philip Berrigan echoed this theme: "I came to the conclusion that I was in direct line with American democratic tradition in choosing civil disobedience. . . . From the Boston Tea Party through the abolitionist and anarchist movements . . . we have a rich tradition of disobedience."[43] David Darst, a fellow defendant, pointed out that "Jesus, too, was guilty of assault and battery when he cast the money changers out of the temple."[44]

Justifying his violation of Alabama's segregationist laws, Martin Luther King Jr., also a man of religion, similarly asserted that "an unjust law is no law at all."[45] But Abe Fortas, Associate Justice of the U.S. Supreme Court, disagreed. In response to King's assertion, Fortas reiterated the long-prevailing arguments against resort to dissent and civil disobedience in a democracy. "Just as we expect the government to be bound by all laws, so each individual is bound by all of the laws under the Constitution. He cannot pick and choose. He cannot substitute his own judgment or passion, however noble, for rules of law."[46]

Vision Seven: Allah's Way and the Devil's Way

Would-be airline hijackers were offered practical advice, in July 1988, by *Al Fajr,* an English-language newsletter distributed to the faithful at London's Regent Park Mosque. An editorial in the Moslem publication assured all readers: "if [a] plane belongs to a country at war with the Moslems . . . [one] is allowed to hijack it." The article continued by asserting that those in conflict with Islam were entitled to no sanctity or protection.[47]

A similar epistle supporting a Holy War, or jihad, was issued a year later by Sheikh Ahmed Ibrahim, a thirty-eight-year-old father of a four-month-old baby, after he was released from Israeli confinement for acts of terrorism. Insisted Ibrahim: "I am ready to kill and be killed in fighting the jihad. . . . Allah is a vengeful God. Jihad is a struggle between Right and Wrong, Justice and Injustice. . . . Killing for the jihad is a holy deed. The Koran says that there are only two ways: Allah's way or Satan's way. I chose Allah's way."[48]

Vision Eight: Tyrannicide as Civic Virtue

In 44 B.C. the Roman Senate ordered a special medal to be struck in honor of Marcus Brutus, a friend of Gaius Julius Caesar as well as one of his assassins. Caesar, the most renowned of ancient Rome's heroes, was assassinated on March 15 in the chamber of the Roman Senate. A contemporary, the historian Seneca, remarked that amongst Caesar's murderers were to be found more of Caesar's friends than his enemies.

A man of military genius and exceptional political acumen, Caesar was suspected of aspiring to kingship and divinity, an aspiration intolerable to republican Rome's oligarchy, from which the assassins sprang. To share equally in their glory and in their guilt, each of Caesar's assassins struck a mortal blow to Rome's fallen idol—twenty-three dagger wounds in all.[49] Believing "that a tyrant is one who means to subvert all conventions himself," observed political historian David C. Rapoport, Rome's citizens would have considered any moral doubts about a tyrant's assassination "as preposterous as the notion that it might be morally wrong to put out fire with water, or to shoot a wild beast from behind."[50]

Vision Nine: Vengeance with Impunity

On the streets of Paris in May 1926, forty-year-old Jewish watchmaker and poet Shalom Scwarzbard assassinated Ukrainian émigré Simon Petlyura. As a youth in his native Ukraine, Scwarzbard had helped organize Jewish self-defense forces against Czarist-tolerated anti-Semitic violence. Escaping from Russia, he settled in France and during World War I volunteered to serve in the French Foreign Legion, earning the Croix de Guerre. But Scwarzbard returned to Russia for a brief time after the Soviet Revolution, taking part in the ensuing civil war. During that period, in the winter of 1919, more than a dozen of Scwarzbard's relatives were among the 50,000 Jews massacred in massive pogroms by Cossack forces led by Petlyura.

Learning years later that Petlyura had settled in Paris, Scwarzbard confronted his nemesis and shot him dead.[51] At the trial, which received worldwide attention, Scwarzbard was portrayed as "an idealist . . . who sacrificed himself on the altar of human liberty."[52] Following a moving address by his counsel, Communist-sympathizer Henri Torres, Scwarzbard was acquitted of all charges.[53] Russian novelist Maxim Gorky lauded the assassination not only as an appropriate "act of vengeance" but also as "a medium for prevention of new massacres."[54]

Vision Ten: Honorable and Dishonorable Means

On the eve of World War II, in the gathering shadows of history's most terrible and ruthless holocaust, the leaders of Great Britain ruled that duplicitous and underhanded means could not be justified even in a struggle against tyranny. Faced with the growing threat of German Nazism, British General Mason MacFarland advised his superiors at Whitehall in 1938 that Hitler was determined to wage war and that if leave were granted to assassinate the Nazi dictator, millions of lives would be saved. The British authorities rejected Mac-Farland's offer, labeling the proposition "dishonorable and un-sportsmanlike."[55] Despite this resolute British answer, similar debates continued to surface with regard to other tyrants, other countries, other times: Cuba's Fidel Castro, Uganda's Idi Amin, Iran's Ayatollah Ruhollah Khomeini, Romania's Nicholae Ceausescu, Panama's Manuel Antonio Noriega, Zaire's Mobutu Sese Seko, and Iraq's Saddam Hussein.

Vision Eleven: The Disingenuous Pseudo-Politicals

"What a glorious opportunity there is for a man to immortalize himself by killing Lincoln," John Wilkes Booth remarked to a friend several years before the actual assassination.[56] Was Booth a genuine devotee of the Southern cause or was he merely a seeker of personal glory? It has frequently been pointed out that not all those who profess to violate the law for political and altruistic causes are genuinely motivated. John W. Hinckley Jr., President Reagan's assailant, belatedly asserted political motives for the shooting, even though he had originally portrayed himself as a disappointed love-struck youth. In communications from St. Elizabeth's Hospital, where he was confined, Hinckley continued to describe himself as a "political prisoner" whom the government wanted "silenced and locked away permanently."[57]

Criminologist Stephen Schafer suggested more than two decades ago that "many simply use . . . the [claim of a political ideal] as an excuse for their own criminal act." Some ostensibly "political" criminals, Schafer warned, are in fact driven by a mere "penchant for adventure," by some irresistible "psychological deviation," or by the desire "for avoiding constructive work."[58] The bloody and senseless adventures of Timothy J. McVeigh and Unabomber Ted Kaczynski, a quarter century later, might well supply additional support for the hypothesis that a significant segment of those claiming the mantle of political offender might indeed be afflicted with social alienation and individual psychopathologies that manifest themselves through political rage.

Vision Twelve: The Price of Eternal Vigilance

Writing a preamble for a new nation's Declaration of Independence in 1776, America's founding fathers proclaimed life, liberty, and the pursuit of happiness to be "inalienable rights." Soon thereafter, France's 1789 Declaration of the Rights of Man and the Citizen enumerated liberty, equality, and fraternity, as well as individual security, freedom to immigrate, and the privilege to resist oppression, as human rights within its new wide-ranging charter.[59] Almost two centuries later, after the Romanov dynasty was deposed in Russia in the name of a proletariat, the authors of the Russian Republic's 1918 Constitution[60] similarly listed (and again affirmed in the 1977 Soviet Constitution[61]) "the working peoples" entitlement to protection against exploitation and to freedom of speech and assembly. Also decreed by the 1918 Constitution were the rights of all citizens to leisure, free education, guaranteed work, and health care.

In the aftermath of World War II's destruction and holocaust, the United Nations sought to safeguard the world against future abuses of power. Specifying the rights of all individuals to freedom of speech, opinion, religion, and travel, the 1948 Universal Declaration of Human Rights (later implemented by two distinct Human Rights Covenants) was viewed by Eleanor Roosevelt, then a delegate to the United Nations, as one of history's highest achievements. To further guarantee these and other human rights, the United States and the Soviet Union in 1975 joined other nations in the Helsinki Accord, which promised:

> The participating States will respect human rights and fundamental freedoms, ... all people always have the right, in full freedom, to determine ... their internal and external political statutes ... and to pursue ... their political, economic, social and cultural development.[62]

In the face of these mounting assurances of justice and liberty, an observer might ask rhetorically, What need remains, and what justification, for political protest, civil disobedience, or more militant forms of resistance and self-help? The world's dismal record of just governance makes an answer to this question unnecessary.

◇   ◇   ◇

What lessons may one draw from these highly distilled and disparate glimpses of political dissidents and their struggles? While subsequent history judged some of these political resisters to be heroes or martyrs, others were condemned as traitors or international criminals. For still others the verdict is not yet in. However any of them are ultimately judged, there is a thread that unites them all, beginning in one of humanity's earliest events and stretching to the present day. The thread begins with Adam and Eve's expulsion from the Old Testament's Garden of Eden (an event finalized by the posting of a flaming sword at the garden gate to enjoin the offenders' return). The expulsion was not decreed as punishment for the couple's transgression against other inhabitants. Rather, their offense was against a higher and divine authority's admonition not to partake of the fruit of the forbidden tree. Ever since, what some believe is an inevitable struggle between autonomy and authority (or liberty and authority, as John Stuart Mill described it) has continued as "the most conspicuous" force in human history.[63]

Rebels with a Cause will seek to identify the protagonists in this struggle (whether just or unjust). In the view of predominant contemporary Western thought, this contest must end in autonomy's ultimate victory. Robert Wolff writes: "If all men have a continuing obligation to achieve the highest degree of autonomy possible [stemming from the fundamental assumption of moral philosophy that men are responsible for their actions], then there would appear to be no state whose subjects have a moral obligation to obey its commands."[64] Other conclusions are advanced by political authoritarians, religious fundamentalists, and members of other philosophical creeds.

This book will present the rebels' claims and weigh their motives, dissect their deeds, and assess the morality as well as the social utility of their efforts. Irrespective of their successes or failures, or of the ultimate validity of their motives, these dissidents have struck and continue striking at existing authority and public order in the alleged pursuit of some ideal—be that ideal high or low. It is this assertion of a superior claim, coupled with the denial of personal or selfish motives, that makes judging these rebels so difficult in the fora of public opinion and in the tribunals of justice, both domestic and international.

Our examination of the diverse manifestations of political criminality will be both historical and contemporary in perspective, and will include such disparate forms as dissenting communications, public protest, resistance to public duties, civil disobedience, insurgency, rebellion, secession, and terrorism. Political criminality will thus be scrutinized through its often contradictory facets: as a category of unorthodox crime and as a form of unorthodox politics, as domestic conflict and as intranational warfare, as a tool of communication and as a style of life, as a deliberate program for reform and as a pathological campaign of hate and destruction.

Part One

Beyond Myth and Denial

The Realities of Political Crime and Rebellion

Thou shalt not revile the gods, nor curse the ruler of thy people.
—Exodus 22:28

That the King can do no wrong, is a necessary and fundamental principle of the English constitution.
—Sir William Blackstone,
Commentaries on the Law of England,
bk. III, chap. 17 (1765–1769)

The rich man in his castle,
the poor man at his gate,
God made them, high or lowly,
and order'd their estate.

—Cecil Frances Alexander,
All Things Bright and Beautiful (1848)

After punishment has been administered the bloodied peasant might be gibbeted for public instruction.

Chapter One

When Conscience and Public Order Collide

Is There Place for Protest and Resistance?

> When the strong command, Obedience is best.
>
> —Sir Henry Newbolt,
> *A Ballad of John Nicholson*

> Obedience,
> Bane of all genius . . .
> Makes slaves of men . . .
>
> —Percy Bysshe Shelley,
> *Queen Mab* (1813)

> All political societies are composed of other, smaller groups
> of different types, each of which has its interests. . . . The will
> of these smaller groups always must be examined from two
> distinct perspectives: for the members of the small group, it is
> a general will; for the large society, it is a private will, which
> is usually found to be just with regard to the smaller group
> but disruptive with regard to the larger society.
>
> —Jean-Jacques Rousseau,
> *Political Economy* (1755)

Joan of Arc Listening to the Voices, tableau vivant (performed in 1900).

The Political Offender in History

Authority and its rules—the political offender's raison d'être—are as old as human society itself, and the origin of the political offender similarly is shrouded by the mists of time. Even in the murkiest depths of prehistory, tribal chiefs and priests set strict limits on their peoples' behavior through the introduction of customs and taboos. Anthropologist Bronislaw Malinowski observed the existence of complex rules of conduct governing private life, economic cooperation, and public affairs even among the most primitive societies.[65] Legal historian E. Sidney Hartland confirmed these findings: "The savage is far from being the free and unfettered creature of Rousseau's imagination. On the contrary, he is hemmed in on every side by the customs of his people."[66]

In the societies Malinowski studied, the most hallowed of all customs were invariably those that prescribed the respective ranks, titles, tasks, and privileges of the various members of the community. "[F]rom the sociological point of view," he asserted, "it would be possible to show that the whole structure of [society] is founded on the principle of *legal status*. By this I mean that the claims of chief over commoners, husband over wife, parent over child, and vice versa, are . . . exercised . . . according to definite rules, and arranged into well-balanced chains of reciprocal services."[67]

Rules and customs established to preserve respect and obedience toward chiefs and other superiors (and often entitling inferiors to some corresponding rights) have been deeply embedded in every human culture and society, and have been documented among people as diverse in time and geography as the ancient Israelites of the Near East, the Samoans of the Eastern Pacific, and the Ashanti of Africa's Gold Coast.[68] These standards were maintained through force as well as mythology, religion, ritual, and law. The ancient Egyptians attributed godly parentage to their leaders, while the Greeks often endowed their rulers with supernatural qualities. When the Israelites' first king, Saul, ascended to the throne, the prophet Samuel thus "took a vial of oil, and poured it upon [Saul's] head, and kissed him and said . . . the Lord had anointed thee to be captain over his inheritance."[69]

In all historical societies those of lesser rank were expected to respect those who allegedly had been divinely selected for leadership.

"Thou shalt not revile the gods, nor curse the ruler of thy people," commanded the book of Exodus.[70] Offenders against those considered divinely privileged were cruelly and swiftly punished. The Bible reports that when a common soldier, expecting to be rewarded for his regicide, claimed to have slain King Saul, the Israelites' first ruler and Saul's rival, David, refused to countenance this transgression against royal and divine authority. Asking, "How wast thou not afraid to stretch forth thine hand to destroy the Lord's anointed?" the youthful king to be promptly ordered the assassin's execution.[71]

Writing during the early part of this century, political scientist Gaetano Mosca observed that in most societies (especially in those grouped along more hierarchical lines than kinship), the ruling classes rarely justified their political authority exclusively by their de facto possession of power.[72] Instead, they sought to advance a metaphysical or ideological formula (the "political formula," according to Mosca) to portray their possession of power as the logical and necessary consequence of the beliefs of the people over whom they ruled. "Among ancient peoples the political formula not only rested upon religion but was wholly identified with it. Their god was preeminently a national god. He was the special protector of the territory and the people. He was the fulcrum of its political organization."[73] In Judeo-Christian societies, Mosca emphasized, the sovereign's reign was legitimated by direct divine anointment or calling. Similarly, in the Chinese polity the emperor ruled as the Son of Heaven, while in Moslem societies the legitimacy of authority was derived by descent from the prophet Mohammed or through delegation by his devoted successors.[74]

The political formulas under which rulers exercise their authority have thus served as the glue that binds society together.[75] As a consequence, dissenters and rebels against those in authority have been viewed as a threat not only to the ruling class but also to the very foundation of the society and government legitimized by the "political formula." The rebel's campaign to erode the very legitimacy of authority has been condemned, accordingly, by "all persons who, from a diversity of backgrounds, have united under common beliefs, attitudes and customs of which the political formula is the keystone."[76]

Treating rebels as public enemies and their offenses against sovereigns as a form of sacrilege was prevalent in the cultures of the eastern Mediterranean—Babylon, Egypt, Judea, Persia—as well as in the primordial African and Melanesian societies. Even so, the sanctity of rulers was not always viewed as absolute or universal. In ancient Greece and in republican Rome, the peoples' experiences with tyrannical leaders led to more qualified and seasoned views regarding dissent and rebellion. Some of the most noted Greek and Roman philosophers, including Xenophon and Cicero, were known to challenge the legitimacy of unjust rulers and governments.[77] Not only were the assassins of tyrants sometimes given the opportunity to flee into exile or to suffer such lesser penalties as fines and confinement, but they were sometimes glorified for their offenses against the once-admired leaders.[78]

"The ancient Greeks and Romans had no word to correspond to [the] term assassination," wrote political scientist David C. Rapoport. "A killing was simply means to an end; its moral significance depended entirely on the *nature* of the person killed. A man who struck a public personality down was either a murderer or a tyrannicide. And the word for tyrannicide was the same as that for 'liberator,' one who freed his country."[79] In early Rome, even those merely advocating or aspiring to tyranny were subject to severe public sanctions. Spurius Cassius, the author of a land reform bill, was assassinated by his own father, who suspected that the law was a step toward tyranny.[80] Because a person regarded as a tyrant was beyond the protection of the law, there was little judicial or other public inquiry into the justification for the assassin's deed.

Opposition to those in power in classical Judea, Greece, and Rome was often not so much a response to political abuses by government as it was an expression of pious revulsion against claims of divinity made by impious rulers. The Hebrews, as well as the early Christians, suffered persecution as rebels largely because they would not submit to the semidivine status of the Caesars. The Judeo-Christians' refusal to offer sacrifices on the altars dedicated to the rulers, the common means by which subjects acknowledged the supremacy of the king or emperor, was often viewed by their opponents as a rejection of temporal as well as divine authority. Yet after Constantine embraced Christianity, the formerly dissenting and persecuted Church Fathers found themselves in a dramatically opposite posture vis-à-vis political authority. Once the emperor had submitted to the overlordship of Christianity, he was held to be protected by Heaven, and the Church Fathers enjoined their followers to practice utmost obedience and loyalty to him.

Despite these religious and political changes, tyrannicide continued to be of intense academic and practical interest throughout the twilight of the Roman era. The educational texts of the declining Roman Empire and of the early Middle Ages suggest that in the course of scholarly training students were frequently made to debate the legitimacy of tyrannicide as an unorthodox political remedy for abuse of power.[81] While the scholastic exercises continued, the judges of the later Middle Ages increasingly began to impose the most barbaric punishments on those who dared disrupt the prevailing feudal hierarchy. Those who would challenge this hierarchy by attacking the existing political, religious, social, or economic order were not to be tolerated.

Over time, Christianity's earlier responses to political assassination and rebellion were increasingly modified by the development of new religious as well as secular doctrines of armed warfare. In warfare, the classical Greeks and Romans practiced total war, in the belief that their enemies possessed no rights. Much like the practice of domestic tyrannicide, the assassination of foreign rulers was considered acceptable. Medieval Christian society, however, saw the evolution of a strict set of rules of chivalry to govern the conduct of warfare between "honorable" opponents. David Rapoport emphasized that a "Christian knight like Galahad or Roland worried about the difference between fair and foul fighting; to an Achilles or a Ulysses the distinction would be incomprehensible."[82]

The growing tendency to distinguish between legitimate and illegitimate causes and means for traditional warfare thus led to a parallel development in medieval society's perception of domestic challenges to the political order. As in international war, patterns of differentiation between legitimate and illegitimate causes for insurgency and between acceptable and unacceptable means for conducting the conflict developed with regard to domestic warfare. These new patterns were reflected in *Policraticus,* a twelfth-century text written by John of Salisbury, secretary to Thomas Becket (himself no stranger to domestic conflict). The learned author contended that although divine justice permitted tyrannicide, the killer could not be one bound to his victim through fealty (feudal ties), nor could he resort to dishonorable methods.[83] Those unwilling to conform to the stringent requirements of chivalry were doomed to carry forever the stigma of dishonor—as well as to suffer an ignominious, painful, and public death.

The knight of the Middle Ages and of the Renaissance—supposed to cherish honor and loyalty above all else—considered an assault against his feudal lord not only a breach of his personal oath but also an offense against the fundamental order of society. In Sir Thomas More's imaginary country Utopia (in his 1516 book of the same name), only foreigners were hired to carry out assassination tasks—which in any case were permissible only to prevent war—and even then hirelings could act only at the command of Utopia's government, since individual conscience could never justify assassination. Moreover, Utopia denied haven to those who had killed foreign rulers in its service, lest the assassins "contaminate virtuous citizens."[84] These extremely negative portrayals of the assassin, claimed Rapoport, produced a drastic decline in political assassinations during the medieval era.[85]

But the romantic medieval ideals of honorable warfare lost much of their appeal after the arrival of the Renaissance and the rise of the standing state army. As secularism and pragmatism spread, the old chivalric values began to wane. New rulers and dynasties frequently came to power by force or treachery, and political violence became widespread. Machiavelli, the first "modern" political theorist,[86] eschewed morality in the new age through his advocacy of any and all available means, fair or foul, to attain the ruler's desired political ends. The growing political ruthlessness of the era was particularly evident when, over a half century, eleven members of the Medici family, the most prominent in Florence, were murdered. Five other family members probably died through foul play as well. Commenting on this death toll, Renaissance historian Jacob Burckhardt concluded that no one "believed any longer in the justice of the law. When a murder was committed, the sympathies of the people ranged . . . instinctively on the side of the murderer."[87]

The Enlightenment heralded yet a greater breach in the traditional links between the dominions of God and those of the king. But only the arrival of the Age of Revolution finally gave rise to the claim that governments were human, not divine, institutions. No longer could critics of authority be readily labeled sacrilegious and evil. The fact that the executioners of England's Charles I were condemned as trai-

tors by the Crown Colony of Virginia yet received sanctuary in the
Puritan Colony of New Haven illustrates the new mood of the
mid–seventeenth century.[88]

With the subsequent rise of modern nationalism, emerging rulers
set out to consolidate the small and fractious principalities of the
Middle Ages and the Renaissance. In this attempt they once more
had to search for new ways and means to shore up the legitimacy of
their governments. But the mythologies and ideologies formerly used
to uphold the older political formulas could no longer hold together
the new national entities. The divine claims of kings had been debunked by the revolutions of the eighteenth century. The old feudal
codes of honor were likewise dissipated by the new social, economic,
and commercial realities. The legitimation of government in the up-
coming republics and constitutional monarchies required new myth-
ical, moral, or ethical foundations. In time, these were articulated
primarily under the dual banners of nationalism (proclaiming one's
natural duty to one's nation) and the social contract (representing
authority as the product of the free consent of the governed).[89]

The Currents of Modernity

In 1776 the American Declaration of Independence proclaimed the
primacy of the social contract and articulated the conditions that the
Founding Fathers believed justified rebellion against authority. By
giving political and jurisprudential endorsement to popular resistance against unjust government (one that deprives the people of
their inalienable rights), the Declaration challenged the fundamental
dictate inherent in the ancient laws of treason that the sovereign was
due absolute obedience. Soon thereafter, the upheavals following the
1789 French Revolution produced a similarly radical awakening in
Europe that fostered more permissive attitudes toward political dissidence and popular rebellion.[90] These developments echoed John
Milton's earlier assertion that "it is lawful ... to call to account a
tyrant or wicked king and after due conviction to depose and put
him to death."[91]

But neither the revolutionary nor evolutionary decline of monarchical absolutism necessarily brought a new tolerance toward political opponents and enemies of those in power. The depredations visited by the new rulers in France and elsewhere on the remnants of

the *ancien régime,* as well as on the general population, presented a new development in deliberate governmental terrorism. For several decades, until the mid–nineteenth century, Europe was to echo with calls for revolutions and counterrevolutions, and to experience mobilizations and brutal encounters between contesting forces. The polarization was not to ease until the beginning of the second half of the nineteenth century, at which time a new political tolerance as well as tyrannical exhaustion became evident. From that point, until liberalism's demise after World War I, Europe indulged a new respect for political offenders and their assertions of "noble" motives.[92]

The reasons for the late nineteenth century's liberal flirtation with the political offender were succinctly articulated by Georges Vidal, a leading French legal scholar:

Whereas formerly the political criminal was treated as a public enemy, he is today considered as a friend of the public good, as a man of progress, desirous of bettering the political institutions of his country, having laudable intentions, hastening the onward march of humanity, his only fault being that he wishes to go too fast, and that he employs in attempting to realize the progress which he desires, means irregular, illegal and violent. If from this point of view, the political criminal is reprehensible and ought to be punished in the interest of the established order, his criminality cannot be compared with that of the ordinary malefactor, with the murderer, the thief, etc. The criminality [of the political offender] has not all the same immorality. It is only relative, dependent on time, place, circumstances, the institutions of the land, and it is often inspired by noble sentiments, by disinterested motives, by devotion to persons and principles, by love of one's country. In conclusion, the criminality is often only passing; the author of a political crime who is rather a vanquished, a conquered man, than a criminal, may become, as a result of a revolution favorable to his ideas, the conqueror of the morrow, who is called regularly and lawfully to direct and guide the state and the public administration of his country. The penal reaction exercised against him is not at all, then, like that against malefactors, who violate the ordinary law. . . . [Penal reaction against the political offender is not] a work of social defense against an attack upon imminent conditions of human existence, but is rather a . . . defense of caste, of political parties, against an attack upon an organization and upon a political regime historically transitory.[93]

In the pursuit of these premises, the German penal system, under both the Imperial Kaisers and the Weimar Republic, considered comfortable confinement in a fortress *(Festungshaft)* as an appropri-ately honorable sanction for the offender whose motives were politi-cal. It was indeed Adolf Hitler's enforced leisure, in a mountaintop fortress after the collapse of his 1923 Munich Putsch, that gave him the opportunity to write his genocidal *Mein Kampf.*

In czarist Russia, generally remembered for its authoritarian, cruel, and oppressive rule, the political offender similarly enjoyed unexpectedly lenient treatment. Despite the Imperial criminal code's imposition of particularly harsh sanctions against political agitation and activism, the political offender was nevertheless accorded the trappings of favored status in practice. Dissident Aleksandr Solzhen-itsyn furnished a colorful description of this favoritism in *The Gulag Archipelago:*

> It was almost a crime to mix politicals with criminals! Criminals were teamed up and driven along the streets to the station so as to expose them to public disgrace. And politicals could go there in carriages. . . . Politicals were not fed from the common pot but were given a food allowance instead and had their meals brought from public eating places. The Bolshevik Olminsky didn't want even the hospital rations because he found the food too coarse. The Butyrki Prison superintendent apologized to Olminsky for the jailer having addressed him too familiarly: You see, we seldom get politicals here, and the jailer didn't know any better![94]

To explain the deferential treatment of political offenders in czarist Russia, Solzhenitsyn pointed out: "To draw a distinction between political prisoners and common criminals is the equivalent of show-ing them respect as equal opponents, of recognizing that people may have views of their own."[95]

Germany and Russia were not alone in recognizing political of-fenses and differentiating between political and common offenders. From early times Japan likewise endowed political offenders with a mantle of heroic honor entitling them to benefits not available to common criminals. Initially only offenders of the samurai class and others of high status were accorded this distinction, which included special confinement without forced labor, or *kinko.* Eventually all offenders against the security of the state were granted a similarly privileged status.[96] The laws of Belgium, France, and Italy also cre-ated separate categories of political crimes and accorded individuals in those categories a special and more respectful treatment.[97]

During the past two centuries international law has also differentiated between the political offender and the common criminal. Since the mid–nineteenth century, treaties among Western nations have virtually assured political offenders that, upon their escape from the countries against which they acted, they would be secure from extradition and trial by their pursuers.[98] In 1989 the U.N. General Assembly Resolution on Human Rights exempted all offenders from capital punishment for any of the offenses committed by them.[99] The authoritative voice of the Vatican joined soon thereafter in support of the political dissident. In a 1983 papal pronouncement supporting a comprehensive amnesty for Polish political prisoners, Pope John Paul II spoke out against the imposition of capital punishment on political offenders throughout the world.[100] In 1998, during a visit to Cuba, he likewise urged the release from Cuban prison of all those confined for political offenses.

Despite nearly a century of modern leniency, the final decades of the twentieth century have witnessed a gradual deterioration in the legal status and treatment of political offenders. The respect and tolerance accorded political opponents and insurgents by Russia's czars and Germany's Weimar Republic were not reciprocated by their Communist and Nazi successors. Following the 1917 Soviet Revolution, the leaders of the new Soviet state, themselves formerly pursued as revolutionaries, became zealous pursuers of new political opponents. Both Marxist and Nazi totalitarianism, much like medieval justice before them, reserved particularly harsh penalties for those who dared challenge the newly instituted Leninist-Stalinist or Hitlerian rule. Solzhenitsyn reported that in the Soviet Gulag "any protest that as a 'political' you ought not to be mixed up with ordinary criminals has resulted only in laughter on the prisoners' part and bewilderment on the part of the jailers." Under the Stalinist dictatorship, "'All are criminals,' the jailers reply—sincerely."[101]

Prodding Beyond Myth and Denial

When Italian criminologist Cesare Lombroso's classic work, *Il delitto politico e le rivoluzioni*,[102] was published in 1890, political and revolutionary crime seemed so foreign and remote to Anglo-American audiences that no English-language translation was ever undertaken. In England the first work on this subject, a slim monograph titled *Political Crime: A Critical Essay,*[103] was not published until 1923. Not until 1955 was a French-language study of political crime, Pierre Papadatos's *Le délit politique,*[104] published in Geneva, and it has yet to be rendered into English. Purveyors of American history and law, afflicted by an insular myopia and cultural pomposity, continued to portray political offenses and offenders as alien concepts, associated with less fortunate and less perfect societies. More recently, however, scholarly and popular interest in political rebellion and resistance have begun to take root in the United States and elsewhere.

The interest first erupted during and following America's turbulent 1960s. Within a period of twelve months, the first two scholarly American volumes on the topic of political criminality, Stephen Schafer's brief yet very important *The Political Criminal*[105] and Francis A. Allen's exploratory *The Crimes of Politics,*[106] were published. An outpouring of popular biographical and journalistic expositions of political activists and their campaigns preceded, accompanied, and followed these scholarly efforts. Manifestoes such as George Breitman's *Malcolm X Speaks,*[107] Eldridge Cleaver's *Soul on Ice,*[108] George Jackson's *Blood in My Eye,*[109] Michael V. Miller and Susan Gilmore's *Revolution at Berkeley,*[110] Jessica Mitford's *The Trial of Dr. Spock,*[111] Daniel Berrigan's *The Trial of the Catonsville Nine,*[112] Harold Jacobs's *Weatherman,*[113] Les Payne and Tim Findley's *The Life and Death of the SLA,*[114] and Ellen Frankfort's *Kathy Boudin and the Dance of Death*[115] sent ripples through the information and entertainment media, reciting and romanticizing the use of illegal means to accomplish political ends. There was also a substantial investment of federal funds in a national commission to study the causes of violence in America,[116] and in a governmental task force to assess the reasons for, the dangers of, and the requisite responses to political disorder and terrorism.[117] In 1982 an interagency task force on terrorism was constituted under Vice President George W. Bush.[118]

More ambitious academic analyses of political criminality in America surfaced in the late 1970s and early 1980s: Julian Roebuck and Stanley C. Weeber's *Political Crime in the United States*[119] and Austin Turk's *Political Criminality.*[120] Sorting through what seemed to be the last events of a turbulent era, the first book assembled and proposed a bibliographic catalog of classifications, but failed to develop its utility for practitioners of law and criminal justice, while the second advanced an innovative and thought-provoking theoretical framework, but failed to place it within historical perspectives or relate it to clinical evidence. To address these shortcomings came the first two volumes of my trilogy, which this volume, *Rebels with a Cause,* completes. In 1986 *The Tree of Liberty: A Documentary History of Rebellion and Political Crime in America*[121] set forth the documentary evidence of the ubiquity and constancy of political criminality in the United States, but attempted no synthesis of the subject. In 1995 *The War Against Authority: From the Crisis of Legitimacy and the New Social Contract*[122] presented a more analytical discussion of the perpetual struggle between authority and autonomy worldwide.

The initial eruption of interest in political crime during the 1960s seemed to wane, however, as the societal convulsions associated with the war in Vietnam subsided. Because political turmoil continued throughout the world—with nearly half of the world's nations contending with insurgent warfare, languishing under military rule, or otherwise struggling to introduce democracy or make democracy work—it was only natural that media and scholarly interest shifted from domestic to overseas struggles. Beginning with Barton Ingraham's comprehensive analysis *Political Crime in France, Germany and England in Modern Time,*[123] the nature of much of this global political unrest has been studied and documented. Volumes such as John Laffin's *Fedayeen*[124] and Sean Edwards's *The Gun, the Law, and the Irish People,*[125] more recent examinations such as J. Bowyer Bell's *The Irish Troubles*[126] and Ludmilla Alexeyeva's *Soviet Dissent,*[127] and numerous other accounts of escalating crises have complemented this endeavor. But efforts to develop a comprehensive theory of political crime and rebellion, and to offer consistent policy responses, have been few and for the most part unsuccessful.

Currently, political extremism, fanaticism, and conflict have not only infected particular communities, whole countries, and even subcontinents, but have threatened overall world security. American and other travelers, corporations, and peacekeeping forces have been caught in the spreading web of violence. Moreover, the current resurgence of actual and threatened political unrest in America, coupled with experiences throughout the nation's long heritage of rebellion, suggests that a future emergence of politically motivated violence is neither unlikely nor impossible. Yet in the face of the country's vulnerability, neither America's scholars nor its government have considered domestic political criminality and upheaval to be of great interest or urgency, excepting those marginal forms of indiscriminate political violence labeled "terrorism." As a consequence, America's understanding of political turmoil and disorder abroad, and its preparedness for future episodes of political activism and domestic violence, have remained pathetically deficient.

The Center Cannot Hold: Accommodations with Reality

The doctrinal inflexibility that has blinded American policymakers to the realities as well as the historical roles of the domestic political offender has also denied the political offender an appropriate hearing in the halls of American justice, acting thereby to impoverish political debate and block possible reform. Denial of the political offender's existence and legitimacy has forced extremism where conciliation would have been more productive. Labeled and hunted as common criminals and denied the opportunity for an orderly public airing of their grievances, political dissidents have often been unduly and unnecessarily radicalized. The forces of law and order have been equally driven to extreme measures of control and retaliation. Such extremism has neither engendered respect for the institutions under attack nor enabled the pursuit of necessary remedies for the restoration of internal harmony.

The goddess of justice seems to be wielding her sword blindly. Perhaps her blindfold should now be allowed to slip a bit, to accord her a less inhibited and more realistic glance at the political offender. Accommodations with reality might permit the identification of political dissidents as a special category of offenders who are to receive differentiated and more appropriate treatment—sometimes more lenient and other times more severe. Such differentiation might seek to reconcile the continuing orthodox denials of political motives with Henry David Thoreau's populist urging: "Must the citizen even for a moment, or in the least degree, resign his conscience to the legislator? Why has every man a conscience, then?"[128]

The positive ramifications of giving special and serious attention to the "political offender" and his or her "criminality" are manifold.

Public debate on controversial and volatile political and social issues (ranging from school prayers to abortion clinic protests, from flag desecration to amnesty for deposed tyrants) could become more mature and less strident. Recognizing the reality of political criminality might ameliorate the intensity that arises when one group, whether in the majority or in the minority, is able to punish another through the imposition of criminal sanctions against status, beliefs, or politically motivated actions. If mass protests and civil disobedience could be viewed as categories of political action and resistance, we might avoid tarring the participants in the more intense forms of political debate and action with the same brush we apply to murderers and thieves.

Classifying and subdividing the wide spectrum of political dissidence—from peaceful dissent to indiscriminate violence—would not only be domestically desirable but would also harmonize domestic laws with the nation's international obligations and practices. Domestically, the nation could improve the operations of the different branches of its system of justice, permitting the police, courts, prisons, and military to make adjustments for various gradations of this peculiar class of offender. It is also likely that the procedures and institutions required for the effective regulation, adjudication, and sanctioning of political resisters and dissidents would become fundamentally different from those required for other offender populations.

There is one more reason why the classification and treatment of political offenders has become a pressing issue recently. When undifferentiated from common criminals, political offenders have often been subject to overzealous, oppressive, and unnecessary governmental responses in the name of public order and security. This zeal for oppression is no longer outside the awareness and concern of the international community. Until the recent past, sovereign governments have been immune to international scrutiny and intervention with regard to the domestic control of political opponents. But the world community's traditional reluctance to interfere in the domestic affairs of sovereign nations is undergoing radical change. A nation's domestic conduct toward its own citizens (including those who might be considered political offenders) has increasingly become a matter of international notice and action. No longer may governments blithely hide behind the facades of "national security" and "internal affairs" to deprive some or all of their people of such human rights as are guaranteed to them by international custom and law. With these changes, both the community of scholars and the community of nations must take a fresh and critical look at those claiming to be political prisoners and political offenders, as well as at those in power who deny the legitimacy of such claimants' grievances or even their very existence.

As the third millennium approaches, it is evident that "the center cannot hold."[129] With the breakup of bipolar superpower hegemonies that have dominated this planet for more than a quarter century, governments have seen a dissipation of the rationale of "external threats" used to justify internal repression. At the same time, the stability of governments and of social order around the globe is threatened by growing consciousness of intranational divisions along ethnic, racial, religious, and economic lines. With the resulting worldwide crisis of authority, the singular characteristics of political criminality urgently call for attention.

Despite this urgency and despite the modern advances in the social and behavioral sciences, in criminology and in law criminality has for the most part continued to be treated as a monolithic and impregnable mass of deviant behaviors and governmental responses. This perception has severely held back the understanding of the etiology of crime and delinquency and has retarded effective societal responses and controls. The medical sciences have advanced only when able to give up a similar naïveté, under which such global diagnoses as "lunacy," "fever," and "plague" were commonplace. It is generally recognized today that designations such as "mental illness" or "cancer" consist of diverse strains of pathology requiring differentiated therapies. Each manifestation of behavioral delinquency similarly represents a complex combination of individual and social, genetic and environmental, economic and other factors—consequently demanding particularized and diverse responses for attaining crime prevention and social control.

Only during the current century have American and other criminal justice agencies initiated increasingly determined processes for the specialized control and treatment of distinct types of crimes and criminals. Not until the beginning of the twentieth century were juvenile offenders separated from the masses of adult criminals for special study and rehabilitation. Not until the early 1930s were new endeavors utilizing distinct therapeutic approaches introduced for the treatment of alcoholics and drug addicts. Currently there are substantially more individuals in America subject to specialized juvenile, mental illness, alcohol, drug, and other therapeutic treatment programs than are confined to common jails and prisons.

Admittedly, the new and specialized systems of control and treatment have not eliminated the growing menace of juvenile crime or the damage caused by alcoholism, drug use, and sexual abuse. But the creation of separate juvenile, substance abuse, and other specialized treatment and social control regimes has supplied policymakers and the police, sentencing judges, and correctional officials with added insights as well as alternatives for the treatment of these afflictions—shattering in the process some idyllic assumptions about the total eradication of crime and deviance. Despite many unresolved problems, there continues to be widespread agreement that properly administered, specialized regimes are more humane, economical, and effective in the treatment of the diverse categories of delinquency and crime than was the older criminal monolith.[130]

Equally energetic steps toward a recognition and differentiated control and treatment of other distinct classes of crime were taken some forty years ago when white-collar criminality was first defined and scientifically studied. Since then much light has been shed on this area of criminal conduct and numerous innovative approaches have been attempted.[131] Organized crime next received special attention,[132] resulting not only in vastly improved data about collective criminality, but also in the formation of more effective enforcement procedures and mechanisms. Most recently, female criminality has been singled out for particular attention.[133] The hope persists that these specially focused efforts may produce more effective crime prevention and criminal justice responses, improving not only surveillance and policing but also prosecution, adjudication, and corrections.

Similar benefits are likely to follow from a realistic understanding of political criminality and rebellion. Attention to the phenomenology of political crime and approaches to the classification of its many and diverse manifestations are not merely academic undertakings. Greater insights into the etiology and dynamics of political protest and resistance might produce more effective governmental responses, as well as restraint. Better understanding might not only aid in the formulation of appropriate police, prosecutorial, judicial, and correctional measures, but might also help in resolving pressing questions regarding the political offender's status in domestic as well as international law.

It is unlikely, however, that scientific exploration in the social and behavioral arenas will generate such dramatic payoffs as seen in the natural sciences. Changes in public policy and social practices are generally more difficult and expensive to introduce than modifications in silicon chips or medical protocols. Even a complete understanding of a particular class or type of deviance is not likely to result in readily effective prevention and eradication techniques. Individual habits and customs of society may not be as malleable as the products of the physical world. Moreover, the limitations imposed by constitutional law, as well as by society's ethical and moral considerations, may preclude resort to many newly discovered or older social control methods (e.g., forced resettlement, chemical sterilization, compulsory gene transfers).

Scientists seeking to better defend society against deviance and delinquency cannot expect the same degree of freedom with regard to human psychosurgery and social engineering that industrial engineers are permitted with regard to modifications in their machines or workplaces. It is not likely that any society will be able to eliminate the diverse genetic abnormalities or familial, social, economic, ethnic, and racial deprivations that partially account for alienation, social hostility, and rebellion. Neither should one expect society to carry out the drastic measures required for the undoing of complex psychosocial pathologies that give rise to deviant pursuits. But greater scientific insights into the origins and functioning of political resistance and criminality—in its many disparate and at times contradictory manifestations—are nevertheless likely to produce some important, if not immediate, fruits for those committed to the advancement of communal order as well as individual conscience and autonomy.

Yet the rebel will remain. As the next chapters demonstrate, nearly anyone can become a political offender—through action, speech, writing, or other communications, or due to their mere identity and existence.

Chapter Two

The Riddle
of the Sphinx

Categorizing Political Offenses and Offenders

*"When I use a word," Humpty Dumpty said, in a rather
scornful tone, "it means just what I choose
it to mean—neither more nor less."*

—Lewis Carroll,
Through the Looking Glass (1872)

*Hold thou the good: define it well;
For fear divine Philosophy
Should push beyond her mark, and be
Procuress to the Lords of Hell.*

—Alfred, Lord Tennyson,
In Memoriam A.H.H., Canto LIII (1869)

*The Light of Lights
Looks always on the motive,
not the deed,
The Shadow of Shadows
on the deed alone.*

—W. B. Yeats,
The Countess Cathleen (1889–1892)

Half People, Half Faces, Karl Stojka, oil and acrylic (1989).

Beyond Deification and Demonization

We have examined the political offender's role as Promethean bearer of progress and stirrer of the simmering sociopolitical cauldron. This portrayal, of course, casts the institutions of "authority"—the rebel's eternal antagonists—in a most unflattering light. Whenever the rebel is perceived to stand for reform and progress, the existing institutions of authority (political, social, economic, religious, or familial) are left with the rather less glamorous role of regressively resisting change. But as we know from the lessons of history, not all resistance to change must be viewed as either stifling or evil.

In the first place, not all and not even most exercises of authority turn out to be abusive, tyrannical, or malevolent. In many countries, communities, and smaller political groups, both the institutions of governance and the holders of the reins of power have been sensitive to the public good and have given the people an appropriate voice in their future. In these situations, where those in power make an honest attempt to accommodate evolving needs and demands by expanding and transforming the existing political framework, the establishment's resistance to unorthodox means of change can be viewed not as undue insistence upon an anachronistic and abusive system of "law and order," but as persistence in preserving the previously attained liberty and justice. Such steadfastness (often labeled "conservatism") is certainly nothing to condemn.

Those representing existing authority and its institutions, however reasonable and just, are nevertheless invariably and expectedly demonized by those calling for change. Aspiring rebels usually paint those in power in shades of ungodliness, evil, and corruption. The legitimacy of rebels, the available public support for their cause, and their potential success are inexorably tied to the people's acceptance of the propagandistic and demonic portrayal of those whom the rebels struggle against. A rebel celebrating his victory must show his former adversary in the worst possible light, to reflect upon himself a glory that much brighter.

The demonization process of the challenged authority is well illustrated in the ancient accounts of the Hebrews' struggles against pharaonic enslavement, their rebellions against their exploitative Hellenistic rulers, and their wars against the conquering Roman le-

41

gions. So persistent was the Pharaoh in his tyrannical abuse of the Israelites that, according to biblical accounts, ten plagues had to be
brought upon the land of Egypt before its ruler would let the children of Israel go.[134] Regardless of the historical accuracy of these accounts of the Hebrews' wars against their evil antagonists, it is evident that without a corrupt and evil Egyptian Pharaoh and
Hellenistic Antiochus there could be no just Exodus, no eventual triumph for an oppressed people, no Passover, and no Chanukah.

It is at the feet of another demonized authority—the corrupt, self-
serving, and indigenous Sadducee priesthood cooperating with an
alien Roman occupying army—that Christianity lays responsibility
for the crucifixion of Jesus, with which came the celebrated promise
of his glorious return. The subsequent heroism of many early Christian political offenders, the martyrs who resisted the "pagan and de-
generate" rites that perpetuated a corrupt Roman social and political culture, is similarly celebrated.[135] After the Christians had
solidified their power in Rome, they in turn found themselves portrayed as emissaries of evil by new groups of challengers—first the
mendicant friars and later the leaders of the Protestant Reformation.
Professing revulsion at the decadence and corruption of the Papacy
and its hierarchy, the reformers rose to undo the grip of the See of
Rome, portrayed by them as the lair of the Anti-Christ, the Christian
demon of ultimate evil.

Many of the immigrants to the New World brought with them
similar condemnations of the Old World and its institutions of authority, whether political (royalty and nobility), religious (Catholicism and Protestantism), or economic (feudalism and social class).
Claiming to possess the true spirit of reform in flight from a morally
decaying and doomed Babylon, the colonists went on to commit
their own abuses of power in their newly founded Eden. Resorting
to new iniquities, including the genocide of indigenous peoples and
the institution and continuance of slavery, these immigrants in turn
became the targets of demonization by new generations of political
rebels. When the Native Americans rose in rebellion against the expansionist "Manifest Destiny" of the United States, they demonized
the new interlopers as effectively as the Israelites had demonized the
Pharaohs.

That conquering rebels condemn and in some cases slander their
opponents has never been an indication of their ability to ensure hu-

manity or justice. Throughout history, the victorious rebels have often and quickly stepped into the shoes of those whom they had previously demonized. The instigators of the French Revolution claimed to be leading an uprising against privilege, insensitivity, and tyrannical authority. Yet the reign of terror imposed by the successful revolutionaries matched if not exceeded the abuses of Louis XVI and the somewhat exaggerated evils of his Bastille. It would take Napoleon's "whiff of grapeshot" to sweep away the remnants of the self-corrupted revolution, but only to replace it with another form of evil— imperial arrogance and overreach. The American Civil War, popularly depicted as a struggle for the liberation of African Americans from the inhumanity of slave labor, was followed by political powerlessness and continuing social degradations for a new subject class of "freemen." The 1917 Russian Revolution, portrayed as a workers' and peasants' uprising against a thoroughly abusive autocracy, quickly created its own and even more terrifying reigns of terror, resulting in the slaughter of the peasants and the virtual enslavement of the workers.

The process of demonization has not ceased in modern revolutionary struggles. The availability of an ever growing mass media has made deliberate campaigns of demonization (often through the dissemination of "disinformation") the primary thrust in any revolutionary agenda. Political offenders and the forces in power increasingly describe each other in the stark, polarizing rhetoric of a revolutionary-counterrevolutionary dichotomy. To enhance their own legitimacy, dissidents describe their adversaries as tools of "Evil Empires," as practitioners of racism or other intolerable doctrines or creeds. Conflicts over power, succession, status, autonomy, secession, ownership, and control of land and other resources—material or nonmaterial—are invariably portrayed as struggles of "liberators" against "enemies of the people," as wars of "true believers" against "infidels." Whether accurately or not, dissidents frequently depict their adversaries in power as "communists," "fascists," "racists," "tyrants," or "sexists," while painting themselves as "reformers" and "redeemers." Even personal struggles for political power, often devoid of ideological content, are characterized by their partisans as "campaigns of justice" and "wars of liberation." The modern revolutionary can almost completely avoid the fire and sword of outright battle for more subtle victories delivered by propaganda. The relatively peaceful fall of the Berlin Wall and the demise of the Soviet Empire were largely due to the effective resort to the media and world opinion by the "rebels." So successful were the protestors that no one considered them proper rebels.

At times, demonization can indeed serve as a useful tool for the mobilization of humanity's righteous ire (e.g., by placing Naziism and racism beyond the human pale). The U.N.'s designation of apartheid as a crime against humanity well illustrates the utility of demonic labeling, which helped fortify world resolve against racism and enhanced the struggle for social and economic justice in South Africa. Yet demonic labels can also be used for the character assassination of political opponents, as was the case of the U.N. General Assembly declaration equating Zionism—which claims to be a national liberation movement for dispersed Jews—with racism, though the declaration was ultimately revoked.[136]

We must guard against the temptation to view all rebels and political offenders as heroic champions of humanity, for many self-described "reformers," "liberators," and "messiahs" do not merit inclusion in the ranks of those truly struggling for justice and fellowship. And we must be equally prepared to dispel efforts to demonize all those exercising power, regardless of their objectives and means, as indiscriminate enemies of humanity. Neither Germany's Weimar Republic nor Czechoslovakia's pre–World War II republican regime warranted the demonic portrayals attributed to them by their Nazi adversaries. In many contemporary countries and societies one would be equally hard put to describe the forces of authority as less deserving, less lawful, and less just than the armies of those who have set out to challenge the established order. Especially in the face of the growing challenge to liberal authority by "ethnic cleansers," religious extremists, and other political or cultural fanatics, some international effort to separate the deserving from the undeserving may be in order. A more thorough reporting and objective assessment of governmental uses and abuses of power is the central theme of my previous volume, *The War Against Authority*.[137] But here we must urgently proceed with our specified mission—categorizing the illusive political offenders and defining the rules of warfare that should control the conflicts between them and those in possession of power.

The Quest Beyond the Law That Is

In the face of the persistent and total governmental and jurisprudential denial, usually accompanied by sheer ignorance, of the existence of political crime, assertions such as those of Sirhan Sirhan (the assassin of presidential candidate Robert F. Kennedy), John W. Hinckley Jr. (President Ronald Reagan's assailant), and Yigal Amir (the murderer of Israel's Yitzhak Rabin) of political rather than personal or psychopathological causes can neither be examined nor authoritatively responded to. Just as difficult to address are claims to the mantle of political offender, whether convincing, questionable, or even ludicrous, of James Earl Ray (Martin Luther King Jr.'s assassin), Lee Harvey Oswald (charged with the murder of President John F. Kennedy), John Brehmer Jr. (the assailant of Governor George C. Wallace), Mehmet Ali Agca (Pope John Paul II's assailant), and Timothy J. McVeigh (convicted of the Oklahoma City bombing). Can such claims be weighed by the offenders' own perceptions (often vague and self-serving), by their deeds, or merely by the political or public status of their victims?

Since neither scholarly literature (spanning such disciplines as philosophy, history, politics, sociology, and criminology) nor official legal sources (whether domestic or international legislation and judicial decisions) have come to grips with the definition and character of political crime, few thoughtful and consistent policies and programs regarding those asserting claims of political criminality, whether merited or unmerited, have evolved. The prevailing options, therefore, have been either to adopt the negative and absolutist position of America's law and public policy (however counterintuitive or illogical) that no offense is political, or to adopt a more permissive approach and thereby open a Pandora's box of unsubstantiated, often unjustifiable, and usually indeterminable claims to the mantle of political offender. Fearing the latter, and thereby failing to develop the objective analytic tools needed for any rational decisionmaking, America and other nations have tended to assess claims of political causes and motives in light of their own subjective ideological, ethnic, racial, or other loyalties. "One of the most distressing social syndromes of the past decade," wrote Francis A. Allen, referring to the American scene, "has been the apparent propensity of persons at

both ends of the ideological spectrum to temporize in their condemnations of violence when the acts in question were understood as advancing or intended to advance their own political or social objectives."[138]

Yet this parochial relativism is becoming more and more difficult
to live with in an age in which the mass media increasingly extend
their reach into homes everywhere, turning formerly distant and obscure conflicts into tangible and gripping experiences for growing
and ever more security conscious audiences throughout the world.
The globalization of the war between authority and autonomy
makes it imperative that we seek ways to better differentiate between just and evil objectives and means, and correspondingly between true and false political offenders. Among the host of questions—moral and legal, criminological and military, theoretical and
pragmatic—posed by the "political offense" and the "political offender," none is more complex than the threshold efforts to accurately define these terms. One of the first tasks in this multifaceted
survey of political crime and its perpetrators must therefore be definitional. As previously mentioned, the terms "political crime" and
"political criminal" have been totally denied or largely ignored in
American history, criminology, and law. On the other hand, some
writers and political activists have asserted such broad claims for political criminality and political offender status as would make the
terms nearly all-encompassing and therefore essentially meaningless.
In this chapter we will attempt to steer a middle course, neither constrained by professional blinders nor overwhelmed by self-serving
claims. The definitional task will thus begin with popular under-
standings, liberally extrapolated.

In the *Encyclopedia of the Social Sciences,* published in the United
States in 1933, the article on "political offenders" made no reference
to America; the text and all the bibliographical references pertained
to events, offenses, and offenders in foreign countries, including
Cuba, France, Germany, Ireland, Italy, Poland, and Russia.[139] It was
not until 1979 that *Webster's New Collegiate Dictionary* first acknowledged the existence of the "political criminal," defining this
person as "one involve[d] or charged . . . with *acts* against the government or a political system" (italics added).[140] Although this
rather unilluminating dictionary entry might provide a definitional
point of departure, even a cursory perusal of the realm of "political

crime" suggests that the political criminal cannot always be identified through action. Political crimes might consist of the failure to act—failure to carry out legally imposed duties such as paying taxes or registering for the draft. Communications inciting violence or other unlawful conduct, and even speaking or writing regarding prohibited subject matters, can also be deemed criminal. The ancient and contemporary crimes of sedition and treason are examples. Furthermore, such prohibited communications need not consist of advocacy or conspiracy to overthrow the government or depose existing leaders. Merely pleading for the reform of entrenched political, religious, social, or economic policies might be deemed criminal conduct: advocating liberty for slaves in the pre–Civil War South, urging free economic markets in Stalinist Russia, engaging in Christian proselytizing among Saudi Arabia's Moslems, opposing the circumcision of women in Africa, publishing newspapers without governmental permits in Thailand, or questioning the prophecy of Mohammed in Libya.

Even status can constitute a crime in some places. For Native Americans, blacks, and women in the United States, and for the untouchables of India and other minorities throughout the world, the very fact of *being* has sufficed to turn them into political offenders. Perceived as criminals because of their descent or status (or the desire to engage in activities permitted to others), members of these groups have been penalized for such conduct as being alive, remaining upon their land, pursuing education, or insisting upon their right to vote. It is to describe such persecution of individuals or groups on the mere grounds of their identity or status, or because of their engaging in political, cultural, or religious activities protected under internationally acknowledged rights, that the distinct terms "political trial," "political prisoner," and "prisoner of conscience" have been coined.[141]

To comprehend political criminality, one must view the term "political" quite liberally. Innumerable actions or failures to act motivated by religious, economic, social, or racial concerns could be perceived by those in power as threats upon their authority. Even in the United States, a journalist's mere defiance of court orders to disclose the sources of a news story might qualify as contempt of the authority of the court. The 1983 refusal of Christian fundamentalists in Nebraska to comply with certification standards imposed by a secular government upon religious schools resulted in the arrest of the offending clergy.[142] Even citizens' actions against nongovernmental institutions, personnel, or practices might be deemed politically or socially objectionable and therefore criminal. Discrimination directed against an ethnic or racial group, as well as strikes, picketing, or other civil unrest directed against a protected institution such as a private employer or an abortion clinic, can constitute a crime when those in power define such conduct as undermining to the political stability of the state.

Moreover, the government's power to sanction political offenders is not limited to the tools and penalties offered by the criminal law. Politically suspect individuals may be subjected to a great variety of noncriminal and nonpenal burdens and disabilities as well. In the United States, for example, Southern loyalists, Communists, and others whose allegiance to the government was thought to be in doubt were prohibited from holding public office and other employment. Japanese Americans were subjected to curfew, travel limitations, and exile during World War II, and Native Americans were subjected to relocation and more severe sanctions throughout most of the nation's history.

Conventional wisdom has acknowledged the difficulty of defining political criminality and classifying its perpetrators. Some scholars and practitioners have argued that the phenomenon cannot be objectively defined, relying instead on the albeit facile and uninformed aphorism that "one person's freedom fighter is another's terrorist." These difficulties in reaching a consensus on a definition of political criminality led Italian criminologist Francesco Carrara to assert in the late nineteenth century that political crime was "indefinable."[143]

Such definitional hardships can be readily attributed to both ancient and contemporary political doctrines and institutional myths. Definitional confusion is also deeply embedded in conflicting cultural values and social fabrics. Making the task especially complex are unresolved theoretical as well as practical disagreements regarding fundamental questions: What are the requisites of legitimate authority? What are the limitations upon majority rule? What are the reciprocal rights and responsibilities of the state and its citizens? What are the minimal prerequisites for democracy? What causes justify a citizen's defiance of authority? What means of resistance are to be tolerated? The most treacherous shoals in this murky definitional sea, as previously noted, are the boundaries that divide political and nonpolitical criminals, just and unjust causes of protest and resistance, and approved and proscribed means of dissent and rebellion.

We have seen that in ancient civilizations divine and secular authority—whether represented by the tangible but immeasurable force of God's prophet or the more immediate worldly power of the king, whether personified by the sacred priest or the tribal chief—were often indistinguishable. Moreover, the temporal result of challenging either authority was usually the same—death or exile. Secular law and justice, which encompassed the commands of those in power, was therefore often confused with higher law and justice, which generally encompassed the commonly shared, transcendent, and divinely ordained values. Since secular power historically professed ordination by divine authority, rebellion against either was perceived as sacrilege.

Yet even the earliest biblical tradition voiced a dissatisfaction with this blurring of the line between divine commandments and temporal authority. The prophets of ancient Israel and Judea frequently found themselves pitted against unworthy and unjust earthly rulers. "Hear the word of the Lord, O King of Judah," insisted Jeremiah.[144] Likewise, Daniel prophesied to the king of Babylon the unthinkable: "Mene, Mene, Tekel Upharsin—God hath numbered thy kingdom, and finished it."[145] In the New World, millennia later, Jonathan Mayhew, minister of Boston's West Church, proclaimed from the pulpit to mid-eighteenth-century America that it was "blasphemy to call tyrants and oppressors God's ministers" and, therefore, when "iniquity comes to be . . . established by . . . law . . . it is a sin not to transgress it."[146] In his *Letter from a Birmingham Jail,* Dr. Martin Luther King Jr. reasserted the same position two centuries later: "A just law is a man-made code that squares with moral law or the law of God. An unjust law is a code that is out of harmony with the moral law."[147]

The fierce prophetic insistence on the accountability of temporal political power to divine authority and its transcendental commandments acted to endow with greater legitimacy those setting out to oppose and overthrow usurpers of political power and abusers of true justice in the name of a higher law. With secular law categorized as subordinate to the higher authority of divine or "natural law" (a system of rules derived from either divine principles or the nature of man and society), the duty of citizens to obey government and its orders was irreversibly challenged. It was this revolutionary principle that the writers of the American Declaration of Independence clearly endorsed: that the citizenry is endowed with inalienable rights, and the denial of these rights by those in power justifies the people's altering or abolishing such abusive governance.

For most of humanity's recorded history the tensions between the requirements of the higher authority of natural law[148] and the impositions of temporal power continued unabated. But with the emergence in the late nineteenth century of what legal and political writers have come to call the "positive law" theory[149] (asserting that only existing laws—i.e., laws actually adopted by those in power—are binding), the higher authority of natural law was challenged and denied. The citizen's duty of obedience to government and all its decrees became positive law's unchallenged doctrine. The revolutionary suggestion that since existing laws do not necessarily equal justice, and may therefore be derogated, has accordingly become the greatest heresy in the view of positivist philosophy, which continues to naïvely assert that all enactments of the state—whether just or not—are universally and equally binding. The essence of this positivist argument was articulated in Supreme Court justice Abe Fortas's assertion that no individual can "substitute his own judgment or passion, however noble, for rules of law."[150]

Through their absolutist submission to existing law (not on the grounds that it is infallible but on the premise of the social need for law and order), positivists have blinded themselves to the questions of morality and justice that are the very essence of governmental legitimacy as well as the foundations of political criminality. The preachers of law and order and most law-abiding citizens nevertheless continue to be intrigued and bedeviled by the manner in which political resistance and rebellion, unlike other forms of criminality, frequently seem to emerge in the service of society's positive, moral, social, and cultural objectives. Could there be instances, many continue to ask, when an objective is so morally or practically valuable, or so widely acclaimed, as to justify resort to unlawful, violent, or even wicked means for its attainment? And if so, how are we to divine these worthy causes, and the means they might justify, and distinguish them from unjust objectives and means?

Causes Just and Right

One formula proposed for categorizing political criminality and rebellion would seek to distinguish between just (or "right") causes that catapult men and women into action and unjust (or "wrong") causes that propel actors to protest and resist authority. The difficulty with this approach, of course, lies in what sociologist W.E.B. Du Bois, in his biography of abolitionist John Brown, called the "riddle of the sphinx": How are we to know right causes from wrong ones?[151] More importantly, how are we to discern the difference in sufficient time to pass not merely contemporaneous and transitory judgments but judgments that will withstand the vagaries of changing times and attitudes? Because political crime is a wide-ranging phenomenon—encompassing status and verbal dissent, individual dissidence and collective action, civil disobedience and insurgent militancy—it has inherently resisted simple division into positive and negative categories. Nevertheless, there have been some interesting attempts to make this distinction.

Some thirty years ago, historian Richard M. Brown addressed the question of "just" and "unjust" causes in a report prepared for President Lyndon B. Johnson's National Commission on the Causes and Prevention of Violence. Though Brown's analysis only addressed violent political conduct, his work arguably applies to nonviolent forms of politically motivated behavior as well. Advancing an eclectic viewpoint, combining populist as well as moral and utilitarian perspectives and criteria, Brown suggested that American communal strife fell historically into two major divisions: positive and negative.[152] Positive violence served constructive goals, while negative violence was "in no direct way connected with any socially or historically constructive development."[153] Illustrious examples of positive violence, Brown asserted, included the Revolutionary War, the Civil War, the Indian wars, vigilantism, and the agrarian and labor reform movements. In the category of negative violence he counted the campaigns of organized crime, communal feuds, lynchings, the exploits of bigotry (whether triggered by racial, ethnic, or religious intolerance), assassinations, and urban riots.

According to Brown, positive violence derived its claim to legitimacy from its contributions to constructive goals, as contrasted with nonconstructive objectives. But Brown's test poses a host of threshold problems: Is there a universal and timeless test by which one can measure constructiveness? If not, is constructiveness to be determined contemporaneously with the violent or prohibited act in question, or is it to be viewed through historical hindsight? Is a unanimous or majority opinion required to determine constructiveness, or could a strong minority view qualify? Finally, is constructiveness a matter for expert opinion, or should popular notions be given primary weight?

Although these troublesome definitional problems were left unresolved, Brown offered a second definition for "positive violence," using the term to describe activities that advance "ends that have been widely accepted and applauded."[154] This second test focuses on whether the violence is used to effect widely accepted or popular ends. Although such an approach avoids some of the pitfalls inherent in the constructiveness test, it does so at the risk of embracing as positive those manifestations of violence that initially gain popular support yet are judged atavistic in a historical perspective (e.g., Ku Klux Klan terrorism). The popularity test also risks excluding causes that are deemed contemporaneously unpopular but that are later recognized as constructive (e.g., slave rebellions).

Brown failed to address these shortcomings and contradictions in his classification system.[155] The goals of several of the movements that he classified as positive, including the Revolutionary War and the Civil War, were indeed widely, although obviously not uniformly, applauded by contemporary society. Other manifestations of violence that he designated positive, including the agrarian and labor reform movements, were the product of struggling, politically feeble communities whose views gained wider acceptance and sympathy only with the passage of time.

Conversely, some activities labeled positive by Brown (including vigilantism and the Indian wars) received wide approbation when undertaken, but not so later. The vigilantes proclaimed themselves "believers in the doctrine of popular sovereignty" and asserted the "right of the people, the real sovereigns" to protect the country against "villains."[156] In contrast to the shorter history of vigilantism, the Indian wars, which began in Tidewater, Virginia, in 1607 and culminated in a final massacre at Wounded Knee, South Dakota, in 1890, constituted the longest and most remorseless racial conflict in

American history. Both vigilantism and the Indian wars have been subjected to growing criticism in assessments of America's progress toward a just and pluralistic society. Brown's system seems to inherently rely on the clouded and subjective judgment of those actually experiencing the political strife, rather than on the more objective criteria derived from historical perspectives. This significant flaw subjects Brown's classification system to criticism for being time-bound and biased.

Apart from the general categorization of political offenses by cause—positive and "right" or negative and "wrong"—one is frequently confronted with the more precise question of categorizing the objectives of the political offenders themselves. What specifically are the offenders' motivations? What specifically do they expect to attain through their activism?

In an attempt to classify political criminality on the basis of objectives or motivations, Nachman Ben-Yehuda, in his book *Political Assassinations by Jews*,[157] offers five major classes. The first, "elite substitution," describes activities, including political assassinations, designed to replace the existing leadership, often without aiming to create substantial systemic or ideological changes. The second class, "tyrannicide," deals with particularly violent activities against despots or dictators intended to bring about better, usually less repressive and more rational, rules and rulers. The third class, consisting of "symbolic" or "propaganda by deed" violence, encompasses carefully focused attacks against particular political figures or institutions with the aim of drawing attention to selected and pressing political problems. The fourth class, "terrorism," refers to mass and indiscriminate violent activities, including assassinations, designed to challenge an existing political system and demonstrate the government's inability to rule. The final class, "anomic violence," identifies assassinations and other forms of political violence carried out by lone actors who use political rhetoric to justify deeds stemming from private, idiosyncratic, inarticulate, or irrational motives. We would add a sixth class to supplement the Ben-Yehuda list: the class of "crimes of revenge"— activities through which political actors seek not to affect some future outcome but to offer retribution for past misdeeds.

Ben-Yehuda's classification of political offenses according to the objectives or motivations of the actors supplies an added dimension to Brown's effort to categorize political offenses according to cause.

Although Ben-Yehuda and other proponents of this six-point classification have offered it primarily as a descriptive rather than prescriptive tool, one would be justified in drawing from it further policy conclusions. Of the six classes of objectives advanced by
Ben-Yehuda, only tyrannicide stands out as a usually positive and
just objective. Terrorism and anomic violence, on the other hand,
clearly loom as unjust and negative objectives. The remaining
classes, elite substitution, symbolic or propaganda violence, and
crimes of revenge, cannot be readily assessed or assigned to either
the just or the unjust camp. Judgment on offenses of these classes
must often be withheld until the reviewer is able to weigh and assess
the character of the existing political regime, the surrounding circumstances, and the availability of peaceful means for political
change and restoration of justice.

Unjust Causes:
Finding the Hallmarks of Evil

The proposed identification of negative violence reveals similar flaws
when closely examined. Some of the activities enumerated by
Brown, such as horse thievery, kinship feuds, lynch mobs, organized
crime, and racial or ethnic violence, are easily accepted as negative.
Disparate as they appear, these exploits generally represent egoistic
pursuits devoid of the broad ideological or communal goals that
characterize positive political criminality. Other activities labeled
negative by Brown are not so easily categorizable. As noted earlier,
momentary passions and prejudices may have clouded social judgment in distinguishing negative from positive violence.

Professor Brown tellingly includes slave revolts (extending from
the New York rebellion of 1712 through Nat Turner's 1831 uprising
in South Hampton County, Virginia, and beyond) as examples of
negative violence.[158] Many of these rebellions are likely to be viewed
today as having served "constructive" goals. Yet at the time these rebellions were speedily and ruthlessly suppressed, as they failed to
arouse sympathy or produce improvements in the lot of the enslaved
African Americans.[159]

Though many of Brown's examples of negative violence are beyond debate, positive claims can and have been asserted for still
many other types of violence that he includes in this category. And

overlooked within his class of condemned violence is the phenomenon of "social banditry."[160] English historian Eric J. Hobsbawn, who coined this designation, applied it to the class of pseudomythical outlaws who were admired not only by the underprivileged but by large segments of general society and who are remembered as heroes rather than villains in popular literature.

Heroic Robin Hoods who robbed the rich and gave to the poor were enshrined not only in English traditions but in practically all cultures throughout the world, in a host of incarnations. On the American scene the social bandit continues to be represented in popular accounts and folktales about the James brothers and Billy the Kid. To Confederate sympathizers in post–Civil War Missouri, and to the Grange-minded farmers of the Midwest, the exploits of Jesse and Frank James symbolized a just war against the unpopular invaders from the Northeast—the railroads and the banks.[161] This heroic perception of Jesse James was immortalized in the popular ballad:

> *Jesse James was a lad who killed many a man*
> *He robbed the Glendale train.*
> *He stole from the rich and he gave to the poor;*
> *He'd a hand and a heart and a brain.*

> *Jesse was a man, a friend to the poor;*
> *He never would see a man suffer pain;*
> *And with his brother Frank he robbed the Chicago*
> *   bank,*
> *and stopped the Glendale train.*

> *It was on Saturday night; Jesse was at home*
> *Talking with his family brave.*
> *Robert Ford come along like a thief in the night and*
> *laid poor Jesse in his grave.*[162]

Billy the Kid similarly stood as the just hero to the poor herdsmen and villagers of the Southwest. Later, during the Great Depression, Bonnie and Clyde likewise became the romantic avengers of the farmers and the poor who had been exploited by depersonalizing financial institutions.

Can these popular positive perceptions of the social bandit be reconciled with Brown's definitions of negative violence? Also, how valid is Brown's demarcation between vigilantism (positive violence) and lynching (negative violence)? Some may agree that the two represent polar opposites. Yet to others, a Colorado vigilante's mid-nineteenth-century account illustrates the uncommon merging of positive and negative objectives and methods:

> We never hanged on circumstantial evidence. I have known a great many such executions. . . . I don't believe one of them was ever unjust. But when they were proved guilty . . . there was no getting out of it. No, there were no appeals in those days, no writs of error; no attorney's fees; no pardon in six months. Punishment was swift, sure and certain.[163]

Ambiguities prevail throughout the arena of political crime. The demarcation between positive and negative causes reflects diverse and ever evolving values, of which popular judgments in particular are capable of dramatic and constant change. Ku Klux Klan activities against African Americans, carpetbaggers, and Federal troops in the post–Civil War South, now described as early examples of domestic American terrorism, had political objectives that were widely supported and applauded by the South's disenfranchised landowning whites. Conversely, America's slave rebellions, historically condemned for their violence and occasional brutality, are no longer likely to be perceived as a negative phenomenon. Although abolition was not widely supported at the time of these uprisings—even in the North—one might today view the rebelling slaves' cause more positively, while perceiving as negative the Klan's violent opposition to emancipation and freedom.

Although one might similarly tend to accept the initial characterization of urban riots as negative, even here noted exceptions stand out. The riots provoked by the Sons of Liberty (protesting British tax policies in the leading colonial cities of pre-revolutionary America, including Charleston, New York, Boston, and Newport) served as precursors to the American Revolution. Scrutinizing the urban unrest of the 1960s, historian T. M. Tomlinson similarly observed: "What produces riots is the shared agreement by most Negro Americans that their lot in life is unacceptable, coupled with the view by a significant minority that riots are a legitimate and productive mode of protest."[164]

The line separating the positive from the negative shifts drastically with individual or group perspectives and with the passage of time.

What the underprivileged or emerging classes of any period will likely consider as an indispensable and positive display of resistance will often be viewed as negative or excessive by the established interests of the time. As previously noted, those seeking to retain and conserve established values, powers, and privileges are likely to view any redistribution of political, economic, social, or religious rights as disruptive and negative. But in the eyes of reformers, those supporting the status quo often seem bent on maintaining injustice and fostering social stagnation in a dynamic and ever-changing world. And because these diversely held judgments regarding positive and negative objectives are capable of dramatic change over time, historically illegal and even violent acts can be transformed into hailed and celebrated acts.

Despite these definitional difficulties, it may still be possible to point to some crimes as political and others as non-political or "common," to some causes as constructive and others as negative, to some objectives as just and others as unjust. The difficulty of the riddle of the sphinx—of distinguishing right causes from wrong—does not justify the abandonment of the moral and legal search for a better classification and understanding of rebellion and political criminality. American and world history stand firmly for the conclusion that extralegal means and violence have often served as catalysts for political progress and as harbingers of social and economic justice. This lesson of history must find its way into contemporary law and policy.

Identification by Deed: The Political Offense

Before setting out boldly to further define and classify political criminality, one must determine whether the quest would reap greater benefits by focusing on the deeds or actors in question. Are greater insights likely to be gained from an effort to identify political offenses, thereafter assuming all perpetrators of such offenses to be political offenders? Or would it be more useful to identify the actors, the political offenders themselves, thereafter assuming all deeds perpetrated by such persons to be political offenses?

Similar questions regarding the methodology of classification have been raised before in other sectors of law and criminology, particularly with regard to white-collar crime, juvenile delinquency, and female criminality. White-collar crime was initially perceived as offender- rather than offense-oriented. It was therefore the identity or characteristics of the offender, rather than of the offense, that endowed white-collar criminality with its distinctive nature. Scholars concentrating on juvenile and female criminality have likewise dwelled on the identity of the offender. In contrast, most other categories of crime (including homicide, drug trafficking, and computer crimes) have been differentiated primarily according to the characteristics of the offending conduct rather than those of the perpetrator.

Past experience, as we shall soon see, offers inconclusive answers to our question: Should the offender or the offense be the driving force behind the definition of political criminality? It can be argued that focusing on the offense and its characteristics promises to yield a more universally acceptable and less ideologically tainted definition than would an approach dwelling on the actor. But whether or not it might be easier, in practice, to reach consensus as to what constitutes a "political offense" rather than as to what makes a "political offender" remains to be seen.

International law, which governs the extradition practices regarding escaped offenders (including political offenders), has invariably placed its emphasis upon the definition of the offense rather than on the identification of the offender.[165] A determination that an asserted offense is political is what qualifies an offender for protection under extradition law.[166] Yet despite the 150-year-old and nearly universal practice of refusing the extradition of those charged with political offenses, no consensus has developed in international law, much less in domestic laws, regarding the criteria for defining this category of crimes.

A variety of classification formulas advanced by legal scholars and practitioners are nevertheless worthy of examination. An initially appealing yet ultimately ineffectual approach to the definition of political offenses relies upon drawing a clear distinction between deeds that challenge the state, its institutions, and its security, and those that threaten private individuals and their property. The first category of offenses are labeled "political offenses," while the latter are designated "common crimes" or "conventional crimes."

"As long as there have been states, there have been crimes against the state," noted Barton Ingraham and Kazuhiko Tokoro in their study of political crime in the United States, Western Europe, and

Japan.[167] These writers then enumerated the major strands of anti-state crimes as identified in different legal systems: treason, *prodosia test poelos, perduellio, lésè-majesté,* and *Verrat.* Throughout history a significant number of additional crimes sometimes considered infractions against individual interests, including heresy, gambling, arson, counterfeiting, false testimony, and sodomy, have sometimes been considered offenses against the sovereign authority.[168] Nevertheless, even such an expanded list remains unhelpfully inconsistent and inconclusive.

Some scholars have sought to broaden the definition of political criminality to include not only treason and its allied offenses but a host of other acts that conceivably constitute a threat to the security and authority of the state. Yet such expansion could make the list hopelessly long. Crimes, unlike civil wrongs, are by definition offenses not only against the private citizen but also against the collective interests of the community and the state. It is for this reason that criminal prosecutions are conducted by the public prosecutors, in the name of the state, and the ordained sanctions are determined by the state, not by the victims.

"Criminal law," pointed out criminologists Marshall Clinard and Richard Quinney, "is . . . an aspect of politics, one of the results of the process of formulating and administering public policy."[169] Stephen Schafer, a lawyer and sociologist, similarly submitted that the definition of a crime is nothing more than a translation into legal terms of the political ideology of those in power.[170] Much to the same effect, Richard Quinney proposed that "crime is a definition of human conduct that is created by authorized agents in a politically organized society."[171]

Marxist doctrine, following a comparable vein, has not only placed crime within a broad political context but has also claimed the whole complex of government and law, civil as well as criminal, to be a tool of political power.[172] The standards of behavior required of citizens and enforced by the legal system accordingly flow "from the political organization of . . . society."[173] Consequently, any deviance from state-ordained institutions or values might be viewed as an offense against the political order. It follows, under Marxist thought, that inasmuch as all laws are designed to protect institutions and value systems articulated by the prevailing political authority, all crimes, in the broadest sense, are political offenses.

Adopting such a far-ranging definitional scheme that labels all deviant and proscribed behavior as political crime is likely to be as intellectually and pragmatically counterproductive as the opposite practice of denying the very distinctiveness of political criminality. Such definitional overreach would deprive serious students and practitioners of political justice of the potential benefits likely to flow from a focus upon a narrower and more distinct class of political crime. Classifying and treating all delinquent conduct as political crime (much like earlier attempts to classify all criminality as mental illness)[174] is bound to deprive not only scholars but also agencies of justice of more discriminating, more effective approaches for dealing with the unique problems posed by the "genuine" class of political offenses. Finally, if all crimes are defined as political, there would be no need to separate, for either more severe or more lenient punishment, those offenders with truly just motives.

To maximize public utility it is therefore necessary to seek a definitional middle ground between underinclusion and overinclusion. With this in mind, the axiomatic denomination of particular types of conduct as *per se* political offenses—a practice that prevails in the international law of extradition—has gained a considerable following. This approach specifies as political certain enumerated activities (e.g., treason, sedition, and espionage), and designates as political those offenders who engage in such conduct. Amnesty International, in its interventions on behalf of political prisoners worldwide, similarly restricts its categorization of political offenders to those who engage only in nonviolent protest and resistance.[175]

Having surveyed the categories of acts that could be considered *per se* political offenses, we must next consider a system that would examine and classify general criminality based on the actor's intent or motive. In the context of the traditional Anglo-American legal approach to the definition of criminal offenses, two distinct elements—an *actus reus,* the prohibited act, and a *mens rea,* the prohibited or evil intent—must occur concurrently before a crime is deemed committed. It is evident that a *per se* approach to the definition of political offenses tends to neglect the second required element. When certain acts are defined as political offenses merely by designation and without regard to the offender's intent or motive, the role of *mens rea* is greatly diminished if not totally eliminated in the process.

A *per se* approach tends to classify all acts of treason, espionage, sedition, presidential assaults, flag desecration, and draft evasion as political offenses. It would not matter whether the offender acted for reasons of altruism and patriotism or for personal animosity and greed. Such an indiscriminate outcome—overlooking the political offender's unique claim to noble motives—would negate the very arguments advanced in support of according political protesters and resisters a favorable standing. Under this approach, one would not be able to summarily reject such ill-founded claims for political offender status as those of John Wilson (convicted in the 1990s of espionage for money, as opposed to ideology) or John W. Hinckley Jr. (the "love"-struck offender who claimed originally that his attempt to assassinate President Reagan was prompted by a desire to impress screen actress Jodie Foster). Such a faulty *per se* test might tend to give credence to Hinckley's later claim from prison: "I've become a political prisoner. . . . There is no difference between John Hinckley and Andrei Sakharov. We are both political prisoners in every way."[176] At the extreme end, the *per se* approach overlooks base, nonpolitical motives such as those of Benedict Arnold, Aldrich Ames, or, for that matter, Judas—the quest for pure profit.

The *per se* approach to the classification of political offenses becomes even more objectionable when extended beyond a narrow and restricted range of prohibited activities. The shortcomings of this approach are illustrated by the detailed list of the activities that have been considered political offenses in Europe during the past two centuries.

From his excellent study of French, German, and English law—extending from the mid–nineteeth to the mid–twentieth century—criminologist Barton L. Ingraham derives twelve primary categories of political offenses: (1) acts of betrayal to an enemy (i.e., desertion, espionage, revealing official secrets, and joining enemy armed forces); (2) acts endangering the head of state and principal members of the government (including attempts and conspiracies against their life, limb, or liberty); (3) economic crimes (including counterfeiting of money and the official seal, currency violations, and acts inimical to the industrial and economic welfare of the country); (4) sexual crimes (including relations with the sovereign's wife or children and the offense of miscegenation); (5) crimes of verbal expression (including sedition and libel, insults to the dignity of the head of state, and incitement to mutiny and rebellion); (6) religious crimes (including heresy and impiety, particularly in countries with a state religion); (7) rebellion and other overt resistance to state authorities (i.e., illegal assemblies, riots, and acts of terrorism); (8) crimes of subversion (including refusal to execute the law and issuing illegal laws and decrees); (9) participation in illegal organizations; (10) individual or group usurpation of state authority (including the recruitment of private armies and the levying of unauthorized taxes); (11) misprision (the failure to denounce plots and conspiracies against the government); and (12) miscellaneous offenses such as bribing governmental officials, election fraud, dueling, and unauthorized participation in foreign wars.[177]

While one can certainly imagine circumstances under which most of the offenses included in this comprehensive list might be considered political, one can be equally certain that not all and not even most of these offenses would justify characterization as political offenses without attention to the actor's motive. The inescapable conclusion is that one must have reference to both the act *(actus reus)* and the actor's intent or motive *(mens rea)* before justifiably attaching the "political" label. Indeed, Ingraham suggests as much by concluding his comprehensive list of political offenses with a category that includes practically all common crimes, as long as the primary motive for their commission is political.

Spotlighting the Actor:
Status or Motive?

Forty years ago a new light was shed on workplace and business-related criminality when criminologist Edwin Sutherland first identified and began to study the "white-collar" offender. Drawing on Sutherland's classification and on subsequent research, criminologists have developed new policing, prosecutorial, and correctional methods in the past decades to deal with this particular breed of offender. It is relevant to the political offender's definitional dilemma that Sutherland's focus was on the status and position of the white-collar offender (being one vested with business or corporate authority and trust) rather than on the character of the criminal deed itself.[178]

We have seen that some scholars and practitioners have similarly proposed to identify political criminality through an emphasis on the offender, by pointing primarily to either status or motives and objectives. One such school of thought, following the Marxist lead, would reserve the label of political offender to exploited classes or populations: slaves, the proletariat, those dominated by colonialism, those abused by racism. It is thus the actor's socioeconomic class or status that would confirm his or her political offender status. Historically, such a classification approach could have produced unexpected results, such as the wholesale granting of political offender status to all Attica prisoners, advocation of the questionable political claims of America's urban ghetto arsonists, and possibly even the vindication of self-confessed rapist Eldridge Cleaver. Yet it is this very approach (described in greater detail in Chapter 7) that has been embraced by advocates of the emerging international humanitarian law as a means for enhancing the international status of anti-colonial and anti-racist activists.

Henry David Thoreau, concentrating on the offender's motive rather than his or her status, defined political offenses as "crimes of conscience." Amnesty International similarly refers to political offenders as "prisoners of conscience." Criminologist Stephen Schafer labels these offenses as "crimes of conviction or ideology." More specifically, Schafer, as well as others, contend that it is the offender's motive or intent *(mens rea)* rather than the deed *(actus reus)* that primarily distinguishes the political offender from the common offender.[179] Only when the offender's action is driven by ideology, conviction, or the pursuit a public cause—instead of venality, personal greed, or gain—would the offense qualify as political.

But how is one to determine whether political motives or objectives supply the drive for the proscribed activity? Conceding the primacy of motive over deed, Canadian scholar Austin T. Turk sought to further distill political motives from the characteristics of the offender's defiant actions.[180] In his study of political criminality, Turk identifies four primary forms of political defiance: dissent, evasion, disobedience, and violence. Dissent refers to protest against the structures, activities, or persons who represent authority. Evasion identifies attempts to circumvent the demands of those in authority, including such conduct as failure to pay taxes or report for military duty. Disobedience consists of more explicit and confrontational acts in contravention of government rules or demands, while violence encompasses particularly aggressive manifestations of disobedience.

Another quest for political motives through concentration on the techniques utilized by revolutionary activists was undertaken by Thomas H. Greene.[181] Greene specifies four primary techniques resorted to by political revolutionary movements: coup d'état, violence, guerrilla warfare, and terror. Coup d'état encompasses unconstitutional or otherwise illegal efforts to alter forms of authority or change the existing hierarchy, carried out by conspirators with existing or former political standing. Violence refers to occasional, incidental, and usually poorly organized resorts to militant means (such as Hitler's 1923 Putsch), while guerrilla warfare constitutes variations of irregular domestic, as contrasted with international, warfare (such as Nicaragua's Contras or Afghanistan's Mujahideen). Terror seeks to combine indiscriminate violence with a deliberate plan for the psychological disorientation of the public, with the intention of persuading the population that the rebels are strong and those in authority are vulnerable and replaceable.

Both the Turk and Greene approaches, relying primarily on categorizing forms of resistance rather than on addressing the actors' motives, suffer from several of the inadequacies inherent in the earlier definitional schemes that emphasized acts over actors. At the same time—through their concentration on "political" and "revolutionary" defiance and activism—Turk and Greene help establish the role of motive and create at least an initial presumption that those participating in collective protest or militant resistance tend to be politically motivated. Still, more particular evidence regarding individual motives is needed to avoid the indiscriminate granting of political offender status to every tax evader, draft dodger, or urban rioter.

There are compelling reasons to believe that a discrete definition of political criminality cannot be reached without undertaking a critical examination not only of proscribed activities but also of particular offenders and their motives. By focusing on the offender, one would be able to avoid specifically enumerating the activities that qualify as political. Directing attention to the offender would permit an examination not only of the general causes leading to rebellion but also of the offender's specific motives. Such examination would undertake to distinguish between a citizen victimized by governmental abuse of power, an altruistically and humanely motivated rebel, a conscientious objector, a hired spy, a professional guerrilla, a venal exploiter, and a profit-seeker in collaboration with the enemy. It would separate Benedict Arnold from Ezra Pound, General James Wilkinson (Aaron Burr's friend who was in the pay of the Spanish Foreign Office to incite division in the early Republic) from Jefferson Davis, James Earl Ray from John Brown, John W. Hinckley from John Wilkes Booth.[182]

It must be conceded, however, that broad political causes, as well as specific individual motives, remain diverse, complex, and difficult to identify and classify. Based on his general typology of political violence, Fred R. von der Mehden cataloged a wide range of motives: primordial motives (relating to or derived primarily from cultural, racial, ethnic, and religious conflicts); separatist and secessionist motives; revolutionary and counterrevolutionary motives; coup-oriented motives; issue-oriented motives (e.g., abortion and land reform); and personality-oriented motives (e.g., magnicide and regicide).[183] But formulating a typology of motives underlying all categories of political protest and resistance, not just political violence, will be a difficult and complex task. Hopefully we can uncover some foundational stones for this task by investigating the social and psychological evolution of the political offender (see Chapter 3).

Equally intriguing would be an effort to catalog causes and motives according to the subjective claims advanced by political offenders themselves. Once again the available evidence is likely to be biased and confusing. Perpetrators have sought to justify political protest and rebellion on many diverse and often dramatic grounds: conformity to the immutable demands of some religious or other higher moral order; compliance with the requirements of international or constitutional law; response to the collective needs and imperatives of a given people or community; obedience to the demands of individual conscience; assertion of an individual's or community's self-evident right of self-defense against abusive authority. Yet how accepting should readers, society, or the agencies of justice be of an offender's self-characterization and his or her statement of motives? How authentic or credible was the claim of the Virginia driver arrested in 1984 for employing his car as a battering ram against the doors of a Fairfax County school, who argued that his offense was intended to protest the 1961 Bay of Pigs invasion of Cuba, as well as the Vietnam War?[184] And even if authentically advanced, how much

weight should be given to such preposterous claims in courts of law
or in the fora of public opinion?

Tests of Nexus and Proportionality

Structuring a system for classifying "political" offenses and offenders and for categorizing "constructive" or "just" causes and deeds is,
as we have seen, a task made nearly impossible by disparities in
value systems and by historical fluctuations in public opinion. Neither can exclusive attention to a single criterion such as "cause,"
"motive," "act," or "actor" guide us sufficiently to distinguish between the genuine political rebel or protester and the common criminal who acts in the interests of selfish motives and destructive
causes. If none of these criteria can alone suffice to endow an act of
dissidence, disobedience, or rebellion with "political" merit, the categorization of political crimes must resort to more refined, more
complex, multifaceted formulas.

Some such formulas, previously advanced, warrant at least cursory examination. Yet a truly promising approach to the classification of political criminality might require progression beyond the examination of causes, motives, actors, and deeds. Such an approach
might consist of a combination of three or four elements: a concurrence of a constructive or publicly acclaimed cause, an altruistic motive, a dedicated actor, and a reasonably commensurate deed.

A different approach might further refine the various elements discussed above. For example, it might be required that the "just"
cause involve the assertion of universally recognized rights (such as
the right to resist genocide or the right to struggle against colonialism or racism) rather than the attainment of parochial objectives.
Still, political activists do not always pursue such universally acclaimed causes. They often serve narrow and sectarian objectives.
Yet such limited objectives may not be induced by negative and self-
serving motives, as illustrated by the contemporary contest in America and worldwide between the pro-life and pro-choice forces. Perhaps an actor's commitment to a universal objective or even to a
narrower but altruistic communal objective should be the first test
for political offender status. Of course, as in the conflict between the
pro-life and pro-choice forces in contemporary society, the task of
determining which side is serving a common communal objective, or

whether both are, still remains. Some "judgment calls" will still need to be made, and the majority or public opinion will still need to carry a great deal of weight in making the necessary determination.

From the initial task of delineating the causes and motives asserted by a would-be political offender, we need to proceed to an examination of available and utilizable means of protest and rebellion. Gauging the appropriateness of the political offender's means or deeds might indeed be as much at issue as assessing his or her motives. To overcome the preposterous and nihilistic proposition that deserving ends justify resort to any and all means, we might insist that an act of protest or rebellion be responsive, in intensity and breadth, to the evil perceived by the would-be political offender. We might further require that the deed be reasonably related to the attainment of the relief or objective sought.

Particularly appealing might be a formulation of "reasonableness," perhaps dividing it into two distinct and required elements: nexus and proportionality. Nexus signifies the proximity or phenomenal linkage between the offender's deprivation (his or her cause and objective) and the remedial or defiant means chosen for attaining his or her goals. The second element of the test for reasonableness, proportionality, measures the balance between the offender's deeds and the perceived evils.

A combination of nexus and proportionality offers a ready yardstick against which political offenders and offenses of all stripes might be measured. Nexus permits us to measure the proximate relationship between an existing evil, the professed political objective, and the offender's prohibited act. Such interrelationship might produce an ordering or ranking of all types of political resistance, with the nexus descending from those acts designed to accomplish direct and demonstrable political change to activities with more remote, or activities devoid of, remedial connections. When the offender's objective is to counter oppressive political censorship, the most proximate response might be the production of uncensored underground publications. The nexus is looser, however, when oppressive censorship is countered by the assassination of the governmental censor, the bombing of a post office, or the kidnaping of a foreign journalist—all of which might prove appealing in dramatizing the domestic struggle yet are likely to produce only limited remedial effects at best.

Proportionality offers a different yet related tool for categorizing and ranking the propriety of various manifestations of political resistance and rebellion. Proportionality weighs the intensity of various forms of political militancy against the evils they seek to remedy. Leading an unlicensed march against racial discrimination would be one rung on the ladder of proportional responses. Peaceful picketing of an abortion clinic might receive a similar classification. But such direct action as occupying a prohibited bench in a segregated public bus or preventing a patient from entering an abortion clinic must be viewed as a more escalated response on the proportionality scale. Throwing rocks at a segregated school, setting fire to a public bus, and bombing an abortion clinic or assassinating its director would constitute more extreme and therefore more questionable responses on the proportionality scale.

One more classifying principle to be considered, which is closely allied to the doctrines of nexus and proportionality, is that of "harm minimization." This principle insists that resort to extralegal and, in appropriate circumstances, violent means, be conditioned on the actor's exhaustion of available pacific or less militant remedies. Further, harm minimization requires that political activists in a democratic society—where lawful relief avenues prevail—be granted a much narrower license to engage in prohibited protest, disobedience, violence, and rebellion than their counterparts under authoritarian or totalitarian regimes.

Taking notice of the host of available definitional and classification schemes, criminologists Marshall Clinard and Richard Quinney suggest that society's policymakers and lawyers place their primary emphasis not upon a uniform and comprehensive prototype of political criminality but upon such subcategories of political offenses and offenders as are relevant to the particular situations involved.[185] Nonviolent draft resisters could thus be differentiated from political activists who engage in bank robberies, and offenders who take part in bombing campaigns and assassinations could be differentiated from those who engage in peaceful demonstrations. Each distinct category of offenses and offenders would be treated distinctively. Although such a piecemeal approach might have great practical appeal, and might be already identifiable in the existing system of international extradition practice and law as well as in the emerging body of international criminal law, attempts to formulate a comprehensive classification of the whole spectrum of political resistance and rebellion have not ceased and are not likely to—nor should they, as this volume well demonstrates.

A fragmented approach to this volatile and critical issue can only result in greater confusion and injustice, and may lead to further political problems in the near future. The time has come for both academia and the leaders of the world to make a serious and broad effort to determine and define the nature of political offenses and offenders. The escalating dissent, violence, and challenges to the legitimacy of authority worldwide require that the international community set out to meet one of the most formidable issues of the past as well as the coming millennium: warfare and chaos. As Chapters 3 and 4 demonstrate, dissidence and violence have not been exclusive to any nation or any time.

Part Two

Perspectives of a Unique Offender

There are both heroes of evil and heroes of good.
—François Duc de la Rochefoucauld,
Reflections (1678)

I rebel—therefore we exist.
—Albert Camus,
The Rebel (1956)

"Lenin's General Staff of 1917" published by U.S. Trotskyists in *The Militant*, 1938, showing Stalin as the only remaining Central Committee member of the Bolshevik Party.

Chapter Three

Only Sparks
Fly High

The Making of the Political Offender

> I can't breathe.
> There is a rioting mob inside me ...
> I am the Revolution
>
> —Jean-Paul Marat, in Peter Weiss,
> *The Persecution and Assassination*
> *of Jean-Paul Marat* (1965)

> There are crimes which become glorious by their excess;
> thus it happens that public robbery is called financial skill,
> and the unjust capture of provinces is called a victory.
>
> —François Duc de la Rochefoucauld,
> *Reflections* (1678)

Che Guevara, international revolutionary and leader of Fidel Castro's Cuban rebellion. He was later commander of Bolivian guerrilla revolutionaries.

The Social Threads of Rebellion

"What made an elite [of] prosperous and conservative members of the Establishment . . . turn against their king and start a revolution?" asked historian Richard B. Morris in his study *Seven Who Shaped Our Destiny: The Founding Fathers as Revolutionaries*.[186] After vividly exploring the backgrounds and exploits of Benjamin Franklin, George Washington, John Adams, Thomas Jefferson, John Jay, James Madison, and Alexander Hamilton, he set out to identify common features among this diverse group of American political heroes. According to Morris, the Founding Fathers were all men of principle, dedicated to public service and convinced of the rightness and necessity of their cause. They were bound by a commitment to American independence and a belief in the superiority of republicanism over monarchism.

On a more personal level, these "revolutionaries" all suffered some disappointment in their professional aspirations. Complex individuals, all seven experienced identity crises at various stages of their lives. Morris outlined several other common denominators of these talented and ambitious Founding Fathers. Most did not appear to have had fully satisfying marriages. Despite their heritage of wealth and security, all encountered circumstances in which they felt the need to prove themselves. In the process, all developed an enthusiasm for controversy. Most significantly, their activities and associations brought them in contact with others who also had grievances against the ultimate authority—the Crown and its representatives.[187]

It would be difficult, and scientifically faulty, to attempt to draw significant conclusions regarding rebels and rebellion from so small yet so diverse a group as the Founding Fathers of the United States. Just as futile would be to search for commonality in personality, background, and motivation between America's earliest rebels and political offenders and those who have followed them, here and abroad. Nevertheless, some quests for common threads that link political offenders have been undertaken, with the hope of casting new and useful light on the personalities and environments that give rise to political criminality and rebellion. Various aspects of the social, psychological, and moral makeup of the political offender have been examined by both classical and modern writers. Some of their findings deserve our attention.

Class and Status

A frequent starting point for studies of political offenders has been the analysis of the role of class and status in their lives. Dutch lawyer and criminologist William Adrian Bonger, who published his famous volume *Criminality and Economic Conditions* at the end of the nineteenth century, argued that political offenders represent the powerless.[188] He identified the powerless with the economically "oppressed class," and defined the rebel, or political criminal, as one who struggles against "the political power of the ruling class."[189] Pursuing the Marxist perspective, Bonger sought to understand political crime and rebellion in terms of economic determinism, suggesting that political crime naturally emerges whenever economic and social developments lag behind or run ahead of political developments.[190] He maintained that the oppressed class, because of its limited power, is unable to change the status quo by peaceful and legal means. Consequently, as long as this imbalance in social power continues there remains the "danger that one of those oppressed will kill the autocrat, either to better the situation or to take revenge for what he and his have suffered."[191]

Statistical data demonstrate, however, that although political offenders might often be acting on behalf of underprivileged and powerless classes, they have not necessarily risen from that background. Interesting early evidence is contained in an analysis of 2,564 individuals charged with illegal revolutionary activities against Russia's czarist regime during the period of 1873 to 1879.[192] Members of the ruling or upper classes constituted a startling majority of these offenders, who came from a great variety of backgrounds: aristocrats (28.2%), clergy (16.6%), military (13.4%), peasants (13.4%), urban workers (13.4%), merchants (4.2%), and intelligentsia (3.3%).[193] Study of the vocational and professional backgrounds of 1,703 Russian political offenders sentenced during the 1870s supplied the following breakdown: university students (17.3%), urban workers (16%), high school students (9.7%), teachers (7–8%), peasants (3.7%), and military (2.8%).[194]

Invariably viewing class background and political commitments as closely allied, Soviet Marxists have frequently sought comfort in the myth that the 1917 Russian Revolution had a primarily proletarian background. Less-biased historiographers, however, have pointed to three distinct stages in the Russian revolutionary movement—aristocratic, intellectual, and proletarian—based on the class background of the leaders of each stage. Some have therefore vigorously argued that the Russian Revolution, instead of fitting neatly into the Marxist categorization of "proletarians" rising against an "overclass," was essentially "an intelligentsia revolution."[195]

Similar evidence against the Marxist myth is supplied by other intriguing data of educated sons and daughters of the privileged classes who frequently held leadership positions in the ranks of political dissidence not only in czarist Russia but also elsewhere. Contemporary studies of apprehended terrorists in Italy confirm that a great number of these offenders have come from well-to-do family backgrounds.[196] Likewise, the Colombian M–19 terrorists (who seized the Embassy of the Dominican Republic in Bogota in February 1980 and held fourteen ambassadors hostage) were reported to have consisted "mostly of [the] alienated sons and daughters of prominent families."[197] It can be argued that these scions of the wealthy have the education and time to foment revolution, while the oppressed poor they fight for are too busy surviving to pursue broader communal objectives.

Yet studies that primarily identify political offenders with rich or poor origins have ignored the mounting data showing that the most militant political activists typically have middle-class origins. Social psychologists Karl Schmitt and Carl Leiden were among the first to argue that the ambitious middle class is the greatest source of young rebels eager for opportunity and success. The upper class, they submit, is too satisfied to rebel, and the lower lacks the necessary skills.[198]

Clearly, former assessments of the role of class and status in the formation of the political offender remain inconclusive. The diverse and broad-based memberships of America's civil rights, anti–Vietnam War, environmental protection, abortion rights, gun ownership, and militia movements in the past three decades, as well as the evidence of the broad spectrum of participation in the popular up-

heavals and mass rebellions in Eastern Europe and the former Soviet
Union, might lead one to conclude that socioeconomic class is simply not a factor central to political activism.

Karl and Dwight Armstrong, charged with the fatal bombing of
the Army Mathematics Research Center at the University of Wisconsin in 1970, came from a liberal middle-class background and close-
knit family. Their father, socially and economically independent
since age sixteen, advanced from the position of chauffeur to supervising buyer for a manufacturing company. Proud of his skills and
self-reliance, the elder Armstrong felt that his own outspoken contempt for the Vietnam War had probably influenced his sons. Their
mother responded to her family's activities with utmost pride and
passion. "There never would have been a bombing," she said, "if
people my age had done something, instead of letting our children
do it." Both parents regarded the young researcher who had been
killed in the explosion, and his widow and three children, as "victims of the violence Vietnam bred in people at home."[199]

As if relying on the Armstrongs as prototypes, political writer J.
Kirkpatrick Sale identified four common elements in the families of
anti–Vietnam War activists: (1) a comfortable and professional middle-class background, (2) two employed parents, (3) an evident sense
of social consciousness, and (4) dinner-table discussions that were
likely to be liberal. That milieu, suggested Sale, was "almost predictable for contemporary activists."[200]

These "common denominators" lose much of their claimed universality, however, after one examines more critically the backgrounds of other political offenders in America and abroad. The not
atypical background of America's Diana Oughton, who abandoned
her conservative and authoritarian Republican family for life as a
Weatherman revolutionary,[201] gives credence to the assertion by
criminologists Marshall Clinard and Richard Quinney that "such
characteristics as age, sex, ethnicity, and social class do not differentiate political offenders as a whole from the population in general."[202] Members of antigovernmental militias and participants in
recent protests against abortion clinics and gun control, for example,
fall decidedly outside Sale's categories. Even a cursory review of their
economic and social backgrounds reveals the absence of a permissive
or liberal family milieu, disclosing instead a claimed adherence to
fundamental creeds and sometimes authoritarian value systems.

Perhaps class and status truly play a merely incidental role in the creation of the political offender. Activist leadership often may come not from any particular socioeconomic "class" but from more amorphous and informal clusters of individuals who find their personal paths for advancement blocked by common obstacles. Three decades ago, African American leader Bayard Rustin observed of the American civil rights movement:

> [I]t is not the *lumpen-proletariat*, the Negro working classes, the Negro working poor, who are proclaiming: "We want Negro principals, we want Negro supervisors, we want Negro teachers in our schools." It is the educated Negroes ... [b]eing blocked from moving up, [they] become not only interested in Negro children, but in getting those teaching jobs, supervisory jobs and principal jobs for [their] own economic interest.[203]

Political activists are often those who find a disparity between their background, their educational accomplishments, and their existing social status. Sociologists have coined the term "status incongruence" to describe these situations in which a person's socioeconomic achievement level is inconsistent with his or her expectations based on educational level or such other factors as family, ethnic, or class background. Under this theory, class is more of a catalyst than a determinative factor in the creation of the rebel.

Status incongruence is intensified when social and economic decline befall those in the established and well-heeled classes. It can also occur when the educational and cultural emergence of members of the lower socioeconomic strata is unaccompanied by adequate opportunities for professional and economic enhancement. A survey of Italian political militants thus has revealed that: "The 'open university' policy of Italian universities in recent years has produced an abundance of unemployable and often underqualified terrorists. These universities continue to provide a source of recruits and support for the terrorists."[204]

It is reasonable to conclude that status incongruence generates social and economic restlessness and agitation, conditions favorable for gestating political activists. More specific conclusions about the emergence of political offenders, however, cannot be advanced on the basis of data derived from applying status incongruence to such diverse communities as America's Founding Fathers, Russian revolutionaries, European terrorists, and contemporary American civil disobedients. We might therefore be better advised to seek commonality among more discrete and homogenous categories of activists. The insurgent or armed guerrilla is likely to differ drastically in both personal history and psychological makeup from the political activist who refuses military service, and the offender who engages in lone dissent is not like the offender who joins in collective protest. In particular, rebels committed to violent and militant action may not necessarily resemble those who scrupulously adhere to peaceful action.

Although status incongruence could generally account for much of the turmoil among religious and ethnic militants, the world's youth, urban dwellers, and other categories of rebels and dissidents, focusing on specific manifestations of political activism (e.g., terrorism, treason, and civil disobedience) might lead to a better understanding of the roles of social and educational levels, environment, and societal norms in making the political offender. Rather than seeking a comprehensive psychosocial profile for all political offenders based on class, status, and other factors, we shall attempt the hopefully more productive approach of discerning common characteristics within particular groups of political offenders: presidential assassins, skyjackers, ethnic and religious minorities, and the sometimes-distinguished, sometimes-infamous female activists.

Presidential Assassins

Perhaps the most notorious and exclusive group of "political activists" is the special category of presidential assassins (which includes assailants whose assassination attempts are unsuccessful). This select group has also garnered much previous attention and analysis. After studying the profiles of American presidential assassins, the National Commission on the Causes and Prevention of Violence concluded in 1969 that among these assassins "neither socioeconomic class nor employment seems to establish a common thread."[205] The raw data revealed, however, that of a group of seven assassins, the majority—four—came from artisan or skilled-worker backgrounds, while two came from well-to-do middle-class families and one came from a family who owned a bar and a tenement. One striking shared element was the fact that all seven had lost their employment because of physical disability or some other circumstance one to three years prior to their assassination efforts. Thus, for every member of this troubled group the major lawful avenue for economic livelihood and social advancement—work—had been blocked.[206]

Scrutinizing the individual histories of these presidential assassins, sociologist Doris Y. Wilkinson reported to the commission that each presented an instance of status incongruence—an expectation/achievement gap.[207] Although members of the commission had hoped for a more definite causal connection between that gap and political violence, all they could conclude was that the "question of why the psychic distress derived from status incongruence became politicized in the form of a deadly attack upon a high political officeholder remains unanswered."[208]

Many of America's presidential assassins have also shared relatively recent foreign roots, possibly contributing to their sense of status incongruence. In the first attempt against the life of a U.S. president, by Richard Lawrence against Andrew Jackson in 1835, the would-be assassin was a native Englishman who had moved to Washington, D.C., with his parents when he was twelve years old. John N. Schrank, who in 1921 shot Theodore Roosevelt in another unsuccessful assassination attempt, was born in Bavaria and emigrated to the United States when he was thirteen. Guisseppe Zangara, who attempted to assassinate Franklin D. Roosevelt in 1933, was born in Italy and emigrated to the United States at age twenty-three. Leon F. Czolgosz, who assassinated William McKinley in 1901, was born only a few months after his parents emigrated to the United States from Poland. John Wilkes Booth, who assassinated Abraham Lincoln in 1865, was the son of parents who came to America from England. Sirhan Sirhan, who assassinated Robert F. Kennedy in 1968, was a native of Jordan. Oscar Collazo, who attempted to kill President Truman in 1950, was born in Puerto Rico while the island was under American control. His status as an American is as debatable as his island's. Only four were clearly native-born Americans: Charles J. Guiteau and Lee Harvey Oswald, the assassins of James A. Garfield in 1881 and John F. Kennedy in 1963, respectively;[209] and Lynette "Squeaky" Fromme and John W. Hinckley Jr., the assailants of Gerald Ford in 1975 and Ronald Reagan in 1981, respectively.

Foreign birth or ancestry looms undeniably large in the portrait gallery of past presidential assassins and assailants. So striking is the historical evidence of this fact, that after the assassination of presidential candidate Robert F. Kennedy, the National Commission on the Causes and Prevention of Violence noted, perhaps somewhat simplistically, that the potential presidential assassin should be profiled as "short and slight of build, foreign born, and from a broken family."[210] One might conclude from this portrayal of the typical presidential assassin in America that unlike regicides and violence committed against official figures and symbols of political authority elsewhere, American presidential assaults are carried out by pseudo-political activists—who are merely venting personal anger, dissatisfactions, grievances, hatreds, and dysfunctions. On the other hand, one could argue that, despite the missing causal connections, the American assassin's act represents a misplaced attribution of fault upon a figure of ultimate authority, a substitution of responsibility for the ills and dissatisfactions resulting from confrontations with institutions of lesser authority.

It is thus evident that one must be careful not to insist on ascribing the behavior of the assassin, and by analogy the behavior of the offender taking extralegal and militant action against the established authority in general, to a single cause. The friction between the rebel or political offender and the enforcer of authority is not always directly related to political factors, as successive discussion will demonstrate. An awareness of the amorphous constitution of the political offender community, and of the great diversities in human motivations and interactions, might constitute the best safeguard against simplistic and premature answers to the complex questions posed by political offenders and their offenses.

Pirates in the Sky

As a group, skyjackers lend themselves to simple study. Their crime is easily classifiable and their fate is almost always capture. Thus it was with considerable intensity that David G. Hubbard, a Texas psychiatrist, conducted extensive psychiatric interviews in the late 1960s with 52 American and Canadian skyjackers, out of about 160 in custody at the time.[211] He compared the results to findings of similar interviews with a nearly equal number of Black Panthers and members of the militant French-Canadian Front for the Liberation of Quebec. In his conclusions, Hubbard took issue with previous attempts to divide skyjackers into such diverse groups as "emotionally disturbed," "fleeing felons," or "political activists." These classifications, Hubbard asserted, were spurious. Since there are millions of emotionally disturbed persons in each country, why do only a handful elect to participate in skyjacking or related violence? Since there are thousands of fleeing felons, why do only a very few commit air piracy? Since many millions are committed to political change and activism all over the world, why do only a small number use terrorist tactics? The "real question," according to Hubbard, is "what do these tiny handfuls of men have in common?"[212]

It is this commonality that Hubbard sought to identify. He concluded that regardless of their national, racial, or cultural backgrounds, skyjackers shared great psychological similarities with one another. For example, skyjackers raised overseas (in Scotland, Guatemala, or Cuba) shared much with those raised in North America (in Savannah, Georgia; Seattle, Washington; or Ottawa, Canada). Neither were his conclusions affected by offenders' ethnic or racial origins. Several unexpected similarities emerged among Hubbard's interviewees. Many had grown up in violent families with chronically alcoholic fathers and religiously zealous mothers. Hubbard debunked the popular concept of the skyjacker as a strong, tough, left-wing idealist in flight from persecution. Those interviewed turned out to be timid, sexually inadequate, and generally ineffectual. They resembled the would-be skyjackers portrayed in the film *Dog Day Afternoon,* who resorted to skyjacking, at a time of total personal unraveling, as a decisive act of redemption. Each of the skyjackers interviewed, Dr. Hubbard asserted, had a "better, more tolerable body image and self-image *after* the crime than he had before."[213]

Hubbard claimed that his findings were used to help design a profile of the potential skyjacker. Put to task in the anti-skyjacking campaign developed jointly by the U.S. government and the airline industry, the profile was given considerable credit for reducing the number of offenses against U.S. aircraft from the annual high of forty in 1969 to a mere four in 1976, and thirteen in 1979.[214]

Of all the categories of political offenders, skyjackers, according to Hubbard, appear easiest to pigeonhole. His conclusion, however, should not go unchallenged. Skyjackers, despite their apparently common backgrounds, appear to be driven by different demons. It is highly unlikely that lone and disgruntled skyjackers are the same sort of actors as the organization-bound terrorists who hijacked TWA flight 847 to Beirut in 1985.

Ethnic and Religious Minorities

The prominence of ethnic and religious minorities within the leadership of revolutionary and insurgency movements further highlights the possible contribution of status incongruence to political activism. Among the most noted leaders of the 1917 Russian Revolution, several were members of the country's minorities. Leon Trotsky was of Jewish extraction, and Joseph Stalin was a non-Russian ethnic from the mountainous hinterlands of Georgia. Vyacheslav Constantinovich von Plehve, who at the turn of the nineteenth century shaped czarist Russia's anti-revolutionary and counter-terrorist policies by directing the Oprichnina, the czarist secret police,[215] recognized the unique social and ethnic background of the country's political activists. Inspecting a prison for political detainees, he commented: "I view all political offenders as ambitious aspirants seeking status—is it not true that each of them had dreamt of becoming a representative in Parliament?"[216] Von Plehve considered the growing community of expelled and dropout university students as a particularly rich pool for revolutionary recruitment.

Responding to a Jewish delegation's complaint about government inaction during the 1903 anti-Jewish pogroms, von Plehve, then serving as Minister of the Interior, sought the delegates' assistance in curtailing the growing political activism within the Jewish intelligentsia. "Much is said about Jewish cowardice, but this is not true. The Jews are the most courageous people. In Western Russia, 90 percent of the revolutionaries are Jewish and, in all of Russia, they constitute 40 percent," von Plehve affirmed.[217]

A disproportionate number of the former Soviet Union's human rights activists and political dissenters were likewise members of ethnic, cultural, or religious minorities. Anatoly Scharansky, a Russian Jew who was shuttled from one Soviet penal institution to another and was eventually released from political exile through an international exchange of prisoners, is a recent example. He stands as a model for millions of Jewish and other minority political dissenters and protesters in the former Soviet Union.[218]

In other countries as well, the avant-garde of political militancy often contains a disproportionate number of minority populations.

This phenomenon is reflected in the divergent militias of Lebanon, the cadres of Maoist Shining Path terrorists in Peru, the Tamils of Sri Lanka, the Miskitos of Nicaragua, and the native Indians of Chiapas, Mexico. At times, these minority activists rise in response to specific campaigns of governmental oppression. Often, however, the activists do not speak exclusively for their narrow constituencies but lead broad national campaigns for reform or revolution.

Apart from their distinct identity within the larger national community, there may be few or possibly no other common threads that link minority activists. Surely Stalin, the cunning and eventually paranoid Georgian, had a different background, makeup, and motivation than Trotsky, the urban Jewish theoretician and strategist. In America, likewise, the differences between a Native American protester and an African American civil rights rioter hardly need clarification. So, despite the temptation of another easy classification scheme, identifying political offenders based upon minority status offers no ready conclusions. Perhaps most, if not all, political offenders must be examined individually rather than as members of discrete economic, social, or ethnic groups.

Jael and Her Sisters: Female Liberators

In biblical accounts, Jael, the wife of Heber the Israelite, "smote a nail" into the temples of Sisera, the captain of an oppressive enemy who sought refuge in her tent.[219] Judith, the apocryphal heroine, likewise slew the Assyrian conqueror Holofernes to prevent the destruction of her native Jerusalem.[220] Other exceptional women known from later historical accounts include universally famous leader Jean d'Arc and Marat's lone assassin, Charlotte Corday.

Yet the political isolation of women in Eastern cultures and their diminished public place in most of Western civilization have generally obscured whatever roles they had in the arenas of political activism and crime. It was indeed the diffident treatment afforded American women by their male colleagues in America's nineteenth-century abolitionist movement that subsequently gave rise to widespread feminist political activism—the suffragist movement itself. Later, at the end of the nineteenth century, the anarchist movement brought female political militancy into sharper focus.

Sergei Nachaeyeff, anarchism's master strategist, found it especially important to concentrate upon the role of women when discussing the revolutionary's relationship with various segments of society.[221] He divided women into three categories. The first, those who were "frivolous, thoughtless, and vapid," Nachaeyeff compared with men of privilege, whom he found fit only for exploitation. In the second category were the "ardent, gifted, and devoted" women, who had not achieved the "passionless and austere" dedication required of revolutionaries. These women he compared with men who, even if doctrinally and ideologically committed, were mostly idle word-spillers rather than activists. This group he perceived as capable of supplying potential supporters but not useful fighting troops. "Finally," wrote Nachaeyeff, "there are the women who are completely on our side. . . . We should regard these women as the most valuable of our treasures; without their help it would be impossible to succeed."[222]

Recent history has seen the dramatic expansion of female roles in public life. In America, as elsewhere, early images of thousands upon thousands of unidentified women struggling in the fields or in the rank and file of trade unionism gave way to portraits of such diverse militant activists as Emma Goldman, Ethel Rosenberg, and Angela Davis taking their place in the front lines of political rebellion. In 1975, criminologist Freda Adler, in her book *Sisters in Crime,* wrote:

> Another area in which young women have begun to express their aptitude for assertive behavior is political protest. In the storm of dissent which swept across the country in the late sixties, the adolescent female was an enthusiastic participant in the demonstrations and the coequal cell-mate in the jailings. Initially, during the early sixties, the movements were planned, led, and executed by males while females performed their traditional functions as office workers, coffee makers, and overseers of routine chores. But by the end of the decade, a by now familiar transformation had occurred.[223]

American women played unreluctant roles in the leadership of the most radical student, antiwar, and political revolutionary cadres of the 1960s and 1970s. Diana Oughton and Kathylin Wilkerson were prominent in the hierarchy of the militant Students for a Democratic Society. The roles of women in the pro-choice and pro-life movements of the 1980s and 1990s have been even more dominant. Throughout the world, criminologist H. H. A. Cooper noted, the female protester and terrorist is no longer content "just to praise the Lord and pass the ammunition."[224] Cooper further discerned "a cold rage" about some of these women militants, which even the most extreme and alienated of their male colleagues seemed incapable of emulating.

The women members of West Germany's Baader-Meinhof terrorist gang testify to this type of total commitment. In a West German study of forty major terrorists, twenty-four were female and sixteen were male. The proportionality is particularly striking when one compares political with nonpolitical violent crime. In Germany, women accounted for 60 percent of all terrorists, but constituted only 7 percent of robbers and 20 percent of criminals perpetrating other types of violence.[225]

Women have played an increasingly important role in nonviolent political activity as well. In the former Soviet Union, Natalia Gorbanevskaya helped organize the *samizdat*, the underground press, in the late 1960s. Dr. Yelena Bonner, a Soviet pediatrician, was instrumental in establishing the unauthorized Helsinki Watch Group, a citizen organization that monitors Soviet departures from the human rights provisions of the Helsinki Accord. Bonner became better known when she married Nobel Peace Prize winner Dr. Andrei Sakharov, another Russian human rights activist.

In Britain, women have played noted leadership roles in the civil disobedience movement, including the campaign against the installation of U.S. cruise missiles. Women from many segments of British society participated in protest gatherings at nuclear weapons facilities, most notably at Greenham Common, where they established permanent encampments on the perimeter of the base and persisted despite periodic evictions by police. Many have been jailed for setting up human roadblocks and breaching base security—both as a means of protest and as a demonstration of the vulnerability of the missile sites to less responsible interlopers.[226]

The norm today in the United States is for women to take the same risks as men, whether in response to protests against nuclear armaments, in sheltering Central American refugees who travel the new Underground Railroad of the sanctuary movement, in chaining themselves to fences around abortion clinics, or in other manifestations of prohibited political campaigns. Although no statistics reflecting female participation in current political resistance movements are available, it is evident that the sexes are being treated equally by the criminal courts. For example, in what appeared to be a deliberate message, a federal judge in Arizona allocated identical sentences to women and men for smuggling illegal aliens into the country.[227]

◇   ◇   ◇

Though significant numbers of particular subclasses of political offenders (such as presidential assassins and skyjackers) might fall into narrowly defined socioeconomic, religious, or gender categories, other and broader classes of political offenders belie such categorizations. Not only are political offenders represented by both sexes, but they also emerge from widely diverse class, family, ethnic, religious, and social backgrounds. And they are apparently inspired and driven by an equally diverse variety of causes and beliefs.

The evidence suggests that political offenders can be "outsiders" in a given society, such as women or ethnic and religious minorities, or "insiders" from the predominant ranks of gender, race, class, or faith. Though status incongruence may serve as a valuable common denominator for many of these actors, it cannot explain such diverse phenomena as the middle-class activism of England's Greenham women, the militant zeal of India's poor Moslem and Hindu masses, the broad spectrum of participation in American civil disobedience, the aristocratic presence among the leadership of the French Revolution, or the significant role of the intelligentsia in czarist Russia's November Revolution. This historical and worldwide diversity leads to the conclusion that a profile of the political offender cannot be accurately painted without giving adequate attention to individual psychological factors and to group dynamics that contribute to individual and collective outbreaks of political criminality and rebellion.

Psychological Cartography

Since the futility of searching for common social threads among the broader, or even the more discrete, groups of political criminals has been demonstrated, the individual makeup or psychological characteristics of the rebel is the next logical topic for examination. Criminologist Stephen Schafer, writing in 1974, asserted that "the state of mind of the offender and his emotional balance" has perhaps been the most challenging question for those trying to understand political criminality.[228] Nearly a century earlier, as if anticipating Schafer's complaint, the recognized father of scientific criminology, Cesare Lombroso, ambitiously set out to divide all offenders into three major classes: the born criminals, the insane, and the criminaloids.[229] His born criminals were those who exhibited atavistic physical characteristics and possessed a deficient moral sense. The criminality of the insane was attributed to physiological or mental defects, thus relieving the actors of personal responsibility. Finally, the criminaloids were those possessing weak natures, who were therefore "candidates for good or evil according to circumstances."[230] Within the criminaloid class Lombroso included the category of "criminals by passion," encompassing, for example, the brother who murdered his sister's rapist, the unmarried mother who strangled her illegitimate infant, and the husband who killed his unfaithful wife. Lombroso acknowledged, however, that the passion driving the criminaloids was not always personal. "Sometimes," he noted, "the [passionate] motive is a patriotic one."[231]

Seeking to identify members of each criminal class by physiognomy, Lombroso not only pointed out the born criminals' atavistic attributes but also described criminals of passion as handsome beings with lofty foreheads and serene and gentle expressions. Criminals of passion were further endowed with acute sensitivity and characterized by a high degree of excitability and exaggerated reflex action. Psychologically, criminals of passion possessed an excessive amount of those qualities that are considered desirable in "good and holy persons—love, honor, noble ambitions, patriotism. . . . [T]he motive [of the passionate criminal] is always adequate, frequently noble, and sometimes sublime."[232] Despite the naïveté of Lombroso's physiognomic methods of classification and the parochialism of his racial and cultural conclusions, several of his theses regarding the political offender have withstood the test of time.

Lombroso recognized that just as not all criminals of passion were patriotically or politically—rather than personally—motivated, not all political offenders were impelled solely by passion. He saw the ranks of political criminality as diverse:

[It] recruited from all ranks and conditions—men of genius, intellectual spirits who are the first to realize the defects of the old system and to conceive a new one, synthesizing the needs and aspirations of the people; lunatics, enthusiastic propagandists of the new ideas, which they spread with all the impetuous ar-

dor characteristic of unbalanced minds; criminals, the natural enemies of order, who flock to the standard of revolt and bring to it their special gifts, au-
dacity and contempt of death. These latter types accomplish the work of destruction which inevitably accompanies every revolution: they are the faithful
and unerring arm ready to carry out the ideas that others conceive but lack the
courage to execute.

Finally, there are the saints, the men who live solely for high purposes and
to whom the revolution is a veritable apostolate. . . . They are consumed by a
passion for altruism and self-immolation, and experience a strange delight in
martyrdom for their ideals.[233]

Although viewing passion as a prominent feature of the political
offender, Lambroso recognized that political unrest and insurrection
attracted the passionless and opportunistic as well. At the opposite
end of the spectrum he acknowledged that "passion" could explode
into insanity, and that those with unbalanced minds or emotions often sought the opportunity to play important roles in the revolutionary or other extremist political camps. Witness the collection of psychopaths assembled by the Third Reich.

During the final stages of his career, Lombroso focused increasingly on political and revolutionary offenders,[234] and upon anarchists in particular.[235] He became inclined to accord even greater
weight in revolutionary movements to the role of those with atavistic physical characteristics and abnormal psychological makeups,
stressing the central place of common criminals:

The crimes of anarchists tend to mingle with ordinary crimes when certain
dreamers attempt to reach their goal by any means possible—theft, or the murder of a few, often innocent, persons. It is easy to realize, therefore, why, with
a few exceptions, anarchists are recruited from among ordinary criminals, lunatics, and insane criminals."[236]

For all their sophisticated research and elaborate diagnostic techniques, modern psychiatry, psychology, and criminology have done
little to advance the understanding of political offenders beyond
Lombroso's intuitive groupings. The distinctions drawn between
genuine political offenders and common criminals (or mentally abnormal activists, according to the Lombroso grouping) generally remain subjective, and are usually biased by cultural and ideological
preferences and proclivities. The marked tendency to label all that is
different and unorthodox as either "crime" or "insanity" thus continues unchallenged.

American scholar Robert K. Merton led another, more contemporary attempt to vanquish this bias and to distinguish the political offender from both the common offender and the mentally ill offender.[237] In an effort to chart the full panorama of dissident behavior, Merton first distinguished between "aberrant" and "nonconforming" conduct. He described aberrant conduct (which he attributed to both common and mentally ill offenders) as a pathological form of behavior. Secretive, selfish, and antisocial qualities usually typify aberrant conduct, according to Merton. Nonconforming behavior, however, is an entirely different matter. Nonconforming offenders often announce their dissent publicly rather than seeking to hide their deviance. They also directly challenge the legitimacy of the norms and laws they violate. This is in sharp contrast to common criminals, who usually acknowledge the legitimacy of the laws they break. Finally, and perhaps most importantly, nonconforming offenders claim to depart from prevailing social norms for communal rather than selfish reasons. They often assert their adherence to a higher morality, one that surpasses existing social values.

Merton placed the conduct of the politically motivated offender under this "non-conforming" label. Political dissidence, unlike aberrant or pathological criminality, he concluded, "is not a private dereliction but a thrust toward a new morality or a promise of restoring a morality held to have been thrust aside in [prevailing] social practice."[238]

Merton's well-known "Typology of Modes of Individual Adaptation"[239] charts the distinctions between the law-abiding citizen, the common criminal, the mentally ill deviant, and the ideologically motivated (or rebellious) offender. Table 3.1 presents, in a somewhat modified manner, Merton's summation of the responses of various categories of actors—conformists, criminals, mentally ill, and rebels—first to societal goals and then to the institutional avenues (or means) that society permits for the attainment of these goals.

Merton suggested that the law-abiding citizen, or "conformist," accepts both societal goals and institutional means. On the other hand, the common criminal, Merton's "innovator," generally accepts the shared cultural values and goals of society but rejects and resists the institutionally approved means. These common offenders assimilate the majority's cultural goals (including values such as "success" and "economic wealth") without equally internalizing the societal norms governing the means for attaining these goals (such as "educa-

TABLE 3.1   Merton's Typology: Individual Responses ("Adaptation") to Societal
Goals and Means

Categories of Actors	Categories of Response ("Adaptation")*	Modes of Response to Societal Goals	Modes of Response to Institutional Means
Conformists	Noncriminal ("Conformity")*	Acceptance	Acceptance
Criminals	Criminal ("Innovation")*	Acceptance	Rejection
Mentally ill	Mentally-ill ("Retreatism")*	Rejection	Rejection
Rebels	Political criminal ("Rebellion")*	Rejection and substitution of new goals	Rejection and substitution of new means

*Merton's original terminology.

tion" or "work"). The mentally ill offender, or Merton's "retreatist,"
shirks from—or is unable to cope with—both the cultural goals and
the institutional means of society. The political offender, Merton's
"rebel," falls into an entirely different category. These actors frequently discard the goals of the dominant culture, substituting their
own reformist or revolutionary ideals. At the same time, they also reject the means endorsed by society, advancing new and noninstitu-
tional means for the pursuit and propagation of the new ideals.

Although distinguishing the political offender's outlook and motives from those of other offenders, Merton did not specify the dynamics of the political offender's psychological evolution. This is our
next task: to consider the distinct stages in the process of becoming a
political offender. We shall now turn away from the search for social
and psychological commonalities and from generalized attempts to
distinguish the political offender from the common criminal. Instead, we will direct our attention to the process of change that takes
place when an actor becomes a political offender.

Dynamics of Radicalization

A Sense of Difference and Obedience to a Higher Morality

The fierce individualism of the rebel, expressed through his or her
social and psychological background as well as through the means
he or she chooses for rebellion, is a central theme of this chapter. Yet

even as we acknowledge this uniqueness, there appear to be certain characteristics and phases in the life of a political offender that justify special attention. Among these are the offender's proclivity to see him- or herself as one apart from the common mass of humanity; an encounter with kindred individuals or collectives, whether secret cabals or field armies, with whom the offender can readily join forces; and an exposure to some powerful experience that jars the offender's consciousness and places a wedge between him- or herself and the forces of authority. The rebelliousness of political offenders is often generated by their sense of difference as well as by a feeling of moral superiority over the people and powers with which they contend. The latter perception often flows from the offender's view of the existing order as corrupt and unworthy of obedience, and from his or her claimed adherence to a higher calling.

The leaders of the American Revolution rejected the British laws that they perceived as the product of an oppressive and illegitimate parliamentary process. Similarly, the leaders of the Confederacy left the Union under the claim that it had betrayed the social covenant of the Constitution. Abolitionists defied the law because of their moral repugnance for slavery and their religious and social commitment to the brotherhood of man. In this country and abroad, draft resisters and pacifists have rejected the morality of either particular conflicts or war *per se,* proclaiming the moral superiority of dissidents over conformists. As we shall see, rebels may support their superiority over existing authority and law by relying on not only long-standing religious, philosophical, and jurisprudential doctrines that elevate morality above prevailing law, but also personal convictions and experiences.

A sense of uniqueness has been noted by many political activists during their youth. Describing one of his heroines, J. Anthony Lukas writes in *Don't Shoot—We Are Your Children!:* "Sue was gripped with a sense of her own specialness. . . . [T]he other children [did not] make much out of this specialness. . . . But Sue felt it intensely."[240] In some instances, this sense of uniqueness, specialness, or difference is related to the early development of a young person's social and political awareness. It may be viewed also as originating through an alienation from one's family, peers, or community.

SDS leader Diana Oughton rejected the privileged position enjoyed by her family in their hometown. The other children in school would teasingly refer to her as "Miss Moneybags." When she was six, she reportedly inquired of her nanny: "Ruthie, why do we have to be rich?"[241] She frequently expressed her wish to be like the "ordinary people." Kathylin Wilkerson, a central figure in the Weatherman organization, similarly reported: "I've been a radical most of my life. I was young during the Korean War; for 6 or 7, I was highly conscious of the A-bomb. Gradually I became alienated from the suburban middle-class lifestyle and the values it offered."[242] Both women would eventually join the more radical Weatherman Underground.

This sense of uniqueness might be generated by an awareness of a "higher calling" rather than by worldly conditions. "I have only one choice—my ministry in response to God," wrote political activist David Dellinger, one of the Chicago Seven charged with conspiracy for his role in interfering with the 1968 Democratic Convention. "If the government puts me in jail for following that ministry, that is its choice, not mine."[243] Jim Corbett, convicted for his role as a Sanctuary worker attempting to aid illegal Central American immigrants and sent to prison, believed that "if you really think that God is calling you to serve the needs of refugees then you must meet their most apparent need, which is to avoid capture, inevitable torture and death."[244] Father J. Guadelupe Carney, an American Jesuit priest who joined a Honduran guerrilla group shortly before his death at the hands of the Honduran army in 1983, likewise summarized his calling: "To Be a Christian Is to Be a Revolutionary."[245]

The political offender's sense of uniqueness is often self-described in terms of individual morality. Personal "integrity" and "honor" are key expressions in the dictionary of the political offender. "To be a man, with honor, means to say no to the ugly gnawing creature that is the U.S. foreign policy," wrote draft resister James Taylor Rowland.[246] Activists have also fondly quoted Che Guevara: "This type of fight gives us the opportunity of becoming the human species, and it also permits us to graduate as men."[247]

Much of the political offender's strength is derived from the steadfast belief in his or her own unique moral purity. Dietrich Bonhoeffer describes the "responsible man" who speaks and acts out against injustices when others remain silent. "Who stands his ground? Only the man whose ultimate criterion is not his reason, his principles, his conscience, his freedom or his virtue, but who is ready to sacrifice all these things when he is called to . . . action in faith and in exclusive allegiance to God."[248]

As previously noted, the political offender's response to the higher calling manifests itself not only in his or her self-image but also in his or her interaction with the world. The radical activist, believing that he or she adheres to a superior and distinct value system that rejects established societal goals and methods, decides to affect the establishment from the outside, not the inside. Daniel Ellsberg writes about his decision, while working with U.S. Agency for International Development officials in Vietnam, to challenge the system and to seek an end to war:

> The AID man there . . . said: "Don't do this Dan. You're just the sort of man we want here for this kind of advice. We need you, the government needs you, and you can do good work in this relationship. . . . This gives you access, it gives you a chance to say what you think to the officials. . . . Don't cut yourself off. Don't cut your throat." I had to say to him "I'm not cutting my throat." [Ellsberg's response was simple:] "life exists outside the executive branch. You know, there is nourishment. You can sustain life out there."[249]

As part of their uniqueness, political offenders accept, and at times welcome, the personal sacrifices required by their causes. Martyrdom is indeed more than a professional risk; it is a reward. Karl Armstrong, bomber of the Wisconsin University Mathematics Center, explained his mission: "I was born on the day they hung the Nazis at Nuremberg. . . . The only real resolution I ever made in my whole life was that I would be prepared to give up my life so that wouldn't happen here in America."[250]

Although rejecting existing social values—thereby demonstrating their uniqueness—political offenders appear to possess an acute sense of personal responsibility toward others and toward what they consider to be a flawed society. "I intend to devote all my time to the peace movement," proclaimed one of Anthony Lukas's unidentified young activists. He continued, "I will not run to Canada. This is my country and I love it dearly. Because of this love I cannot stand by and watch people kill people in the name of freedom."[251] As the commitment to social betterment assumes all-consuming proportions, the would-be offender's personal identity merges into the public mission. "For the first time," reported one of Kenneth Keniston's young activists, "I really began to feel a part of the Movement. . . . I began to be able to trace my own roots in terms of being able to feel actually *of* it, not only in it."[252]

A similar vision of the interrelationship between the offender and his or her public mission was offered by Samuel Melville, a leader of the prisoners revolt at Attica Penitentiary. In his search for self-respect and dignity, Melville eventually concluded that his identity was merged with the struggle for social justice. "I don't think you can have inner peace," he wrote, "without outer peace, too. . . . There is not individual change without social change."253 Melville, the man who persuaded Jane Alpert to bomb federal office buildings, died in the Attica riots in September 1971.

The Individual and the Collective

In attempting to draw an accurate profile of the political offender, we have explored, among a host of other factors, the social backgrounds and the psychological makeups of various categories of political activists. We will later explore the assertion that practically all human beings are capable of becoming political offenders—of resorting to proscribed and even violent means to express their dissatisfaction with, disdain of, and opposition to evil, corrupt, and sometimes even merely unresponsive governance. Yet the existing literature supplies little insight into the relationship between individual and collective factors in the making of the dissident, civil disobedient, freedom fighter, and terrorist. Must the political activist belong to a community of like people to claim the status of political offender? Might any individual proclaim a set of political, social, cultural, or religious values and beliefs, however idiosyncratic or deranged, in justification of his or her resort to rebellion and violence? Is the political offender's credibility to be derived from his or her individual conscience, or from his or her communal dogmas and backing?

In his exhaustive study *Political Assassination by Jews: A Rhetorical Device for Justice*,254 Israeli sociologist Nachman Ben-Yehuda notes that most of the recorded political violence among the ancient Israelites as well as among modern Israelis has been expressed through members of organized groups. "One . . . factor to remember," writes Ben-Yehuda, "is that violence, crime, and delinquency have not been traditional hall marks of the Jewish cultural matrix, in or outside Israel. . . . Second, it is quite clear that *individual* Jews are very reluctant to get involved in political assassination events . . . very rarely did we encounter the 'lone assassin'. . . . If political assassinations are carried out, [the event] usually emerges from ideological groups, and it particularly occurs within a fierce struggle for national independence, in a conflict over the definition of moral boundaries of the collective. Within this context, political assassination events emerge as a tool in an alternative system of popular, political and social justice."[255]

No similar assessments of the relationships between the individual and the collective among political activists in other cultures have been found. In discussing the definitions of political offenses prevalent in international extradition law (Chapter 6), we shall see that Anglo-American jurisprudence, in particular, limits the application of the term "political offense" to members of warring and contesting groups rather than to individual activists. This limitation acts to curb the rights of "loners" to resort to unorthodox and violent political means. Yet in domestic systems of justice, where considerations of political motive predominate over questions of group membership, equal consideration might be given to the lone political activist and the offender acting as a member of or on behalf of a broader community.

The American experience can provide notable insight into the relationship between the individual and the collective in the political crime arena. In the 1960s, anti–Vietnam War activist Jane Alpert fell in love with Samuel Melville, an activist on the fringe of the radical left. When Melville became involved with two fugitive French Canadian separatists, Alpert, fearing she would be excluded, plunged into his cause by bombing several federal office buildings. In retrospect, she reported, "the threat of being left out, especially at a time when Sam was drifting away from me, was enough to make up my mind."[256]

In withdrawing from a corrupt society and political system and making a new commitment to establishing a better moral order, few political offenders seek an individual apotheosis, as was the case with Alpert. Instead, at this stage the rebel often seeks others who share common visions. Not surprisingly, the rebel often finds that they are looking for him or her as well. Perhaps by joining others in a common cause and by taking collective efforts to the public stage, political offenders affirm their self-worth and belie the prospect that their alienation from society will be viewed as the outcome of a personal flaw.

For many political offenders, hearing a higher call and even be-holding a vision of the future are not sufficient to lead them to radi-cal action. Despite the rejection of larger society, the dissenter still longs to belong and seeks membership in movements or causes to overcome or avoid social isolation. The involvement in a collective organization or conspiracy often supplies the potential activist with a gratifying opportunity to conform to the norms of a group, albeit an illegal or socially rejected group, as well as the opportunity to be perceived by others as a contributing member of a cadre with a pos-itive agenda. Commencing as a "follower," the new recruit may as-sume a more central role at a later time.

Interestingly, even those who have carried out the paradigmatic lone-wolf political offense—presidential assassination—have been described by the National Commission on the Causes and Preven-tion of Violence as people who tried at some point to identify with some cause or ideologically based movement. Yet these assassins, despite such acknowledged efforts, seemed unable to participate with others in the orderly pursuit of a cause.[257] John Wilkes Booth identified strongly with the Southern cause but was unable to stay in uniform. Charles J. Guiteau tried unsuccessfully to become a member of the Oneida religious community. Leon F. Czolgosz was a disillusioned Roman Catholic.[258] Moreover, virtually all these as-sassins denied their own responsibility for these or other life fail-ures. Several suffered from a high degree of self-loathing, resulting in an escape to fantasy. Anxious to purge themselves of this loathing, and incapable of sustained work toward a long-range goal, the assassins developed the compulsion for one tremendous burst of frenzied activity that was intended to accomplish some-thing of great worth.

Often, the opportunity to join with others in a common enterprise that includes dissent, disobedience, violence, or rebellion is critical to the incipient political criminal's radicalization. Direct exposure to hardcore radicals, in a prison or military setting, or under other fa-vorable environmental factors such as those supplied by religious, academic, or rural enclosures, can serve as an important step in the process. In the 1980s and 1990s, small rural communities in the Midwest and in other parts of Middle America gave rise to "state militias" consisting of antifederal and anti–United Nations zealots. In the 1960s, academic institutions provided a fertile hothouse for the growth of the anti–Vietnam War protest movement. Twenty years later, Unabomber Ted Kaczynski focused his antiscientific animosity on academic institutions and their occupants.[259] Religious congregations supplied a similarly supportive environment for sanctuary workers and Central American peace protestors in the 1980s. Churches played such a major role in political activism that an Oakland County deputy sheriff noted to a reporter: "Now if we want to know when there's a crime wave of civil disobedience coming, we consult the liturgical calendar."[260]

Witness for Peace, a grassroots effort to keep U.S. armed forces out of Nicaragua, took shape in religious retreats, among other settings. One participant in a meeting held in late 1983 at the Kirkbridge Retreat Center in northeastern Pennsylvania (for the alleged purposes of Bible study, prayer, and political action) reported:

> We ... together drew up a statement pledging ourselves to a plan of action in the event of a United States invasion of Nicaragua. That "contingency plan" was subsequently presented to each of our constituencies in the churches and sent to every member of Congress, to the Departments of State and Defense, to the CIA, and to the president, informing them of our intentions should they undertake direct military action against Nicaragua.[261]

These religious activists, in their "Pledge of Resistance," called for peaceful occupation of the field offices of all U.S. senators and representatives until they voted to end American intervention in Nicaragua. A year later, in December 1984, the civil disobedience pledge was expanded to include the occupation of "pre-designated U.S. federal facilities, including federal buildings, military installations, offices of the Central Intelligence Agency, the State Department, and other appropriate places."[262] By January 1986 more than 70,000 people had signed the pledge, making Witness for Peace one of the largest publicly open organizations of potentially active political conspirators in American history. One wonders how many of these activists would have had the courage to act alone, without the support provided by mass numbers and the shelter derived from sympathetic media coverage.

Obviously, not all associations of prospective political offenders operate in the open. Some are decidedly unwilling to submit either their tenets of belief or their membership lists to open scrutiny. The right-wing organization Posse Comitatus and the subsequent "state militias" have sought unusual levels of secrecy, making pursuit and investigation by the authorities a difficult matter. It is reported that:

> Indeed, the Posse has no discernable leader, and only the vaguest structure. Michael Beach, a retired machinist from Portland, Oregon, is thought to have founded the Posse in 1969. Yet there is no evidence that he ever exerted or tried to exert much control over the group. The Posse has no national headquarters, no executive board, no letterhead. In two years of investigating the radical right, I have never come across a Posse Comitatus booth at a convention or even a central mailing address for the group. There are loosely organized state branches in Oregon, California, Wisconsin, and Missouri, but the Posse consists mostly of local bands among friends and acquaintances. A typical Posse meeting involves eight or ten men sitting around a kitchen table, complaining of injustice and planning to exercise rights that, by law, they don't have. Recruitment is entirely by word of mouth and personal contact.[263]

Some of these political action associations, whether overt or covert, formed at universities, churches, or kitchen tables—and even if loosely organized—provide a support structure for rebellious activism. The activist's sense of special destiny and of separation from the conformist society now become reinforced by a new camaraderie and organizational affirmation. As with a feedback loop, bonding by common goal and deed intensifies the potential offender's identity as different and special. One friend of the Berrigan brothers, activist opponents to the Vietnam War, wrote about their exclusive "club," consisting only of those who had ventured out into danger in the name of a cause: "You can't criticize the Berrigans this year. They look down on anyone who hasn't risked as much as they have. They'll barely break bread with you if you haven't burned your draft card. Talk about ghettos! That ghetto of martyrs is the most exclusive club of all."[264]

Sociologists Marshall Clinard and Richard Quinney point out that the political offender often seeks to enhance his or her sense of self-worth by soliciting strong sympathy and support from "the people."[265] In any society, there may be a wide segment of the population ready to respond in the way the political criminal hopes. Segments of society that do not share majority values or that are excluded from political power may welcome and even celebrate those standing for political dissent and disobedience.

In the United States, the historic "peace churches" (the Church of the Brethren, the Society of Friends, and the Mennonites) have long provided community support to war resisters, including those opposed to World War II, the Korean War, and the Vietnam War. Similarly, the African American community has offered at least psychological support to the rebels and rioters of the incendiary 1960s. The Southern rebels in the Civil War relied not only on community support but also on the statelike apparatus of the Confederacy. Many subsequent and contemporary dissidents and insurgents—whether in South Africa, Vietnam, Quebec, Afghanistan, Ireland, Nicaragua, or Israel's West Bank—have been successful in portraying themselves as representing not only individual but also broader religious, ideological, ethnic, or communal dissension from the ruling regime. Thus political activists, including terrorists, may find gratification in believing themselves to be representatives of a wider collective—much as soldiers in uniform are confident they speak for their nation or country.

The Seminal Event

How do an individual's sense of uniqueness and revulsion against real or imagined injustice, when enforced by the comradeship of others with similar experiences and stimulated by membership in a rebellious group, suddenly erupt into political resistance, crime, or rebellion? The transition from alienation and disaffection into radicalism and rebellion is often brought about by a seminal event that triggers or intensifies the rebel's process of "politicization." At times the event consists of a dramatic occurrence that shocks or deeply affects the potential activist. Witnessing a sixteen-year-old boy's self-immolation in front of Syracuse Cathedral, in protest against the Vietnam War, served as the seminal event in Daniel Berrigan's career as a political offender. Berrigan subsequently visited the boy as he lay dying in a hospital. There Berrigan "smelled, for the first time . . . the odor of burning flesh."[266] When the boy later died, Berrigan felt that the tragic sacrifice had not been in vain. The youth's death had "brought something to birth" in him. He had been transformed. He would carry on the boy's fight. Timothy J. McVeigh, who bombed the Alfred P. Murrah Federal Building in

Oklahoma City in 1995, similarly viewed the federal government's massive and deadly assault upon the Branch Davidians in 1993 as the clarion call for his transformation from mere dissident into direct resistance warrior.[267]

In other cases the igniting element is supplied by simple events that most individuals would view as quite ordinary. Diana Oughton was shocked by what she observed during her travels in Guatemala. It was there that she began to "see for the first time that the rich are afraid of the poor, and that the poor hate and envy the rich."[268] Dr. Benjamin Spock's sudden realization that "the whole *world* was in peril" because of the global nuclear threat, spurred him to join the peace movement.[269] Karl Armstrong maintained that the tragic events at Kent State initiated his radicalization. He was shaken by the killing of students, which to him "meant that the U.S. Government had declared war on the students. . . . It was then that I made the decision to destroy AMRC [the Army Mathematics Research Center at the University of Wisconsin]."[270]

One woman's account typifies the mindset of hundreds of others who in the recent past fought pitched battles of civil disobedience at the Greenham Commons nuclear weapons facility in Britain:

> [W]hen I was about seven and a half months pregnant, I watched *Horizon,* about the "Protect and Survive" plans. We in Wales would not be hit directly, and it became very plain to me that I would have to sit and watch my children die. Children are much more susceptible to radiation than adults, and I would have to watch them die in agony and then die myself. Suddenly it became obvious to me that I had to do something for my children.[271]

The seminal event has more than symbolic significance. It becomes a lens through which the activist reexamines the entire society. In the case of some revolutionaries and terrorists, a distaste for and opposition to one aspect of society may be extended to other social and political institutions. The gap between ideals and reality becomes intolerable. At that stage the revolutionary is no longer willing to accept partial or reasoned reform, instead requiring a total restructuring of society. "[S]uddenly, for all of us," reported Daniel Berrigan, "the American scene was no longer a good scene. It was, in fact, an immoral scene. . . . Ours was a scene that moral men could not continue to approve if they were to deserve the name of men."[272]

Although a single and dramatic seminal event may help explain the triggering of outrage in theretofore naïve or trusting people, what about the deeper and more gradual processes that transform politically sophisticated moderates into firebrands? Here too seminal events may play a role. We have seen how the process of radicalization feeds on an initial self-perception of uniqueness, a belief in moral purity, and a sense of personal responsibility. This self-image is not unique to the political offender—it is frequently shared by the politically orthodox reformer. Often, however, frustrating experiences, or a particularly upsetting event, may result in the erosion of the reformer's faith in the system within which he or she works. When faith in law and order erodes, in either the politically experienced or the uninitiated citizen, a seminal event can supply the catalyst for breaking with the past—impelling the would-be political offender into action.

For the founder of the radical environmental group Earth First! the political erosion grew slowly out of personal experiences in the field of conventional Washington politics. Dave Foreman, former chief lobbyist for the well-respected Wilderness Society, described his experience:

> [T]ime and time again, we'd come out of those meetings having made all the concessions, rather than having gained any. We bent over backward to be reasonable and credible and politically pragmatic. And by contrasting that timid stance with the emotional, hard-line, no-compromise approach taken by the mining, timber, and livestock industries . . . in their lobbying efforts, it wasn't hard to figure out why they were winning and we were getting only the crumbs. . . . Our group would [therefore best] operate outside the political system and make it known that we had fundamental differences with the worldviews of the political/industrial establishment.[273]

Between Passion and Insanity

Reviewing the diverse traumatic paths that often lead to the radicalization of an otherwise "normal" person begs a lingering question. Will any individual, sufficiently provoked and under appropriate circumstances, resort to rebellion, or is something else required to nourish and trigger the actor's outburst? Rebels might view this "something else" as a nobility or courage lacking in the common individual. The authorities, on the other hand, might rather see such radicalization and rebellious actualization as the result of a flaw, an abnormal zeal, a mental aberration, or—more pejoratively termed— an insanity.

Since public opinion, as well as modern psychology, might view the political offender's behavior as egocentric, monomaniacal, or megalomaniacal—even though history may later view it as altruistic, patriotic, and farsighted—it is not surprising that the political offender's mental health is often put to test by society and by those in authority. Often, as was poignantly illustrated in the recent cases of Timothy J. McVeigh, Unabomber Ted Kaczynski, and Russell Eugene Wesson Jr., the mentally ill assassin of two federal Capitol police officers, there is considerable room for doubt as to the offender's mental condition.

Two Studies in Idealism, Zeal, and Disillusion: Tuller and Rockwood

In June 1976, Charles A. Tuller, a white fifty-two-year-old former high official in the federal government, went on trial in Houston, Texas. With his sons Jonathan, age twenty-one, and Bryce, twenty-two, Tuller was charged with hijacking an Eastern Airlines plane from Houston to Havana, Cuba. In the process an airline ticket agent had been killed by the hijackers. Before the hijacking the three defendants, then residing in Alexandria, Virginia, had killed a bank manager and a police officer while unsuccessfully trying to rob a bank in Crystal City, Virginia.

At the trial, Dr. Duard Bok, a Houston psychiatrist, described Charles Tuller as "partly mentally ill" and suffering from a delusion that he was being persecuted by the authorities for activities that were personally and professionally correct. Tuller perceived the government in general and the U.S. Justice Department, his recent employer, in particular, as corrupt and dishonest. He also believed it was morally correct for individuals to resort to violence to achieve justice. But Dr. Bok testified: "If he had not been mentally ill and delusional, he would not have committed the acts he did." Tuller's former wife described her husband as "highly intelligent," but subject to violent outbursts. She testified that Tuller, a civil rights worker, had became obsessed with the plight of minority groups he was trying to help and "totally lost his professional detachment."[274]

"I feel that what I did, I did with honor, and with the intention of making my country a more humane place," said Charles Tuller after his arrest. *Washington Post* reporter Eugene L. Meyer, interviewing him at the Arlington County Jail, described Tuller as a balding man with a gentle-looking face and wire-rimmed glasses. "I have broken the laws of this country, and therefore I am a criminal," Tuller added. "I have no argument with this, and no doubts about it. But I think that a higher law must consider a man's motivations, his principles, his aims and goals."[275]

A native of Toledo, Ohio, Tuller graduated from the New School for Social Research in New York City, and worked as a Wall Street broker and later operated a small business. Becoming engrossed in the civil rights movement in the early 1960s, he served as vice chairman of the Newark, New Jersey, branch of the Congress on Racial Equality and took employment with the Newark Business and Industrial Coordinating Council, which sought jobs for unemployed African Americans. The businessman turned reformer then served as a troubleshooter for the Community Relations Service of the U.S. Department of Justice and concluded his career working with the Office of Minority Business Enterprise (OMBE) at the Commerce Department.

"Over these years," Tuller reflected, "I began to realize there were basic things wrong, that we were treating symptoms not causes." In the late 1960s, he became convinced that "direct action" by a young, revolutionary "avant garde" was required, since "the idea of a loyal opposition in this country was overall quite ineffectual." In early 1971, Tuller, his sons, and a couple other young men decided to form an action group. They set out to equip themselves doctrinally and militarily so they "could eventually break with our government or what is called law, and try to do something about reconstructing a new system." Although Tuller claimed that the group's physical conditioning and familiarity with the use of arms was purely defensive, and that their intent was merely to "talk with local people and find indigenous leaders to engage in radical politics of change," their revolutionary strategy took a violent turn when he realized that the group lacked the funds to carry out its plans.[276]

By October 1972 the Tullers found themselves in the lobby of Crystal City Bank, guns blazing, in the middle of a shootout. Bank manager Harry J. Candee refused to surrender his keys and Israel P.

Gonzalez, a police officer making his rounds, surprised the impoverished revolutionaries in the midst of their holdup attempt. After killing Candee and Gonzalez, the robbers fled to Houston, as the elder Tuller knew of a surgeon there who could help the injured members of the gang. Since the surgeon was out of town for the weekend, the group decided, apparently on the spur of the moment, to hijack a plane to Cuba.

After shooting a ticket agent in the Houston airport, the group succeeded in escaping to Havana. But their "idealistic views about Cuba" were quickly shattered by personal experiences. They found a Cuba dominated by Russians and by a caste system, with most of the population having little opportunity to "become part of the decision-making mechanism." The Tullers lived on small stipends provided by the Castro government, deciding not to work "because that was the first step to being Cubanized."[277]

At the first opportunity, and with funds provided by the Cuban government, Tuller and his sons left for Nassau and from there went to Miami, passing undetected through U.S. immigration and customs controls. Although they had hoped to pick up their revolutionary mission where they had left off, there was still the problem of a depleted treasury. The Tullers' next "fund-raiser" took place in a K-Mart in Fayetteville, North Carolina. This robbery attempt, too, was foiled, and resulted in Bryce, the oldest Tuller son, being captured by store employees.

On July 7, 1973, the remaining family members decided that they were "not going to leave Bryce behind . . . that's just the kind of family we are." Instead, they turned themselves in to the FBI. Summarizing the events of the previous three years, Charles Tuller concluded, "All I can say is we were three or four people who tried, and the fact that we weren't seemingly very successful I don't think at all [detracts] from the idea that people have got to dedicate themselves in some meaningful way to stopping this [national] suicide we're involved with."[278]

Charles Tuller was first tried in state court in Arlington, Virginia, for the murders of the bank manager and the police officer. He was found competent to stand trial as well as sane and criminally responsible for his deeds. Upon conviction he was sentenced to a minimum of thirty years in prison. Later, in Houston, Tuller was also tried in federal court for air piracy in connection with the hijacking. Once again the court determined that he was sane and accountable for his crimes.

Although the courts concluded that Tuller was sane under the law, the family's escapades leave a lingering suspicion that Tuller and his sons did not have a firm grasp on reality or their place in it. There is little doubt that their activities were politically motivated: They sincerely believed that they were operating on a higher moral plane than the government officials whom they blamed for the callous treatment of society's ills. Nevertheless, even by the most lenient appraisal, their plots and deeds might be considered sufficiently uncommon as to raise doubts about the two courts' conclusions of Charles Tuller's sanity.

Equally bizarre but not altogether different was the fate of a sensitive and highly passionate American soldier who set out single-handedly to remedy not the ills of his home country but the inequalities of a neighboring island, Haiti. Captain Lawrence P. Rockwood was dispatched to Haiti in 1995 by President Clinton to "stop brutal atrocities [and bring about] stability and democracy."[279]

The facts of Rockwood's subsequent offense were simple and undisputed: Without authorization, he left his assigned military post and went into the Port-au-Prince National Penitentiary soon after U.S. forces had landed on the island. Demanding to conduct human rights inspections, and claiming to be on official business, he refused to leave until the entire prison could be inspected. A few hours later, a major from Rockwood's unit arrived at the prison and ordered Rockwood's departure, and only then was the inspection conducted.

According to the U.S. Army's prosecutor, Captain Rockwood "demonstrated exceedingly poor professional judgment [by going into the prison] and demanding to conduct human rights inspections without the authority of [his superior officers]."[280] Rockwood, on the other hand, attempted to explain his conduct not in terms of military hierarchy but in light of his duty to humanity: "I found it difficult not to conclude that the U.S. government could not to some degree be held ethically, morally or legally responsible for the human rights violations being carried out [by Haitian military police] with the knowledge of the [U.S.] command, in the direct proximity of its forces."[281]

Though Rockwood was given a thorough psychological evaluation, no signs of mental disorder were found. At his court-martial,

Rockwood "wrapp[ed] himself in that coat [of human rights],"[282] an unsympathetic newspaper reported. He and his counsel summoned forth the principles of the Nuremberg trials, the Geneva Conventions, and the My Lai massacres. The U.S. Army, on the other hand, cast aspersions on Rockwood's motives and stability, describing his "desire to be a one-man human rights squad" as "unreasonable" and arrogant. As the most telling attack on Rockwood's judgment, the prosecutor noted that the accused's attempt "to be responsible for everyone else's behavior . . . was pretty heady stuff for a captain taking Prozac for depression."[283]

Rockwood was found guilty of military misconduct and was discharged from the service. But as in the Tuller case, many doubts remained regarding a citizen's appropriate duty in the face of manifest evil. Was Rockwood too naïve or too conscientious in his attempt to follow in the footsteps of his idols, whom he kept pictures of on his desk: Hugh Thompson (who won a Distinguished Flying Cross in Vietnam for trying to save civilians during the My Lai massacres), Georges Picquart (who was court-martialed for revealing the anti-Semitic motives behind the Dreyfus case), and Colonel Claus von Stauffenberg (who attempted to assassinate Hitler)? Perhaps one simple additional question might be asked: Should it matter from whence Rockwood's motives came—whether from high-minded morality or from fringe drives of insanity—so long as he sincerely attempted to protect and relieve those abused in confinement?

Insanity or Devotion to a Higher Cause?

Despite the mental health ambiguities underlying such conduct as that of the Tuller family or Captain Rockwood, pathological delusion and insanity may often lie in the background of some political offenders. In 1918 criminologist Maurice Parmalee asserted that mental illness or disorder, of one type or another, was prevalent among most political offenders.[284] After dividing political offenders into three categories—the pathological, the emotional, and the rational—Parmalee observed that the "rational" offenders were clearly the minority.[285] The individuals predominant among those committing political offenses, he concluded, were the "emotional" offenders. He described members of this category as "sympathetic" persons who responded compassionately to human misfortunes and set out to ameliorate them. The "pathological" political offenders, on the other hand, included those who were psychopathologically inclined to acts of violence against individuals of authority and prominence with whom they had little or no personal contact.

The characterization of the political criminal as mentally abnormal has been reiterated by other criminologists and psychiatrists. In 1969 the National Commission on the Causes and Prevention of Violence, which looked into the roots of political assassination in America, noted that most if not all assassins and assailants had experienced a disruption of normal family or parent-child relationships. All were reported to be loners who had experienced difficulty in making friends of either sex, particularly in establishing lasting relationships with women. Relying on this and other evidence, some of the commission's experts declared: "All those who have assassinated or attempted to assassinate Presidents of the United States . . . have been mentally disturbed persons who did not kill to advance any rational political plan."[286]

One of the commission's consultants, Dr. Lawrence Z. Freedman of the University of Chicago, strongly argued that the typical presidential assassins were "mentally disturbed persons" and that, with one possible exception, "there have been no [genuine] *political* assassination attempts directed at the President of the United States."[287] After excepting from his analysis the Puerto Rican nationalists' attack, in which Collazo participated, upon President Truman, Freedman concluded that all other attacks were "products of mental illness with no direct political content."[288] Another consulting psychiatrist went so far as to diagnose the assassins' mental illness as "schizophrenia, in most instances a paranoid type."[289]

Despite the commission's conclusion that a diagnosis of mental illness alone did not explain why certain disturbed persons sought to become assassins (rather than undertake different types of criminal, antisocial, or bizarre behavior),[290] some social and behavioral scientists have nevertheless seen in the commission's conclusion a psychiatric or psychoanalytic overindulgence. Criminologist Stephen Schafer, for instance, criticized the commission for speaking "in orthodox Freudian terms, hinting at the offenders' unconscious need to commit political crimes."[291] Indeed, permitting the commission's consultant to offer paranoid schizophrenia as the specific mental malady of presidential assassins whiffs suspiciously of a snap diagnosis. One wonders how diagnosticians personally unacquainted with their subjects could so precisely define their ailments.

The Utility of Insanity

The question of the political offender's mental health has a direct and pragmatic bearing on many issues, the first of which is the suspect's competence to stand trial. Next, the offender's mental competence reflects on the likelihood and success of his or her insanity defense. Finally, insanity may effect the tailoring of any of the appropriate sanctions that might be imposed on the offender: guilty, not guilty by reason of insanity, guilty but mentally ill, or yet some other disposition. But resort to the insanity label has other uses as well. First, it cloaks what might be an actor's inexplicable violence or dissent with a pseudo-scientific patina that raises insidious questions regarding the rationality of the offender's cause. A mentally aberrant offender, characterized as out of touch with reality, will taint the cause for which he or she stands and fights. To those political offenders who undertake their deed in hope of eventual popular support, a court's finding of, or even the plea of, insanity is an ignominious defeat.

The political offender thus tends to vehemently resist resorting to the insanity plea. When Charlotte Corday was tried for the assassination of French revolutionary leader Jean Paul Marat and her advocate pleaded her insane, she complained that the defense was unworthy of her.[292] The Marquis de Sade was confined to a mental institution rather than a prison allegedly to lessen his own standing as well as to denigrate the standing of his "obscene" plays and novels within the French intellectual community. American abolitionist John Brown, after his conviction for the Harper's Ferry raid, strenuously resisted the urging of some of his sympathizers to enter a plea of insanity. Collazo, the Puerto Rican who attempted to assassinate President Truman, refused to allow his lawyers to plead insanity, despite the psychiatric claim that his goal and plan of action showed little grasp of reality.[293] Sirhan Sirhan, the assassin of presidential candidate Robert F. Kennedy, likewise rejected the double-edged effects of the insanity defense. Only poet Ezra Pound, whose admirers sought to avoid a public treason trial for his seditious World War II radio broadcasts on behalf of fascist Italy, was persuaded to undergo a plea of incompetence and a subsequent confinement in St. Elizabeth's mental hospital in Washington, D.C., in lieu of standing up to his criminal accusers.

In *The Right to Be Different*, a previous study of the treatment accorded such deviant classes as the mentally ill, alcoholics, drug addicts, and "sexual psychopaths" in the United States, this author demonstrated that resort to psychiatric labels and processes for dealing with various classes of social deviants has not been without substantial peril to those affected.[294] The therapeutic and assertedly nonpunitive approach can unwittingly be turned into an oppressive tool in the hands of those in authority, who under the guise of "therapy" may mete out harsher sanctions than usually available under the penal process. Despite the therapeutic label's purported implication of humanitarian protections, most societies have seen to it that a high price—in terms of loss of liberty as well as status—is exacted from suspects for according them the questionable benefits of being considered "insane."

The fallacy, cruelty, and human rights abuses inherent in attributing the deeds of political offenders to mental disorder are widely known. For nearly half a century, the Soviet Union relied on special mental clinics for the detention and reorientation of political, religious, and ideological dissidents.[295] Responding to charges that mentally sound opponents of the regime were being suppressed in insane asylums, the Soviet Union's official daily, *Izvestia,* assured its readers in 1972 that the Soviet institutions contained only those "who have committed socially dangerous acts in a state of derangement."[296] This "socially dangerous" and "deranged" conduct included such innocent activities as membership in the Seventh Day Adventist Church and adherence to its dietary rules, as Birute Poskene, a Lithuanian mother who lost custody of her children and was confined to a mental hospital, was to discover.[297]

It is no wonder, therefore, that even when faced with death, incarceration, or other punishment, political offenders have resisted the label of mental illness. Despite the apparent benefits of an insanity finding (thereby exempting the offender from criminal responsibility and punishment), political dissidents generally prefer to be labeled criminal rather than ill. The former Soviet Union's record of abuses demonstrates to future generations that the unwitting designation of political offenders as insane not only overlooks the true underlying causes of their behavior and risks unnecessary state overreaction to the dangers they pose, but also unduly diminishes their role and status in the estimation of present and future generations.

The Rush to Be Political: Undeserved Honor

Enumeration of the social and psychological factors that contribute to the making of the political offender must not ignore the role of the media in endowing the dissatisfied with identity, a voice, and credibility—possibly even inciting them into action. Successful political action requires a combination of human masses, matériel (funds, printing presses, and weapons), and effective communications. Protagonists in a political struggle can invariably be counted upon to appeal to the broader audiences by lauding the altruism of the rebels and decrying the wickedness of those in power. This is always countered by a diametric barrage from the opposing camp.

It is within the nature of the mass media to reach out and inform the discontented that they are not alone, and indeed even to insist that they should be discontented. In 1937 George Orwell reported:

> Talking once with a miner I asked him when the housing shortage first became acute in his district; he answered "When we were told about it," meaning that till recently people's standards were so low that they took almost any degree of overcrowding for granted.[298]

The vital role of the mass media in the development or expansion of communal conflicts was similarly pointed out by James Coleman:

> Whether the local newspaper creates an issue through editorial activity or sensationalist reporting, or whether it merely seeks out and reports events which create an issue, it is true that many controversies are born when community members unsuspectingly open their newspaper one morning. Similarly, in times of disaster or crisis, the mass media become of crucial importance.[299]

Contemporary mass media technologies provide far greater opportunities for the fanning of popular discontent than those offered by the marketplace rumors and angry citizen parades of earlier eras. In 1937 the power of a newsreel showing Chicago police firing point-blank into a crowd of labor picketers, killing nine, riveted the attention of not only congressional investigators but the whole country.[300] Similarly, the black civil rights movement of the 1960s benefitted from news footage of police using cattle prods, dogs, and clubs against peaceful marchers in Birmingham and Selma, Alabama. The horrors of the Vietnam War brought into the living rooms of America each night were responsible for accelerating and deepening opposition to that war. Some believe that global communications through television and facsimile machine were responsible for the success of the "velvet revolution" in Eastern Europe and the brief success of the democracy movement in the People's Republic of China. Likewise, the 1991 anti-Gorbachev coup attempt in the Soviet Union was foiled in part by the ability of its opponents to keep open the lines of communication from Moscow to the world.

The speed with which news can reach around the world, and the virtual inability of governments to control communications in and out of their countries, give domestic forces a greater chance of success than ever before in seeking sympathy and support abroad. In an era of great competition for media attention, there is nothing like a massacre, an assassination, the bombing of an aircraft or courthouse, or the governmental razing of suspects' houses to rivet the attention of millions. Ted Koppel, host of ABC's *Nightline,* would agree:

> Without television, terrorism becomes rather like the philosopher's hypothetical tree falling in the forest: no one hears it fall and therefore it has no reason for being. And television, without terrorism, while not deprived of all interesting things in the world, is nonetheless deprived of one of the most interesting.[301]

Rapid and ubiquitous communications often accelerate the processes that can escalate disquietude into rebellion. It is no wonder that political dissidents actively seek the media stages of the world, often by creating what has come to be called a "media event"—a happening that has no or little purpose other than to secure mass attention for the political platform of the activists.

The media, for their part, have duly and even eagerly reported the adventures or misadventures of those challenging authority. Episodes of the graduation of political, racial, ethnic, social, and economic unrest into violent assaults and terrorism against persons and property have received widespread coverage in the press, on radio, and on television, and have been accompanied by details concerning the perpetrators' political grievances and agendas. Together with this coverage often comes an unwarranted aggrandizement of the activists, contributing sometimes to the unwarranted heroic myth of political crime and rebellion.

As the strains and stresses of American society came into full bloom in the late 1960s and early 1970s, virtually every social problem was translated—by both activists and the attentive media—into radical political terminology. Claims of racial, economic, social, and gender deprivations all came to be expressed as political issues. With the growth of feminist and gay rights movements, sexual relations and preferences assumed new political dimensions. In addition, Native American rights, prisoner rights, student rights, and rights of the handicapped, fetuses, children, and senior citizens were all cast more as political than medical, racial, cultural, socioeconomic, religious, or historical problems. America's political activists were not reluctant to adopt the rhetoric and style (if not always the violence) of insurgent groups and guerrilla movements around the world—challenging America's police, courts, and prisons, as well as its universities, defense establishment, "military-industrial complex," and expanding federal hierarchy. As these claims were seriously considered by the media, ever larger numbers of offenders began asserting political motives for their deeds, seemingly in an effort to purge the stigmas from their common crimes.

Skyjackers revived the long-dormant practice of sea piracy (carried out in earlier days for personal greed and adventure), transmuting it into aircraft piracy in the name of political protest. These new pirates of the air often sought applause and asylum for their indiscriminate criminality. Others, modern freelance espionage agents, shed their dark and old-fashioned identities as adventurers and illicit entrepreneurs to emerge as "activists" with claims for global peace, disarmament, or similar noble ends. Like America's Ethel and Julius Rosenberg, convicted of sharing atomic secrets with the Soviets, or England's Kim Philby, a highly placed spy who ultimately sought refuge in Moscow, many others have proclaimed themselves "political offenders" dedicated to higher causes rather than common criminals or traitors who served foreign powers for money or thrills.

Whole classes of common offenders pressed their claims of political prisoner status on the theory that their offenses were rooted in and attributable to socially, economically, racially, or politically exploitative systems. Describing themselves as political prisoners, the inmates of New York's Attica Penitentiary sought in 1972 both their release and mass transportation to a politically sympathetic country of asylum. Samuel Melville, later killed in the Attica uprising, wrote in his prison newspaper, *Iced Pig:*

> Of primary importance is t[he] coming awareness of ourselves as *political prisoners.* No matter how heinous t[he] "crime" u have been convicted of, u are a political prisoner just as much as Angela [Davis]. *Every act has a cause and effect.* T[he] *cause* of your "crime" is that u found yourself in a society that offered no prospects for a life of fulfillment and sharing with your brothers and sisters. A society where u were taught to compete and beat t[he] guy next to u because if u didn't, he'd beat u. A society whose every facet and angle is thoroughly controlled by t[he] Pig-dogs of t[he] corporation giants of Amerika.[302]

But even perpetrators of the basest offenses (conceived of personal pathologies and stoked by urges for bestial gratification) frequently received undeserved and uncritical media attention when they portrayed their crimes as a function of some new "political" insight. Eldridge Cleaver, later Minister of Information of the Black Panther Party, advanced the proposition that interracial rape should be viewed as a political protest when carried out by a male of a deprived class or race against a female of the oppressing society. In his letters from prison, Cleaver asserted:

> I became a rapist. To refine my technique and *modus operandi,* I started out practicing on black girls . . . and when I considered myself smooth enough I crossed the tracks and sought out white prey. I did this consciously, deliberately, willfully, methodically . . . rape was an insurrectionary act. It delighted me that I was defying and trampling upon the white man's laws, upon his system of values, and I was defiling his women.[303]

Leaders of the anti–Vietnam War movement (including Father Philip Berrigan, himself imprisoned for destroying U.S. selective service records) gave support to common prisoners' claims of entitlement to political status. Speaking of his prison experiences, Berrigan noted: "So we had that common bond with them [the common offenders], in a very wide sense, almost everybody there was a political prisoner. And almost all of them had the firm conviction of confronting the system, using the best means at hand."[304] Andrew Young, then U.S. Ambassador to the United Nations in 1977, similarly conceded before a worldwide press conference that a large number of prison inmates in the United States were "political prisoners," and the media faithfully gave uncritical credence to this unsubstantiated claim.

Even such pathological misfits as Charles Manson and his followers (the "Family"), who were charged with some of the most heinous and gratuitous murders in California history, found the media listening when they undertook to cast their deeds as revolutionary acts designed to bring down a "corrupt" system. Asserting that his Family's killings would help trigger a racial war, Manson relied on an alleged prophecy contained in a lyric from the Beatles song "Helter Skelter." After a war in which blacks would be exterminated and whites militarily exhausted, Manson and his disciples were to emerge from hiding and ascend to political supremacy.[305]

The image of Charles Manson as a political revolutionary was given considerable credence in the Yippie and leftist fringe literature of the time. Political militant Bernadine Dohrn told a convention of the Students for a Democratic Society that "the Weathermen dig Charles Manson." A San Francisco underground paper, *Tuesday's Child*, which described itself as "the Voice of the Yippies," named Manson "Man of the Year." And after visiting Manson in jail, political activist Jerry Rubin, of Chicago Seven Trial fame, proclaimed: "I fell in love with Charlie Manson the first time I saw his cherub face and sparkling eyes on TV."[306] More important than the validity or intensity of the beliefs of Dohrn, Rubin, and the Yippies was the fact that they were widely broadcast by the mass media to a less than comprehending public.

The culmination of the era's intimate dance between self-styled revolutionaries and the sensation-thirsty media came in the spring of 1974.[307] After kidnaping Patricia Hearst, daughter of *San Francisco Examiner* publishing magnate William Randolph Hearst, a group identifying themselves as the Symbionese Liberation Army (SLA) failed to demand ransom for their captive. Instead they commenced a publicity campaign, filing their taped "communiqués" with various radio stations and other media outlets. The SLA's potpourri of published "objectives" ranged from the destruction of capitalism and corporate institutions to the opening of prisons, from the abolition of marriage to the humane and loving care of the aged and the young. Ultimately they demanded that William Hearst provide free food to welfare recipients, government pensioners, disabled veterans, and released convicts.

In mid-April 1974 the SLA, accompanied by Ms. Hearst, robbed a bank at gunpoint, wounding several people in the process. In a communiqué from Ms. Hearst, newly converted to the revolution and now calling herself "Tania, a soldier in the people's army," the SLA defended the robbery as necessary to support the revolutionary cause, noting that "the difference between a criminal act and a revolutionary act is shown by what the money is used for." A month later the SLA, never numbering more than ten members, was virtually extinguished by the death of six members in a shootout with Los Angeles police, an event that was telecast live.

Despite her claims to have been sexually assaulted and coerced into ostensible cooperation with the SLA, Ms. Hearst was subsequently convicted and sentenced to prison for seven years for her part in the bank robbery. She served twenty-two months before President Carter commuted her sentence. Two months later she married her former bodyguard and slipped back into privileged seclusion. One could probably never conclude for certain whether "Tania, a soldier in the people's army" was a victim, an opportunist, a noble reformer, or merely a confused conformist.

The intense media appeal of self-asserted political offenders and their diverse, sometimes sincere and sometimes convoluted motives is illustrated by the lengthy interview granted to author Robert B. Kaiser by the imprisoned Sirhan Sirhan, the Jordanian assassin of presidential candidate Robert F. Kennedy. Kaiser probed into Sirhan's motives for shooting Kennedy. "Well, with [John F.] Kennedy, I loved him," Sirhan responded. "And to me, President Kennedy was infallible. He was a man, you know, I loved him! And I thought Kennedy, Bob, would do the same, you know, do the same. But, hell, he fucked up."[308] Sirhan was apparently referring to Robert Kennedy's alleged "betrayal," his failure to stand up for the Palestinian cause.

Throughout the remainder of the interview, Sirhan frequently and vigorously objected to Kaiser's personal line of questioning, particularly when pressed to detail his own youthful disappointment with his father's desertion of the family. Several psychologists pointed to this fact as the underlying cause for Sirhan's preoccupation with Robert Kennedy's "betrayal." Sirhan reiterated: "They're all trying to dig into my family background. That had no effect on my actions. . . . Had I killed my wife, had I killed my brother . . . [I could] understand their trying to delve into my background. But, you see, this was political." When Kaiser sought to explore Sirhan's relations with a certain young woman, Sirhan retorted: "Don't talk about women to me." Taken aback, Kaiser asked the reason for Sirhan's objection. "'This is political,' said Sirhan. 'This is politically motivated,' he started to giggle nervously. 'This is heh heh, political, heh heh, politically motivated.'"[309]

In his exploratory monograph *The Political Crime: The Problem of Morality and Crime,* criminologist Stephen Schafer identified a category of offenders he designated as "pseudoconvictional."[310] The "pseudos," observed Schafer, are common criminals who posture themselves as acting out of altruistic convictions. But unlike most common criminals, the "pseudos" need not necessarily have personal or material goals. Instead, they might be motivated by the thrill of adventure: living beyond and outside the law to share in popular fame and adulation. Their claims of political motive, however strenuously asserted, are mere excuses.

Pseudoconvictional criminals can be found not only among those waging war against authority but also within the ranks of those serving the causes of existing political power. Many despots, tyrants, and dictators throughout history have abused power and exploited society not for some political or public objective, but for their own pathological or economic gratification. Similarly, among individuals and groups advancing political causes for their resistance and rebellion against those in power, many may merely be pseudoconvictional claimants. How then are genuine political offenders to be distinguished from the impostors, those who resort to political motives merely as a cover?

The growing politicization of American and global life, as well as the accompanying media exaggeration and editorialization, have unfortunately made the differentiation between the genuine political offender and the imposter more difficult with time. Indeed, despite the persistent denial of the very existence of political criminality by justice systems in America and most other countries, the bizarre luster and sympathetic claims of the political offender have continued to appeal not only to the general public but also to the mass media. Even at the height of America's preoccupation with domestic terrorism and serial crime in the mid–1990s, no other death-row convict received as much attention in the United States and abroad as did newly converted Black Muslim Mumia Abu-Jamal. A former leader

of the militant Black Panthers and a onetime journalist and radio
personality, Abu-Jamal was convicted of murdering a Philadelphia
police officer during the latter's effort to arrest Abu-Jamal's brother.

Mumia Abu-Jamal's conviction was upheld through several appeals. The evidence against Abu-Jamal was termed by the prosecutor
as among "the strongest I have seen in 24 years as a prosecutor." [311]
Others, asserting a police frame-up, compared Abu-Jamal's conviction to that of Captain Dreyfus in anti-Semitic nineteenth-century
France. Despite the absence of exonerating evidence, Abu-Jamal's
advocates urged: "who could wish for a more ideal culprit for the
murder of a white police officer than this black man, a former Black
Panther militant and journalist who was denouncing police violence
against the black community?"[312]

In very short order Mumia Abu-Jamal became a global political
celebrity. Concentrating on his former political activities, the racial
tensions in the United States, and the terminal nature of his sentence,
Abu-Jamal's supporters found sufficient arguments to turn what appeared to be an open-and-shut cop-killing case into a political crime.
The outcry of the alleged injustice imposed upon Abu-Jamal was
compelling enough to rouse even the Italian Parliament to pass a resolution calling on the United States to release the offender, and the
death sentence was ultimately commuted to life imprisonment by
Pennsylvania's governor. As of this writing, it is unlikely that the
guilt or innocence of Mumia Abu-Jamal can be readily resolved to
the satisfaction of all. But his case further underscores the importance of drawing lines of demarcation between the political offender,
the common criminal, and the pseudoconvictional offender.

Stages in Moral Development

Although the forces of authority generally seek to discredit the political offender by pointing to his or her dysfunctions, pathologies, or
disingenuity, other social observers and behavioral scientists see the
rebel in a more favorable light. Criminologist Stephen Schafer
voiced fundamental objections to the characterization of politically
motivated offenders as psychologically unbalanced. Instead, he
viewed political offenders as those who had escaped the stifling conformity that society seeks to impose. Rejecting psychiatric jargon
and labels, Schafer relied instead on what might be described as

"learning theory" to explain the apparent uniqueness of the political offender:

> To think of political criminals in terms of "abnormality" or some kind of mental derangement appears reasonable only to those who forget the pluralistic nature of morality and the inadequacies of the socialization process. . . . [I]n the false assumption that all members of the society are well socialized and thus can and do understand the "command" of morality, the sovereign cannot believe that anybody with a sane mind would rebel against his moral tenets. . . . But those who do not accept these moral principles (*because* their socialization to this morality has been inadequate), and *therefore* do not feel happy with the morality that guides their society, are not necessarily mentally sick. . . .
>
> The political criminal sees no reason for believing that man's true happiness and perfection depend on understanding the place the sovereign assigned to him in this globe. He does not suffer any kind of mental disorder; he is just an inadequately socialized explorer of a vision—a vision that would not emerge if he were adequately socialized.[313]

Although Schafer, in an inherently favorable portrayal, attributed the political offender's uniqueness to "inadequate" socialization, Harvard social psychologist Lawrence Kohlberg viewed the rebel's uniqueness as a product of special and favorable developmental factors. Seeking an explanation for the rebel's retreat from conformity, Kohlberg elucidated what he perceived as common "stages of moral development," clustering around three distinct levels—the preconventional, the conventional, and the postconventional.[314] At the preconventional level, a person responds to existing rules of right and wrong by weighing them in terms of hedonistic consequences (punishment and reward). At the conventional level, maintaining the standards of one's nation, peer group, or family is perceived as valuable and desirable in its own right. Right behavior at this stage consists of doing one's "duty" of maintaining law and order for its own sake.

Kohlberg argued that although all humans go through the same sequence of stages, only a few reach the postconventional level. At this highest level, one is motivated by sensitivity and concern for others, and by a commitment to universal and higher laws.[315] Among this highest class Kohlberg listed Martin Luther King Jr. and Mahatma Gandhi. An individual who reaches this level observes moral values and principles that have validity and application without regard to the authority of the nation or group to which the individual belongs. "At heart, these are universal principles of justice, of equality, of human rights, and of respect for the dignity of human beings."[316] Stirred by this noble image of the postconventional activist, Kohlberg was not seeking only a greater understanding of the process of moral development that leads to this higher stage. He entertained futuristic hopes for creating or nurturing more such righteous individuals to serve as humanity's eternal guardians against tyrants, despots, and other abusers of power.

Despite the opinions of such scholars, who have tended to either discredit or ennoble the political offender, intuition and evidence strongly suggest that neither approach is totally correct, and that the potential for rebellion and dissent exists in all. This conclusion is supported by the historical record of the United States and other countries. The commonality of political crime was also suggested by Maurice Parmalee in the early twentieth century, in his categorization of three classes of political offenders: the rational, the emotional, and the pathological.[317] He found "rational" political offenders the least prevalent. He pointed out, accordingly, that those with highly developed reasoning capacities—as contrasted with those possessing sympathetic and compassionate personalities—were unlikely to resort to violence as a means of social reform except in instances of last resort.[318] Instead, he looked to the "emotional," or compassionate, group as the primary producer of rebels. However, Parmalee maintained that any person might become a political offender for appropriate reasons of individual or collective belief or conviction under particularly stressful circumstances.

A public opinion poll conducted more recently in Florida confirmed Parmalee's observation in its finding that 58 percent of those interviewed professed a willingness to violate state laws that conflicted with strongly held religious or moral convictions.[319] The large numbers and diverse classes of people involved in various types of political militancy confirm that neither psychosocial pathology nor doctrines of failed socialization, status incongruence, and moral development can explain the phenomenon of political criminality. That not all political offenders are moved by a single force or combination of forces must be readily admitted. More important is the inescapable conclusion that nearly anyone might venture forth to resist abuse of power when pressures—internal and external, individual and communal—become unbearable. There is no universally held value or common denominator among those who struggle against authority. In this fight ordinary people pushed too far may join ranks with the embittered, the alienated, the criminal, and the insane. Anyone can become a political offender, a combatant in the war against authority—regardless of status, class, race, gender, religion, or ethnicity. It may indeed be said that rebellion is a nearly universal constant of the human condition, an experience that most of us have shared at one time or another in response to different manifestations—real or imagined—of the abuse of power.

The Two Faces of Janus: Deity or Demon?

Donning her blindfold, the goddess of justice often chooses not to differentiate between the common criminal and the political offender who appear before her. The blindfold further prevents the judging goddess from distinguishing between the benevolent and malevolent rebel. For lack of recognition, those rebelling against authority frequently suffer as common criminals. Worse, most political offenders, particularly if unsuccessful in their rebellious pursuits, are also often relegated to ignominy by those who defeat them. Yet a few manage—in their victory or even in their defeat—to ascend to the lofty status of demigods and are accorded the laurels and rewards of heroes and patriots, often posthumously.

The political offender—drawn from a primal archetype—is both a creator and a destroyer of authority and its culture, a manifestation of Shiva in universal garb. The Greek rebel Prometheus brought fire—that indispensable element of civilization—to the mortal world by stealing it from the gods on Mount Olympus. Biblical Adam and Eve brought humankind the forbidden fruits of the Tree of Knowledge: self-awareness and the ability to discern right from wrong. Noted American psychoanalyst Rollo May enumerated Socrates, Jesus, Buddha, and Krishna among the culture-creating heroes, arguing that throughout history the rebel has been a positive force, a mover and shaker—the *primum mobile* of society.[320] May suggested that, like Orestes in Greek mythology, the rebel is a symbol of humankind's assumption of individual responsibility for one's life. This responsibility, he wrote, is "the life-blood of culture, the very root of civilization."[321]

The fate of the rebel often includes martyrdom. In particular, the idealistic, creative rebel (the one with a better "vision of life or society")[322] almost inevitably becomes a victim of the forces of authority. Prometheus, for his gift of fire to the mortal world, was chained for eternity to Mount Caucasus, where an eagle sent by Zeus, the Greek god—king of gods and mortals—daily devoured his entrails. Similarly, Adam and Eve were cast out of Eden to gain their bread by the sweat of their brow, their return forever barred by a revolving flaming sword. Socrates was given his hemlock, while Jesus met his fate at Golgotha. In the New World, John Brown was hanged as a traitor by the forces of "law and order."

Modern rebels and political offenders often meet similarly tragic ends, though not always at official hands. Mahatma Ghandi and Martin Luther King Jr. were cut down by the bullets of criminal assassins. Their deaths became martyrdoms, attributed to society's resistance to change. These rebels thus satisfied martyrdom, a frequent prerequisite for entry into the annals of history. Rollo May noted the "startling regularity through history with which society martyrs the rebel in one generation and worships him in the next. . . . The list is as endless as it is rich."[323]

While recognizing the rebel's function as a creative hero, we must also recognize the rebel's role as a destroyer. History's most reviled rebel, the archangel Lucifer, was expelled from Heaven for disobedience. "Better to reign in Hell than serve in Heaven," he proclaimed, even though this meant spending eternity immovably frozen in a sea of polluted ice, chewing forever on the world's most distasteful sinners.[324] History is replete with these destructive rebels—tyrants, butchers, and megalomaniacs who pursued and often attained power as an end in itself. For these self-centered and "pseudoconvictional" rebels (the Nebuchadnezzars, Neros, Genghis Khans, Hitlers, and Stalins), destruction becomes in the end more important than creation.[325] Contemporary culture all too often glamorizes this sort of destructive or negative rebel: Among our most popular cultural idols are those who expressed their contempt for the "establishment" and its values—from America's James Dean (the "Rebel Without a Cause") and numerous "heavy metal" and "rap" music groups, to West Germany's Ulricke Meinhof, founding member of the Baader-Meinhof terrorist gang.

The quest for mere power and change, if unaccompanied by a definite and responsible plan for creating something new and better, tends to become futile and destructive—imagine Prometheus without his fire, Adam and Eve without the self-knowledge they gained at such terrible cost. Worse yet, the aim of many rebels is self-interest, to "simply substitute one kind of government for another, the second no better than the first . . . [making] the individual citizen, who has to endure the inevitable anarchy between the two, worse off than ever before."[326] When rebellion is an end in itself, when the ascension to power becomes a self-contained objective, the darker side of the rebel prevails. The act of rebellion then tends to become an infliction of nihilistic terror—designed to destroy, to disrupt, to frighten, to cow, to shock, and to disgust, rather than to create or to renew.

But regardless of the rebel's message and mission, whether creative or destructive, he or she often symbolizes humanity's eternal striving for change, the desire to sweep out the old. This is why, whether the rebel is righteous or venal, popular culture often endows him or her with superhuman proportions. The rebel is portrayed as one who transcends the rules, who proceeds despite the inhibitions of the law, who achieves against all odds, who comes from a unique mold reserved for demigods.

The rebel's image as a figure somehow larger than life has tended to make us insensitive to him or her as the recipient of worldly rewards or punishments. Deifying or demonizing the rebel makes it possible for us to view this defier of authority as a rarity, one who cannot be properly understood or judged by common social institutions and legal tribunals. Law and public policy often disclaim, therefore, the need to take particular account of such men and women of destiny who act beyond the law. History, it is claimed, will make the final judgment anyway. Indeed, it is explained, only time can winnow the creative rebel from the destroyer, the good from the evil.

But does this superhuman myth bear scrutiny? And must we relinquish judgment? Are rebels really created in a unique mold? Or are they mostly ordinary people who find themselves in extraordinary situations? If the latter, then should we not pay more attention to what separates the worthy rebel from the unworthy? Should not our public policy and law respond in greater measure to the rebel's common humanity? And should we not do this in advance of history's final judgment?

Instead of coming to grips with these questions, most institutions of justice have continued to pursue and punish all rebels indiscriminately for their offending words or deeds, or for their very existence. Like the gods on Mount Olympus, we have not deigned to consider the mitigating circumstances of the rebel's grievances, hopes, and motives. By casting all rebels into the pit of ignominy, we have chosen to uphold "law and order" at the expense of truth and change. Yet historically, the rebel—as either creator or destroyer—poses unique problems for society, morality, and law. His or her desire for a new society, new institutions, and new thought inevitably presents a threat to existing society, institutions, and thought. Equally troubling is the realization that many of those who allege pursuit of new and more positive and humane goals do so only ostensibly, to conceal their pursuit of selfish, nihilistic, or psychopathological objectives.

Perpetuating the myth of the political offender as a unique and uncommon actor does not assist us in dealing with the worldly problems posed by political criminality and rebellion. It does not help us determine when the political rebel should be considered a beneficent bringer of civilization and change, and when a destructive and selfish force. Society and its institutions must find a different way of approaching these thorny questions, a means of checking the destructive side of the rebel without stifling the forces of progress, renewal, and change that might move him or her.

Part Three

Villains or Patriots?

Political Offenders in America and Abroad

The highest duty is to respect authority.
—Pope Leo XIII (1810–1903)

All our liberties are due to men who, when their conscience has compelled them, have broken the laws of the land.
—Harry Roberts,
British Rebels and Reformers (1942)

Good men must not obey the laws too well.
—Ralph Waldo Emerson,
Politics (1844)

A tyrannical rule of forty years is preferable to one hour of no rule at all.
—Islamic adage

Marat, aspiring for despotic power during the French Revolution, assassinated in his bathtub. *The Death of Marat*, Jacques-Louis David, painting (1793).

Chapter Four

Piercing
the Monolith

Lessons of the American Experience

Even God cannot change the past.
—Agathon (447–401 B.C.),
attributed by Aristotle,
The Nichomachean Ethics, at vi

*It has been said that although God
cannot alter the past, historians can.*
—Samuel Butler,
Erewhon, chap. 14 (1872)

The Peaceable Kingdom, Edward Hicks, oil on canvas (c. 1826–1828).

The frame of the painting reads:
"The wolf did with the lambkin dwell in peace, His grim carniv'rous nature there did cease; The leopard with the harmless kid laid down, And not one savage beast was seen to frown; The lion with the fatling on did move, A little child was leading them in love; When the great PENN has famous treaty made, With Indian chiefs beneath the elm tree's shade."

The Myth of America's Peaceable Kingdom

Americans have long taken comfort in their belief that the development of their country has differed radically, and for the better, from the admittedly violent and disorderly civilization's evolution as seen in the lands of their European ancestors. A 1969 report to America's National Commission on the Causes and Prevention of Violence pointed out that:

> As comforting as it is for civilized people to think of barbarians as violent and of violence as barbarian, Western civilization and various forms of collective violence have always been close partners. . . . Historically, collective violence has flowed regularly out of the central political processes of Western countries. . . . The oppressed have struck in the name of justice, the privileged in the name of order, those in between in the name of fear. Great shifts in the arrangements of [European] power ordinarily have produced—and have often depended on—exceptional movements of collective violence.[327]

The United States, on the other hand, has generally been depicted by domestic scholars and social commentators as endowed with a manifest destiny and a distinct style. "[A]mericans since the Puritans have historically regarded themselves as a latter-day 'Chosen People' sent on a holy errand to the wilderness, there to create a New Jerusalem," wrote political scientists Hugh Graham and Ted Gurr.[328] On the new continent there was to be the true realization of Isaiah's prophecy: "The wolf and the lamb shall feed together, and the lion shall eat straw like the bullock; and dust shall be the serpent's food. They shall not hurt nor destroy in all my holy mountain."[329]

The growth of the American nation—described by Benjamin Franklin as "founded by the design of providence to cultivate a new earth"[330]—was equated, in characteristic optimism and faith, with the realization of various utopian ideals and programs. Concurrently, there developed what lawyer-historian Richard E. Rubenstein called "The Myth of Peaceful Progress."[331] That myth professed that the United States was unique among nations as a place in which extremely diverse groups had learned to compromise their differences peaceably.

This image saw American society as having been blessed by a blurring of divisions between the multiplicity of economic, social, political, and ethnic groups. That achievement was attributed to a combination of factors, including the fertility of the land and the richness of its resources, the tendency of the people to be hardworking, the fact that neither a true aristocracy nor an impoverished proletariat had set roots in this soil, and finally, the belief that the Constitution and the political system had created ideal instruments for political compromise. Thus, it was believed, "any sizable domestic group could gain its proper share of power, prosperity and respectability merely by playing the game according to the rules."[332] Since America's Constitution had supposedly implemented and perfected the tools necessary to ensure the peaceful sharing and transference of power—a process essential for supporting change and progress—no need remained for violent or unlawful political, social, or economic pursuits.

Although America's identity as a child of political revolution did pose some problem for the country's vision of itself as a land of blessed harmony, this revolutionary heritage has often been explained away as an anomaly caused by an oppressive "foreign" tyrant. With time, the Declaration of Independence's proclamation that "it is the right of the people to alter or abolish" their government, impliedly by either peaceful or violent means, began to seem charmingly anachronistic.[333] A widely held faith in the Constitution's self-correcting mechanisms and its protections against governmental abuse of power has made resort to extralegal means unthinkable for most citizens. And this faith persists despite the fact that the Constitution and its machinery could not forestall the Civil War, the bloodiest intranational conflict of the nineteenth-century world.

Lesser outbreaks of politically connected violence both before and after the Civil War have been more easily overlooked. These episodes have often been labeled "un-American," tacitly implying that they were of alien origin—resulting from ideas brought to America's shores by foreigners, or from actions of immigrant populations resisting integration into a peaceful and homogenized American society. This was a convenient explanation for men like Franklin B. Gowen, president of the Philadelphia and Reading Railroad Company, who in 1875 attributed labor unrest in the coal mines of Pennsylvania to "a class of agitators . . . men brought here for no other purpose than to create confusion, to undermine confidence, and to stir up dissension between employer and the employed . . . advocates of the Commune and Emissaries of the International."[334] Severe and undeniably massive political disturbances were thus considered by scholarly writers and by the public as rare anomalies and foreign intrusions. Moreover, political dissidence and violence were long overlooked as having played a significant role in the domestic political life and socioeconomic development of the country.

These prevailing notions typically remained unchallenged until quite recently. It was the racial and urban riots of the 1960s, combined with campus unrest, that produced a new awareness of the role of political dissent and violence in American history. These upheavals also led to an inevitable reassessment of the traditional (or "change-through-consensus") view of American political progress and reform. When black activist H. "Rap" Brown asserted that mass political violence was "as American as apple pie,"[335] he shocked the nation's sensitivity. Nevertheless, serious scholars soon began to advance similar "revisionist" theories of America's not-so-peaceful progress. The once lonely voice of Reverend Theodore Parker, who proclaimed in 1848 that "We are a rebellious nation; our whole history is treason,"[336] began to be increasingly echoed by prominent historians and social scientists in the second half of the twentieth century.[337]

In 1969 Richard E. Rubenstein concluded: "For more than two hundred years . . . the United States has experienced regular episodes of serious mass violence related to the social, political and economic objectives of insurgent groups."[338] Similar conclusions were reached the same year by historian Richard M. Brown in his report to the National Commission on the Causes and Prevention of Violence: "There has been a vast amount [of violence] connected with some of the most constructive, positive and, indeed, among the noblest chapters in our national history."[339] Moreover, the commission suggested that virtually all significant events in American history had been interlaced with violent people and violent deeds. The nation itself was born in violence, in a guerrilla war against a foreign ruler. Former attorney general Ramsey Clark appropriately noted that "mob violence threatened the Constitutional Convention in Philadelphia in 1787, causing the convention to provide in the Constitution itself for a federal place of government and other places as needed to safely conduct the activities of the new republic."[340]

The very land that the United States now occupies was gained through centuries of aggressive wars of conquest against Native

Americans. Order and stability on the country's frontier were based
heavily on vigilante violence. Efforts to ease the plight of the farmer
gave rise to agrarian uprisings. The violent convulsions of the Civil
War produced more American casualties than World War I and
World War II combined. Yet through this slaughter the national political union was saved and the enslaved African Americans attained
their freedom. At the end of the nineteenth century and in the early
twentieth, the struggle of industrial workers for improved wages and
working conditions, as well as for the right to organize and strike,
produced extensive violence. For a great number of immigrant
groups—African, Irish, German, Slavic, Italian, and Chinese—"as-
similation" into America's melting pot was rarely accomplished
without violent upheaval. "Again and again violence has been used
as a means to ends that have been widely accepted and applauded,"
wrote Brown in his report to the National Commission on Violence.[341]

More recently, neoconservative historians and criminologists have
urged that there is insufficient evidence to warrant the claim that the
United States is an inherently "violent society." Objections have
been voiced, in particular, to the characterization of American history as more violent than the histories of other nations. Criminologist Graeme Newman, for example, argues that the existence of numerous and diverse incidents of public disorder throughout
American history does not establish a continuous thread or tradition
of violence in America.[342] Nonetheless, whether or not the United
States has seen more violence than other nations, and regardless of
whether episodes of American upheaval have been part of a violent
tradition or have resulted from incidental social, racial, and economic tensions, the country certainly has not been immune to the
heritage of political violence common to other civilizations.

Render unto Caesar

Despite the rich history of dissent, civil disobedience, dissidence, rebellion, and revolution in America, the country's scholars as well as
its government have uniformly sought to downplay or even overlook
the very existence of political offenses and offenders within its borders. Both the police and correctional agencies have been unwilling
or unable to distinguish ideologically and conscience-driven offend-

ers from common criminals. American courts, likewise, have persistently refused to listen to, much less consider, the motives of those claiming to break the law in the name of resistance to perceived political, social, racial, gender, or economic injustices.

Various reasons have been advanced for the failure of American law and political historiography to examine the peculiar mission and role of the political offender. More than three decades ago, Harvard University political scientist Adam B. Ulam observed:

> The citizen of the United States lives in an apparently pragmatic and "unideological" environment. If he views his society at all, he probably sees there no irreconcilable conflicts, no "inherent contradictions," only concrete problems always susceptible to concrete solutions. Economic ills will respond to material progress, which is taken for granted; political . . . short-comings can always be remedied by legislation . . . ; even the major social problems such as the racial one will be solved by education, wise legislation and time.[343]

Whether stemming from naïveté or design, both the American public and American law enforcement agencies continue to assert that political criminals and criminality do not exist, and have never existed, in the United States. Yet these assertions are easily refuted by the formidable list, dating from colonial times to the present, of New World candidates for the mantle of political offender. How could one reject or overlook Nathaniel Bacon, who rose against Virginia's royal governor, Lord Berkeley; George Washington, who rebelled against England's King and Parliament; Jefferson Davis, who presided over the rebelling Confederate States; tribal chiefs Hiawatha, King Philip, Osceola, Tecumseh, Sitting Bull, Crazy Horse, and Joseph of the Nez Perce, who led the Native American resistance to the colonizers' westward expansion; John Brown, who raided Harper's Ferry in the hope of inciting a slave rebellion; labor leader Eugene V. Debs, who spoke out against America's involvement in World War I; and Martin Luther King Jr., who led demonstrations in Selma, Alabama, in support of voting rights for blacks?

Should the list of political offenders exclude Benedict Arnold, the American patriot who later sought to betray his country to the British for pride and profit; John Wilkes Booth, who assassinated Abraham Lincoln; Ethel and Julius Rosenberg, who communicated atomic bomb secrets to the Russians; Sirhan Sirhan, the Jordanian immigrant who assassinated Robert Kennedy; and Timothy J.

McVeigh, who bombed the Alfred P. Murrah Federal Building in Oklahoma City? How should one treat radical labor leaders Joe Hill and Big Bill Haywood, and Vietnam War protesters Philip and Daniel Berrigan? What about Daniel Ellsberg, who revealed the classified Pentagon Papers to the mass media, and Randall Terry, who led the disruptive blockades against legally operating abortion clinics?

There have been thousands more, known and unknown. But a comprehensive listing of America's rebels, revolutionaries, and political dissidents has never been attempted. Several persuasive reasons account for America's reluctance to unlock the gates that secure political crime from deep inquiry. First, in the minds of many scholars, policymakers, and government officials, the very identification or recognition of political offenses and offenders seems tantamount to an endorsement of political criminality or, at the very least, an endorsement of special judicial leniency for its perpetrators. Such outcome has been generally viewed as incompatible with the "rule of law."

Second, there is concern that permitting an offender to plead political motives as a defense to prohibited conduct might create havoc with jurisprudential doctrines that insist on universal application of the law. Anglo-American law has generally permitted scrutiny only into the narrow question of an offender's intent (as distinguished from evidence of his or her motive) in order to shelter the law's universality and evenhandedness against individualistic and relativistic excuses and defenses. For the very reasons that courts refuse evidence of an actor's compassionate motives in prosecutions for euthanasia (mercy killing), they remain unbending in their opposition to considerations of "political criminality," a concept with heavy motive-laced and value-laden underpinnings. Recently, however, American jurisprudence has allowed some departure from its exclusive emphasis upon intent by permitting evidence of motive as an element in the definition of so-called hate crimes.[344] Although this departure has resulted in considerable questioning and opposition,[345] it might nevertheless become a wedge for introducing political criminality into American law.

Third, by denying the very existence of political criminality, those in power seek to avoid the troublesome questions concerning the legitimacy of the people's resort to nonparliamentary means of change. In a society that designates itself as democratic, resort to unorthodox opposition is difficult to support. Author Brendan Behan, in his autobiographical book *Borstal Boy,* reflected on Anglo-American law's deliberate blindness toward political offenders. For having been a member of the Irish Republican Army, Behan was placed in confinement with common offenders after his arrest. Responding to the British denial of his claims to political offender status, Behan wrote: "I knew . . . it was the usual hypocrisy of the English [in] not giving anyone political treatment and then being able to say that alone among the empires . . . [England] had no political prisoners."[346]

Fourth, America's continuing unwillingness to differentiate between "political" and "common" criminality is particularly understandable when viewed in its historical context. Many of the original colonies were founded by political exiles. The nation was conceived in treason and midwived by violent revolution. In adolescence, it nearly perished from rebellion. From the perspectives of stability and political order, the United States has not overcome its fear of these skeletons in its own closet. It is no wonder that to counter the fearful lessons of the country's origins, the responsible men and women who shaped and continue to mold the country's law and policy have fostered the belief that existing political mechanisms are, always have been, and always will be ample for all needed reforms. It thus becomes an intolerable heresy to suggest that urgent ends might sometimes justify extralegal means, or that the motives underlying these means should be considered by tribunals of justice.

Finally, America's majoritarian orthodoxy—its commitment to popularly derived and majority-determined norms that bind all members of the community—paradoxically turns all those who fail to observe majority commands, whatever their reasons or motives, into undifferentiated offenders. Obedience to the articulated law, it is argued, is the absolute obligation of all citizens, irrespective of the morality or ultimate validity of the legal command.[347]

Speaking in 1921 against a proposed amnesty for America's World War I resisters, Attorney General H. M. Dougherty summarized the essence of American democracy's uncompromising philosophy: "When the sovereign will of the state expresses itself through duly enacted law it is repugnant to the very nature of the supremacy of the law and its uniform application . . . to permit two standards . . .

to exist side by side—the standard of the law and the standard of some individual or group acting . . . to set up a so-called conscience at a variance therewith."[348] This position on the supremacy of the law over individual or group conscience has not changed in the intervening years. United States Circuit Court judge Simon Sobeloff echoed in 1969: "To encourage individuals to make their own determinations as to which laws they will obey and which they will permit themselves as a matter of conscience to disobey is to invite chaos."[349]

Despite, and possibly because of, America's origins, its law has remained steadfast in refusing to take account of offenders who assert political, religious, moral, or ideological motives as justification for their deeds. American criminal justice has continued, for that matter, to maintain its overall and long-standing monolithic simplicity. There has been little effort in American jurisprudence or legal practice to distinguish crimes of greed from crimes of passion, crimes of mass exploitation and profiteering from collective efforts to reform public policy, crimes induced by economic and social deprivation from motiveless crimes of thrill-seekers, crimes of venality from crimes of idealism. As a consequence, America's unique historical experience with political protest, resistance, and rebellion has hitherto remained unilluminated in the nation's vast archives of crime and justice.

"Render unto Caesar the things which are Caesar's"[350] thus remains the nation's official imperative. It is not surprising, therefore, that the public prosecutor argued before United States District Court judge Morrow in 1894 that "under our laws there can be no crime of a political character."[351] Upholding the argument, the court failed to take notice that treason—the only crime defined by the Constitution—is inherently political, and that the Founding Fathers, traitors in the contemporary judgment of their English rulers, were all political offenders.

Groping in the Dark:
Crimes Without Numbers

The stubborn refusal of America's government and scholarly community to admit that political rebellion and resistance are domestic as well as foreign problems clearly indicates a shortsighted and erroneous conception of this phenomenon. An unwillingness to classify political dissidence as a distinct category of criminality, combined with an insistence upon the unlikelihood of this phenomenon significantly affecting the future of the United States, leaves the nation vulnerable not only to its own domestic stock of militants, such as those responsible for the tragic bombing of the federal building in Oklahoma City, but also to a growing number of new arrivals carrying with them old-world hostilities. Witness two dramatic events of 1993: the assassinations near CIA's Langley headquarters,[352] and the explosion at the World Trade Center in New York City.[353] Both events have been attributed to offenders with marginal American ties.

Yet America's continued unwillingness to open its own Pandora's box of domestic political crime has prevented the collection of relevant statistical and other data from which one could divine the future prospects for politically connected domestic violence and terrorism in America. This gap in information is startling, given the glut of materials on other crimes that have been collected and published in America in recent decades.

Crime and punishment are big business and major employers in America. In 1996, 829,936 police officers and related employees derived their livelihood from combating crime.[354] In 1995 the total number of inmates in state and federal prisons and jails exceeded 1.5 million (up from 315,947 in 1980)[355] and the number of prison guards, correctional officers, and others engaged in the supervision of convicted offenders exceeded 596,000.[356] Some 375,000 persons were serving as judges and as lesser functionaries of the judicial branch, more than 117,000 were engaged in prosecutorial functions, some 15,000 were employed full time in public defense, and more than 7,000 were occupied in miscellaneous criminal justice assignments.[357] An unspecified percentage of the 805,872 members of the American legal profession devoted some portion of their practice to the defense of criminal cases.[358] And the more than 14 million offenses reported to police in 1995 provided the fuel that stoked this elaborate machinery.[359]

In 1969, at what seemed the height of that era's political unrest, United States senator John McClellen warned the country against a terrorist "war against the police" and a "wave of guerrilla warfare" that would slash the nation.[360] Despite this prophecy, no government agency, nor any private organization, set out to systematically tabulate or analyze the kinds or frequency of political crime that followed in America—violent or nonviolent, individual or collective. Because of the lack of record-keeping, the extent of political dissidence and resistance in the United States is impossible to measure today.

How many political offenses have taken place in America during the past several decades? What segment of the country's total criminality is accounted for by political dissidence and rebellion? What do we know about periodic fluctuations and their causes, about growth and decline in this area? One seeking a response to these fundamental questions finds few answers in the existing literature, and few methods in the traditional research approaches. Both private reports and official records relating to political crime are deficient and unrevealing.

Unlike most categories of conventional criminality, for which law enforcement reports, victim complaints, and victimization surveys are used to measure the extent of the criminal problem, political offenses are not identified or counted. The *1978 Statistical Abstract of the United States* listed only one class of crimes defined as "political"—political assassinations and assaults. The compiled data included all attacks "on persons holding political office or upon any individuals or groups for political reasons." The abstract reported a total of eighty-one assassinations and assaults in the United States between 1835 and 1968. This classification of political assassinations and assaults was abandoned in 1972, and no similar information has since been made available.[361]

In 1982 the U.S. Justice Department's *Sourcebook of Criminal Justice Statistics* began publishing data on incidents of domestic as well as international terrorism, defining such terrorism as politically motivated violence that affects American citizens or property. Included in these data have been incidents of kidnapping, hostage-taking, bombing, armed attacks, hijacking, assassination, sniping, threats, hoaxes, and other forms of terrorism. These compilations show dramatic fluctuations in worldwide terrorism involving U.S. citizens, ranging from a total of 47 casualties in 1981 to 386 in 1983, from 34 in 1989 to 1,011 in 1993 (due largely to the World Trade Center bombing), from 11 in 1994 to 70 in 1995 and 533 in 1996 (covering the bombing of the U.S. military complex in

Dhahran, Saudi Arabia). Domestically, 51 incidents of terrorism were reported in the United States in 1982, 25 in 1986, 0 in 1994, 1 in 1995, and 3 in 1996.[362] These wild shifts in crime rates remain unexplained. Although the total number of reported international terrorist incidents affecting Americans was listed at 557 in 1991, nearly half of these occurred during the two months of Operation Desert Storm.[363] In 1997 the total number of incidents was listed at 304. These numbers seem to belie Senator John McClellen's alarmist forecast and provide pathetically little support for the often repeated calls for a total American war against "terrorism."

One will seek in vain among the various official sources for other offenses identified as or connected with political dissidence and rebellion. However, the *Sourcebook of Criminal Justice Statistics* has supplied data on various categories of crime likely to attract politically motivated perpetrators. Under the classification of "skyjacking," a total of 270 occurrences were reported in the United States between 1968 and 1984.[364] Between 1985 and 1990 the total number of occurrences dropped to 20.[365] Bombing incidents may also carry strong political undertones. Of a total of 2,074 successful and attempted bombings reported in the United States in 1975, 76 targeted law enforcement buildings and vehicles, 62 involved other government property, and 11 were against international establishments.[366] The selection of these public targets may suggest political motives, but official records fail to document such connections or to explain the sudden drop in reported bombings to 687 in 1983, or the subsequent rise to 1,528 bombings in 1990, 2,980 in 1993, and 2,577 in 1995.[367] How the tragic bombing of the federal building in Oklahoma City, producing 168 victims, sits in this panorama still remains subject to speculation.

Noteworthy also is the fact that out of 76,842 arson incidents reported in 1996, 4,149 were directed against public structures, once more suggesting a political grievance.[368] The most recent and sudden rush of arson directed against African American churches, mostly in southern states, similarly raised the profile of growing politically and racially motivated criminality in the last decade of the twentieth century.[369] Since assaults on law enforcement officers may likewise be politically related, notice should also be taken of some 65,000 assaults on federal, state, and local law enforcement officers in 1994, many of which were reportedly related to civil disorders and riots.[370]

Still, public records completely fail to list such inchoate crimes as treason, sedition, or political conspiracies, which are inextricably connected to opposition to authority. Neither do official statistics refer to or tabulate such offenses as civil disobedience, draft evasion, and desertion, or politically motivated tax evasion. Even if appropriate statistical categories were established and kept, there would still be gross deficiencies in the collected data. Because of their very nature, many political violations (including treason, sedition, espionage, prohibited trips—such as travel in Cuba—or memberships in outlawed political parties) may not give rise to typical victim complaints. Since it is not primarily persons or property but the overriding governmental authority that is noticeably affected in these cases, full reporting cannot be expected. Governments may not only be unaware of such political crimes, but may actively seek to suppress the information out of fear of public embarrassment or in the interest of continued surveillance.

Generally, most political offenses do not come to the attention of police and public until they develop into open confrontations with agencies or officials of authority. Yet many political offenses are carried out in a clandestine and furtive manner. Behind every known dissenter, rioter, and bomber there may be hundreds of quiet conspirators. For every open confrontation there may be a score of aborted conspiracies. Despite this apparent veil of silence, political offenders, unlike ordinary criminals, are often possessed by an urge to tell the world of their exploits and even claim credit for the offenses of others. In their struggle against authority, political activists have learned to conduct their campaigns not only on battle fronts, but on bulletin boards, newspapers pages, and, most importantly, on the television screen. But in seeking to confuse and demoralize their enemies, political activists are given to grave exaggerations of their numbers and their attainments.

Only once in the history of the United States has a comprehensive survey of political crime been undertaken. A 1969 report by the U.S. National Commission on the Causes and Prevention of Violence concluded that more than 2 million Americans had participated in collective demonstrations, riots, or terrorism to express or advance their various political agendas (ranging from opposition to the Vietnam War to support for civil rights reforms) during the preceding five years. "No more than a fifth of them took part in activities proscribed by law, but their actions reportedly resulted in more than 9,000 casualties, including some 200 deaths, and more than 70,000 arrests."[371] The commission also reported that in the mid-1960s the United States experienced more civil and political agitation than most other nations. Although America was ranked twenty-fourth in the severity of civil disturbances when compared with other nations, its total number of reported incidents exceeded the world average. About 11 of every 1,000 Americans took part in civil or political strife, compared with an average of 7 per 1,000 of the populations in other countries.[372]

The most illuminating comparison, however, came from contrasting America with the seventeen democratic nations on the European continent and the United Kingdom. Overall, America experienced more disturbances than any of the European countries, even though American strife tended to be less intense. Regarding America's worldwide ranking, the commission observed that "[w]ith few exceptions, the countries more strife-torn than the United States have experienced [real] internal wars, like Venezuela, Algeria and Indonesia."[373] How long this remained true one cannot tell. No follow-up assessment has been undertaken; consequently, developments or trends in American political strife cannot be traced with any reliability.

The National Commission on Violence also undertook in 1969 an examination of political violence in the United States through a historical perspective. It conducted a review of newspaper reports from 1819 to 1968, looking for accounts of political violence during that 150-year period. Included in the studied categories were events involving "an attack on an official or group of officials for any reason or an attack on an individual or group of individuals for political or social reasons."[374] Labor-connected violence was included, as were incidents arising from economic, racial, religious, or political conflicts. The commission excluded only the events of the Civil War, ignoring a total of nearly 2 million rebel combatants in the South—nearly one-tenth of the combined populations of the Union and the Confederacy.

The evidence examined by the commission demonstrated that the problem of political violence in America was not new. "By its very persistence," asserted the commission, "it is a serious ... problem for our society ... for its roots run very deep."[375] Even so, the evidence before the commission concerned only collective and openly conducted strife. Charged with investigating public violence, the commission did not survey less visible varieties of unlawful activity carried out for political reasons. Particularly neglected in the 1969 report were individual actions as well as group conduct falling short of violence yet carried out in the pursuit of political protest, reform, and rebellion—such as strikes, draft and tax evasion, and other illegal actions. Thus, in a statistical sense, the historical record of political strife in America remains literally unknown to scholars and policymakers alike.

The Disparity Between Doctrine and Practice

Although American legal theory and doctrine have refused to acknowledge the very existence of political crime, the federal government as well as state governments have responded with remarkable alacrity, throughout the nation's history, to offenses involving political motives or causes. Over time, the country has produced a uniquely severe arsenal of laws, procedures, and sanctions to counter the perceived threats posed by those pursuing political, socioeconomic, racial, or other goals through illegal or unorthodox means.

This severity of treatment was not envisioned when the Republic was founded. Fearing despotism even more than they feared disloyalty and public disorder, the authors of America's Constitution set out to do away with English legal doctrines and practices that silenced freedom of speech and curtailed dissent. Since the abuses of the English system were made possible in great part by unduly elastic definitions of the crime of treason, the United States not only made treason the only constitutionally defined crime, but set out to define that offense narrowly. By constitutional mandate, treason is to consist only of "levying war against [the United States], or in adhering to their enemies."[376] James Wilson, a Philadelphia lawyer who was chiefly responsible for the treason clause in the Constitution, reportedly "never doubted that this was the only political crime against the nation which Congress was empowered to punish."[377]

Despite the initial commitment to keep the greatest variety of political speech and conduct free from official controls, the Federalists, upon their ascension to power, found the original definition of treason too narrow and ineffective to combat what they considered dangerous forms of political opposition and dissent. The passage of the far-reaching 1798 Sedition Act testifies to the shortsightedness of Wilson's appraisal of congressional powers.[378] And as the years passed, prohibitions of new political offenses were grafted onto the initial prohibition of treason, at both the federal and state levels.

These new laws prohibited a wide range of conduct: the education of slaves and even free black Americans; the suffrage of women; the advocacy of anarchy, communism, or other suspect doctrines; membership in suspect organizations; and the disclosure of government secrets. Other laws restricted the mobility and selected activities of Native Americans and various minorities. Still other laws prohibited the counseling of evasion or resistance to military service, taking part in unauthorized foreign travel, the crossing of state lines in order to engage in political agitation, and the commission of hate crimes.[379] Even such a constitutionally protected right as that entitling citizens to petition Congress was at one time banned by overreaching state officials.[380]

Ancient offenses, including the vaguely defined crime of sedition, were revived and restructured beyond recognition as the struggle between those in authority and those in opposition continued to escalate. A post–Civil War law passed to prohibit multiple voting by whites in the South was applied to punish women attempting to exercise the franchise,[381] and the crime of espionage was broadened during World War I to criminalize mere pacifism and antiwar sentiments.[382] Quasi-criminal sanctions for the suppression of political activity and the imposition of stringent controls upon political opponents have been instituted throughout the country's history. Federal and state laws have relied not only on penal sanctions but also on such devices as loyalty oaths, security investigations, prohibitions against holding office, detentions under martial law without the benefits of habeas corpus, restrictions on travel, and the barring of entry or the expulsion of politically suspect aliens.

The American system of justice has frequently designed special laws for the suppression of political offenses when the prohibitions intended to combat these offenses as common crimes are considered inadequate. The common-law offenses of arson and malicious mischief have been supplemented with the crime of sabotage, while kidnapping has been augmented with the new offenses of hostage-taking and skyjacking. Murder and assault have been given such innovative labels as "assassination" and "terrorism" in order to reflect new political orientations. Claiming reliance on either explicit or implicit constitutional authority, the federal government has employed particularly drastic measures against political offenders—measures that would be impermissible in the struggle against common crime—such as suspending the writ of habeas corpus, using militias as political police, trying political offenders by military tribunals (without the protections of the Bill of Rights), mobilizing the military to displace and resettle civilian populations, and conducting comprehensive surveillance programs against politically suspect civilian populations.[383]

The responses of Congress and the executive branch to political offenses and offenders have usually been marked by extreme severity. Many of these sanctions directed against individual and collective political dissent have been episodic and ad hoc rather than deliberate and predictable measures derived from general principles of law and justice. Governmental responses often have been the product of temporary passions, reflecting an excessive zeal of the authorities. Yet few of these measures have received a dispassionate *post facto* reassessment. It is likely, therefore, that governmental measures now recognized as excessive will be repeated to combat future political upheaval.

Although this legacy of unreflective and ad hoc methods of dealing with political criminality has left the various departments and echelons of government without well-considered guidelines for future action, each branch of government and each division of the criminal justice system faces particular and unique questions regarding their encounters with political criminality. For the police, the question of whether so-called political, religious, or otherwise ideological offenders should be accorded differential treatment remains a primary concern. When a group of Native Americans took over a deserted monastery in Wisconsin and proclaimed their "last stand," should police have responded as to a gang of robbers barricaded in a bank?[384] When a militant contingent of the Hanafi Moslems took over public buildings in Washington, D.C., should special negotiations have been conducted with them, and safe conduct offered to them?[385] When the Branch Davidians refused to vacate their militarized compound at the behest of leader David Koresh, should they have been treated differently from an assembly of common criminals?[386] Should distinct eavesdropping and wiretapping laws be required for the surveillance of political offenders? Should mass arrests made during a political rally be handled the same way as arrests in a gambling establishment or a crack house?

The police have had great difficulty in drawing lines between the basic needs of public law and order and the freedom to exercise the legitimate constitutional rights of speech, assembly, parade, association, and conscience. The dilemma of the Chicago police when Dick Gregory demonstrated against racial discrimination in a white neighborhood (which was resolved when the police opted to arrest the peaceful demonstrators rather than the hostile members of the crowd)[387] is not as novel as originally portrayed by the mass media. Similar policing issues were raised during the American Nazi demonstrations in the predominately Jewish town of Skokie, Illinois,[388] and during the recent invasive and occasionally violent protests against abortion clinics.

For the judicial branch, political offenders pose similarly difficult problems. The political activist on trial does not tend to acquiesce by pleading guilty, nor does he or she merely seek what would be considered a fair and orderly trial. In the 1981 Chicago trial of six male and four female defendants suspected of being members of the Armed Forces of Puerto Rican National Liberation (FALN) and accused of seditious conspiracy, violations of weapons laws, armed robbery, and interstate transportation of stolen vehicles, the normal courtroom decorum was dramatically altered. The defendants insisted that they were "prisoners of war" and contested the authority of the federal judiciary to try them. Objecting to their representation by counsel and threatening to disrupt the trial, the accused eventually "were herded into two separate Federal courtrooms, where they sprawled in chairs, reading, napping and doing exercises as the proceedings of their trial were piped into the room by intercom."[389] Moreover, political offenders often view the trial not as a judicial process but as a political platform for voicing their challenges to the legitimacy of those in power. In the 1985 New York trial of seven alleged members of the United States Freedom Front who were charged with the bombings of corporate buildings and military installations, the accused insisted that the real issues were "the Government's 'crime' against black and Hispanic people and United States imperialism."[390]

"In Court," wrote activist priest Philip Berrigan, "one puts values against legality . . . and with slight chance of success. One does not look for justice; one hopes for a forum from which to communicate ideals, convictions, and anguish."[391] Counsel for the defense must confront their clients' view that the representation of political offenders need go beyond the traditional functions of the defense counsel. "When it comes to defending political dissenters like ourselves, lawyers become accomplices in the game against us—if, that is, they play its rules," argued Berrigan.[392] In order not to be co-opted by the "system," defense counsel for political offenders may have to assume unique and radical functions, such as urging the court and particularly the jury—as representatives of the "popular will"—to follow early common-law traditions and thus pronounce a verdict for "justice" by "nullifying" the injustices that "the dead letter of the law" would seek to impose.[393]

The correctional system too can find the influx of politically articulate offenders disruptive to institutional administration. Socialist Ammon Hennacy, sent to prison for anti–World War I agitation, described how the prison warden had scattered the incarcerated conscientious objectors throughout the prison population so they could not reinforce one another's convictions and plot against the prison authorities. "This reminded me," wrote Hennacy, "of the farmer who caught the ground mole and said 'Hanging's too good for you; I'll bury you alive.'"[394] Later in his prison stay, Hennacy indeed organized and led a general prison strike against the administration. The Attica uprising was similarly fueled by the political rhetoric of self-styled political prisoners.[395]

With no guiding principles for the treatment of political offenders, how are correctional institutions to distinguish between deterrence, retribution, incapacitation, and rehabilitation? Many political offenders tend to view their role in prison as that of a proselytizer and leader of others. They may actively solicit confrontations with their jailers, and may even seek further punishment as a means for securing public notoriety and attaining martyrdom. As was the case with Hennacy, Eugene V. Debs, and Martin Luther King Jr., the confinement and segregation of offenders often seems to endow them with heroic proportions, eventually transforming public sympathy into a rallying cry against those in authority.

Political offenders also pose special problems for heads of state, whether the U.S. president, state governors, or foreign sovereigns. The U.S. Constitution empowers the president "to grant reprieves and pardons for offenses against the United States, except in case of Impeachment."[396] No further criteria or limits are imposed upon these presidential powers. Nevertheless, the history of the presidential pardon in the United States, from its first use by George Washington to benefit the participants in the Whisky Rebellion to the Vietnam Amnesties of Gerald Ford and Jimmy Carter, demonstrates that major beneficiaries have been not common offenders but rather those charged with or convicted of political offenses. Some 200,000 Confederates were pardoned by Andrew Johnson. Calvin Coolidge granted a general pardon to all those convicted of draft evasion and espionage during World War I. Harry Truman similarly granted pardons to large numbers of offenders following World War II. Dwight Eisenhower ordered the pardon of some 4,500 Americans arrested for collaborating with the country's enemies. Ford and Carter granted amnesty to some 30,000 Vietnam War draft evaders and deserters. Notable also are Ford's prophylactic pardon of Richard Nixon and Ronald Reagan's pardon of two FBI agents convicted of illegal surveillance of political suspects. Pardon and amnesty for offenders are similarly authorized by the various state constitutions.

Not only are provisions for the granting of pardons and amnesties to common criminals and particularly to political offenders prevalent throughout the legal systems of the world, but the resort to these provisions has become an earmark of the post–Cold War era. Within many countries that have undergone dramatic political transformations, such as the former Soviet Union and the countries of the Communist Eastern Bloc, large numbers of political prisoners have been released from confinement—often to assume the very reins of power responsible for their imprisonment. It was not uncommon therefore for Pope John Paul II to condition a recent effort for reconciliation between the Catholic Church and Cuba's tattering communist regime upon a significant show of goodwill toward Havana's imprisoned political opponents.

Even more dramatic has been the recent and growing tendency of fledgling democracies to forego the traditional urge to punish and retaliate against former oppressors. In such diverse locales as Argentina, Chile, El Salvador, Guatemala, and South Africa, the desire for a new national compromise has resulted not in mass prosecutions of former political enemies but in the pursuit of national conciliation. Newly created Commissions for Unity and Reconciliation, vested with broad amnesty powers and sometimes popularly renamed as "Truth Commissions," have made it their priority not to impose criminal sanctions but to inquire into and document former strife, conflict, suffering, and injustices as a means for effecting "the reconstruction of society."[397]

One might conclude that a critical assessment of the history of political criminality and its treatment in America and throughout the world would suggest to American and foreign lawmakers new approaches and policies to be utilized in shaping future responses to the recurring problems posed by political offenders. Such policy innovations might include a dramatic shift to "noncriminal alternatives," or even a total decriminalization of certain prevalent political offenses.

It has long been evident that criminal sanctions have only limited utility in deterring or reducing criminality. In the political arena, in particular, criminal sanctions might even be counterproductive. Writing in the late nineteenth century, Italian reformer Enrico Ferri, a leader of the positivist school of criminology, advocated the general replacement of criminal penalties with noncriminal alternatives.[398] Favoring positive over negative reinforcements, Ferri is credited with a dramatic call for the construction of public urinals as a substitute for Rome's previous and ineffective emphasis upon criminal penalties as a means of deterring individuals from discharging their waste in the open. Ferri's plea for noncriminal alternatives can be said to have universal applications. As means of social control, the stringent requirements and strict enforcement of weapons licensing and alcohol sales laws are often considered by criminologists as superior to the outright prohibition of guns and alcoholic beverages.

In America, the granting of franchise to women (Nineteenth Amendment, 1920) has undoubtedly proven to be far less costly than the arrest, prosecution, conviction, and incarceration of thousands of female offenders charged with the crime of seeking to cast their vote. Similarly, the ending of Prohibition (Twenty-Third Amendment, 1933) resulted in the substitution of a system that regulated alcohol production and sales for a system that outrightly criminalized millions of alcohol imbibers. The United States, and other nations as well, might reconsider their resort to traditional criminal measures in the war against political opponents, possibly replacing repression and prosecution not only with noncriminal alternatives but also with the institution of greater tolerance and the granting of new liberties.

We learn from history that reliance on the criminal process for resolving political conflicts polarizes communities, exacerbates differences, and often prejudices chances for an ultimate political compromise. Countless individuals throughout the world and throughout history have been unnecessarily subjected to the severe stigmas of common criminality for manifesting views or engaging in behavior that would ultimately become acceptable or even exemplary. Susan B. Anthony, a nineteenth-century American political offender, remains the only woman to have a national coin minted in her image. A dramatic portrait of John Brown, executed for treason in Virginia in 1859, now decorates the Kansas statehouse in Topeka. And a noted political offender of the twentieth century, Martin Luther King Jr., is one of only five Americans to have a national holiday established in his memory.

Discretion or Caprice: The Political Offender in American Foreign Policy?

In its foreign relations, unlike in its domestic policy, the American government has consistently considered political offenses to be a distinct class of behavior, thereby granting the bona fide political offender a special and favored status. On numerous occasions, for nearly a century and a half, the United States has refused to extradite asylum-seekers wanted for the prior commission of political offenses abroad. As late as the 1980s the Department of State continued to deny Great Britain's requests for the surrender of Irish Republican army militants wanted for acts of political violence in Ulster.[399]

However, those who resort to violence for political objectives are not all treated equally for extradition purposes. At the same time the State Department snubbed Great Britain's extradition requests, it approved the extradition of other asylum-seekers, including an Arab charged by Israel with terrorist activities in the Galilee town of Tiberias,[400] who was extradited on the grounds that he had failed to establish the political character of his offenses. With no authoritative and consistent domestic law to fall back on, those charged with the administration of America's extradition process are left adrift with only impressionistic, ad hoc, and variable perceptions to guide them in assessing claims to "political" status. The resulting decisions, by both the judiciary and the executive, have tended to be unprincipled, inconsistent, and even indefensible (see Chapter 6).

One of the most litigated of America's extradition cases involved a notorious Yugoslav immigrant named Andruja Artukovic.[401] From 1941 to 1942, Artukovic served as Minister of Internal Affairs for the short-lived and Nazi-affiliated independent state of Croatia, formed after the occupation of Yugoslavia by Axis forces during World War II. After Yugoslavia's restoration as an independent country, its government sought Artukovic's extradition from the United States, to which he had escaped, on the grounds that he had ordered and supervised the mass murder of some 200,000 Yugoslav citizens—opponents of Croatia's fascist regime. The evidence regarding the Croatian wartime hierarchy of power (and thus direct responsibility for the atrocities) was conflicting. There was, however, compelling proof of Artukovic's complicity in the murderous policy and its execution.

The U.S. District Court for the Southern District of California, which first heard Yugoslavia's request, nevertheless refused extradition. In denying Yugoslavia's request, the court-appointed hearing commissioner relied heavily on a finding that the crimes detailed in the extradition request had "a political character."[402] As a political offender, the commission thus concluded, Artukovic was exempt from extradition. More than twenty-five years of complex legal maneuvering were required before the U.S. government finally ordered, on somewhat unrelated grounds, Artukovic's expulsion from the country and his return to Yugoslavia to stand trial for his wartime crimes.[403]

With the growth of political opposition to authority and insurgency against governments worldwide, America has become the haven of choice for many Latin American, Asian, African, and European political refugees. Even when their home countries do not request their return through extradition, the United States is still faced with the question of whether those seeking shelter should be admitted pursuant to the special laws that accord asylum to political refugees. When escapees knock at America's gates seeking political asylum, or when their extradition is demanded by the regimes they have opposed, America's immigration authorities, courts, and criminal justice agencies face complex legal and humanitarian questions, which they are left to answer without the benefit of adequate and reasoned doctrinal processes. Since its own domestic law persistently denies the very existence of political offenses and offenders, how is America to derive a rational, defensible, and consistent policy regarding foreign seekers of refuge and asylum? When escapees from Cambodia, Cuba, China, Ethiopia, El Salvador, or Haiti seek to enter or remain in the United States, are they to be treated as illegal immigrants, political offenders, or asylum-seekers?

Whether offenses committed in foreign countries should be considered criminal or political is a critical question for determining the legitimacy of a foreign national's initial entry into America. Although America's immigration laws generally exclude the permanent entry of convicted felons, potential immigrants whose crimes are deemed "political" are not usually excluded on that ground.[404] A felon visa applicant coming before an American consul in Bosnia, Kenya, Nicaragua, Romania, the Philippines, South Africa, or Palestine's West Bank is therefore likely to qualify as a nonfelon if his or her offense is determined to be "political."

Within the boundaries of the United States, immigration authorities have the added and growing burden of processing immense numbers of applications by aliens who either entered the country illegally or came as tourists or students and then proceeded to apply for asylum on the grounds that return to their native countries would be politically dangerous. Nearly 143,000 such applicants, coming from some twenty-three countries, were awaiting disposition in 1983—a backlog whose regulation was greatly hindered by the lack of a definite policy and specific criteria.[405] By the early 1990s the backlog was even greater, as growing political turmoil worldwide drove masses of escapees and asylum-seekers to America's shores.[406]

For each asylum-seeker, government agents must determine whether deportation would threaten the applicant's life or liberty on account of his or her political beliefs or activity.[407] When forty-eight Polish sailors from three fishing vessels jumped ship in Boston harbor within a one-month period in early 1989, President Bush and his administration were faced with a familiar, troublesome question:

How is the United States to distinguish between those truly seeking freedom from political oppression, and those merely hunting the fortunes of economic betterment? Timothy Whelan, an Immigration and Naturalization Service official, advised the media that to resolve this dilemma his agency would rely on an advisory ruling from the State Department, taking into consideration Poland's political climate, "the lengths the sailors had to go in order to leave their homeland," and whether they would face prosecution if they were required to return there.[408] But how are we to reconcile this benevolent policy, and the typically similar treatment of refugees from Castro's Cuba, with America's refusal to permit entry to escapees from poverty-ridden and politically volatile Haiti? The ultimate decisions regarding both extradition and asylum are shared by a variety of American courts and diverse agencies of the executive branch. How could one expect consistent outcomes under such a legal regime that, moreover, has rejected the relevance of political criminality in its domestic arena?

Similar difficulties have been noted on the flip side of the coin—when the United States seeks the return of citizens who claim to be victims of American political, social, or racial persecution and who have sought refuge in foreign countries. During the American Revolution, hundreds of thousands of American Loyalists went to Canada and England. During the Civil War, some of those who opposed the Union sought haven in the islands and ports of the Caribbean. More recently, Vietnam War draft evaders went to Canada and Sweden, while Puerto Rican revolutionaries and black activists sought refuge in Cuba and Algeria. If the United States seeks the return of such emigrants from their host countries, it cannot justifiably address the claim of these escapees—that they are extradition-exempt political offenders—by merely and naïvely reciting its own claim—that there are no political offenses and offenders in the United States. In light of the escalating political strife worldwide, and in the face of the growing number of offenders seeking refuge overseas, a reassessment of the political offender's status has become critically necessary. The historical refusal to differentiate between common and political offenders in America and many other countries (including, as the next chapter demonstrates, the nations of Europe) can no longer withstand the storms of political change.

Chapter Five

Cycles of Oppression and Leniency

Europe's Search for the "Honorable Offender"

Let the ruling classes tremble at a Communist revolution.
The proletarians have nothing to lose but their chains.

—Karl Marx and Friedrich Engels,
The Communist Manifesto (1848)

[T]he policy of leniency of bourgeois governments towards
their political enemies appears neither as an exercise of . . .
charity nor as the achievement of a higher stage of
civilization, but as one manifestation of a . . . "death wish"
on the part of a class which had no desire to rule.

—Barton L. Ingraham,
Political Crime in Europe (1979)

The Death of Socrates, Jacques-Louis David, painting.

Political Offenders from
Antiquity to the Revolutionary Era

Reviewing European law and practice from antiquity, through Roman history and the Middle Ages, and up to the modern era, historian Pitirim Sorokin confirmed that political offenders were almost universally subjected to the most extreme punishments the law could command.[409] Dissidents and rebels, often objects of both violent popular condemnation and intense hostility from those in authority, were generally portrayed not only as enemies of the ruler, but also as enemies of the state and its people. Resistance to or protest against those exercising the power of the state was viewed, accordingly, "as an act of hostility, identical to that of an enemy warrior who attacks the tribe, the city or the neighboring state in order to destroy it."[410] During the nineteenth century, however, political offenders attained, albeit briefly, a favorably distinct status within the criminal systems of Europe. This unusual experiment with liberal approaches is of particular interest today as modern society continues to grapple with the application of appropriate sanctions against the various categories of political offenders.

The classical view of the political offender as *hosti humani generis* (an enemy of all mankind) was reflected in the early and broad-ranging European laws that prohibited much of what is today called "political crime." These prohibitions were originally divided into two distinct categories: (1) alliances and intrigues with foreign powers (roughly the equivalent of today's "treason"), and (2) domestic transgressions against the interests of the ruler (including such offenses as sedition and counterfeiting the coin of the realm). The distinction between the two categories was first instituted by Roman law, which differentiated *proditio,* or betrayal to an external enemy, from *crimen laesae majestatis,* or internal offenses against the person or authority of the ruler.[411]

Even as the Roman power ebbed, the countries of continental Europe continued to maintain the Roman separation between "external" and "internal" political offenses. Both French and German law drew distinctions between political crimes involving aid to a foreign enemy (the French crime of *trahison* and the German *Verrat*), and domestic offenses concerning the citizen's relationship to the sovereign or government (the French crime of *lèsé-majesté* and the German *Maiestätsbeleidinung*). Early English law similarly resorted to *lèsé-majesté* to describe offenses against the sovereign's person and dignity and to distinguish them from foreign disloyalty.[412] With time, however, the distinction was dropped and domestic violations were combined with foreign alliances under the English law of "treason."

The encompassing goal of all these laws was viewed as threefold: to protect the king from activities affecting his personal or familial safety and dignity; to protect him against acts of betrayal by his subjects in concert with foreign powers; and to safeguard him against domestic challenges or interferences with the exercise of the royal prerogatives.[413] The emphasis on the personal protection of the ruler was typical of the European political order of the time, throughout the continent: "The picture . . . was one of power jealously guarded by a political ruler against the derogations and usurpations of powerful rivals, rather than one of an abstract entity, such as a 'state,' 'nation' or 'constitution' being protected against ideological assaults and mass revolutions seeking a change in the social and political order."[414] These treason and sedition laws would later be expanded beyond their original task of safeguarding the king's person and family, and by the close of the Renaissance would begin serving much broader functions in the general maintenance of public law and order.

Continental laws protecting the sovereign often ordained summary and harsh punishment for those accused of political disloyalty and resistance. Despite the increasing procedural safeguards made available over time to common criminals, those rebelling against established power were convicted on the basis of the flimsiest of evidence: depositions by criminals, confessions induced by torture, or testimony coerced from children and spouses. Trials were frequently conducted in secret by special tribunals, which denied the offender defense counsel as well as the opportunity to call defense witnesses. Moreover, preventive detention for indeterminate periods through *lettres de cachet,* issued on order of the king and countersigned by one of his ministers, provided a particularly powerful weapon against suspects, as no mechanism was made available to the detainees for refuting the charges.[415]

This disregard of the political offender's procedural rights was rationalized by Cardinal Richelieu's observation that "[t]here are some crimes which it is necessary to punish, then investigate. Among them, the crime of *lèsé-majesté* is so grave that one ought to punish the mere thought of it."[416] Accordingly, the penalties for political crimes in France were extremely gruesome. Execution by drawing and quartering *(l'écartèlement)* was common, and was accompanied by the confiscation of all the offender's property, the disinheritance of the offender's family, and the permanent banishment of close relations from the realm.

German laws governing the treatment of political offenders during the seventeenth and eighteenth centuries were hardly more lenient, based as they were on the same Roman legal concepts that had animated the French system.[417] As in France, *crimen laesae majestatis* in Germany were usually punished by death or banishment, and the offender's property was often confiscated. Again, the procedural protections available to the conventional criminal were denied the political offender. Following the feudal tradition, political offenses were viewed primarily as a breach of faith with the ruler himself. It was this perspective of personal betrayal and loss of honor that turned political offenses into particularly shameful and dishonorable crimes. Not surprisingly, when Frederick the Great of Prussia, under the benevolent influence of Enlightenment philosophers, abolished the use of torture in criminal cases, the practice was nevertheless retained with regard to political offenders.[418]

The Enlightenment did give rise, however, to campaigns against the continuation of absolute judicial discretion and campaigns for an enhancement of the role of the legislature through the promulgation of comprehensive criminal codes. In the new codifications, the old Roman distinction between offenses against the internal order of the state and offenses endangering external security was reinforced. That distinction eventually permitted an important differentiation between what were to be considered less serious and more serious political offenses.[419]

An even more innovative approach to the classification of political offenses was introduced by Prussian law in 1794.[420] A distinction was drawn between high treason, or *Hochverrat* ("an act which tends by violence to change the constitution of the state or which is directed against the life or liberty of the head of state"); treason against the country, or *Landesverrat* (crimes committed against the external security of the state); and seditious speech or conduct, or

Majestätsbeleidigung (offenses against the honor and authority of the sovereign, lesser princes, or other state officials in the discharge of their duties).[421] All three offenses were subsumed under the general heading of "crimes against the state," with specific penalties attached to each. Despite these reclassifications, the punishment for all political offenders remained brutish. For *Hochverrat* and *Landesverrat* the law prescribed humiliating forms of capital punishment, accompanied by imprisonment or banishment for the convict's family. Those convicted of the lesser offenses could expect hard labor in irons.[422]

Unlike Continental law, which had largely drawn upon the Roman legal tradition, English common law did not usually differentiate between external and internal political offenses, encompassing both types within the category of "treason." Despite an early attempt to limit the scope of treason through the Statute of Treasons of Edward III,[423] judicial interpretation steadily expanded the definition of the crime, turning almost all forms of resistance to the government into "constructive treasons." The treason statute was construed accordingly, at various times throughout English history, to encompass a wide range of political actions, including domestic rioting, fomenting rebellion in the colonies, collecting information for the benefit of the king's political opponents, and any armed resistance to the king's agents or laws.[424] With time, almost any resistance to the power of the law could be construed as treason.

Sedition was another major tool in the English arsenal for repressing political dissent. Consisting of any communication designed to or likely to bring about hatred, contempt, or disaffection against the sovereign, the Constitution, or the government and its agents, sedition became a vicious tool of oppression.[425] Said Justice Allybone in 1688: "[N]o man can take upon him to write against the actual exercise of the government, unless he have leave from the government . . . be what he writes true or false. . . . It is the business of the government to manage matters relating to the government; it is the business of subjects to mind their own properties and interests."[426]

Sedition eventually encompassed any and all criticism of the king or his government. Attempts to incite discontent among the populace, to promote hostility between different classes of the populace, or to press for changes in existing law, were all considered acts of sedition.[427] Any censure of the king or his government for their errors, or suggestions for fundamental changes in the state or church, could constitute sedition.[428] It was seditious to suggest that the sovereign had been misled or mistaken in his policies, to point out errors or defects in the law or government, or to call for reform. "About the sole right English judges . . . conceded to the subject was the right of humble and respectful petition made to the Government in proper form," wrote criminologist Barton L. Ingraham in his extensive study of political crime in Europe.[429]

The movement toward constitutionalism, which followed the English revolution of 1688, brought about the first major changes in the procedures applicable to treason prosecution. The Trials for Treason Act of 1696[430] granted the accused the rights to obtain a copy of the indictment no later than five days before trial, to secure a list of the jurors selected to try the case, to present his own defense with the aid of witnesses called by him, and to enlist the assistance of a counsel assigned by the court (a right not applicable to other felony cases until 1837). A conviction for treason required a voluntary confession in open court or the testimony of two witnesses to overt treasonous acts. An additional legal modification in 1708 required that the accused be presented a list of the prosecution's witnesses at least ten days prior to trial.[431]

By the nineteenth century the English laws of treason and sedition contained more elaborate safeguards than the laws of any other European country. Despite these reforms, the cruel treatment of those convicted of political crimes persisted. In comparison to the punishments imposed in England, observed Ingraham, "even the aggravated forms of capital punishment prescribed by French and German law at the time seem indulgent." [432]

The French Revolution and
Flirtations with Liberalism

The decades preceding the French Revolution saw the increasing influence, throughout Europe, of the liberal writings of the French encyclopaediasts and the other social and political thinkers of the era, including Montesquieu, Voltaire, and Beccaria. Equally indicative of the era's thinking were the reform-minded criminal codes instituted by such "enlightened monarchs" as Russia's Catherine the Great, Austria's Joseph II, and Prussia's Frederick the Great.[433] Yet the widespread turmoil, violence, and terror evidenced in France and throughout Europe during the immediate postrevolutionary period had major repercussions on the life and laws of the Continent.

France's internal convulsions and subsequent victories over its neighbors spread panic—accompanied by waves of political repression—through the monarchical regimes of the rest of Europe, near and far. As France became the center of revolutionary zeal and propaganda, other Continental regimes vacillated between the conviction that resort to repression would provide immunization against the spread of the contagious doctrines of republicanism and popular rule, and the futile hope that leniency would best safeguard public tranquility. When the Bastille—the infamous Paris prison for the detention of political offenders—fell to the Revolution on July 14, 1789, a mere seven prisoners emerged. This small number bespoke well of the monarch, Louis XVI, who was viewed as being "in the forefront of the movement for judicial reform."[434] Somewhat ironically, the monarch's reign, which would be cut short by the Revolution, was marred by little political repression. It is likely, asserted André Maurois, that "Louis XVI was not overthrown for being despotic, but for being ineffectual—for being unable to use his powers to force the changes long overdue."[435]

The Revolution initially advocated tolerance toward political dissent. The newly formed National Assembly, which had taken over the powers of the monarchy, nobility, and clergy, was dominated by followers of liberalism. Half of the National Assembly's members were lawyers, and they produced oppressive as well as liberal changes in the years immediately following the Revolution. Punishment was legally redefined as a solely personal sanction against the offender, thus eliminating attainder and other penalties against innocent members of a convicted person's family. An early decree had granted extensive procedural safeguards to all those accused of crimes, including the rights to obtain a copy of the accusation, to enlist the assistance of counsel, to confront state witnesses, to call witnesses for their own defense, and to receive a public trial.[436] *Lettres de cachet* were abolished in 1790, and the right to jury trials was extended to all felony cases, including those of treason.

The reforms culminated in a new criminal code, adopted on October 8, 1791.[437] Political offenses, whether implicating the internal or external security of the state, were now classified as "crimes against the state" and were no longer viewed as injuries to the personal authority of the sovereign. Capital offenses were drastically reduced in number—from over one hundred crimes to thirty-two—although most crimes against the state remained subject to the death penalty.

The relative liberality of France's 1791 code was reflected also in the elimination of offenses based solely on prohibited belief or speech. One was no longer prohibited from expounding doctrines and views unless they inflamed the public to immediate riot or rebellion against authority, nor was it any longer a crime to hold membership in proscribed organizations. Yet these post-revolutionary reforms, initiated during the newly instituted constitutional monarchy, were destined to be cut short by continuing political turmoil. Less than one year later, a mass uprising in Paris led to a new constitutional convention. The convention ordered the monarchy abolished, and decreed that September 22, 1792, be the first day in the calendar of the new French Republic. The following January saw the execution of Louis XVI.

These events ushered in the infamous Reign of Terror, administered by the all-powerful Committee of Public Safety.[438] The newly emerging despotism swiftly created a battery of laws giving the regime sweeping new powers against alleged counter-revolutionaries. First among these was the Press Law of March 29–31, 1793, which prescribed death for those who wrote or published materials advocating the dissolution of the state, the restoration of the monarchy, or the revival of any other authority that infringed on the new sovereign powers of the people.[439]

The next step in the campaign of repression took place on March 10, 1793, when the Revolutionary Tribunal was established.[440] During its seventeen-month existence, 1,254 people (among them former queen Marie-Antoinette) were condemned to the guillotine. There was no appeal from this court, whose jurisdiction included "every counterrevolutionary enterprise or attack upon the liberty, equality, unity, or indivisibility of the republic . . . as well as all plots tending to . . . [further] the establishment of any other authority hostile to the liberty, equality and sovereignty of the people."[441] The mission of this court (and basis for its procedures) was summarized by a decree issued on October 10, 1793: "Revolutionary laws ought to be speedily executed."[442]

Three weeks earlier, on September 17, 1793, the Law of Suspects had been passed, providing that all "suspected persons" found at large be placed under detention.[443] The definition of "suspected persons" was long and vague, and included such categories as "partisans of tyranny," "enemies of liberty," those who could not account for their means of support, those who had not discharged their civic duties, those who had been denied certificates of good citizenship, "disloyal" ex-nobles and their families, and those who had emigrated after the Revolution. The Law of Suspects also called for local "Committees of Surveillance" to compile lists of suspects for each district. The "suspects" were to be placed in houses of detention or guarded in their own homes. Under the new law, the central Committee of Public Safety in Paris served as the clearing house for information on arrests and seized evidence. Though some 300,000 persons were eventually declared "suspects," the number actually imprisoned never exceeded 100,000. Many of those detained were never tried and only a few were put to death.

As a member of the Committee of Public Safety, lawyer Georges Couthon reasoned that the function of the courts was to protect society, not its enemies, and that the effective protection of society from its internal enemies required the elimination of legal formalities, which were, in his opinion, no more than chicaneries invented by lawyers.[444] Thereafter, to speed up adjudications, the prosecution no longer had to call witnesses to establish its cases unless the existing documentary evidence was considered insufficient. The right to cross-examination and the right to counsel were eliminated, thus greatly hindering the accused in the presentation of a defense, and the tribunal was limited to only two sentences: acquittal or death. It was this last oppressive law that brought about the downfall of Robespierre on July 27, 1794. Historian R. R. Palmer wryly noted that, despite the comprehensive terror and its repressive laws, the Committee of Public Safety had not "put to death enough of its enemies to establish its rule as a permanent regime."[445]

The oppressive laws enacted during the Reign of Terror were eventually abolished by the successor regime. A new code of criminal procedure, the *Code des délits et des peines,* enacted on October 25, 1795, indeed reinstituted most of the liberal principles of 1791.[446] Although threatened by plots and attempted coups, the Directory—the five-man executive council that had ruled France under the 1795

Constitution—had nevertheless become increasingly dependent upon the army for protection. And it was from the ranks of the army that Napoleon Bonaparte emerged at a time noted for the "popular craving for order and [the] almost unbounded cynicism of former revolutionaries."[447] After dissolving the Directory, Napoleon consolidated his power as First Consul in 1800 through a set of new laws to curtail the publication and distribution of political journals, limit the powers of juries, and deport suspect persons. A special court was created to deal with brigandage and political offenses, while France's criminal system was again fundamentally restructured through the introduction of new criminal codes—the Napoleonic procedural *Code d'instruction criminelle* in 1808 and the substantive *Code pénal* in 1810.

Although the drafters of these codes retained harsh sanctions for political offenders, they nevertheless acknowledged the special characteristics of political crime. Commenting upon the penalties of banishment and forced transportation to overseas possessions, they observed: "A man can in effect be a bad citizen of one country and not be one in another . . . the presence of one guilty of a political offense ordinarily constitutes only a local danger which can be eliminated in the state to which he is banished."[448] The codes therefore excepted those condemned to transportation from the requirement of branding *(la flétrissure)*, on the grounds that "[p]olitical offenses . . . do not suppose the complete renunciation of all principles of honor and morality; [and] they do not have, as with other crimes, their necessary cause in the depravity of the heart." The codes noted further the hope of the transportee "being restored to his rights of citizenship in the place of exile."[449] However, recognizing the inefficacy of traditional penalties as deterrents for the ideologically motivated, the drafters of the Napoleonic codes favored the confiscation of the political offender's property, on the grounds that "legislation . . . ought to . . . seek to restrain the ambitious . . . for whom the fear of death holds no terrors, by the prospect of the poverty which, on his account, will pursue his family."[450]

After returning to power in 1815 upon Napoleon's final military defeat, the embittered aristocrats pressured the new monarch, Louis XVIII, brother of the executed Louis XVI, to institute a new era of repression. However, admitting his responsibility as a constitutional monarch, Louis XVIII tried to implement a spirit of political compromise in the country. One critical question concerned a proposed amnesty for the former officials of Napoleon's regime. The new ultraroyalist legislature initially supported a list of more than eleven hundred people to be excluded from the clemency grant, but the king ultimately managed to limit the purge to nineteen leaders who had previously been turned over to the courts for trial, and to thirty-eight others sentenced to banishment. The broad amnesty law subsequently enacted became a model for successive French regimes.[451]

In 1830, after a short reign by another brother of Louis XVI—the Count of Artois, who ruled as Charles X—a Paris mob composed of discontented journalists, students, and workers rioted in opposition to the new regime's effort to restore the *ancien régime*. The July Revolution brought to the throne the Duke of Orleans, member of a junior branch of the Bourbons, who ascended to the throne as Louis-Philippe. Designated "King of the French" rather than "King of France," this new "citizen king" was devoted to the revolution. His government reflected the shift of political power from the old aristocracy to the new bourgeoisie and brought into power the leaders of the liberal opposition to the former royalist regime, including Casimer Perier, Laffite, Guizot, and Lafayette. Dedicated to constitutional monarchy and to the control of the electoral process by the middle classes, the new government was committed to legal reforms preventing the oppression of political opponents and curtailing censorship.[452] The new regime also granted jury trials for press infractions and political crimes *(délits politiques)*.[453]

The term "political crime," used explicitly for the first time in the history of law, was to encompass offenses against the internal and external security of the state, conspiracies and attempts on the life of the king and his family, conduct defined under the term "civil war," offenses of criticism and provocation against public authority through religious sermons and pastoral letters sent abroad, the display or distribution of seditious materials and signs, and any other offenses against the dignity of the royal authority.[454] This new liberal attitude toward political offenses was further manifested in the 1832 revision of the Penal Code. Confiscations of property previously accompanying convictions for political crimes were abolished. Moreover, three lesser political offenses were exempted from capital punishment: conspiracies *(complots)*, as contrasted with attempts *(attentats);* the counterfeiting and passing of counterfeit moneys; and the counterfeiting of the state seal.[455]

Under the 1832 revision of the Penal Code, a mild form of confinement, detention *(détention),* was made applicable to political offenders.[456] This contrasted with the older and more severe forms of imprisonment used against conventional criminals: forced labor *(travaux forcés)* and solitary confinement *(réclusion).* A sentence of detention was to be served "in one of the fortresses situated on the continental territory of the kingdom." The law further provided that, subject to specified legal regulations, political offenders be permitted to "communicate with persons placed within the place of detention or with those outside."[457] As an alternative to detention, the new law authorized deportation or transportation to France's overseas possessions.[458]

For those detained in France, an 1833 regulation specified confinement in the central section of the Mont Saint-Michel fortress, "entirely apart" from the buildings occupied by the other convicts.[459] Under the 1833 law, political offenders were also exempted from forced labor, but work was permitted "as a means of distraction and recreation for prisoners who demand it."[460] The law reiterated the emerging policy that offenders who differed from common offenders "as to education, social position and habits" should not be subject to the usual penal regimen imposed upon common criminals.[461]

The harsh treatment initially accorded political offenders by the European regimes in the pre– and post–French revolutionary periods was only the first swing of a pendulum that would continue to oscillate for the rest of the modern era. In most European countries, periods of conservatism and repression alternated with periods of liberalism in which political protesters and rebels gained respect for their special motives and unique societal functions. Louis-Philippe's regime brought the first major liberalization in the legal treatment of political offenders. Criminologist Barton Ingraham attributes this dramatic liberal development during Louis-Philippe's reign to the shaky and questionable legitimacy of the nineteenth-century French regimes:

> A government comes into power as a result of the unnatural death of its predecessor; its legitimacy is therefore under a cloud from the start; it attempts to heal the divisions within the society; it fails, encounters growing opposition

and is forced to rely on legal repression to protect its existence; this may be successful for a while, but, as soon as the unity of the ruling group dissolves and the government loses the support of its main prop (a loyal army), it is overthrown, usually by an uprising in Paris. The dreary repetitiveness of this pattern may have had a lot to do with the development of extremely relativistic attitudes toward political crime, particularly the "internal" political crime of challenge to, or hindrance of, political authority.[462]

The new French leniency toward political criminality was given a similar interpretation by Greek political scientist Pierre Papadatos. In these periods of great political, economic, and social torment and discord, with regimes shifting from conservatism to liberalism and back again, hedging one's bets appeared a pragmatic and wise policy. Papadatos suggested that the new liberal attitudes toward political offenders were a product of the revolutions in the first half of the nineteenth century. Since "[t]he parties in power had found themselves alternately conquerors and vanquished," Papadatos wrote, "political offenders seemed unlucky players rather than criminals. [The victors] condemned their political opponents because they had been defeated in the struggle; happy, in their turn, were those who proclaimed themselves the legitimate government and who defended themselves in the name of the same moral laws formerly invoked against them."[463]

Intent on undoing the evils of the First Republic's Reign of Terror, Louis-Philippe and his ministers hoped that reforms calling for the moderate treatment of political offenders would produce the societal tranquility France had so long sought. This was not to be, as the new regime found itself "more exposed and disarmed than any of its antecedents had ever been."[464] Increasingly, those in authority felt forced to resort to more severe measures for disarming and controlling real and potential political opponents. New criminal laws were established to control public criers and bill-posters engaged in political propaganda. Strict controls were imposed upon unauthorized associations, and seditious speech was again prohibited. Once again, the pendulum had swung toward repression.

The government's attempt to prevent a relatively minor political banquet in Paris ignited a mass revolution that in the end gave rise to the Second Republic.[465] Upon gaining power, the former political agitators once more initiated their rule with concessions to political freedom. Within days of the revolution, all violators of the press laws as well as all other political offenders were released and amnestied. The death penalty was abolished for political offenses on February 26, 1848, and on November 4 this prohibition was incorporated into Article 5 of the new Constitution.[466]

Yet the popular unrest continued unabated. Ultimately, Prince Louis Napoleon was elected president of the Republic toward the end of 1848, and he served in that office until he seized power as Napoleon III in a December 1851 coup d'état that initiated a new era of political repression. The Second Empire alternated between conservatism and liberalism, bringing much economic prosperity but little freedom to the political life of the country. The regime was particularly weakened by a growing popular opposition to its authoritarian style.

After France capitulated to German troops under the leadership of Wilhelm I and his chancellor, Otto von Bismarck, at Sedan in 1871, the revolutionary Paris Commune took over the French capital. In the resulting chaos, the nation's assembly met in Bordeaux and deposed Napoleon III, declaring him responsible for the ruin, invasion, and dismemberment of France. After a "Bloody Week," in which some 30,000 Parisians were killed, the nation's Third Republic was ushered in. From 1871 until World War I, France witnessed a flourishing of economic and political liberalism, threatened only by the persistent and indiscriminate violence of the emerging anarchist movement.

Winds of Reform in Great Britain, Storms of Repression in Ireland

English attitudes toward political criminality were to be most severely tested by the situation in Ireland. Although Anglo-Irish tensions had existed since the twelfth century, England's efforts to extend its influence to Ireland were largely ineffective until the seventeenth century, when Scottish Presbyterian missionaries began to achieve measurable success.[467] Eventually, Cromwell's invasion and subsequent redistribution of land pushed the indigenous Catholic population further west of the Shannon,[468] and English laws drastically limited the rights of the Irish people to vote and hold property.[469]

Even though some of these restrictions were lifted in the latter part of the eighteenth century, there remained a great deal of resentment toward the English for their domination of Ireland. The discontent found vent in localized agrarian movements such as the Whiteboys, the Rightboys, and the Steelboys, who protested English penal laws, land laws, and rent notes. Becoming more and more radicalized, militant, and organized, these groups also served to embolden parallel republican and reform movements on the main island of Great Britain.[470]

Following the French Revolution, Irish leaders took part in a 1796 French plan to invade Ireland, an invasion stymied at the last minute by storms that scattered the French fleet. During this period, English prime minister William Pitt was reported to have been afflicted with visions of "thousands of bandits" sacking and burning the City of London.[471] Indeed, riots were not uncommon. Each new attempt to suppress the increasing spread of political opposition seemed to provoke even more vigorous opposition. New controls against seditious writings and speech were instituted in England and Ireland, as were laws against imported revolutionaries and suspected seditionists. An alien registration law passed in 1793 was to safeguard England against dangerous French émigrés.[472] Habeas corpus was suspended, the detention of suspected persons without trial was authorized,[473] and political meetings were restricted.[474] In 1797, Ireland's Insurrection Act conferred more sweeping powers upon the authorities and made the taking of oaths of allegiance to prohibited societies a capital offense. Habeas corpus in Ireland was partially suspended in October of that year.[475]

In February 1798, England set out to "disarm" Ulster, the seat of United Irish activity. A responsive rebellion broke out in May. Although the revolt was quickly suppressed through the arrest and internment of large numbers of United Irish leaders,[476] its effects were far-reaching and ultimately led to the 1801 Act of Union between Ireland and England, which foreclosed direct Irish Catholic participation in the governing of Ireland. The 1798 revolt did little to calm English anxieties about uprisings at home, and spurred further restrictions on political freedoms throughout the islands.[477] In 1800, Parliament even eliminated, in cases involving attempts on the king's life, the ancient requirement that the testimony of two witnesses accompany all treason convictions.[478]

Neither the decline of the revolutionary threat from the Continent, upon the commencement of Napoleon's reign, nor the conclusion of the war with France, brought tranquility to England. The return of some 200,000 retired wartime soldiers and sailors swelled the English labor market with unemployed and restless workers. Economic conditions further deteriorated as improvements in manufacturing techniques and the shrinking of foreign markets increased unemployment. To many observers it seemed that the country was ready for social and political revolution. "The country at this time was in a state of great excitement," wrote legal historian Henry Cockburn. "I have never known a period at which the people's hatred of the Government was so general and so fierce."[479] The governmental response was further repression.[480]

Sir Robert Peel's assumption of the office of Home Secretary in 1822 marked the beginning of a new spirit of reform in the British criminal justice system. Attainder had been abolished,[481] and more than half of some two hundred capital offenses had been ascribed lesser penalties. Due to the 1814 amendment of the Treason Act, traitors could no longer be beheaded or disemboweled while alive. Hanging replaced beheading and those dragged to their place of execution were to be afforded the benefit of a sledge.[482] Other criminal penalties, even for treason and sedition, had also been relaxed. Although causes for political turmoil and uprising abounded, they were adroitly turned aside by social and economic reforms before outright rebellion could erupt. The dawning Victorian Age ushered in a period of unprecedented British prosperity and power, signaling the effectiveness of the socioeconomic and political-legal reforms. Excepting Ireland, not a single execution for a political offense occurred in Great Britain between 1820 and 1916, when Roger Casement was hanged for treason.[483]

The British reformist approach to political dissent and rebellious turmoil in England was inspired in part by the early writings of Utilitarian philosopher Jeremy Bentham, who had pointed out that the punishment of political offenders was "superfluous" as well as "expensive."[484] Bentham argued that one who spreads "pernicious opinions or mischievous doctrines" should be allowed to speak out because "it will be to the interest of a thousand others to refute his theories, and so, it may well be to establish the truth more firmly than ever."[485] The evil of any penalty imposed, Bentham further asserted, was likely to be "greater than the evil of the offense." Severe penalties, he thought, might cause discontent among the offender's allies and supporters, as well as among foreign powers whose good-will the authorities desired. Excessive punishment was also wasteful, according to Bentham, because it deprived the political offender's country of his potential contributions.[486] The leniency that Bentham prescribed eventually came to be a fixture of English practice, al-though no formal recognition or differentiation was granted to "po-litical offenders" as a group. Although severe penalties for crimes like sedition and high treason remained on the books, the harsh sen-tences mandated for those convicted were invariably mitigated by the agencies of justice or by the Crown.

Moreover, many convicted English "seditionists" were members of the educated and professional classes: journalists, publishers, and lawyers. Prison authorities often allowed these offenders a special regime suitable to their means and station in life. The leniency to-ward those jailed for sedition was evidenced by the case of essayist and poet Leigh Hunt, who was convicted of seditious libel and sen-tenced to two years' imprisonment in 1812. While in prison, he was permitted to continue writing and editing his paper, the *Examiner*, and to receive friends and other visitors. Hunt's books, his piano, and fresh flowers were allowed into his cell to make his stay as com-fortable as possible.[487] The case of Arthur Alfred Lynch, nearly a century later, further typified this pattern. A member of Parliament, Lynch was sentenced to death in 1903 for aiding the enemy during the Boer War in South Africa. After serving three months in prison, Lynch's sentence was commuted and he was released on parole. Re-elected to Parliament in 1909, he was commissioned a colonel in the British army in 1918.

Germany: From Principalities to One Reich

Throughout this era, German responses to political offenses and of-fenders, much like those of the French and English, swung back and forth between conservatism and liberalism. The early German laws concerning political crime, like the French laws, were derived from Roman principles.[488] However, the more manifestly feudal character of the Germanic culture produced an even greater effort to preserve through strict laws the hierarchical order of society. German codes thus included offenses such as *Lästerung* (insulting one's lord) and *Mord am Landesherrn* (murdering the lord), which were considered particularly grave threats to the social order and resulted in the of-fender's loss of status and honor.

With time, the already severe penalties against political crime were often made harsher. As noted above, when Frederick the Great pro-hibited the use of torture in Prussian criminal proceedings, he never-theless retained the practice in cases of political crime.[489] Bavaria's 1813 Penal Code,[490] one of the most influential codes of the century, imposed death by decapitation upon those convicted of high trea-son, requiring also, prior to execution, the public exhibition of the condemned person, who was to carry a sign inscribed "Guilty of High Treason." Further, the traitor's family was compelled to change their name, and a column of infamy was erected upon the offender's grave.

During the French Revolution and its Napoleonic aftermath, vig-orous waves of both liberalism and nationalism surged through the German principalities, as expectations of a freer, unified Germany rose amongst the country's students and intelligentsia. But the Con-gress of Vienna, at which Austria's Metternich predominated, reaf-firmed the structure of Germany as a loose federation under Aus-trian hegemony. To suppress the exuberance of the universities and their students, the Karlsbad decrees allowed the administrative dis-missal of teachers, without a hearing, for propagating "doctrines hostile to the public order and subversive of existing governmental institutions."[491] Prior press censorship was instituted, and a Central Investigating Commission was created to inquire into "the origin and ramifications of the revolutionary plots and demagogical associ-ations directed against the existing constitutions" of the German states. As a result of these and similar enactments, working toward German unification or belonging to societies whose goals would en-tail the loss of sovereignty by the existing and disparate states, be-came crimes of high treason. Pan-German patriotism thus became a capital offense.[492]

By the middle of the nineteenth century, however, public attitudes toward political offenders were beginning to change, both in the German scholarly literature and in legislative enactments. Because of the particularly influential role of legal scholars in the German sys-tem of justice, their views on political crime carried considerable weight. But these scholars were not all of the same view. The conser-vatives called for increasingly severe penalties for political offenders.

They pointed out that while common offenders merely violated laws without denying their validity, political offenders denied the very legitimacy of the state and its laws. Because political offenders thus presented themselves as superior to the dictates of existing or "positive" law and sought to impose their private and subjective will upon the general will of society, they were deemed to be more dangerous and evil than conventional offenders.[493]

Many liberal and radical scholars, on the other hand, considered the moral compulsion and noble objectives motivating political offenders to be of utmost importance. Political criminality, in their view, reflected defects in society and in the state, rather than in the offender. Accordingly, combating political crime often required the reform of the state. Political offenders were therefore not to be viewed as criminals but rather as critics or as enemies of the existing state. And thus they were to be considered and treated as prisoners of war. Although these liberal jurists, including French legal scholar Georges Vidal, were not willing to accord dissenters the right to oppose society by violent means, they nevertheless believed that the preventive measures required to restrain political dissidents should not be classified as criminal sanctions.[494]

Even some of the more traditional writers recognized political crime as being not so much a violation of moral norms as a disruption of the pragmatic political order imposed by the state and those in power. Given the special nature of political crime, they called for differential treatment of those charged with these offenses. The severe punishment of political criminals, some pointed out, indeed frustrated the state's ultimate objective of achieving national consensus. A more moderate approach to political opposition was thus recommended as a tool of future reconciliation.[495]

These pragmatic considerations combined in time with Germany's older penal policies, which favored persons of high status, to liberalize the system of sanctions applicable to political offenders. "Germany, being a status-oriented society, retained for at least fifty years beyond the French Revolution . . . lenient forms of punishment for high-status offenders," observed Barton Ingraham.[496] Based on Roman law, which differentiated between *honestiores* (high-status offenders) and *humiliores* (low-status offenders), the German system sought to continue in prison the distinctions existing in open society.

Detention in a fortress *(Festungshaft)*—without the irons and the arduous labor forced upon common criminals—developed in eighteenth-century Germany as a special punishment for *honestiores,* the nobility, and other offenders of high status. During the first half of the nineteenth century, this punishment was extended to other persons, particularly members of the educated classes, who with altruistic motives committed crimes not deemed dishonorable. Although these lenient laws did not specify a differential sanction for political offenders as such, the long-established traditions of *custodia honesta* accrued in time to the benefit of the political prisoner.

The experiences of the German state of Württemberg well illustrate the progressive changes in the treatment of political offenders. Although the 1810 laws concerning offenses against the state and its king imposed severe penalties, they authorized the milder penalty of *Festungsarrest* for high-status offenders. In 1824 the law was changed to permit penalties of fortress detention whenever the circumstances of the offender and the nature of the crime merited more lenient treatment. Attention thus began shifting from the offender's status to his or her motives and the character of the crime. The trend was carried further in 1849, when the law was changed to altogether eliminate social status from sentencing considerations.[497]

With the 1871 unification of Germany, the perception of political crime was drastically altered. Unification demonstrated that the previous regime's repression of Pan-German activism was wrong and ineffective. The creation of the German Reich, despite the former laws that proscribed unificationist patriotism, gave rise to a new public recognition of the fallibility of the law. Greater tolerance for competing and conflicting ideas and programs gained support not only among radicals and liberals but among the more conservative segments of the population as well.

The unification of Germany also brought about an important change in the new federal Penal Code, which reflected the period's strong preoccupation with issues of political activism and dissent. The debates on the code's adoption were lengthy and fierce, and the final language was the product of political compromise. For many of the offenses against the state, and usually whenever extenuating circumstances were found to exist, detention in a fortress became an alternative penalty. The code provided specifically that where a choice was allowed by law between detention in a fortress and confinement in a penitentiary, the latter sentence was not to be allowed unless it was established that the offense had arisen "as the result of a dishonorable state of mind."[498]

Prison sentences for political offenders thus became the exception rather than the rule. Penitentiary confinement was required only when the crime of high treason involved the murder or attempted murder of the sovereign, when a serious act of treason was committed against the state *(Landesverrat),* or when serious rioting occurred against public officials.[499] The death penalty was to be imposed only for the murder or attempted murder of the kaiser or the reigning prince of the offender's native state or state of residence.[500] But despite this growing liberalism in the overall treatment of political offenders, the new German law continued to display great hostility toward secret societies[501] and toward the political activism of the clergy.[502]

Aware of the spread of radical economic and political doctrines, Germany prohibited secret societies and incitement to class violence.[503] Seeking to build up German nationalism, Bismarck addressed the international affiliations of both socialism and Catholicism as threats. New provisions of the Penal Code made it an offense for members of the clergy, in their preaching or writing, to make "affairs of the state the subject of comment or discussion in a manner dangerous to the public peace."[504] Furthermore, all Jesuits were banned from the territories of the Reich and all religiously affiliated schools in Prussia were placed under the supervision of the state.

The Twentieth-Century Retreat from Liberalism

I have previously noted the succinct and well-articulated justifications for the nineteenth century's liberal flirtation with the political offender advanced by leading French legal scholar Georges Vidal. To briefly reiterate:

> [The political offender's] criminality cannot be compared with that of the ordinary malefactor, with the murderer, the thief, etc. The criminality [of the political offender] has not all the same immorality. It is only relative, dependent on time, place, circumstances, the institutions of the land, and it is often inspired by noble sentiments, by disinterested motives, by devotion to persons and

principles, by love of one's country. In conclusion, the criminality is often only passing; the author of a political crime who is rather a vanquished, a conquered man, than a criminal, may become, as a result of a revolution favorable to his ideas, the conqueror of the morrow, who is called regularly and lawfully to direct and guide the state and the public administration of his country.[505]

With the approach of World War I, this liberal outlook was already in decline. The specter of a global "war to end all wars" intensified the spirit of nationalism, resurgent around the globe, and brought with it a wariness of critics and opponents of existing state authority. Those not recognizing the need to close ranks in the face of impending foreign threats were perceived as subversives—or even as enemy agents. Even in the United States, the opposition of pro-labor interests and pro-German sympathizers to war was viewed and treated as seditious and treasonous.

In France, as elsewhere in Europe, the mobilization of national determination and resources spurred a growing intolerance of political opponents by both the population and the government.[506] Once the war had failed to attain an early resolution, this intolerance began to take a serious toll on those who continued to criticize their government's military activities or political objectives. Political leaders opposed to the war were subjected to charges of treason,[507] and the expropriation of property was reinstated as a penalty for those convicted of violating French external security laws.[508]

After the Armistice, in the face of the new socioeconomic turmoil, the politics of intolerance continued to expand. French Fascist conspiracies, patterned after the successful exploits of the Hitler's Brownshirts, gave rise in the 1930s to new counteractive measures by the government. After the French army had to be called in to defend the legislature from an attack by a Fascist mob, major changes were instituted in provisions dealing with political criminality, particularly in peacetime espionage law.[509] The definition of "espionage" was expanded (to include the disclosure of industrial and economic information) and its penalties were increased (to permit once more the imposition of *relégation,* or transportation to overseas colonies). Moreover, procedures were further streamlined in order to deal with these offenses "quickly and with the least fuss possible."[510] Organizations dedicated to violent insurgency, paramilitary activities, or any other undermining of the French Republic were subject to dissolution,[511] and their members could be imprisoned for up to two years. But the most drastic measures against political criminality were not instituted until after Hitler's invasion of Czechoslovakia in March 1939.

As war with Germany seemed inevitable, the French government moved to better protect itself against persons and activities likely to jeopardize the national security. Special emergency powers, already available under the Constitution, were assumed by the executive on March 19, 1939.[512] Penal Code provisions concerning crimes against the external security of the state were drastically expanded soon thereafter.[513] The new law reinstituted capital punishment for the more serious violations of the law of treason,[514] while the penalty of forced labor (previously applicable only to common crimes) was extended to offenses against the country's foreign security.[515] Most significantly, all felonies and misdemeanors against the external security of the state—whether committed in time of war or peace—were now to be tried by military tribunals. The dramatic reversal of France's earlier lenient policies toward political opposition was made complete by revising Article 84 of the Penal Code, which provided: "For the purpose of imposing punishment, felonies and misdemeanors against the external security of the state shall be treated like ordinary felonies and misdemeanors."[516]

After the country's victorious conclusion of World War II, many expected a return to leniency in France's treatment of political offenders. But this hope was not realized. General Charles de Gaulle's Provisional Government conducted mass trials of wartime collaborators, casting a new light on the often temporal meaning of "political crime." Post–World War II ordinances, clearly *ex post facto* in character, established the new offense of "national disgrace" to criminalize such conduct as was ordained either legal or mandatory under the wartime Vichy government.[517] Thousands who had served the occupying Germans or Marshal Pétain's collaborationist government were prosecuted. French citizens could not claim, as a defense to charges of collaboration, that their actions had complied with the existing law under Vichy and the German occupation.

During the post–World War II period, France was further preoccupied not only with the punishment of wartime collaborators but also with the more immediate dangers posed by the emergence of new political threats to the well-being of the Republic. Continuing emergencies in France's overseas possessions, combined with troublesome domestic unrest, ultimately resulted in an even harsher stance toward opponents of the regime. Though liberal attitudes lingered a short time for purely "domestic" political offenders, the traditional line of demarcation between offenders against domestic security and offenders against external security gradually lost its meaning. As manifestations of international causes and movements, such as communism and fascism, erupted on French soil, the line between domestic and foreign security threats became almost totally blurred.[518]

The French were vigorously attempting to control the growing political unrest that threatened both metropolitan France and its North African possessions and ultimately culminated in the end of the Fourth Republic. The various governments under the new Fifth Republic instituted increasingly harsh emergency measures, including the pretrial internment of nationalist Front pour la Libération Nationale sympathizers in Algeria.[519] Successive legal enactments during the de Gaulle regime extended the internment of suspects to France itself,[520] and the government increasingly resorted to the constitutionally authorized "special powers" available in the instance of national emergencies.[521] By 1958, military tribunals had assumed jurisdiction over offenses related to the Algerian violence.[522] Suspects could be detained in police stations for an extended time without access to their families or lawyers, and without formal criminal charges.[523] Finally, even the conditions for the divestment of French citizenship from suspected and convicted political offenders were broadened in 1961 as an added weapon in the government's arsenal.[524]

The most extreme legal measure during the Algerian unrest was the ordinance of June 4, 1960, which drastically revised the Penal Code and the Code of Criminal Procedure and abandoned the traditional division of crimes into those threatening external security and those threatening internal security.[525] The revisions also required that all offenses against state security, whether felonies or misdemeanors, be tried by military courts in time of war, and by a special "Court for the Security of the State" in time of peace.[526] The earlier right to a jury trial was abandoned. Only a shadow now remained of the nineteenth-century policies that had given political offenders preferential treatment—both in terms of substantive provisions and procedurally—over ordinary criminals.

Great Britain, a tenacious empire, faced less of a domestic crisis after the conclusion of World War II, but it too had particular sensitivities regarding those fighting for independence from British rule. Political offenders in British possessions and dependencies such as India, Pakistan, Ghana, Nigeria, Jordan, and Palestine were increasingly subjected to different and harsher controls than were common offenders. In many of the remaining territories of the empire, emergency regulations, patterned after Britain's experience in Northern Ireland, permitted the long-term confinement or so-called administrative detention of suspected political offenders without appraisal of charges, trial, or conviction.[527] These administrative detentions were used to devastating effect in Northern Ireland, where at one point as many as 15,000 political suspects were held in administrative detention at a time. Other emergency provisions for dealing with the Irish unrest also continued to be enacted.[528] Although British rule eventually came to an end throughout its far-flung empire, except in Northern Ireland, many of Britain's former structures and traditions have persisted in its newly independent colonies. These have included not only such beneficent institutions as the civil service and resort to the rule of law, but also the inordinately frequent willingness to resort to emergency provisions in order to deprive political suspects of otherwise commonly applied and constitutionally ordained criminal procedures.

Germany's Road to Totalitarianism and Back

The winds of political disorder and change evidenced in the Western democracies were even more stormy in Germany. The Weimar Republic, established in 1919 after Germany's World War I defeat, was unable to control the political chaos that followed the collapse of the country's military and industrial establishments. Throughout Germany, the political left-wing–organized Soldiers' and Workers' Councils plotted to take power in the country's industrial centers. Socialist regimes were established in the states of Bavaria, the Ruhr, Saxony, and Thuringia. Moreover, leftist elements of the Social Democratic Party (the Spartacus League) attempted to establish a national workers' government through a socioeconomic revolution in the Soviet style. During the ensuing unrest, Spartacus leaders Rosa Luxembourg and Karl Liebknecht were murdered in Berlin.

The Weimar government could not obtain support from the moderate or left-of-center elements in the country to control the evolving chaos. Neither did the new government receive the backing of the more conservative or right-of-center parties, which with great contempt alleged that the Weimar centrists had stabbed Germany in the back during the world war. Desperately seeking to protect itself against the political extremes of both the left and the right, the Weimar regime attempted to institute its own political controls by passing the "Law to Protect the Republic" in 1922.[529] The new law was to be administered by a special "High Court for the Protection of the Republic." The Weimar government's problems in bringing these new political weapons to bear were exacerbated by the limitations imposed by Germany's prevailing federal Constitution. Coordination of efforts at the federal and local levels never effectively materialized. It is thus reported, with regard to the last election before Hitler took power, that

> the Prussian Government, by a decree of July 30, 1930, barred all civil servants from supporting Nazi and Communist organizations. The wearing of Brown Shirts in Prussia was also forbidden, and so the SA [Hitler's Brownshirts] made do with white shirts. But the Central Government was not ready to take similar steps, and this duality largely canceled out the effects of regional measures.[530]

The federal-state jurisdictional divisions that weakened the Weimar government were aggravated by a rift within the governmental apparatus itself—between reformist liberals in the Reichstag and the conservatives who remained in control of the country's military, police, and judicial agencies. Kurt Tucholsky, a highly respected essayist of the era, accused the conservative-dominated judiciary of administering "political justice" as a means of protecting causes it was sympathetic to:

> [Tucholsky] maintained that an observer could tell much of the character of a country from its legal procedure. . . . [He] constantly compared the treatment by the court of the left- and right-wing offenders. Liebknecht's [leftist] followers received [long] prison sentences. . . . "The Kappists [rightists] we let go free." Tucholsky reported that men who revealed the hiding places of secret arms were arrested while those in possession of the weapons went free. Reactionary students who trampled the [new] republican flag were left untouched, while tramplers of the [discarded] imperial colors received three months. Tucholsky came to believe that the behavior of the courts toward the right was

tantamount to giving it free reign to behave as it wanted no matter how criminal the action.[531]

The executive branch showed similar sympathy toward violent right-wing organizations. When the federal government finally attempted to outlaw Hitler's SA Storm Troopers *(Sturmabteilung)* and the SS *(Schtzstaffel)* in April 1932, President Hindenburg promptly removed General William Groener, the minister who had announced the measure.[532]

Particularly ineffective was the enforcement of an emergency law enacted by the Weimar government that specifically prohibited private citizens or groups from dispersing lawful meetings,[533] a tactic increasingly used by the National Socialist storm troopers to combat their political adversaries. This disruptive tactic brought Adolf Hitler and his followers into the Burgerbrau Cellar in Munich on November 8, 1923. Breaking into a meeting of Bavarian reactionary leaders, the Nazis forced those in attendance to support their march on Berlin. Once freed, the Bavarians withdrew their support, and Hitler's march on Munich the following day was dispersed by the police, ending his attempted *Putsch*. Adolf Hitler himself was sentenced to serve five years in fortress confinement *(Festungshaft)*, a term that was later reduced to less than one year.

It was not outright illegality but rather the exploitation of the democratic process itself that ultimately brought the National Socialist Party to power. The middle class (pauperized by inflation), the youth (largely unemployed), and the veterans (disappointed because of lack of attention) swelled the Nazi ranks. The National Socialists increased their seats in the Reichstag, the national parliament, from 12 in 1928, to 107 seats in 1930, to 230 seats in 1932, to 288 seats in 1933. They thus became the largest party in the Reichstag, though they never achieved a majority.

On January 30, 1933, Adolf Hitler was sworn in as chancellor of Germany by ailing general Paul von Hindenburg, the country's president. At his disposal was not only the power to rule by emergency decrees, authorized by Article 48 of the Weimar Constitution, but also a host of other drastic laws enacted by Germany's desperate Weimar Republic in its quest to disarm its adversaries. It was with the aid of these and other newly enacted measures that Hitler turned what appeared a lawful assumption of power into a *coup d'état*.[534]

After their seizure of power, the Nazis immediately addressed the shortcomings of German federalism. The former difficulties in federal-state coordination were quickly overcome by decree on February 28, 1933: "if a state fails to take the necessary steps for the restoration of public safety and order, then the Central Government is empowered to take over the relevant powers of the highest state authority."[535] Another important measure introduced by the new Hitlerian regime was modeled on the previously repealed Weimar "Law to Protect the Republic." The new "Emergency Decree to Protect the German People"[536] incorporated many of the provisions of the earlier law, but it was expanded through a new and ominous provision for taking into "protective custody" *(Schützhaft)* anyone suspected of plotting to alter the Constitution. This new authorization was to serve as the first step toward the establishment of the Third Reich's infamous concentration camps, and marked the end of any rational treatment of political opponents.[537]

Once "protection" against the Reich's enemies had been established, the next step in the consolidation of Nazi power was the Reichstag fire of February 28, 1933. The internationally publicized event was also utilized to trigger the "Emergency Decree of the Reich President for the Protection of the People and the State,"[538] under which capital punishment was extended to a large number of political offenses previously subject to lesser sanctions. The decree was quickly followed by the Enabling Act of March 23, 1933, in which the Reichstag essentially yielded its remaining legislative powers to what had finally become a dictatorship.[539]

The National Socialist Party was designated the only lawful political party in Germany on July 14, 1933.[540] Under the political theories propounded by the Nazis, Germany's "national community," not the state, became the source of all law and the focus of all loyalties. The party was viewed as the sole expression of the "national community," and betrayal of either the party or the state constituted treason. Since all social status under Naziism was theoretically derived from the community, the political offender—a rebel against the *Volk,* or people—was to be denied all dignity and humanity.

Under this new view, political offenders were to be subjected to more stringent police, court, and prison proceedings than were common criminals. Political offenders could be held in preventive detention for indeterminate periods. A People's Court of Justice *(Volks-*

gerichthof) was granted exclusive jurisdiction over all treasonous offenses, trials for which were to be held in closed sessions and under
summary procedures that could even exclude the defense counsel.[541]
Additional laws aimed at controlling speech and dissent were soon
passed, some of which strongly resembled the old English laws of
sedition (the German *Heimtueckegesetz*).[542] A contemporary observer reported that "eighty percent of all persons accused of any
kind of political offense are condemned under it."[543]

With these measures directed to silence all dissent within the German citizenry, the next targets for the Nazi purge were the institutions of government and the structures of the party itself. The campaign of *Gleichschaltung*, or of unification and incorporation of all
social institutions, began with the removal of all Jews and "politically unreliable" employees from the government, including the pha-
lanxes of lawyers who had participated in the liberal Weimar system.[544] The party itself was eventually purged on the "Night of the
Long Knives," during which Ernst Röhm, the leader of the SA, was
executed by Theodor Eicke and Michael Lippert, the commandants
of the Dachau concentration camp.[545] Most of the victims of the
purge went to their deaths believing that there had been some mis-
take, loudly proclaiming their allegiance to the fuhrer as they were
hauled away in the dead of night. The purge was retroactively made
"legal" by a law of July 3, 1934, proclaiming that "the measures
taken on June 30 and on July 1 and 2 to strike down the treasonous
attacks are justifiable acts of self-defense by the state."[546] The last
remnants of legality had been cast aside.

Writing in 1979, criminologist Barton Ingraham, confounded by
the Weimar regime's weakness in the face of what at first was merely
a gang of street brawlers, concluded that liberal "bourgeois"
regimes generally suffered from a self-defeating "strange chivalry"
toward their internal political enemies—a sort of "death wish."[547]
He argued that such liberal bourgeois governments inherently lack
the desire to rule and are more interested in trade and commerce
than in political struggles for power. But this highly controversial explanation of the rise of German Fascism is challenged by the factual
context of the Nazi rise to power.

Though Hitler had claimed that the German people were tired of
democracy, the truth is that the country had never wholeheartedly

accepted it. The profoundly militaristic and hierarchical culture that had existed under the kaisers was uniquely adaptable to the emerging Fascist ideology and social structures. Revolving around concepts of duty, honor, and the protection of the Fatherland, this national heritage was warped by a worldwide depression, the terrible and wasting hyperinflation of the early 1930s, and the punitive "peace" imposed upon Germany by the victorious Great Powers at Versailles. Weimar's relatively lenient treatment of its domestic political enemies was a reflection of political realities—of the regime's enormous institutional weakness in the face of intolerable social, economic, and political conditions.

If there had been a death wish on the part of the liberal forces in Germany after World War I, it had evaporated by the end of World War II. When the Federal Republic of West Germany came into being after the Allied occupation, the liberal treatment of political offenders in the pre-Nazi era was not reintroduced. Mindful of the past weaknesses of the Weimar Republic in the face of enemies from both the left and the right, Germany's new leaders sought to safeguard the nation's democratic regime against those who would seek to subvert it.

In its Basic Law *(Grundgesetz)* of 1949, Germany guaranteed to its citizens the basic rights of life, liberty, and freedom of religion, conscience, speech, press, and association.[548] The law specifically exempted from its protections, however, "associations, the objects or activities of which conflict with the criminal laws or which are directed against the constitutional order or the concept of international understanding."[549] The Basic Law further specified that "[w]hoever abuses the freedom of expression . . . in order to attack the free, democratic basic order, shall forfeit these basic rights,"[550] and also that "[p]arties which . . . seek to impair or abolish the free and democratic basic order or to jeopardize the existence of the Federal Republic of Germany, shall be unconstitutional."[551]

Commenting on West Germany's new policies regarding political offenders, Ingraham observed: "The Founding Fathers of the Bonn constitution had resolved to defer no more to the principle of the absolute neutrality of the democratic state in the face of political parties, regardless of their nature and objectives."[552] In decreeing the dissolution of groups like the neo-Nazi Socialist Reich Party and the

German Communist Party, the nation's Federal Constitutional Court reaffirmed that Germany would no longer rely on vulnerable governance but was to become a "valiant democracy."[553]

Darkness at Noon in the "Workers' Paradise"

Many perceive the Nazi regime as the ultimate evil—as the greatest and most cruel attempt to extinguish humankind's ethnic, political, social, and religious pluralism. The Soviet Union's attempt to create similar uniformity through the making of a "New Man" was to end as an equal or even greater failure.

Since the founding of their state, and long before the Communist Revolution, Russia's czars had their own harsh methods for containing political crime and criminals, which featured only ephemeral glimpses of leniency.[554] The Okhrana was an extraordinarily effective body of political police, despite its eventual (and probably inevitable) failure to preserve the monarchy. So prevalent was the czarist penetration of suspect political organizations that "the farcical position was reached . . . in 1908–09, . . . [when] four out of five members of the Bolshevik Party's St. Petersburg Committee were Okhrana agents." In fact, when *Pravda* was first published in 1912, its editor (Roman Malinovskii) and its treasurer (Miron Chernomazov) were both police agents.[555] The Bolsheviks merely refined the czarist art of political control—and terror—to extraordinary levels.

The Communists' system of repression began to take shape in the earliest days after the Revolution. The ensuing civil war against the remaining loyalists and alleged counter-revolutionaries provided the justification for the Bolsheviks to rule by decree. After the first and only Constituent Assembly had been dissolved, Vladimir I. Lenin's signature on brief communiqués could alone spell death for thousands who stood in the way of the state. Under these decrees the regime began its first purges, indeed rounding up political enemies and shooting them by the thousands. "On the Arrest of the Leaders of the Civil War Against the Revolution" was among the first decrees. Issued by Lenin on November 28, 1917, it condemned the leadership and membership of the rival Kadet (Constitutional-Democratic) Party to death as "enemies of the people."[556] George Leggett, in his authoritative work on the period, noted that "the term 'enemies of the people,' used in the tradition of the French Revolution, literally put its victims outside the law, with every man's hand against them."[557]

An old Russian proverb suggests that one has "to break some eggs to make an omelet." The total history of the Soviet regime, in its struggle to build the promised Communist society, was to see the breaking of an inestimable number of eggs. On December 7, 1917, Lenin's new government established the CHEKA (the All-Russian Extraordinary Commission for Combating Counter-Revolution, Speculation, Sabotage, and Misuse of Authority), and appointed as its chairman Feliks Dzerzhinsky. Through its other incarnations as the GPU, the OGPU, and later the NKVD, this organization would ultimately become the feared KGB (Committee for State Security).[558] The new CHEKA quickly began to fulfill its mandate "to suppress and liquidate all attempts and acts of counter-revolution and sabotage throughout Russia, from whatever quarter."[559]

As in other times and other places, external and internal threats to the new revolutionary government seemed to justify the institution of a "reign of terror." The pressures of the Russian civil war and the threats created by competing political forces were to prove a perfect complement to the Bolsheviks' ideas about the inevitability and desirability of a "dictatorship of the proletariat," making repression appear both ideologically legitimate and necessary. Leon Trotsky, commanding the Red Army throughout the civil war, referred admiringly to "that remarkable invention of the French Revolution which makes men shorter by a head," and spoke darkly of things to come: "In not more than a month's time terror will assume very violent forms, after the example of the great French revolution; the guillotine, and not merely the gaol, will be ready for our enemies."[560]

The reign of terror was at hand. "Whites" (non-Communists), Kulaks (small landowners), and other suspected and actual "counter-revolutionaries" would suffer under the wrath of the new regime. After an attempt on Lenin's life had failed, the remaining non-Bolsheviks—Kadets, Social Revolutionaries, and the Mensheviks—were, for the most part, summarily shot, an action justified by Lenin's previous decrees declaring these unfortunates to be "outside the law."[561] Despite the protestations of the reformists and social democrats who had participated in the Revolution, the Red Terror had begun.

Lenin preferred to forget that Marx, even when advocating violent revolution, generally disapproved of the use of revolutionary terror, and strongly criticized its application by the Jacobins in the French Revolution, regarding such use as a sign of weakness and immaturity in the regime that practiced it. . . . Lenin, recalling Marx's phrase of 1848 about the French Terror being simply the bourgeoisie's plebeian way of settling scores with feudal absolutism, proposed that, after the coming revolution in Russia, the Bolsheviks—"the Jacobins of contemporary Social-Democracy"—should, like the French Jacobins of 1793 . . . use terror to settle accounts with the autocracy.[562]

The rhetoric issuing from the organs of the Bolshevik Party grew increasingly bloodthirsty as the Red Terror continued: "[L]et there be floods of blood of the bourgeois—more blood, as much as possible."[563] The Bolsheviks' deliberate choice to rule through terror became a fixture of the Soviet system, with even more bloody purges continuing after Lenin's death. "Recourse to terror had figured prominently in Russian history. Terror had raged in the savage cossack-peasant risings of Stenka Razin and Pugachev, and in their suppression by the iron hand of autocracy. . . . Now Lenin summoned the cruel atavistic terror of the Russians, harnessing it to his purpose."[564]

Lenin's terror was only a prelude to the greater and more murderous regime of his successor, Joseph Stalin. Robert Conquest, in *The Great Terror,* estimates the number of Stalin's victims at over 20 million.[565] During his twenty-three years in power, Stalin further perfected totalitarian methods for controlling dissent. A huge system of prison camps was created, the Gulag. The lethal cold, starvation, and forced labor experienced by those sentenced to these institutions were well described by Aleksandr Solzhenitsyn in *The Gulag Archipelago.*[566]

The former czarist device of internal passports was reintroduced to control all movement within the socialist state. This mandatory and comprehensive system of controls classified all Soviet citizens into rigid categories, including: *yevrey* (Jew), *tsigan* (Gypsy), *rabochiy* (worker), *sluzhashchiy* (civil servant), *krestyanin* (peasant), and *uchashchisya* (student).[567] The classifications, made by the security officer who filled out the passport form, evolved into a veritable caste system for an allegedly classless society.

The Soviet Union's attempt to exercise absolute control over the lives and minds of its citizens represented, much like the Nazi campaign, the ultimate striving for absolute power by those favoring authority over autonomy, conformity over freedom, dictation over debate, uniformity over pluralism. As with other such attempts to extinguish the inexorable force of human rebellion, the Soviet experiment was destined to collapse. Yet in its pursuit of internal security and social control, the Soviet Union differed dramatically from other countries that have struggled with the question of political protest and resistance.

Traditional Western jurisprudence has long faced the argument that political crimes, as distinguished from common crimes, have special characteristics and demand differential treatment. But in a totalitarian society where the state owns all property and controls all institutions, no transgression can be characterized as nonpolitical. Any offense against persons, property, or ideology is necessarily perceived as an offense against the state, and hence a political crime. No leniency can be extended to an offender, therefore, on the grounds that his or her offense was politically motivated.

Soviet criminal law nevertheless labeled some crimes as particularly political and therefore deserving of the harshest of penalties. Though President Gorbachev proposed substantial revisions to the criminal codes, several "Especially Dangerous Crimes Against the State" as well as a number of lesser political offenses endured therein until the very demise of the Soviet Union. These included failure to return from a foreign country,[568] industrial and military espionage, the grave injury of a public official "for the purpose of undermining or weakening Soviet authority,"[569] possession or distribution of anti-Soviet propaganda,[570] sabotage or subversion "intended to obstruct the normal work" of economic entities,[571] and, all-inclusively, any organized political opposition. The Soviet psychiatric system served as yet another potent weapon in the government's suppression of political protest and dissidence. The law established several procedures by which the authorities could rid themselves of troublesome dissent, such as committing offenders to psychiatric hospitals or subjecting them to compulsory medication as alcoholics and drug addicts. Most psychiatric patients thus consisted of: advocates of human rights or democratization, nationalist activists, would-be emigrants, and religious believers.[572]

Born in idealistic fervor, the Soviet Revolution sought to create a politically and economically new man, *Homo Sovieticus*. This revolutionary promise, quickly extinguished by Lenin's Red Terror, ultimately led to Stalin's campaign to destroy the very soul of the political man—to eliminate all thought not planted by authority, to crush even the possibility of dissent. In the case of the Soviet Union, this historically familiar development led not only to repressions at home, but also to the crushing of the 1953 East German uprising, the 1956 Hungarian revolt, and the Prague Spring of 1968. The common theme seen in Soviet and other Communist tales of unfulfilled revolutionary promises turning into oppressive nightmares is no less evident in the contemporary era, in which governments continue to grapple with their own legitimacy as well as with that of their political opponents.

But despite the Soviet Union's unusually harsh treatment of its political opponents, the Communist "bloc" of nations was never as monolithic as it may have appeared to Western observers. The Soviet Union was unable to impose absolute uniformity upon its satellites. Emigration restrictions, a fixture in the Workers' Paradise, varied considerably in countries like Romania and Cuba. The Romanian government permitted and at times actively encouraged the emigration of selected populations—including ethnic Germans, Hungarians, and Jews. The Cuban policy under Fidel Castro likewise placed few barriers in the path of those choosing to depart for political or economic reasons. All this leads to the inevitable conclusion that the diverse treatments accorded political offenders offer exceptional insights into why the perpetual struggle between those in power and those seeking to share in its benefits constitutes such a critical and compelling issue in the history of governance and of mankind.

Part Four

Reconciling Public Order with Higher Law

*The study . . . of the American Revolution . . . may teach
mankind that revolutions are no trifles: that they ought
never to be undertaken rashly; not without deliberate
consideration and sober reflection; nor without a solid
immutable, eternal foundation in justice and humanity; nor
without a people possessed by intelligence,
fortitude and integrity.*

—John Adams, in Virginius Dabney,
*The Patriots: The American Revolution
Generation of Genius* (1975)

It is a strange desire to seek power and to lose liberty.

—Francis Bacon,
Essays (1625)

Liberty, too, must be limited in order to be possessed.

—Edmund Burke,
Letters to the Sheriffs of Bristol (1777)

There Was No Way Out, Karl Stojka, oil and acrylic.

Chapter Six

The Political Offender's Quest for Sanctuary

Asylum or Extradition?

I have loved justice and hated iniquity:
therefore I die in exile.
—Pope Gregory VII, last words (1085)

[T]reasons . . . are sufficiently punished by exile.
—Thomas Jefferson (1792)

A free country can never agree to surrender foreigners
to their prosecuting home state for deeds done in the
interest of the same freedom and liberty which
the subjects of the free country enjoy.
—Lassa Oppenheim,
International Law (1905)

"*If you start granting amnesty to people for following their conscience, pretty soon <u>everyone</u> will be following his conscience.*"

From *The New Yorker*.

Safe Haven for Agents of Change

Although posterity may grant them some credit and perhaps even posthumous laurels, reality is not usually kind to rebels and political offenders. Whether true resisters to governmental terror and abuse, valiant pursuers and upholders of new and uncommon values and institutions, or merely selfish seekers of the spoils of power, political offenders have invariably been subjected to harsh persecution by those in authority. Failing to consider the severity of or the reasons for the offense, the forces of law have generally meted out unduly strict sanctions to those daring to challenge the prevailing order, unleashing their wrath against all opponents—whether peaceful or violent, virtuous or vicious. It matters little if the offense is nothing more than participation in (or a suspected sympathy for) some reform-minded movement, consists merely of unauthorized speech or some other prohibited communication, or is based only on some immutable but unfavored or suspect facet of the offender's very being or status, such as religion, race, ethnicity, or socioeconomic standing. Driven to desperation in their search for domestic relief, political offenders are often compelled to escape their oppressors by seeking haven abroad. Particularly in periods of great and widespread turmoil, as exemplified by the current worldwide political maelstrom, the community of nations is brought face to face with dramatic influxes of thousands and even millions of displaced men and women searching for shelter and sympathy outside their native lands.

Accounts of political dissidents taking flight from their home, village, or country to escape repression, punishment, or enslavement can be found in many of humankind's legends and histories. Some rebels have sought refuge in the unpopulated deserts or forbidding forests of their native lands. Others have eluded their pursuers by escaping abroad. The list of fugitives includes many who would become heroes as well as those who would remain villains—the Old Testament's King David, Switzerland's William Tell, Dutch jurist Hugo Grotius, French novelist and social reformer Victor Hugo, Vermont's Ethan Allen, Kenya's Jomo Kenyatta, Egypt's Anwar Sadat, the former Soviet Union's Vladimir Lenin, and Iran's Ayatollah Ruhollah Khomeini.

The biblical account of Jonah,[573] who sought in vain to escape the hazards of his divine calling—to forecast to the people of Nineveh the destruction of their depraved city—symbolizes the dilemmas facing those endowed with a political or prophetic mission. Resisting his assignment, Jonah hid aboard a ship sailing away from Nineveh, only to be discovered, cast overboard, and eventually swept back into the condemned city in the belly of a whale. When the modern dissident escapes from the wrath of those in authority, he or she faces great uncertainties as well. Will the rebel be afforded safe haven abroad, or will he or she be expelled and delivered to his or her pursuers?

From antiquity through the Middle Ages, chieftains, princes, kings, and others in authority were generally reluctant to provide hospitality and protection to dissidents wanted by other tribes and peoples—a caution well founded. Escaped offenders were often seen as potential troublemakers and as a threat to their new host countries, and granting sanctuary to foreign dissidents could earn a ruler the enmity of powerful neighbors. Further, the rulers of diverse lands, whatever their relations with one another, shared an inherent interest in upholding the sanctity of political power and in preventing the enemies of authority from going unpunished. On the other hand, sheltering an unfriendly neighbor's adversary could prove a useful gambit in the political game between rulers.

Since the earliest of times, these diverse considerations produced informal as well as formal systems for the intertribal, intersovereign, and international surrender or exchange of foreign fugitives. Bowing to these political realities, democratic Athens, a paragon of political virtue, considered itself well advised to proclaim its readiness to cooperate in the capture, surrender, and punishment of the culprits wanted for the attempted murder of the ruler of its autocratic yet powerful neighbor—King Philip of Macedon. Perhaps the earliest agreement regarding the extradition of offenders between sovereigns was contained in the peace treaty between Egyptian pharaoh Ramses II and Hittite prince Hattushilish III, which was signed around 1280 B.C.[574] The treaty, preserved in hieroglyphics carved on a stone tablet at the Temple of Amman in Karnak, Egypt, established the mutual duty of the two rulers to return to each other escapees from imperial justice. Nevertheless, both the Egyptian pharaoh and the Hittite prince made surprising humanitarian concessions in their

treaty by solemnly forswearing the mutilation of surrendered offenders, the massacre of their families, or the destruction of their
homes.[575]

Despite a few formal surrender agreements, most of antiquity's
captures and returns of escaped offenders took place through sporadic and informal exchanges. Jealous of their sovereign rights,
rulers were reluctant to enter into agreements that limited their absolute discretion to offer or deny safe haven to whomever they might
choose. Consequently, not until modernity did even advanced countries such as Great Britain become parties to extradition treaties.
Only five extradition agreements were entered into by Britain during
the more than six hundred years between 1174 and 1794.[576] Other
countries remained similarly reluctant to formally obligate themselves to the surrender of escaped offenders. Altogether, fewer than
ninety extradition treaties were recorded throughout the community
of nations in the period between 1718 and 1830.[577]

While the surrender of refugees, whether through formal or informal extradition, can be traced far back into antiquity, so too can the
practice of churches and municipalities granting asylum or sanctuary
to selected escapees from the wrath of authority. Compassion and
liberal treatment have often been extended not only to aliens but
also to specified classes of relatively blameless domestic offenders.
Well known is the Mosaic code's establishment of six cities of refuge
within the land of Israel to which those who took human life without malice could escape from the victim's vengeful relatives.[578] In ancient Babylon, Greece, and Rome, as well as in the Arabian Penin-
sula, escaped slaves, debtors, political refugees, and others deserving
such relief were granted similar shelter in the temples of the various
deities.[579]

Some scholars point to these early church-affiliated sanctuaries as
evidence of an ongoing cleavage between divine compassion (in
granting asylum) and princely intransigence (in denying shelter).
One scholar even suggested that asylum was nonexistent in Egypt,
India, and Persia, which he considered representative of Asia's and
Africa's "more developed" civilizations (due to their total merger of
religious and temporal authority).[580] But whether one accepts this
highly questionable conclusion that asylum had its origins in the less
developed societies (meaning the more decentralized and less totalitarian communities), there is ample evidence of early secular as well

as religious forbearance toward morally blameless persons escaping bondage or cruel punishment.

The advent of Christianity, whose adherents themselves were subjected to three centuries of persecution prior to the Roman Empire's official recognition of the religion, gave renewed support to the institution of asylum. Constantine's Edict of Toleration, which in A.D. 313 authorized churches to grant shelter to fugitives, marked the beginning of a new era. Later in the century, Theodosius formalized the church regulations concerning asylum. After the solidification of ecclesiastical authority in Europe, the Christian Church further expanded its doctrines of asylum. The Councils of Toledo (in A.D. 638 and 681) broadened the categories of those entitled to protection and established a safe haven around churches—a radius of thirty-five steps—within which the seizure of offenders was prohibited. Christians who violated asylum rights were subjected to excommunication by the church. Throughout the brutal and dark years of the Middle Ages, the clergy vigorously exercised its authority to offer asylum to the persecuted, the oppressed, and the vanquished.[581] But with the emergence of the nation-state, and in response to the zealous national assertions of sovereignty, churches began to relinquish their long-standing privileges in matters of asylum.

While asylum lost ground in the Christian world, a diminution in the role of shrines and temples as centers of refuge was taking place in Hindu, Moslem, and Buddhist societies as well. The status of contemporary religious asylum in the East is evidenced by India's recent refusal to recognize Sikh temples as places of shelter and by Saudi Arabia's use of its police in routing out fundamentalist dissidents from its mosques. Yet a modern reemergence of asylum, founded on new, nonreligious doctrines and considerations, has taken place in the post–World War II era. The foundations for this emerging support of asylum have been supplied by the uncanny merger of political pragmatism with a new outburst of international humanitarian sensitivity.[582]

The willingness to offer shelter and the refusal to return an escaped foreign offender have become issues with obvious and grave pragmatic political implications. Leniency toward fugitives from an unfriendly neighbor is merely the implementation of the Machiavellian principle that the enemy of one's enemy is a potential friend. For the republican regime of postrevolutionary France, granting shelter to fleeing antimonarchists of other countries seemed nothing less than a sound investment in the future of republicanism throughout the world. To the democratic nations fighting the Cold War, the granting of asylum to refugees from Communist totalitarian regimes was similarly a self-serving mission. The Soviet Union's 1977 Constitution likewise promised a haven to all defeated participants in an external "revolutionary [or] national liberation movement."[583] The Soviet grant of asylum thus constituted a consolation for all those who had failed in their struggle against imperialism and capitalism.

Beyond political pragmatism, a growing worldwide revulsion against the oppression of innocents has given a new and accelerated impetus to the old engines of asylum. The Mosaic law's nexus between moral blamelessness and the right to asylum has been reasserted in America and elsewhere in modern times. In pre–Civil War America, the abolitionist Underground Railroad, which offered escaped slaves shelter in the North, found its justification in the widespread moral condemnation of the institution of slavery. More than a century later in the United States, a similar moral imperative drove the members of the "Sanctuary Movement," a grassroots collection of religious and community activists, to offer shelter in their churches and homes to illegal immigrants fleeing social and political oppression in Central America.[584] Public sympathy toward refugees and other seekers of political shelter, manifested mostly in the United States and Europe in the second half of the twentieth century, demonstrates not only the continuity of the moral basis for the institution of asylum but also the growing role played by the international community and its laws in affairs that had traditionally been reserved exclusively for domestic sovereignty.

The Emergence of International Asylum

The modern institution of political asylum is directly traceable to the doctrine originally known as "the right of supplicants," which was ardently cultivated by Dutch jurist Hugo Grotius (1583–1645), a towering figure in the development of modern international law. A native of Amsterdam, Grotius was influenced by the Dutch capital's lenient policies toward religious dissidents from other countries, and his views were further shaped by the fact that Grotius himself was ultimately forced to seek political asylum in France. Grotius invoked the authority of previous jurists to support his claim that individuals should have the right to choose their country of nationality,[585] and that all states have a common duty to admit deserving refugees into their midst.[586] Despite his commitments to these and other principles of individual liberty, many of which foreshadowed the rights proclaimed by the eighteenth-century revolutions, Grotius denied citizens the right to rebel against unjust authority.[587] But as a humanitarian, he was unwilling to abandon citizens to the mercy of abusive rulers.

He proposed therefore that the international community provide succor to those suffering under tyrannical rulers. By extending asylum to those escaping injustice, Grotius pointed out, the host states would be both expressing their displeasure of foreign tyrannies and serving the humane needs of deserving members of the international community. However, Grotius limited the privilege of asylum to those he considered as suffering from "undeserved enmity." Observing that "the name of supplicants is rightly due only to those whose mind is innocent, [but] with whom fortune is angry," Grotius insisted that those "whose life is full of wicked acts have no way [by] which they may find pity or asylum."[588] Supplicants granted asylum had the further duty to "submit to the [host country's] established government and observe any regulations which are necessary in order to avoid strife."[589]

The Grotian principles of international asylum were expanded upon by scholars such as Christian von Wolff (1679–1754) and Emmerich de Vattel (1714–1767). Wolff, a professor at the new German university at Halle, was an early proponent of the theory that all state authority is the product of a rational contract between the rulers and their subjects. Although conceding that this contract might indeed be breached by those in power, Wolff, like Grotius, insisted upon the subject's duty of total obedience to the state, thereby denying citizens the right to rebel. But as a member of the German Enlightenment, Wolff, again like Grotius, sought to protect the oppressed by urging the extension of asylum "to those who have fallen into misfortune, [and] to those escaping misfortune."[590]

Vattel, a Swiss diplomat, and second only to Grotius in stature as an international jurist, was another avid supporter of asylum. He elaborated on the duty of the community of nations toward individuals who had been forcibly driven from their countries, as well as toward those who voluntarily sought asylum "to escape some punishment, or to avoid some calamity."[591] About the religious and philosophical foundations of the asylum doctrine he wrote: "A man, by being exiled or banished, does not forfeit the human character, nor consequently his right to dwell somewhere on earth. He derives this right from nature, or rather from his Author, who has destined the earth for the habitation of mankind."[592]

From these foundations the modern doctrines of asylum began to emerge. But progress toward consistent and widely accepted standards for the granting or withholding of asylum was slow. Though both international declarations and domestic developments continued to advance the theory and practice of asylum through the eighteenth and nineteenth centuries, widespread support for and the actual availability of asylum and sanctuary for oppressed political, religious, ethnic, and cultural minorities did not emerge until later. Only after the convulsive effects of the two world wars, and of such intervening upheavals as the Spanish civil war, was the international community finally galvanized into a dramatic reformation of asylum policy. In the post–World War II era in particular, the plight of persecuted minorities and others struggling for individual and group rights began to receive serious attention in world affairs. The memories of ethnic and religious persecution associated with Nazi and Fascist totalitarianism spurred some countries to unilaterally proclaim their willingness to accept those fleeing oppression,[593] although no collective or international duty to do so had emerged.[594]

The French Constitution of 1946 provided one of the first provisions for political refuge, specifying in its preamble the right of asylum for "anyone prosecuted because of his activities in the cause of freedom."[595] The 1947 Italian Constitution, in Article 10, granted similar rights to the "foreigner who is denied in his own country the effective exercise of democratic freedoms provided for by the Italian Constitution."[596] The German Federal Republic guaranteed asylum to the "politically persecuted,"[597] and several Latin American nations modeled their laws after the Constitution of pre-Castro Cuba, which recognized the right of asylum for "those persecuted for political reasons."[598]

The countries of the former Communist Eastern Bloc legislated more parochial guarantees of asylum. The Soviet Constitution and its 1977 Fundamental Law extended the right of asylum to foreigners "persecuted for upholding the interests of the working people and the cause of peace, or for participation in a revolutionary and national liberation movement."[599] The 1954 Constitution of the People's Republic of China further subjected the granting of asylum to the discretion and political proclivities of those in authority by promising shelter to any foreign national "persecuted for supporting a just cause."[600]

Even before World War II, political strife in various parts of the world stimulated efforts to protect the oppressed and to ensure the availability of sanctuary for those divested of political power. These efforts resulted in changes to both domestic and international laws. Latin American states, for example, not only acted to secure the right of asylum in their domestic laws but sought to codify that right in international treaties and conventions. On February 20, 1928, the Sixth International Conference of American States at Havana adopted a convention on asylum that safeguarded the right of refuge for political offenders.[601] Among all signatories, only the United States expressed reservations regarding the recognition of asylum as part of international law.[602] A decade later, the Second South American Conference on Private International Law, held in Montevideo on August 4, 1939, similarly adopted a treaty on political asylum and refuge.[603]

Despite these and similar efforts to extend protection to the politically persecuted, the granting of asylum continued to be viewed as a discretionary privilege vested exclusively in the discretion of each nation-state. Although individuals were entitled to apply for asylum and nation-states possessed the authority to grant it, no person had the inherent right to this protection. The denial of the individual entitlement to asylum was based, supposedly, on the legal theory that

> [i]nternational law is a law of states, not of individuals. . . . This law governs inter-state relations, not the relations of individuals who compose states . . . individuals have no direct access to it, no direct rights under it. They may be beneficiaries of certain rights and obligations which exist between states under this law, but [they are] not the depositories of such rights and obligations.[604]

Despite frequent reiterations of this stringent doctrine, the second half of the twentieth century has seen a growing departure from the traditional view of the loose relationship between the individual and international law. The contemporary law of nations has imposed increasing international duties upon individuals and, correspondingly, has enhanced the international rights of individuals. Moreover, beginning with provisions set forth by the League of Nations in 1919, which for the first time in world history sought to implement a permanent system for the protection of minority rights,[605] individuals had already been accorded procedural safeguards entitling them to petition international organs and to present claims before them.[606]

The 1966 International Covenants on Human Rights,[607] which sought to implement the right of persons to "seek and enjoy" asylum (as proclaimed in 1948 by Article 14 of the Universal Declaration of Human Rights),[608] included a specific provision regarding the right of asylum. This inclusion has been viewed by some as an implied recognition of the granting of a new individual right to "receive" or "be granted" asylum. Such expansionist assertions of the individual right to asylum, as contrasted with the earlier and more restrictive principle of the state's exclusive right to extend or deny shelter, generally proved unacceptable.

Prior to the adoption of the 1966 human rights covenants, three nations (Chile, Uruguay, and Yugoslavia) introduced before the United Nations Commission on Human Rights a joint proposal to guarantee asylum to "all persons accused or persecuted because of their participation in the struggle for national independence or political freedom or because of their activities for the achievement of the purposes and principles set forth in the Charter of the United Nations and in the Universal Declaration of Human Rights." The proposal also undertook to deny the right of asylum to persons alleged to have committed acts contrary to these same purposes and principles.[609] These liberal provisions were not adopted, however.

A similar approach by the Soviet Union called for guaranteeing the right of asylum to "all persons persecuted for their activities in defense of democratic interests, for their scientific work or for their participation in the struggle for national liberation." This proposal would have denied the right of asylum to those charged with war crimes or with offenses counter to the goals and principles of the United Nations.[610] This effort to define asylum as an individual right also failed to gain acceptance.

Rather than vest all politically persecuted persons with the right to asylum, the community of nations set out instead to offer lesser safeguards for the benefit of those who could qualify for the sympathetic title of "political refugee." A refugee was defined as a person who, owing to a well-founded fear of being persecuted for reasons of race, religion, nationality, membership of a particular social group or political opinion, is outside the country of his nationality and is unable or, owing to such fear, is unwilling to avail himself of the protection of that country; or who, not having a nationality and being outside the country of his former habitual residence is unable or, owing to such fear, is unwilling to return to it.[611]

Under this definition, an individual must demonstrate a well-founded objective fear of persecution to qualify as a refugee.[612] An individual must also be located outside his or her country of nationality or, if stateless, outside his or her country of residence.

Proponents of the right to asylum remain unsatisfied with the lesser protections secured by the recognition of an individual's refugee status, and call for granting politically endangered persons significantly greater benefits. The refugee laws act generally to prevent only the expulsion of political refugees who previously have secured legal or illegal entry into a given country.[613] An international entitlement to asylum, on the other hand, might impose a duty upon a sovereign state to admit those persecuted and hiding abroad, as well as those sailing toward the harbors or knocking upon the gates of the haven country. Until such new international asylum rights are formulated and adopted, each country remains essentially free to bar the entry of political escapees and refugees seeking sanctuary. Under America's current laws, only those who have already gained admission into a country must be accorded procedural due process by this host nation, including the guarantee of nonrefoulement—meaning that the refugee will not be expelled to his or her home country if he or she can substantiate an objective fear of persecution.[614] But for the thousands facing violence and oppression in their home countries with no passage of escape, and for those who have tried and failed to gain entry into haven states (such as Vietnamese known as the boat people in the Far East or the Haitian refugees on the high seas), much of the civilized world offers no relief similar to the shelter available to escaped slaves and other deserving asylum-seekers in antiquity.

Asylum and Political Refuge at the End of the Millennium

Recently, the institution of asylum has undergone dramatic changes worldwide in both doctrine and practice in response to newly unleashed political and socioeconomic tensions and disorder. The unprecedented worldwide escalation of tribal, ethnic, and religious strife has put unbearable strains upon the fragile asylum system of old. That nearly 1.5 million Rwandan refugees, out of a total national population of fewer than 9 million people, suddenly congregated around the border of Zaire in a period of mere weeks in 1994, typifies these postmodern realities.[615] In the same year, the United Nations High Commission for Refugees assisted more than 22 million refugees (twice the number reported in 1990, and four times the number reported in 1980)[616] who had been displaced from their native lands. Moreover, the very character of the asylum-seeker for whom the system was originally intended has changed so drastically that traditional criteria and procedures are no longer effective in dealing with this delicate and volatile international situation.

The initial theories and practices of asylum were conceived centuries ago mostly for the benefit of an elite class of refugees that no longer predominates today. The primary claimants of asylum at the end of the twentieth century no longer resemble such past asylum-seekers as Hugo Grotius, Jean-Jacques Rousseau, and Sigmund Freud. Waves of refugees escaping tribal hostilities, "ethnic cleansing," civil wars, governmental persecution, and genocide, as well as poverty and economic hardships, have been emigrating from their native lands in ever-increasing numbers, in the hopes of securing elsewhere a greater measure of safety and a better life—politically, socially, and economically. Rwandans, Cubans, Haitians, Kurds, Bosnians, Salvadorans, Mozambicans, Liberians, and Cambodians are only the most recent among the scores of peoples who have sought escape from the inhospitable and dangerous webs of their previous lives.

In the face of exploding internecine conflicts, the deficiencies of asylum doctrine have become readily apparent. The situation has become so tenuous and unpredictable that the very survival of the institution of asylum has been called into question by scholars and practitioners.[617] The backlog of cases, concerns over financial resources, and increased xenophobia in receiving countries have resulted in a negative and, at times, hostile stance toward asylum laws and their beneficiaries across the globe. A glance at existing laws and practices regarding political asylum aptly reveals the inadequacies of prevailing standards.

The current U.S. asylum law is based upon the 1980 Refugee Act,[618] which in turn is rooted in the 1967 United Nations Convention Regarding the Status of Refugees.[619] The stated goals of the 1980 Refugee Act were to fulfill America's obligations under international law, first by establishing standardized procedures for the admission of asylum-seekers, and then by removing ideological biases in the process of granting asylum.[620] Persons who have fled or are fleeing political persecution have three distinct avenues through which they may enter and be granted asylum in the United States: (1) upon initial admittance into the United States as a refugee; (2) through the forestalling or withholding of deportation if already in the country and otherwise being required to depart due to illegal entry or the expiration of previously authorized stays; and (3) upon the granting of asylum after formal admittance into the country. Each of these three methods of securing political refuge is distinct and must not be confused with the others.

The refugee laws of the United States are contained in the Immigration and Naturalization Act, which outlines the process for securing haven in the country.[621] Refugee status is available only to people outside the United States who comply with the particular prerequisites for the "refugee" designation.[622] To qualify, an applicant must be located outside his or her native country and must be "unable or unwilling to avail himself or herself of the protection of that country because of persecution or a well-founded fear of persecution on account of race, religion, nationality, membership in a particular social group or political opinion."[623] To cope with the tremendous number of refugee claims, which far exceed America's hospitality, capabilities, and readiness, the president and Congress determine through "consultation" before the end of each year, the number of refugees to be admitted into the United States the following year. Only predetermined numbers of refugees who raise a "special humanitarian concern" are admitted under this special procedure.[624]

The withholding of deportation, as a form of relief for those fearing governmental persecution abroad, is governed by the Immigration and Naturalization Act and is derived from the international legal principle of nonrefoulement. This principle stipulates that an alien must not be returned to his or her country of origin if upon such return his or her life or freedom would be endangered because of race, religion, nationality, membership in a particular social group, or political opinions.[625] To qualify for the withholding of deportation, the alien must demonstrate that it is "more likely than not" that he or she will be persecuted for one of five specified reasons.[626] If these tests are met, the withholding of deportation to the alien's native country becomes mandatory. It is not mandatory, however, that the alien be offered haven in the United States; he or she might be sheltered in a "safe" third country instead. Moreover, the withholding of deportation does not accord the alien the right to apply for permanent residence.[627]

To be eligible for the maximum category of refuge, that of asylee, the applicant must be either on American soil or at the country's border or point of entry,[628] and must meet the definition of "refugee" elaborated earlier.[629] The grant of asylum requires proof that there would be a "reasonable possibility" of persecution if the applicant were returned to his or her native country, a lesser standard than that required for the withholding of deportation.[630] Moreover, a grant of asylum is discretionary and can be conferred only upon a favorable determination by the U.S. attorney general or his delegate after an administrative hearing.[631] Recipients of asylum are permitted to apply for permanent residence in the United States.[632]

The procedural safeguards available to refuge-seekers vary according to the circumstances and categorization of the applicant. Since those who seek a withholding of deportation or a granting of asylum are necessarily physically present in the United States, they are entitled to a greater number of procedural protections, which inherently extend the length of the process and the duration of their stay in the country.[633] Those who have not successfully landed upon American soil (having been interdicted offshore by the military or other governmental agents) must face more preemptory exclusionary proceedings in which procedural rights are severely restricted.[634] It is significant that the direct grant of asylum by the United States is limited to applicants already on American soil or at its points of entry. The United States, unlike some other countries, does not grant asylum at its embassies or consular facilities, although American ambassadors may accord temporary asylum in exigent circumstances.[635]

That America's refugee and asylum policies are not carried out evenhandedly has been a long-standing allegation. Singled out for particular criticism has been the alleged practice of denying asylum to applicants from oppressive regimes with which America seeks to maintain cordial relations, while liberally granting asylum to applicants from Communist-dominated and other "hostile" nations.[636] In 1990, President George Bush and his administration sought to modify some of these objectionable practices.[637] The reforms were designed to eliminate ideological considerations from the disposition of asylum cases and thereby diminish the "reflection of . . . American foreign policy" in the granting of asylum.[638]

Despite these and similar efforts abroad to simplify and reform the procedures for the granting of refuge to politically displaced persons, the unprecedented increase in the number of asylum-seekers worldwide has created a global crisis. In 1991 the cases pending before the United States Immigration and Naturalization Service alone stood in excess of 329,000.[639] The upsurge in the number of applicants has produced a growing perception that many of those desiring asylum in the United States are mere seekers of economic advantage rather than desperate victims in need of political shelter. One proposed remedy for the incredible backlog of cases in the United States has been a call for eliminating or severely restricting the availability of the typically long and time-consuming process of judicial review in asylum cases.[640] Another remedy has been a call for the early expulsion of asylum-seekers who fail to supply accurate documents or who otherwise make frivolous claims.[641]

The status of asylum-seekers abroad mirrors their tenuous standing in America. In 1992 Germany dramatically altered its asylum policies in response to the massive influx of refugees from its former Communist neighbors in the East. Prior to this about-face, Germany had adhered to one of the world's most liberal asylum policies. The country's post–World War II Constitution guaranteed the right to asylum to all those who were "persecuted on political grounds."[642] But since the asylum-granting process was meticulous and lengthy, the intervening rights and entitlements of applicants became very costly for the country's treasury. For decades the German government housed, clothed, and fed asylees at its own expense during the pendency of the asylum process, a period that often lasted more than three years. These economic benefits accompanying the lengthy asylum process seemed to encourage an ever-growing number of asylum applicants.[643] By October 1992 around 50,000 refugees were entering Germany each month, and the total number of applicants for political asylum numbered 438,191—an increase of 71 percent over 1991. Moreover, the number of asylum applicants in Germany in

1992 exceeded the total number of asylum applicants in all other European countries combined.[644]

To counteract this massive influx and its accompanying burdens, Germany amended its Constitution in 1992, abridging the right of asylum through new standards. The new law, which went into effect in July 1993,[645] reflects major changes in Germany's political climate. Although the right of asylum has not been eliminated from German law, applicants who originate from oppressive countries but who enter Germany from "transit" countries that do not persecute political opponents are no longer eligible for asylum. To implement this policy, Germany maintains a list of transit countries for which there is a rebuttable presumption of nonpersecution.[646] These developments, accompanied by more restrictive procedural standards, bring Germany in line with current standards established by the European community to curtail the institution of asylum.

Today asylum is increasingly perceived within the European community as an emerging threat to the Continent's common good and harmony. Critics of these restrictive policies have voiced their growing alarm as well:

> Fearful that a continuing commitment to refugee protection threatens the viability of a union premised on external closure, states have taken the facile approach of elaborating a policy of generalized deterrence: all persons seeking entry from less-developed states—whether or not they have a valid claim to refugee status—will be stigmatized as potential threats to European communal well-being, and their prospects for ingress consequently constrained.[647]

Other commentators similarly suggest that if the nations of Europe fail to achieve a common asylum policy, individual countries will deem themselves invited to establish restrictive laws based upon "the lowest common denominator in the criteria and procedures used to determine refugee status on a regional basis."[648]

Western proponents of liberal asylum policy view the Maastricht Treaty,[649] which has commingled asylum issues with criminal matters, as evidence that the Western European community and its citizenry are increasingly viewing asylum-seekers as economic profiteers. Eastern European countries are likewise grappling with the social, economic, and humanitarian pressures produced by mass population displacements. Prior to the collapse of the Soviet Union, Eastern European countries readily granted asylum to those with so-called socialistic persuasions. The crisis in former Yugoslavia, the growing ethnic tensions elsewhere, and the mounting economic hardships within the region have also acted in recent years to dramatically curtail the availability of asylum in Central and Eastern Europe.[650] Only the Bosnia and Kosovo brutalities acted temporarily to awaken the European conscience.

At the end of the millennium, the institution of asylum stands, however, at a crossroads. Its importance has perhaps never been greater, yet its legitimacy and efficacy have never been more strained and subject to challenge. The profusion of asylum-seekers, compounded by their changing character, has overwhelmed the world community's goodwill. When Dante sought asylum and refuge in Bologna upon his political exile from Florence, he was not accompanied by multitudes of refugees. Today whole communities, indeed nations, are expelled or forced into exile for political, economic, and a variety of other reasons. The system designed to accommodate Dante can no longer bear the burdens of modernity.[651] While the demand for asylum throughout the globe continues to rise, the availability of asylum continues to decline. Lost in the shuffle is the political offender's hope for a safe haven while he or she continues to await a new and better world order.

The Expansion of Extradition

Asylum and extradition can best be portrayed as opposite responses to the pleas of those who assert political motives to justify their quest for foreign shelter. The doctrine of asylum supports the refuge-seeker's appeal for a safe haven outside his or her home country. The doctrine of extradition, on the other hand, requires a host country to surrender to the home country fugitives charged with offenses against the requesting regime. Although asylum and extradition have been practiced since antiquity, the world community has found itself increasingly torn between the conflicting demands imposed by these contrasting doctrines. Such conflicts are inevitable when existing scholarship and doctrine cannot readily distinguish between an asylum-seeker's allegations of "political persecution" at home and his or her government's counter-assertions that the asylum-seeker is nothing more than a "common criminal" at best, and an "international criminal" at worst.

The need for coherent and consistent formulas for resolving these disagreements has grown increasingly evident in recent years. Questions of asylum and extradition are no longer viewed as having merely individual or domestic implications. The granting of asylum and extradition requests today implicates not only the resolution of pressing humanitarian dilemmas but also the maintenance of public order worldwide. It is feared that the ready availability of asylum abroad might escalate escape and emigration by disgruntled populations and even promote protest, unrest, and resistance movements at home. Conversely, the ready granting of extradition and the return of persons charged with political offenses might discourage and reduce the incidence of rebellion and political criminality in the requesting countries. The United States record pertaining to the granting of asylum and the denying of extradition for America-bound Irish rebels and dissidents helps illustrate the impact that the policies of host countries can have upon the maintenance of law and order in the offenders' countries of origin.

Most host nations grant or withhold requests for asylum and extradition based upon their own national assessments of the events taking place in the home countries of those involved. This self-centered and self-serving approach has produced an uncertain and uneasy balance between these two conflicting international policies. Countries can essentially choose to either ignore or even support the status quo within neighboring nations by denying asylum to escaping political activists. Conversely, they can elect to indirectly encourage resistance to authority and even endorse revolution in other nations by readily granting asylum and refusing the extradition of unsuccessful rebels. We can best understand how this precarious international balance between asylum and extradition came about by briefly reviewing the history of extradition.

Frederic Martens, a leading nineteenth-century scholar, suggested that the history of extradition can be divided into three periods.[652] During the first period, stretching from antiquity until the end of the seventeenth century, extradition (taking place mostly through informal executive exchanges rather than through the enforcement of treaty obligations) was resorted to chiefly to accomplish the surrender of political offenders and heretics. In the second period, covering the eighteenth century and the first half of the nineteenth century, bilateral treaty-based obligations were established between nations

mostly for the extradition of "common" rather than political offenders. The treaties of that period were general agreements between
neighboring states designed to control roving bands of military deserters who posed a danger to travel and transportation. The third
and latest phase of extradition commenced around the middle of the
nineteenth century when the advent of railways and steamships
made public travel, and thus international escape for offenders, easier and more accessible. In this third period, extradition assumed its
new role as part of a concerted international scheme for the suppression of major transnational crimes and criminals. "The increasing
mobility and elusiveness of common criminals presented States with
an urgent problem of controlling their movements," wrote Australian extradition expert I. A. Shearer. "[A] state which did not take
effective measures against the incursion of foreign criminals would
quickly find itself a seething haven for the undesirables of other
lands."[653]

The leaders of liberal jurisprudence initially voiced strong misgiv-
ings about the expansion of extradition. Cesare de Baccaria, the Italian founder of modern penology, opposed extradition so long as oppressive procedures and capricious penalties afflicting returned
fugitives prevailed in their home countries.[654] Responding to similar
concerns, democratic countries such as England and the United
States remained reluctant to constrict their previously liberal traditions of granting asylum to the politically oppressed. But as the Continental penal system underwent liberalizing reforms, humanitarian
concerns against surrendering suspects became less pressing. Furthermore, the growing flow of immigrants to England and the
United States brought an end to the sense of geographic isolation
and security experienced earlier in these countries. A new awareness
of the potential domestic dangers posed by alien fugitives made the
new call for wider extradition practices more appealing.

The 1794 Jay Treaty between England and the United States was
the first extradition agreement for either nation. Contained in a general treaty of amity, commerce, and navigation, this agreement provided that each government would "deliver up to justice" to the
other country all escaped persons charged with murder and
forgery.[655] To safeguard against unsubstantiated demands, the treaty
required that surrender be based on such evidence that would be sufficient to have the person arrested and charged had the crime been

committed in the host country. Despite their early agreement, neither England nor the United States pursued further extradition treaties with other countries until the middle of the nineteenth century. Indeed, the term "extradition" was not introduced into American statutes until 1848,[656] and only in 1870 did the term, which evidently saw its earliest use in France at the end of the eighteenth century, acquire formal legal standing in England.[657]

In 1842 the Webster-Ashburton Treaty between England and the United States replaced the expired Jay Treaty.[658] The list of extraditable offenses was expanded to include arson, piracy, robbery, and uttering forged papers, in addition to murder and forgery. England and France entered into a similar treaty in 1843.[659] Subsequently, England entered into two other extradition treaties, one with Denmark in 1862 and another with Prussia in 1864.[660] Although these early treaty efforts were sporadic, the passing of the English Extradition Act in 1870,[661] which signaled the advent of broad parliamentary support for extradition, stimulated England to enter into extradition treaties with thirty-four more countries between 1870 and 1910.[662]

Although America's initial experience with extradition was limited to two treaties with England, its extradition obligations were soon to undergo a major expansion. In rapid succession, treaties were concluded with France in 1843, the Hawaiian Islands in 1849, Switzerland in 1850, and Prussia in 1852. By 1870 the United States had entered into extradition treaties with seventeen countries. Shortly thereafter, the leading English extradition expert, Sir Edward Clarke, conceded: "In the matter of extradition, the American law was . . . better than that of any country in the world; and the decisions of the American judges are the best existing expositions of the duty of extradition, in its relations at once to the judicial rights of nations and the general interests of the civilization of the world."[663] Over the next hundred years, America's extradition treaty relations with other countries grew geometrically, reaching eighty-one foreign states by 1970.[664] "These treaty relations," wrote I. A. Shearer, "represent without doubt the most consistent and most comprehensive effort by any State to cooperate with other States in the suppression of fugitive criminals."[665]

Arguably France was even more aggressive in its pursuit of international cooperation on this subject. In the eighteenth century,

France concluded numerous extradition treaties with adjoining countries, and in 1841 the French Ministry of Justice boasted that even when extradition treaties were lacking, the cordial relations maintained with officials of foreign nations enabled France to always obtain "by individual arrangements, the surrender of offenders."[666]

In the nineteenth century, France actively expanded its extradition relations with remote overseas countries, including the United States in 1843, Columbia in 1850, and Venezuela in 1853.[667] By 1870 France had developed extradition treaties with twenty-eight nations. Even more important was French leadership in developing new substantive standards as well as procedural safeguards applicable to extradition. These included (1) the exemption of political offenders from extradition; (2) the right of countries to refuse extradition of their own nationals; and (3) limiting of the post-extradition trial and punishment to the specific offenses for which extradition was granted (the principle of "specialty").

As the modern structure of extradition law evolved, three distinct national enabling regimes emerged. For a small group of countries, domestic legislation is deemed necessary to establish the national power to extradite as well as to specify conditions and limitations upon the practice. But once the extradition power is legislatively defined, the country's executive may engage in extradition practices without any further authorization. For a second group of nations, extradition powers are attributed to the bilateral or multilateral treaties themselves (e.g., the Jay Treaty between England and the United States).[668] These treaties usually set forth the types of offenders subject to extradition and the procedures under which extradition is to take place. Multinational conventions, on diverse topics of common global concern, supply a third and growing source of authority for contemporary extradition. These conventions (dealing with such matters as slavery, counterfeit currency, traffic in narcotic drugs, and the punishment of aircraft hijacking)[669] impose upon the signatories the obligation to either prosecute or extradite all known offenders within their reach.

At the end of the twentieth century, international treaty-making has thus been combined with domestic legislation to create an intensive and quite effective worldwide network of extradition agreements and practices. This rapidly emerging international system for the detention and surrender of those seeking to escape the criminal sanctions of their native countries might, at first glance, seem to pose an insurmountable obstacle to the political offender's quest for a friendly shelter. Yet the expanding duty of states to turn common offenders back to their pursuers has been accompanied by a corresponding growth in the international protections available to those claiming to be political offenders.

Sheltering Political Offenders: "The Onward March of Humanity"

Until the dawn of the modern era, as previously noted, international extradition was utilized largely as a weapon against escapees wanted for treason or rebellion, rather than against common offenders.[670] Thomas Hobbes, as well as Hugo Grotius, reflected the thinking of their times in considering political offenses as graver than ordinary crimes, thus justifying more severe and comprehensive penal responses.[671] "Historically," wrote American legal scholar Cherif Bassiouni, "extradition was the [particular] means resorted to for the surrender of political offenders. These were persons guilty of crimes of *lèse majestè* which included . . . treason, attempts against the monarchy or the life of the monarch, and even contemptuous behavior toward the monarch."[672] This role of extradition is reflected in the 1834 trilateral treaty between Austria, Prussia, and Russia limiting extradition to those accused of high treason, armed rebellion, acts against the security of the throne, and acts of *lèse majesté*.[673] The three monarchies' shared interest in safeguarding their power against political challengers was evidently of a higher order than their concern for the capture of mere common criminals.

"The French Revolution of 1789 and its aftermath," wrote Bassiouni, "started the transformation of [political crime from what] was the extraditable offense *par excellence* to what has since become the nonextraditable offense *par excellence*."[674] Revolutionary fervor, in combination with revolutionary doctrines, dramatically changed the public perception of the political offender. The new attitude was expressed most succinctly in France's 1791 Jacobin Constitution, which declared in Article 120 that the French Republic "grants asylum to foreigners banished from their countries for the cause of freedom. [Asylum, however,] . . . will be denied to tyrants!"[675] Affirming his own commitment to "the cause of freedom," even the authoritarian Napoleon condemned the Senate of the city of Hamburg for surrendering to the British government three Irishmen accused of involvement in the Irish rebellion of 1798. "Virtue and courage are the support of a State; servility and lowness are its ruin," he pronounced. "You have violated the laws of hospitality in such a way that even the wandering tribes of the desert would blush with shame."[676]

The rhetoric of the new revolutionary governments in France and America continued to raise critical questions about the legitimacy of governments and about the people's right to rebel. Traditional notions regarding the absolute authority of rulers began giving way to new philosophies that vested the people with a mantle of sovereign power. Consequently, the legitimacy of a government was no longer considered permanent and absolute but instead "relative to the rightness of its actions and the consent of the governed."[677] Moreover, although those in power continued to vigorously battle their domestic challengers, they could no longer ignore the likelihood of a political role reversal through revolution or coup d'état. As those vested with authority contemplated the possibility of hostile successors in office (creating a likelihood of their own need for political refuge), the old and firm support for the extradition of political opponents underwent reexamination and change.

Despite the new revolutionary stirrings, treaties committing countries to extradite political offenders continued to emerge through the middle of the nineteenth century. The most adamant insistence upon the duty of nations to surrender political fugitives continued to come from the three autocratic members of Europe's Holy Alliance (Russia, Austria, and Prussia), who were frequently threatened by social and economic uprisings and thus shared a common fear of revolution.[678] Indeed, as soon as France's Bonapartist regime was crushed, the 1815 Congress of Vienna began a vigorous campaign to restore the old order in all respects. In particular, the alliance sought to root out rebels and revolutionaries from the European continent (particularly to prevent the escape of those who had participated in the Austro-Hungarian and Russian political upheavals). In the pursuit of this objective the alliance even pressured the Swiss Confederation, until then a haven for those seeking political shelter, to impose stiff immigration controls.

At the 1820 Congress of Troppau, the Swiss were asked to suppress political agitation among German refugees in the Grisons Canton. The following year the Holy Alliance sent a diplomatic note to the Swiss, requesting the expulsion of refugees who had fled from the political turmoil in Austrian-ruled Piedmont. In 1822 the alliance proposed that all European states "assist" the Swiss in expelling political refugees. Only Great Britain declined the request. To apply additional pressure, France mobilized its troops near the Swiss border in 1823, while Chancellor Metternich of Austria declared that the Swiss Confederation would lose its neutrality status if it continued to harbor and support political refugees. The Swiss Confederation ultimately succumbed to these demands, voting in 1823 to prohibit the immigration of political refugees from surrounding nations.[679] In 1849, Russia and Austria joined to seek the extradition of some 5,000 rebels who had found refuge in Turkey after a failed anti-Habsburg rebellion in Hungary. Supported by Great Britain, Turkey refused to extradite the Hungarian dissidents in what became one of the nineteenth century's major successful tests of the political offender's protection from extradition.[680]

The surge of liberal thinking and popular sympathy for political offenders at the time is well illustrated by the dramatic events surrounding the *Galotti* decision. Having rebelled against the government of Naples, Galotti fled to France. In requesting Galotti's extradition, the Neapolitan government promised to the French that Galotti would be tried only for his common, nonpolitical offenses. After Galotti's return by France, Naples violated its pledge. Tried for his role in the 1820 revolution, Galotti was sentenced to death. The French immediately revoked their extradition decree and demanded Galotti's return. When Naples refused to comply, France sent battleships to Naples and threatened to declare war. Galotti's sentence was promptly commuted to exile,[681] and France declared it would never again request or grant the extradition of political offenders.

The Galotti episode spurred an 1834 treaty between France and Belgium that created the first explicit international prohibition against the extradition of political offenders.[682] Though no such limitation was contained in the later 1843 treaty between France and England,[683] another treaty that same year between France and the United States specifically exempted from extradition those accused of "any crime or offense of a purely political character."[684] This became the first official recognition of the political offender's unique standing under U.S. law, supplying renewed evidence of the country's traditional liberalism in matters of political refuge and asylum. However, the American commitment to the protection of the political asylum-seeker was hardly absolute or permanent. Neither the subsequent 1849 treaty with the Hawaiian Islands nor the 1852 treaty with Prussia mentioned political offenses at all. But the exception did appear in the 1850 treaty with Switzerland and in the 1855 treaty with the Two Sicilies.

In 1849 the British prime minister, Lord Palmerston, advanced his own government's liberal inclinations in support of the political offender's right to a safe haven: "The laws of hospitality, the dictates of humanity [and] the general feelings of mankind, forbid such surrenders; and any independent Government which of its free will were to make such surrender, would be deservedly and universally stigmatized as degraded and dishonored."[685] Soon thereafter, England and France concluded a treaty that included, for the first time in English diplomatic practice, provisions for the exemption of political offenders from extradition. The treaty included also the principle of "specialty," which limited the prosecution of extradited offenders to the crimes specified in the extradition request.[686] Parliament failed, however, to approve the necessary legislation for the implementation of this treaty, in part because the treaty's requirement of prima facie evidence of guilt before the granting of extradition was considered overly onerous.

Despite the parliamentary failure, Britain's leadership continued to profess a profound sympathy for the political offense exception. Incensed at Gibraltar's British governor for extraditing several escaped rebels to Spain in 1815, Sir James Mackintosh—echoing Napoleon's earlier condemnation of the city of Hamburg—declared before Parliament: "Shall a British general perpetrate a violation of the right of supplicant strangers at which an Arab sheik would have shuddered!"[687] English support for fugitives condemned by unjust laws was also manifested in several British responses to demands for the return of runaway American slaves. In September 1853 an American slave, John Anderson, escaped from his master. Three weeks later he encountered a Missouri plantation owner by the name of Diggs, to whom he offered himself for sale so that he could be near his wife. Rejecting the offer, Diggs instead captured Anderson as a runaway, intending to turn him in for a reward.[688] Anderson escaped again, with Diggs and four of his slaves in pursuit. Cornered, Anderson stabbed Diggs fatally in the chest and back and thereafter made his way to Canada, where he lived as a free man for seven years.

In 1860, Anderson was arrested in Canada on an extradition application from Missouri. Sympathetic Canadians filed a writ of habeas corpus on Anderson's behalf. Chief Justice Robinson of the Canadian court of the Queen's Bench noted that under the municipal law of Missouri Diggs had been authorized to arrest Anderson. Under Canada's law, the killing of a man legally authorized to make an arrest was considered murder, and murder was an extraditable offense. Any circumstances justifying Anderson's action were therefore for a Missouri jury rather than a Canadian judge to consider. Furthermore, the Canadian court was not persuaded by the argument that even if acquitted of murder in Missouri, Anderson would revert to slavery upon his return to the state.[689] The Canadian decision calling for Anderson's return to Missouri generated widespread attention and concern in England. The Secretary for the Colonies promptly instructed the governor of Canada to withhold the warrant for Anderson's extradition, noting that London required more time to consider the matter. Soon thereafter, the Canadian court reversed its former decision on technical grounds and discharged the prisoner.

In an earlier case, named after an American slave ship, another British encounter with escaped American slaves produced an even greater outpouring of sympathy for those striking out for liberty. The *Creole*, an American slave ship en route from Hampton Roads, Virginia, to New Orleans, was seized by members of its human cargo. In the uprising, the captain and his mate were wounded and one of the slave owners was killed. When the ship sailed into Nassau, the British governor put aboard a guard at the request of the American consul, and two magistrates were appointed to make further investigations. Nineteen slaves who were implicated in the mutiny and murder were confined in Nassau after the governor refused to hand them over to U.S. authorities, and the remaining slaves aboard the ship were freed. Ultimately, the nineteen originally accused of piracy were acquitted after a trial before an English court.[690]

Despite the consternations created in England by unpopular and unjust foreign requests for the return of rebelling slaves, two more decades were to elapse before Great Britain formally committed itself against the extradition of political offenders, be they slaves or freemen. Only in 1868 did the English House of Commons Select Committee on Extradition urge legislation to expressly exempt political offenders from extradition.[691] Two years later the British Extradition Act of 1870 recognized that political offenders deserved special exemption,[692] although Parliament neglected to specify in detail who was to be accorded this privileged "political" status.

From Doctrine to Practice: The Many Faces of Political Offenses

Although the fundamental distinction between "common" and "political" offenses had been recognized both internationally and in the domestic laws of several countries by the end of the nineteenth century, the precise definition of the terms "political offense" and "political offender" remained unclear and parochial. In most international treaties, as well as in domestic legislation, the terms appeared undefined, evidently reflecting a desire to allow the various sovereigns considerable flexibility in their application. This desire to permit each nation the opportunity and freedom to construe "political offenses" as it wished, as well as to give nations the option to modify the term to suit changing circumstances, continues to this day.

The first American legal document regarding political offenses—the 1843 treaty with France—referred to "purely political crimes and misdemeanors," without offering further guidance on what constituted those offenses.[693] The Belgian extradition law of October 1, 1833, being the progenitor of all modern statutory and treaty provisions dealing with political offenders, similarly utilized the broad terms "political offense" and "acts connected with a political offense" but failed to define them.[694] The British Extradition Act of 1870, which articulated the English doctrine regarding the nonextradition of political offenders, likewise made general reference to offenses "of a political character."[695] The outcome of all this doctrinal nonspecificity has been to vest in the judicial and executive branches of the various countries the power to mold and modify, on a case-by-case basis, their own notions of political criminality.

The language of the American, Belgian, and British formulations focuses on the political nature of the offenses committed, rather than on the status, affiliation, or motives of the perpetrators. At first glance, this would suggest that all those whose acts fall within a specified category of "political offenses"—whatever their motivations (be they altruistic or venal) or affiliations (be they "loners" or members of political collectives)—might be exempt from extradition. On the other hand, offenders motivated by purely political or ideological causes could not escape extradition and punishment if their acts did not fall within the category of "political offenses." But these self-evident conclusions have not taken hold in the evolving worldwide interpretation of the law of extradition.

In the absence of a predominant formula, a variety of approaches that aid in the identification of political offenses and offenders have been developed in the academic literature as well as in the practice of nations. Scholars have sought to distinguish between offenses that might be viewed as "purely" political and those deemed as "related." Little agreement has been generated in this pursuit. Seeking to encompass within the "purely" political category those acts that directly threaten the existence or security of the state, while supposedly posing little direct danger to the well-being of individual citizens, scholars initially restricted this class to treason, sedition, and espionage.[696]

Even greater uncertainty has developed with regard to "related" political offenses, a category of antistate activities that tend also to impact directly upon innocent citizens and their personal well-being. In the European literature especially, the "related" group was further divided into "mixed" offenses *(délits complexes)* and "connected" political offenses *(délits connexes).*[697] Mixed offenses, though directed against the state, are usually thought to be acts that in themselves constitute common crimes. Closely allied to the purely political offenses, mixed offenses might include the assassination of heads of state, the kidnaping of political leaders, and similar offenses that, despite their injury to individuals, are directed primarily against the state. Connected political offenses, on the other hand, have as their ultimate goal only a desire to secure, change, or redistribute political power. Such connected conduct as bank robberies and extortion against citizens places the burden of the offenses on private individuals instead of the state.

The difficulties in distinguishing mixed from connected political offenses have caused this distinction to fall into general disuse. But the earlier delineation between "purely" and "related" political offenses continues to have its adherents. Even though contemporary jurisprudence has abandoned the rigidity of these earlier classifications, the nexus or "relatedness" of an act of resistance to a stated political cause, as well as its effect upon innocent citizens (somewhat related to the question of proportionality), continue as important questions in the definitional approaches to political offenses.

Distinct from these scholarly attempts, the world's major legal systems (relying either upon executive or judicial decisions and interpretations) have continued to develop a variety of other doctrinal classifications in their efforts to differentiate political from common offenses. Not surprisingly, this organic process, carried out by nations with divergent legal and political traditions, has not converged upon a unified approach. Three general strains of thought have emerged, however: the Anglo-American "political incident" theory, the Continent's "political motivation" theory, and the "injured rights" principle (which serves to supplement the other two approaches).

The Political Incident Doctrine

In Anglo-American jurisprudence, two conditions must converge in order to convert an otherwise criminal act into a political offense. First, a political revolt, movement, or disturbance must exist, and second, the offense must be committed not only in the course of such a disturbance but "in furtherance" of it. The 1891 *Castioni* decision supplies an oft-repeated illustration for this traditional English test. Castioni, a citizen of the Swiss canton of Ticono, led disgruntled local residents in an armed attack on a government building, resulting in the fatal shooting of a public official. When Castioni sought refuge in Great Britain, the English court refused to surrender him, holding that "crimes otherwise extraditable become political offenses if they were incidental to and formed part of a political disturbance."[698]

The subsequent 1894 *Meunier* decision restated this test, stressing the need for a political disturbance that involves "contending parties."[699] Some have considered this requirement for a political disturbance with contending parties as a damper on the claims of the lone or unaffiliated political rebel. Yet the restrictive *Castioni-*

Meunier doctrine remained in force until 1955, when England's doctrine was radically reassessed in *Ex parte Kolczynski*. In *Kolczynski*, Communist Poland sought the extradition of the mutinous crew of a small Polish fishing trawler. The crew, after putting the captain and some other seamen under restraint, had sought political asylum in an English port. Under the *Castioni-Meunier* rationale, the seamen would have had to demonstrate that they were part of an organized struggle against the government of Poland. Since no such resistance movement existed at the time, the refugees called for a more liberal definition. Responding to the argument of the crew members that they had rebelled against those in authority, and taking notice of "the law prevalent in the Republic of Poland today," Lord Goddard denied the Polish government's request for extradition. He concluded that it was "necessary, if only for reasons of humanity, to give a wider and more generous meaning to the words ['offense of a political character'] . . . without in any way encouraging the idea that ordinary crimes which have no political significance will be thereby excused."[700]

I. A. Shearer described the *Kolczynski* decision "as the high water mark of liberality" in the English definition of political crimes, for its departure from the traditional requirement that a political offense had to be concurrent with a broad-based political uprising.[701] The decision affirmed, however, that acts for which extradition would be denied must be politically motivated and directed toward political ends. It was also apparent that the political offender's protection against extradition was to be liberally interpreted where return was sought by totalitarian governments.

Shortly thereafter, however, the English courts rejected an attempt to further extend the newly expanded political offense exception to religiously motivated behavior. The case of *Schtraks v. The Government of Israel* involved an Israeli government request for the extradition of one of its nationals who had sought refuge in England.[702] Wanted for kidnapping and perjury, Schtraks argued that his offenses were political. Before fleeing to England, Schtraks had defied an Israeli court order to return a young man to his natural parents. Having previously lived with the Schtraks family, the boy in question had been given a strictly orthodox Jewish upbringing. Fearing that his religious life would be disrupted by a return to his secular parents, Schtraks spirited the boy out of the country. Since Israel's religious political parties supported the accused's position (calling public meetings on the subject throughout the country) and the issue was debated in that country's Knesset, Schtraks persisted in his claim that the offense was political.

Rejecting Schtraks's arguments and granting Israel's extradition request, the House of Lords acknowledged that religion and politics were closely allied in the state of Israel. It conceded also that some of the country's political parties were founded on religious ideologies, and that the question of religious education was a controversial political issue. But the House of Lords unanimously concluded that the offense had not been committed for a political purpose. The evidence, in the court's opinion, strongly suggested that the crime was privately motivated rather than being intended as an act of political resistance and protest.

The American courts had voiced their general adherence to the English definition of political offenses as early as 1894. Echoing the 1891 *Castioni* decision, the U.S. court presiding over in *In re Ezeta* defined "political offenses" as acts committed "in the course of civil war, insurrection or political commotion."[703] This standard remains virtually unchanged in American extradition law and practice to this day, despite numerous efforts to liberalize the law by abandoning the civil war or insurrection requirement, as sometimes has been done in England. In 1963 an American court commented favorably in *In re Gonzalez* on the English stance in the *Kolczynski* case and called for a similar liberalization of the political exception in America, especially with regard to fugitives from totalitarian regimes. Reviewing the evidence before it, however, the *Gonzalez* court concluded reluctantly that the facts did not disclose "a case in which the acts in question were blows struck in the cause of freedom against a repressive totalitarian regime."[704]

In the United States, as in England, the initial extradition decision is made by the courts. But the leading role of the judiciary in England has not been duplicated in American law, where the executive branch has the power to override judicial denials of the political offense claim. This, of course, has broadened the opportunity of offenders to be granted political shelter in the United States.[705] Still, the joint authority of the judiciary and the executive has tended to produce controversial results and politically charged determinations. In 1908 a U.S. magistrate approved the czarist Russian government's request for the extradition of Krishian Rudewitz, a Russian revolutionary wanted on charges of murder, arson, burglary, robbery, and larceny. But Secretary of State Elihu Root, under pressure from public opinion, decided to override the magistrate's decision. In the exercise of his executive power, Root concluded that the offenses were political and Rudewitz was permitted to remain in the United States.[706]

Despite the greater potential for leniency afforded by America's combination of judicial and executive discretion, the country's tradition of defining political offenses on an ad hoc and case-by-case basis seems inadequate today, especially in the face of mounting rebellion and internal political turmoil worldwide. Taken over time, America's extradition decisions have not been principled and consistent. The political offense exception has often been applied to the deserving and undeserving alike. In one contemporary decision, smacking of political partiality, an American court refused to extradite to Batista-ruled Cuba two members of Fidel Castro's revolutionary group wanted for the murder of a prisoner.[707] Another controversy was engendered by Yugoslavia's request for the extradition of Andrija Artukovic, a former interior minister in the Nazi-affiliated Independent State of Croatia who was charged with the mass murder of some 200,000 political opponents in the World War II era.[708] The U.S. Department of State, supporting Yugoslavia's request for extradition, argued that Artukovic's offenses were not "necessarily connected with a [political] struggle for power." The State Department argued further that even an alleged "political" intent could not excuse the genocide of national, ethnic, racial, or religious groups.[709] But the U.S. magistrate assigned to the case concluded that insufficient evidence was submitted regarding the accused's guilt, and furthermore "that the crimes charged [were] political in character."[710] After nearly twenty years, and following a new extradition request filed by Yugoslavia in 1977, the United States finally granted the extradition and deported Artukovic to Yugoslavia.[711] On May 14, 1986, he was convicted and sentenced to death by firing squad, but the sentence could not be carried out due to Artukovic's death in prison.[712]

In these and other instances, America has been criticized for its idiosyncratic and ad hoc application of extradition law. Other significant problems have been noted as well. The requirement for a "con-

nection" between the charged crime and an ongoing public disturbance has been challenged by I. A. Shearer, who observed critically
that

> if the situation which puts the fugitive in opposition to the requesting govern-
> ment is not accompanied by violence, . . . if the offense is not committed in the
> course of and incidentally to . . . a violent disturbance, the offense . . . cannot
> be characterized as political. Thus an act which preceded and perhaps precipi-
> tated the violent disturbance would not qualify as a political offense.[713]

This need for a connection played an important role in *Jimenez v.
Aristeguieta,* which involved Venezuela's request for the return of its
former president Marco Jimenez.[714] Overthrown by a coup, Jimenez
fled to the United States, but the new Venezuelan regime demanded
his extradition on the grounds that he had committed common
crimes during his term in office, including the receipt of "kickbacks"
on government contracts. An American court granted extradition,
pointing out that there was "no evidence that the financial crimes
charged were committed in the course of and incidentally to a revolutionary uprising or other violent political disturbances."[715]

The requirement of a connection between the offense and an ongoing political movement or uprising creates particularly difficult
problems when the haven country recognizes the existence of "contending parties" but the requesting government is unwilling to concede such a fact. For several decades the British government had
thus voiced complaints against American tolerance toward Irish militants who sought shelter in the United States. The unwillingness of
U.S. courts to grant English requests for the extradition of escaped
Irish offenders became a sensitive matter in the traditionally friendly
Anglo-American relationship. In 1979 for example, the United Kingdom, in *In re McMullen*, sought the extradition of a member of the
Provisional Irish Republican Army (PIRA) for a bomb attack on a
British army station that resulted in the death of a civilian. The federal magistrate in California, citing *Castioni*, denied extradition on
the grounds that a political disturbance existed in Northern Ireland
and that, despite the death of a civilian, the bombing had been directed at a military target.[716]

In 1981 a federal magistrate in New York had before him
Desmond Macklin, an alleged member of the PIRA who had been
accused of the illegal possession of firearms and the attempted mur-

der of a British soldier. Relying again on *Castioni* the magistrate ruled that the alleged acts were political offenses and thus nonextraditable.[717] In 1983 a California federal court was confronted with another PIRA member, William Joseph Quinn, who was wanted on charges of murder and conspiracy stemming from a series of bombing incidents. Again the court denied the extradition, finding that the bombings were directed primarily at British governmental targets.[718] The final case in this Irish quartet appeared before a New York federal court in 1984 in regard to PIRA member Joseph Doherty, who was wanted for the death of a British army captain in an ambush of an army patrol in Northern Ireland. Once more, the court denied extradition on the grounds that the offense constituted a "political offense exception in its most classic form."[719]

Responding to growing charges that America had become a safe haven for Irish terrorists, the United States finally agreed to an overhaul of its 150-year-old extradition treaty with England.[720] Despite strong popular and congressional opposition, a supplemental treaty was signed between the two countries on June 25, 1985, and ratified later by the U.S. Senate.[721] The supplemental treaty's first article limits the hitherto undefined political exception clause by excluding from it several classes of conduct what American courts, at earlier times, had usually recognized as political and therefore nonextraditable offenses. The excluded offenses, defined as "crimes of violence typically committed by terrorists," included aircraft hijacking and sabotage, offenses against internationally protected persons, hostage-taking, murder, manslaughter, malicious assault, kidnaping, possession of firearms, explosives, or ammunition, and serious property damage. Under the new agreement, those charged with these specified offenses were no longer to be exempted from extradition to England, whether or not they were part of an ongoing political uprising. The revised treaty thereby limits protection from extradition only to those resistance fighters willing to forswear most forms of violent struggle. Of course, political activists committed to only peaceful means or civil disobedience are not likely to be sought out for extradition in the first place.

It has been argued that the inconsistency and capriciousness of U.S. extradition law and practice became particularly apparent in cases involving deposed foreign dictators in search of an American haven. In 1980 the United States refused Iranian demands to extradite the Shah of Iran, whose torture and murder of political opponents took place not in the course of a violent disturbance but served rather as a precipitating factor for the Islamic revolution that finally toppled the Peacock Throne.[722] In 1986 the United States similarly refused to consider the return of Ferdinand Marcos, who had been charged with several "common" criminal offenses, to his native Philippines.[723]

Despite these many shortcomings, the Anglo-American political incident theory has nevertheless been echoed in the practice of other countries, including the civil law nations of Latin America. Although the Latin American legal tradition has manifested greater tolerance toward political asylum than have English and American common law traditions, it is the Anglo-American rather than the Continental view of the political exception that has taken root there. This common law–derived South American position is illustrated by Argentina's 1957 request for the extradition of Guillermo Patricio Kelly and others from Chile. Kelly, an avowed anti-Communist, was sought by Argentina for robbery and murder committed during a raid on the Communist Party's headquarters in Buenos Aires.

The Supreme Court of Chile, acceding to the Argentine request for Kelly's extradition, pointed out that the crimes charged against Kelly "did not occur during an attack . . . on the security of the State, such as to be considered connected to a . . . political offense. They took place at a time of public tranquility." The court observed further that the extradition exemption applies only to a purely political offense or to one that is intimately connected with a political disturbance. Extradition was thus granted on the grounds that Kelly's alleged "murder and theft were isolated acts" during a period of public peace.[724]

The Political Motivation Doctrine

A very different formula for identifying political offenses and their perpetrators has been applied by the civil law countries of the European continent. While Anglo-American jurisprudence has relied on an essentially objective test—determining the existence of a "political revolt or disturbance"—the European approach has dwelled on the more subjective criterion of the offender's "motivation." Looking to the offender's particular motives, the European test seeks a strong connection between the asserted political cause and the offending conduct.

The elements of the Continental doctrine were carefully enumerated by the Swiss Federal Tribunal in the 1908 case of *V.P. Wassilief*.[725] To qualify as political, the court held, an offense had to be committed with the express purpose of modifying the political or social organization of the state. Furthermore, the offender's activity had to be directly connected to that objective. The third criterion, which came to be known as the principle of "predominance," required that the political significance of the offense must outweigh the public interest in punishing the conduct. This suggests that offenses involving violence, or other means disproportionate to the ends sought, would in most likelihood be considered common offenses. Applying all three criteria to Wassilief, who stood accused of murdering a chief of police, the Swiss court ordered his extradition. In its judgment the court stressed that the accused did not commit his crime in pursuit of purely political goals, nor was murder a necessary action in light of other means of redress available to him.

Adhering to the same principles, Swiss courts again rejected the political defense in a 1923 case in which the French government requested the extradition of Alviso Pavan, an anti-Fascist journalist wanted in France for the murder of an Italian Fascist. A crime, the court held, "is invested with a predominantly political character only where the criminal action is immediately connected with its political object. Such [a] connection can only be predicated where the act is in itself an effective means of attaining this object or where it is an incident in a general political struggle."[726] Accordingly, Pavan's murder of a member of an opposing political party did not constitute a political offense, and Pavan was turned over to France.

Similar reasoning was applied in the 1933 *Ockert* decision, although a different outcome was reached. Ockert, a left-wing German activist sought by Germany for the killing of a member of the National Socialist Party in a street fracas, fled to Switzerland. The Swiss tribunal noted that the clashes between the two antagonistic groups were not casual disputes based upon local or personal enmity, but were part of a larger political struggle approaching the status of civil war. Referring also to German press headlines that highlighted the offender's "Marxist Murder Tactics" and the victim's "Sacrifice in the Service of the New Reich,"[727] the Swiss court concluded that the homicide constituted a political offense.

Although the Swiss courts initially followed the Anglo-American requirement that political offenses be part of a broader struggle for political power, later decisions increasingly recognized an exception in the case of fugitives from totalitarian regimes in which open political struggles were impossible. *In re Kavic,* decided in 1952, held widespread passive resistance to be appropriate substitute to the violent struggle requirement.[728] In *Kavic,* Yugoslavia demanded the return of an airplane crew that had diverted a domestic flight to Switzerland, charging the crew with misappropriation of state property and endangering the safety of public transport. The Swiss court refused the extradition request, pointing out that the common-crime characteristics of the charges were outweighed by their political dimensions. Noting that minimal danger was posed to the passengers' lives and property by the experienced crew's straying from the flight plan, the tribunal also described as too restrictive the traditional requirement that the political offense be incidental to a violent struggle. Endorsing a less stringent standard, the court noted that with

> [t]he growth of totalitarian states . . . those who do not wish to submit to the regime have no alternative but to escape it by flight abroad [yet] this more passive attitude . . . is nonetheless [more] worthy of asylum than active participation in the fight for political power used to be in what were . . . normal circumstances."[729]

An added criterion, that of "proportionality," was eventually added by the Swiss courts to the earlier standards of "motivation" and "predominance." The merger of the three principles is well illustrated by the 1961 *Ktir* decision.[730] Ktir, a French national and member of the Algerian Liberation Movement (FLN), took part in the 1960 execution in France of another FLN member suspected of disloyalty. Following the murder, Ktir escaped to Switzerland and was soon confronted with a French demand for extradition. Contending that France and the FLN were at war at the time of the offense, Ktir argued that his deed, the killing of an enemy, constituted a political offense. He urged further that if extradition were granted, he should be exempted from the death penalty in France, since the offenses for which he was wanted were not capital offenses in Switzerland.

Concluding that Ktir's offense "did not satisfy [the] requirement of proportionality," the Swiss court granted the French extradition request. In so ordering, the court once more restated its test for identifying political crimes:

> Political offenses include offenses which, although constituting acts falling under the ordinary criminal law, have a predominantly political character . . . in particular as a result of the motives inspiring them and the purpose sought to be achieved. Such offenses . . . presuppose that the act was inspired by political passion, that it was committed either in the framework of a struggle for power or for the purpose of escaping a dictatorial authority. . . . A further requirement is that the damage caused be proportionate to the result sought, in other words, that the interests at stake should be sufficiently important to excuse, if not to justify, the infringement of private legal rights. When murder is concerned, such a relationship exists only if homicide is the sole means of safeguarding more important interests.[731]

The carefully articulated Swiss formula is reflected in the laws of the other European countries. An early French test for identifying political crimes was contained in a 1927 law that exempted from extradition offenders whose acts were committed in the course of an insurrection or civil war.[732] Italian law also echoes the Swiss approach, as does the Dutch 1966 extradition law, which reiterates that, in deciding issues of political criminality, courts must determine the motives of the actor and the nature of the injured interests. Denmark's 1947 extradition law is similarly phrased, making the classification of an extraditable offense dependent upon a careful balancing of the need for public order against the citizenry's right to oppose political oppression.

Sweden, in a 1957 law and related court decisions, has developed some of the most liberal standards against the extradition of political offenders. German extradition policies, working in tandem with the country's liberal asylum laws, which have readily permitted the extension of shelter to all those who are "politically prosecuted," have similarly discouraged the extradition of those eligible for asylum.[733] Asylum practice in Belgium, despite the country's initial introduction of the restrictive *clause d'attentat* (discussed later), has also been noted for its liberality.

The contemporary Continental doctrines regarding the nonextradition of political offenders are now encapsulated in the 1957 European Convention on Extradition.[734] The convention reflects the continuing struggle between the forces of law and order and their adversaries, those who call for resistance to abuses of governmental power. The outcome is an effort at compromise. The convention specifies:

> Extradition shall not be granted if the offense . . . is regarded by the requested party as a political offense or as an offense connected with a political offense.
>
> The same rule shall apply if the requested state has substantial grounds for believing that a request for extradition . . . has been made for the purpose of prosecuting or punishing a person on account of his race, religion, nationality or political opinion, or that person's position may be prejudiced for any of these reasons.
>
> The taking or attempted taking of the life of a Head of State or a member of his family shall not be deemed to be a political offense for the purposes of this Convention.[735]

Reaffirming the traditional standards of national sovereignty, the European Convention on Extradition thus continues to look to the domestic law of the haven state as the sole and ultimate decision-maker in granting the asylum-seeker's request for the political offender exception. While the convention displays considerable liberality by including within its scope both "purely" and "connected" political offenses, it also codifies the restrictive *clause d'attentat*.

The Injured Rights Doctrine

Over the years the injured rights doctrine has emerged to supplement and modify the European extradition doctrine.[736] By focusing on the political offender's victims, the injured rights doctrine sets out to limit nonextraditable offenses to transgressions against the representatives, properties, and institutions of the state. Those causing deliberate injuries to individuals or institutions not directly involved in the governmental process are not protected from extradition. The emphasis on the political offender's targets not only departs from the Anglo-American approach and its emphasis upon the objective circumstances surrounding the offending act, but also contrasts with the Continental theory and its emphasis on the offender's subjective motive.

A leading example of the injured rights approach is provided by *In re Giovanni Gatti*. A Communist activist, Gatti was charged with attempted homicide by the Republic of San Marino. After his escape to France, San Marino demanded his extradition. In granting the request in 1947, the French court reiterated that "political offenses . . . are directed against the constitution of the Government and against sovereignty. . . . The offense does not derive its political character from the motive of the offender, but from the nature of the rights it injures."[737] The *Gatti* decision appears to hark back to the early scholarly attempts to distinguish between "purely" and "related" political offenses—between those activities that primarily affect the state and its institutions, and those involving common criminality that violates the rights of innocent people. Under the injured rights test the recognition of the political defense is ensured only when the state is the primary or only victim. The defense becomes attenuated, however, when the effects of the offender's criminality are borne mostly by uninvolved individuals.

◇   ◇   ◇

The many and diverse approaches discussed thus far, reflecting various efforts to translate the doctrine of the political offense exception into practice, demonstrate that the political offender has not yet found a secure place in international jurisprudence. In this chapter, the reader has been invited to contrast the objective yet relatively simple and inflexible political incident test of the common law, with the Continent's more subjective political motivation formula, a more flexible formula that offers a greater likelihood for the denial of extradition. The simplicity of the common law, in the final analysis, may reflect a particularly determined effort to restrict the application of the political offense exception. On the other hand, the Continental approach, which gives greater weight to motives and seeks to curtail individual harm, may demonstrate a greater willingness to accommodate the political dissenter whose motives are sincere and whose conduct is carefully prescribed to protect the innocents. It is clear that differing approaches to the philosophical and pragmatic dilemmas posed by the political offender continue to bedevil the nations of the world. The international community, which has long been seeking an accommodation with and balance between the rights of protest and rebellion on the one hand, and the maintenance of public order and the protection of innocents on the other hand, has not yet come up with a generally acceptable solution. As political violence and disorder spread worldwide, the search for a doctrine that strikes the proper balance has become increasingly important.

The Decline of "Politicals" in the Age of Terror

In the search for a balanced and universally acceptable definition of political criminality, one must take notice of the radical changes in attitudes toward political offenses in the last 150 years. Although the belief that political offenders should be exempt from extradition retained wide acceptance in the international community throughout the nineteenth century, scholars, as well as increasing numbers of nations, have been coming to the conclusion that certain classes of political actors, particularly those engaging in indiscriminate and reprehensible acts of violence, should be excluded from these benefits. This exclusion of some categories of "politicals" was the product of a growing fear of public disorder and possible anarchy posed by an escalating and often indiscriminate resort to political resistance and rebellion.

The *clause d'attentat,* first formulated by Belgium in response to the attempted assassination of France's Napoleon III in 1856, limited the political offense exception by denying political offender status to assassins as well as assailants of heads of state or their immediate families.[738] The *clause d'attentat* was the first effort to restrict the limits of public tolerance toward those who challenge authority. Under Belgium's *clause,* which other nations soon adopted, protection from extradition was no longer to be made available to those who had perpetrated violence against kings, presidents, and other heads of states or their families.[739]

Criticizing the limitations imposed by the *clause,* I. A. Shearer complained:

> It may be questioned whether there are not times in the history of some countries when assassination is the only practical means whereby the rule of a tyrant may be ended. On the other hand, if assassination should always be regarded as an excessive measure, not deserving of protection under extradition

law, it may be questioned why the operation of the clause is restricted to heads of State and their immediate families [and does not] include . . . all government ministers and perhaps other officials as well.[740]

Yet despite continuing objections (which questioned both the founding premise of the rule and the logic for its limitation) the *clause d'attentat* became enshrined in the international law of extradition. Political activists were thus placed on notice that no amount of governmental repression, abuse of power, or even state terror can justify violence against the very individuals serving as the wielders and symbols of state power.

The emergence of militant anarchism in the late nineteenth century spurred the creation of yet another class of political offenders who were to be denied the traditional protections from extradition. The globe-trotting and indiscriminately violent anarchists, openly repudiating all governments and social organizations, were seen as qualitatively different from the more traditional political dissidents. Even the geographically distant United States was not spared the menacing presence of the anarchists—witness the 1901 assassination of President William McKinley by Leon Czolgosz, an expatriated anarchist. Viewed with profound abhorrence by a broad spectrum of political persuasions, ranging from monarchists to republicans, from conservatives to liberals, world opinion concluded that anarchists had to be stamped out.

In 1894 the English courts were presented with the question of whether anarchist militants should qualify for the political offense exception. *In re Meunier* involved a French request for the extradition of an anarchist who had escaped from France to England after exploding bombs not only in an army barracks but also in a crowded cafe. The English court refused to recognize Meunier's claim that his crime was political. Judge Cave wrote:

[I]n order to constitute an offense of a political character, there must be two or more parties in the State, each seeking to impose the Government of their own choice on the other. . . . [But in] the present case there are not [two parties] . . . for the party with whom the accused is identified . . . by his own voluntary statement . . . is the enemy of all government. Their efforts are directed primarily against the general body of citizens."[741]

The decision reflected the prevailing view that anarchism was not a political movement but rather a general threat to all nations. Further support was gained for the *Meunier* decision in 1902 when the Pan American Convention explicitly excluded all anarchistic acts from consideration as political offenses.[742]

The fate of the anarchists was the writing on the wall to alert all political activists that specified types and forms of political militancy would fall outside the internationally tolerable boundaries of political conflict. Although the political offender continued to be treated with leniency and special consideration at the beginning of the twentieth century, the growing social, economic, and political turmoil in the era between the two world wars gave rise to a new global groping for political tranquility. Because governments were dependent for their survival upon the cooperation of fragile coalitions of divergent parties, they were no longer willing to tolerate the heavy domestic costs of militant political oppositions. The political offender increasingly seemed less an agent of unavoidable revolutionary reform and more a threat to and a destroyer of public order.

Growing international restrictions on the activities of the political offender and a constriction of the political offense exception became the order of the twentieth century. As global diplomacy, travel, and business expanded dramatically, crimes against diplomatic, transportation, and communications institutions increasingly came to be seen as threats to the well-being of a newly interdependent world. International outlawry, a concept dating back to the ancient crime of piracy, was metamorphosed into international "terrorism" and became a fixture of international law.[743] Multinational conventions have increasingly gone beyond the ancient prohibition of piracy, long viewed as constituting the first "crime against all nations," to create such new offenses affecting the modern international community as counterfeiting,[744] white slavery,[745] narcotics traffic,[746] aircraft hijacking,[747] hostage-taking,[748] and the mailing of letter bombs.[749] These crimes were universally condemned, and thus the duty of enforcement, including the extradition of suspected perpetrators, was imposed upon all nations. The continuing movement to restrict the political offense exception and to assist in the surrender of offenders charged with heinous crimes was also hastened by domestic legislation exemplified by the French Extradition Law of 1927, which provided that offenders charged with "acts of odious barbarism and vandalism prohibited by the laws of war" were not to be granted exemption from extradition.[750]

The world community's growing resolve to fight indiscriminate and vile political protest, resistance, and rebellion was greatly strengthened as early as half a century ago by the assassination of Yugoslavia's King Alexander during his 1937 visit to France. Particularly offensive to the forces of law and order was France's inability to secure the suspected "political" offenders' extradition from Italy, to which they had fled. Accordingly, the League of Nations proposed in 1938 an international convention against what were then perceived as extreme and intolerable forms of political militance. The proposed Convention Against Terrorism barred all resort to violent political means, as well as inducement, encouragement, and assistance of such means.[751] The convention's objective was to deprive all violent political offenders of their former respect and tolerance within the international community of civilized nations, and to ensure that perpetrators of terrorist acts would no longer be sheltered from extradition.

The League's idealistic hopes for an international regime that would condemn as well as prevent political violence were ultimately destroyed in the conflagration of World War II. The war and the postwar era evidenced the futility of the League's dream of reducing political violence worldwide. At the war's conclusion, many of the underground resistance movements that had been mobilized against Nazi, Fascist, and Japanese occupations were replaced by new militant forces fighting for national liberation. As tribes, ethnic communities, and entire nations sought to define and carve out their political destinies and territories, the remains of the far-flung European empires were shattered by upheaval and rebellions. The anti-colonial struggles, ranging from India's relatively peaceful campaign of civil disobedience to more violent outbursts in Asia and Africa, accounted for a dramatic growth in the number of independent countries—from the mere 65 members of the League of Nations upon its demise, to some 185 members of the United Nations currently.

The more traditional campaigns against colonialism and for national self-determination now combined with the emergence of a new body of internationally proclaimed human rights that reinforced the nineteenth century's image of the political offender, a warrior for these rights, as a "noble" actor. Yet at the same time, as previously noted, increased global interdependence (in the social, economic, and political arenas) acted to produce a dramatic expansion in the willingness and force of international law to curtail the range of means and weapons available to political offenders in their campaigns against authority and other real or imagined enemies. As the international community developed new laws and procedures for apprehending and punishing those who transgressed against the existing global order, the newly emerging body of "international crimes" acted to diminish the former safeguards available for the protection of political offenders.

The expansion of a universally condemned class of international crimes was hastened by the Nuremberg tribunal and its judgments at the conclusion of World War II. Building on the previously existing law of war, the Nuremberg tribunal affirmed that "war crimes," as defined by the 1907 Hague and the 1949 Geneva Conventions (enumerating offenses against foreign nations, foreign nationals, and prisoners of war), constituted international offenses. The tribunal affirmed that "crimes against peace," such as aggressive wars, also constituted internationally proscribed offenses. Finally, it recognized a new category of offenses—"crimes against humanity," a classification that for the first time in world history made it possible to punish a state for its abusive conduct against its own citizens.[752]

Designated as enemies of all mankind (much like the anarchists before them), those who engaged in war crimes and other acts of international criminality could no longer expect sanctuary from any nation. Stripped of the political offense protection, these enemies of all nations could be subjected to prosecution wherever they sought to hide. Reinforcing these principles of universal accountability, the 1951 Convention Relating to the Status of Refugees specifically denied refugee status and the protections available under it to all those who had "committed a crime against peace, a war crime, or a crime against humanity."[753] Nearly a quarter century after the Nuremberg judgment, the U.N.'s General Assembly further expanded the boundaries of international criminality by designating South Africa's institution of apartheid as a crime against humanity.[754] It has thus become abundantly clear that through resort to principles developed in earlier international campaigns against piracy and slavery and by calling forth the authority of the Nuremberg tribunal and the standards developed by subsequent conventions, the international community can place not only unlawful belligerents but also an entire category of political militants (such as activists in the causes of apartheid or colonialism) outside the traditional protections afforded to lawful belligerents under the law of war or to political offenders under the extradition exceptions.[755]

The political offender's standing was further curtailed by the 1948 Genocide Convention,[756] which set out to safeguard the survival and well-being of national, ethnic, racial, and religious communities. By making it an international crime to take the life of members of such communities, to cause them serious bodily or mental harm, or to deliberately inflict upon them conditions calculated to bring about their destruction, the Genocide Convention specifically eliminated genocide and related crimes from the list of protected political offenses. Moreover, the convention obligated all nations to grant requests for the extradition of those charged with genocide offenses.[757] In 1988, after nearly four decades of American hesitation, the treaty was finally ratified by the U.S. Senate.[758]

The worldwide campaign against war crimes, crimes against peace, crimes against humanity, apartheid, and genocide has thus crafted a category of international outlaws that echoes the ancient classification accorded to brigands and pirates. These criminals are summarily placed outside the bounds of civilized society and are to be shunned by all people. Yet this development of international outlawry has been a relatively easy task compared with the difficulties nations have experienced in reaching international agreement about the criteria for the more general classification of "terrorism," a term referring to a wide range of politically related acts of indiscriminate violence carried out in the alleged pursuit of political causes directed against innocent parties, or "soft targets," outside the arenas of the conflict. In 1930 the Swiss Federal Tribunal ruled that terrorist offenses fell outside the political offense exception. Approving the granting of extradition in the case of one charged with terrorist activities, the court noted that "acts which are not . . . directed to the realization of a particular political object . . . but which serve merely terroristic ends . . . cannot give rise to asylum."[759] The Supreme Court of Argentina took a similarly firm stance, declaring in 1968 that "extradition will not be denied where we are dealing with cruel or immoral acts which clearly shock the conscience of civilized peoples."[760]

Expanding on the nineteenth century's *attentat* exception to political criminality, several contemporary treaties have excluded all acts of assassination from the category of political offenses.[761] An example is the extradition agreement of the Council of the League of Arab States, which was approved on September 14, 1952, and to which Egypt, Iraq, Jordan, Saudi Arabia, and Syria are signatories.[762] Though the agreement specifies that political offenders are not to be extradited between the member nations, it stipulates that the assassination of heads of state or their families, attempts on the lives of heirs to the throne, premeditated murder, and other acts of terrorism are not to be recognized as political offenses.[763]

As world attention concentrated on the specter of terrorism in the decades between 1960 and the end of the century, several futile attempts have been made to produce a comprehensive definition of this much-feared phenomenon. Though "terrorism" was identifiable through its indiscriminate and disproportionate violence against belligerents and neutrals alike, its denial of protection for innocents, and its proclivity to export violence beyond the boundaries of the contesting parties, a precise definition could not be universally agreed upon.[764] In its continuing war against random and exported violence, the community of nations therefore chose to concentrate not so much on defining this difficult, multifaceted, and amorphous phenomenon, but on outlawing specifically defined types of terroristic conduct, such as aircraft highjacking, hostage-taking, endangering diplomatic personnel, letter-bomb campaigns, and similar types of conduct considered adverse to the security of all nations. In so doing, the world community demonstrated a remarkable readiness to condemn and punish as terroristic various classes of activities that would have been political offenses had they not threatened or served to disrupt essential internationally protected persons, institutions, or instrumentalities (e.g., diplomats,[765] aircraft,[766] the mail service,[767] hostage-taking,[768] etc.). By designating these selected forms of political militance as internationally proscribed, international treaties imposed a duty on all signatory nations not only to apprehend those charged with such conduct but also to subject them to either extradition or prosecution—a duty summarized by the maxim *aut dedere aut punire* (extradite or punish).

These developments at the end of the twentieth century supply ample evidence of a growing international recognition of the duty of all states to protect the world community against common enemies, a recognition that dates back to ancient efforts to suppress piracy. Emmerich de Vattel, writing in the mid–nineteenth century, urged that persons who commit offenses against the human race "may be exterminated whenever they are seized."[769] Vattel elaborated:

> Although the justice of each nation ought in general to be confined to the punishment of crimes committed in its own territories, we ought to except from this rule those villains, who, by the nature and habitual frequency of their crimes, violate all public security and declare themselves the enemies of the human race. [The latter] attack and injure all nations by trampling underfoot the foundations of their common safety.

Adhering to Vattel's mandate, the world community has defined an increasing number of internationally significant offenses as "universal" in the concluding decades of the twentieth century. The notion of universal or international crimes was reinforced by the concept of universal jurisdiction, which obligated all nations to take appropriate action (extradition or punishment) against offenders within their boundaries or within their reach. This development, which testifies to the willingness of nations to forego political differences in extreme instances, has resulted in a growing effort to condemn, punish, and deny "political" status to those offending against such indispensable institutions and needs of the world community as the safety of diplomatic personnel, the security of the high seas, and the protection of civil aviation.[770]

Some proponents of political militancy have argued that the new international willingness to curb the privileged status previously accorded to political offenders has overextended the war against terrorism. They suggest that the lines between political offender, freedom fighter, insurgent, and terrorist are being blurred and intentionally confused by the ideological and rhetorical excesses of the forces of law and order. This confusion, they argue, makes all claims to political purpose and motive, however valid, seem inherently suspect. Allowing such confusion to continue, they argue, may indeed threaten the world community's basic moral instincts and weaken the resolve of those committed to a global campaign against tyranny and abuse of power. Such confusion, some fear, erroneously places a noble rebel like George Washington on the same moral level as the terrorist skyjackers who sent Pan Am flight 103 and its innocent passengers plummeting to the earth at Lockerbie, Scotland.[771]

It has been said that "history is written by the victors" and that the legitimacy of a political struggle and its participants can only be established by their success. If this is true, then the primary effort of this volume is doomed to failure, and one will be never able, in a consistent and forward-looking manner, to distinguish the political hero from the villain. Yet this volume remains steadfast in its dedication to the opposite conclusion. Evidence supports the proposition that just political offenders can be identified and distinguished from both international outlaws and common criminals, and that they can therefore be accorded differential treatment in domestic as well as in international law and practice.

Chapter Seven

Justifications and Absolutions

The Political Offender's "Higher Law" Defenses

*We are not to be compared with ordinary criminals. . . . Our aim
is to destroy a political regime after which our society will
exist under a superior regime. We claim that our case should
be heard before a court responsible to no one country by
the whole world—a court based on pure justice and pure ethics.*

—Eliahu Bet Zouri,
Israeli assassin of Lord Moyne (1944)

Defence, not defiance.

—Motto of the Volunteers
of America Movement (1898)

Declaration of the Rights of Man and Citizen, 1789.

The Law and Morality of
Disobedience and Resistance

Political dissent and opposition, and even militant defiance and violent resistance (whether individual or collective), may be considered "justified" when carried out in response to governmental abuses of power.[772] When the rebel wages war against a totalitarian or authoritarian political system, his or her pleas for justice and assertions of a "higher law" that supports resistance can be doubtlessly acknowledged and even accepted. Some commentators have indeed spoken not only of the "right" but also of the "duty" of the individual and the community to disobey oppressive rulers and regimes.[773]

But the justifications are not as readily apparent when disobedience takes place in countries and communities that have pronounced themselves to be "democratic" and whose governments display some or considerable adherence to the "rule of law." Political writers as well as governmental spokespersons in such assertedly free societies have long insisted that disobedience and resistance to the law (as distinct from efforts to secure change through authorized parliamentary or judicial means) are wholly unwarranted and illegitimate.[774] English jurist T. H. Green spoke out in 1907 on the errors of all forms of disobedience:

> Supposing then the individual to have decided that some command of a "political superior" is not for the common good, how ought he to act in regard to it? In a country like ours [England], with a popular government and settled methods of enacting and repealing laws, the answer of common sense is simple and sufficient. He should do all he can by legal methods to get the command canceled, but till it is canceled, he should conform to it.[775]

Responding similarly to the intense popular opposition to his country's military presence in South Vietnam, Australia's prime minister declared in 1970: "As to inciting people to break the law, I think there can be no excuse whatsoever for those in a community where the opportunity exists to change the law through the ballot box."[776]

The citizen's duty of obedience in a democracy, under this view, is derived mainly from the doctrine of the "social contract," an alleged agreement under which the state, in assuming its sovereign authority, undertakes to protect and serve the citizen. In return for this protection, the citizen accepts the duty to obey the commands of those in authority, a duty that is reinforced by a continuing mutuality of interests between the citizen and his or her government.[777] Derived from the "social contract" and reinforced by the supposed societal benefits flowing from the maintenance of the rule of law is the further doctrine that democracy permits no departure from existing laws and regulations. This doctrine has been voiced in response to a variety of disobedience, including the recent abortion clinic protests and the anti–Vietnam War and racial protests of the 1960s, which combined to shake America's tranquility. In *Concerning Dissent and Civil Disobedience,* Justice Abe Fortas of the U.S. Supreme Court reiterated that "[p]rotesters and change-seekers must adopt methods within the limit of the law."[778] Fortas insisted further that violations of the law in pursuit of social change were impermissible in societies that supply both lawful avenues for the expression of individual and mass protest and institutions for the implementation of popularly desired reforms. In conclusion, he called for the scrupulous observance of all existing legal norms, which he described as the "bone structure of a democratic society."[779]

Only in the exceptional instance where a particular law is itself "basically offensive to fundamental values of life or the Constitution"[780] was Fortas willing to concede a moral justification for disobedience or active resistance to the law's requirements. However, even in these cases, Fortas rejected the claim that such moral justification would constitute a legal defense. He stressed forbiddingly:

> Anyone assuming to make the judgment that a law is in this category ["basically offensive to fundamental values of life or the Constitution"] assumes a terrible burden. He has undertaken a fearful moral as well as legal responsibility. He should be prepared to submit to prosecution by the state for the violation of the law and the imposition of punishment if he is wrong or unsuccessful. He should even admit the correctness of the state's action in seeking to enforce its laws, and he should acquiesce in the ultimate judgement of the courts.[781]

Fortas's absolutist insistence upon the supremacy of "positive" or existing law, as contrasted with a higher "natural law," fails to deal with the "unthinkable"—the sad truth that democratic systems can and do break down wherever and whenever corruption, majority insensitivity, minority manipulation of power, gerrymandering, voter apathy, or social, economic, racial, and gender imbalances warp the mechanisms and operations of just governance. Even where majority rule truly exists, it is not impossible for a majority to vote in laws and implement procedures that are discriminatory, immoral, and even unconstitutional. America's treatment of blacks, Native Americans, and women throughout most of its national existence clearly demonstrates the imperfections that may persist even under an alleged democratic or majority rule.

From Fortas's perspective, abolitionist John Brown was not entitled to militantly challenge the institution of slavery. Under the Fortas's unbending doctrine, Brown should have further acquiesced in the judgment of the Virginia court that convicted him of treason. Similarly illegitimate would be Mohandas K. Gandhi's nonviolent campaign of *satyagraha* and Dr. Martin Luther King Jr.'s violations of the unreasonable laws that prohibited his protest marches against racial discrimination. Yet Dr. King chose the questionable path of civil disobedience, seeking to pursue through it his quest for a higher justice. Despite his objections to Dr. King's illegal action, Fortas nevertheless lauded Dr. King's decision to accept imprisonment for his actions "without complaint or histrionics."[782] Fortas cites this as evidence of Dr. King's commitment to the supremacy of the rule of law. It is more likely, however, that Dr. King chose not to protest his imprisonment in order to dramatize his struggle rather than to profess his respect for the legitimacy of Alabama's corrupt police and prison systems. One may acquiesce to imprisonment for a variety of reasons, as Dr. King did. Yet such submission to punishment stops short of admitting "the correctness of the state's action in seeking to enforce its laws," as Fortas urged. On the contrary, as historian Howard Zinn warned, acknowledging unjust authority and acquiescing to its evil decisions indeed carries a great social danger, because "[w]hen unjust decisions are accepted, injustice is sanctioned and perpetuated."[783]

The lives—and deaths—of Dr. King, John Brown, Joan of Arc, Socrates, and other rebels who fought injustice demonstrate the stubborn unwillingness of those in authority, even if they represent democratic or majority rule, to listen and respond to their critics until they find themselves in a state of siege. The guarantees of free speech and press and the availability of the ballot box do not always constitute sufficient means of redress, nor do they supply a com-

pelling argument for totally stripping the citizen of the right to resort to other means to combat the abuse of governmental power.
Even Alexander Hamilton recognized the supremacy of the original
sovereign authority that was vested in the people. Hamilton wrote
emphatically in *The Federalist:* "To deny this would be to affirm
that the deputy is greater than his principal; that the servant is
above his master; that the representatives of the people are superior
to the people themselves."[784] The moral and communal ends served
by majority governance and the rule of law do not necessarily outweigh either the need or the justification for popular corrective action, especially when great evil persists in a society and the remedial
processes and protections are in fact unavailable to its aggrieved citizens.

Some radical observers have indeed argued that the latter is most
often the case—that the procedures and protections available to citizens in Western democracies have frequently proven to be inadequate for curing mounting political and social ills. Citing the plight
of African Americans, Howard Zinn suggested that "[w]e have been
naive in America about the efficacy of . . . representative government
to rectify injustice."[785] He argued further that resort to the ballot
box often fails to produce changes in public or foreign policy.
"[M]ost of us—when we are honest with ourselves—feel utterly
helpless to affect public policy by the orthodox means. The feeling is
justified."[786]

Even a government committed to a democratic constitution cannot guarantee justice to all segments of society. A generation ago,
English constitutional law scholar K. C. Wheare pointed out the
need for nonorthodox remedies against the tyranny of the majority,
even in a country as free as his own:

[C]an we in fact say that a permanent minority, unable to obtain what it wants
under a Constitution, must continue always to obey that Constitution? The
answer surely is no. There are circumstances in which it is morally right to
rebel, to refuse to obey the Constitution, to upset it. A Constitution may be the
foundation of law and order in a community, but mere law and order is not
enough. It must be good law and good order. It is conceivable surely that a minority may be right in saying that it lives under a Constitution which establishes bad government and that, if all else is tried and fails, rebellion is right.
No doubt it is difficult to say just when rebellion is right and how much rebellion is right, but that it may be legitimate is surely true.[787]

Those who challenge the right of rebellion in a democracy defend not only the infallibility, absolute binding power, and the eternality of the initial social compact, but also the legitimacy and morality of majoritarian principles and majority decisions, even when they exclude major segments of the population, such as blacks, women, or indigenous peoples. Those challenging the notion of absolute obedience argue that abuse of power is as likely to occur under republicanism and democracy as under an oligarchy or monarchy, and that the tyranny of a so-called majority is no less tolerable than other tyrannies.

This questioning of the presumed symbiosis between the doctrine of the social compact and the principle of majoritarian rule is not a modern phenomenon. Thomas Jefferson, probably the most democratically inclined of America's Founding Fathers, spoke frequently of the dangers of "elective despotism," pointing out that "one hundred and seventy-three despots would surely be as oppressive as one."[788] Writing in 1894, when women and Native Americans were denied the franchise, Matthias N. Forney similarly complained: "What does majority representation mean? It means that the majority shall have everything and the minority nothing."[789] An even broader hypothesis of the ills of majoritarianism was advanced by Simon Sterne: "The process of creating a majority demoralizes most of those who compose it; it demoralizes them in this sense, that it excludes the action of their higher moral attributes, and brings into operation their lower motives."[790] Yet Forney and Sterne were merely following in the footsteps of Leonard Courtney, who two decades earlier had pointed out:

> You cannot trust any exclusive party to act with justice to those who are wholly in their power, and whose cause cannot be pleaded before them. If the minority have not someone to speak up for their feelings and desires, the majority will act with injustice towards them; and it is not so much from any set purpose to be unjust as from the natural incapacity of men to understand the needs of their neighbors. . . . As the old proverb says, "No one knows how the shoe pinches except him who wears it."[791]

Thus, while so-called compelling public interests in preserving the social compact and the general acceptability of majoritarian rule have usually been advanced as dispositive arguments against resort to nonparliamentary dissent, the validity of this position is less than certain.

The justification of majoritarianism may be acceptable in relatively homogenous societies, in which a system of safeguards for the protection of minorities could possibly suffice as a countervailing force. But in most contemporary countries, which have pluralistic and diverse compositions of populations, one must search for more effective systems of power-sharing in order to balance existing diversities and conciliate competing interests. Absent such systemic reforms, majoritarianism often fails as a reliable principle for maintaining the broadest necessary public confidence in the legitimacy of power.

Critics have long been concerned not only with the general potential for abuse of power under majority rule, but also with the inability of the judicial process in the United States and elsewhere to protect, in a timely manner, fully comprehensive rights to life, liberty, property, and the pursuit of happiness, even when these rights are guaranteed in a nation's most hallowed documents. Of the United States, some have argued that the judicial branch, as well as the legislative and executive branches, have not always upheld the equal and just values inherent in the country's Constitution. Critics point readily to many shameful episodes in the history of the U.S. judicial system. Where was the Constitution, they ask, when the Supreme Court, under Chief Justice Taney, ruled that escaped slave Dred Scott was returnable "property" rather than a human being?[792] What protection did the Constitution offer those accused and convicted under the questionable 1798 Alien and Sedition Acts,[793] or those illegally detained as rebel sympathizers under President Lincoln's questionable executive orders during the Civil War?[794]

The U.S. Supreme Court, critics point out, unanimously upheld the conviction and ten-year sentence of socialist leader Eugene Debs for denouncing U.S. involvement in World War I. Debs was indicted for "inciting to insubordination," disloyalty, and mutiny, yet the most offending words he used in his Canton, Ohio, speech were that his audience was "fit for something better than slavery and cannon fodder."[795] Even such great guardians of liberty as Justices Holmes and Brandeis joined the rest of the Supreme Court in affirming as constitutional the Espionage and Sedition Acts of 1917–1918,[796] which restricted the freedom of speech of American dissenters. During World War II, U.S. courts again found it impossible to provide timely relief for the loyal Americans of Japanese extraction who were confined in relocation camps.[797] Once more, immediately after the conclusion of the war, the Supreme Court affirmed the constitutionality of the now discredited Smith Act, which made it a crime to "teach" subversive doctrines.[798]

These intrusions upon the rights of American citizens took place despite ringing and explicit constitutional guarantees to the contrary. Governmental departures from constitutional safeguards have often been justified on the grounds that political freedom and tolerance must from time to time yield to more compelling societal interests, including public safety and order. In 1919, Justice Holmes sought to disarm political critics and dissidents by analogizing them to the man who falsely shouts fire in a crowded theater.[799] But the problem is that not all those shouting fire do so falsely. Often, indeed, theater owners as well as governments may stoutly refuse to admit the existence of a dangerous fire. Since governments may deny or even be unaware of a "fire" that rages in the streets, in public or private institutions, or in the hearts of its citizens, should the better-informed citizen be pledged to silence and inaction?

America's Founding Fathers, in their pursuit of a just and responsive government, were not so unworldly as to believe in their ability to totally and eternally eliminate inequity and evil, and to insist on the inflexibility and total binding power of the rule of law. In cases of national emergency—specifically in instances of rebellion and invasion—the Founding Fathers were willing to vest in government the power to suspend the historical safeguards supplied by the writ of habeas corpus.[800] If such occasional governmental departure from principles of legality is to be tolerated, should not the people of America and other democracies—the original and true sovereigns of these nations—be permitted similar resort to extralegal measures under exigent circumstances? Should not individuals and groups be permitted the same degree of self-defense against governmental abuse or government-tolerated injustice that their representatives—their delegated agents in office—are permitted in defending government against its enemies?

Dissidence, Political Crime, and Rebellion as Obedience to "Higher Law"

Despite its questionable theoretical and pragmatic foundations, the traditional "law and order" argument continues to assert that citizens of democratic states must channel their protest and dissent only into such avenues as the prevailing codes of law have defined as "lawful." But these dictates and codes, which the adherents of positivism hold so dear, are neither historically nor jurisprudentially the exclusive foundations of moral and legal authority. On the contrary, many political offenders claim adherence to transcendental legal and moral rules, applicable to all people, that do not derive their legitimacy from the positive laws made by humankind and temporal regimes. Whether these principles or rules are held out to be universally obvious or are alleged to have been specially revealed only to a select few, political offenders may view them as constituting higher commandments, imperatives, or truths that must be obeyed by all. The sources of these commandments might be divine revelations, religious texts, ethical doctrines, socioeconomic imperatives, ethnic or racial heritages, characteristics of human nature, laws of science, or any of a thousand claimed beliefs, values, or rights that the secular and transitory authorities may choose to ignore or suppress.

The revealed word of God is an especially powerful source for assertions of such higher law. Jeremiah thus claimed: "Then the Lord put his hand, and touched my mouth. And the Lord said unto me, Behold, I have put my words in thy mouth."[801] With this divine authorization the prophet subsequently sought to justify his seditious speech against the reigning king of Judah: "I will deliver Zedekiah . . . and his servants, and the people . . . into the hands of Nebuchadnezzar, King of Babylon, and into the hands of their enemies . . . and he shall smite them with the edge of the sword; he shall not spare them . . . neither have mercy."[802]

Like Jeremiah, many political offenders have sought justification for their beliefs and deeds in the commands of divine authority. Such higher law, ordained by divine powers, might be contained in scripture and other professed revelations and bodies of eternal wisdom, including the Old and New Testaments, the Bhagavad Gita, and the Koran. The history of many creeds, and of their followers—Eastern and Western, ancient and modern—is replete with individual and communal opposition to, and rebellion against, the secular law whenever it failed to comply with articulated divine principles. Socrates, a renowned and respected Greek philosopher, challenged prevailing secular law, which he considered to be in conflict with divine commandments. He proclaimed: "Men of Athens, I shall obey God rather than you."[803] The Koran similarly asserts, in the words of the prophet Mohammed, that the true believer "should not obey the commands of god's creation which contradict the command-ments of the creator."[804]

In the mountains of Jerusalem in the second century B.C., Judas Maccabaeus rebelled successfully against the ruling Syrian despot, Antiochus IV, rather than accede to his demand to place an idol in Jerusalem's holy temple. Other decisions to obey divine rather than secular law have often carried great costs and severe penalties. In the fifteenth century, thousands of Spanish Jews sought exile from Is-abella and Ferdinand's Spanish regime when they were offered the "opportunity" to convert to the Christian faith or else depart the country. The American Pilgrims sacrificed their positions and posses-sions in the Old World to observe their own divine commandments on a new continent. The Christian minorities in pagan Rome knew they would suffer for their religious beliefs and practices, just as surely as do the Bahai faithful in contemporary Iran or members of the Coptic community in present-day Egypt.

Throughout the ages, the faithful have chosen to suffer personal danger, criminal sanctions, and possible extinction in the pursuit of their divine commandments. These offenders, seeking to follow their religious scriptures and codes, which often governed personal life, ethics, social behavior, and economic conduct, were just as "politi-cal" as their secular contemporaries who seek to justify their dissent and defiance through various sources of higher law and rights: secu-lar laws of nature, reason, science, or some inalienable right to life or personal choice.

"Gods are, culturally speaking, symbols of our ideal yearnings and visions," wrote psychoanalyst Rollo May.[805] Thus, while the faithful expressed their ideal yearnings through divine symbols and laws, others have sought to build their visions of a higher order upon sec-ular foundations. Especially with the coming of the Enlightenment, the new apostles of nature, reason, and science began to put forth their "ideal yearnings and visions" through a secular vision of "higher law," which they often derived from an increasingly evolv-ing universal moral consensus. As basis for this temporal image of higher law as an overriding system of moral rules based on innate reason, the Enlightenment philosophers could hark back to Plato, Aristotle, and the Stoics' natural law *(jus naturale)*.

The Greek natural law philosophers argued in favor of a cosmic moral law that was "harmonious with nature, diffused among all,

constant, eternal."[806] Cicero, who transplanted this idea of natural
law into the political and legal realms, viewed *jus naturale* as a system of laws dictated by pure reason, describing it as "the guide of
life and the teacher of the duties."[807] The Stoics, relying on Aristotle,
argued that unjust positive laws that contradicted natural laws were
not valid. Aristotle, in his *Rhetoric,* had further advised that when
advocates had "no case according to the law of the land," they
should "appeal to the law of nature."[808] It was indeed through the
cohesion of these universal concepts of natural law that the narrow
tribal Roman civil law *(jus civile)* was transformed over time into an
international law *(jus gentium)* applicable to all people.[809]

In its later, Christian version, natural law long retained its original
claim of being a rational and scientific doctrine, though it was now
viewed through the prism of Christian theology. Beginning with St.
Augustine, natural law furnished the underpinnings for Christian
doctrine. Augustine distinguished between eternal or divine law
(containing the highest and most binding of principles), the lesser
"natural" law (that part of the divine law comprehended by man's
reason, heart, and soul), and, lowest on the scale, temporal or positive law.[810] The Christian doctrines of natural law eventually
reached their zenith in the writings of Thomas Aquinas, who asserted that human or positive law "was not law" and certainly was
not binding on conscience.[811]

The intellectual predominance of the natural law doctrines remained evident throughout the Renaissance and the Age of Reason.
Both Dutch legal philosopher Hugo Grotius and his English contemporary Thomas Hobbes sought in natural law the means to restrain
both the overreach of the modern state and the excesses of voracious
men. Natural law served as the basis for the international jurisprudence developed by Grotius.[812] Hobbes likewise employed natural
law as a foundation for his domestic political philosophy, stressing
the close relationship between natural law and civil law in under-
writing the power and legitimacy of the state (which he labeled the
"Leviathan"):

The Law of Nature, and the Civill Law, contain each other, and are of equal
extent. For the Lawes of Nature, which consist of Equity, Justice, Gratitude,
and other Morall Vertues . . . are not properly Lawes, but qualities that dis-
pose men to peace, and to obedience. When a Common-wealth is once settled,

then are they actually Lawes, and not before; as being then the commands of the Common-wealth . . . [t]he Law of Nature is therefore a part of the Civill Law in all Common-wealths of the world. Reciprocally also, the Civill Law is a part of the Dictates of Nature. For Justice, that is to say, Performance of Covenant, and giving to every man his own, is a Dictate of the Law of Nature. . . . And therefore Obedience to the Civill Law is part also of the Law of Nature. Civill and Natural Law are not different kinds, but different parts of the Law; whereof one part being written, is called Civill, the other, unwritten, Naturall.[813]

Natural law continued to assume many new and diverse faces and formulations over time.[814] John Locke's doctrines of "liberty" were an attempt to synthesize and systematize the natural law doctrine by placing it into the form of a social contract.[815] Immanuel Kant, similarly looking for the origins and definition of natural law, is credited with endowing the doctrine with rational and consistent dimensions, yet Kant professed that this rational basis was no longer attributable to some divine or preexisting "nature."[816] These diverse formulations of natural and higher law have been embraced not only by philosophers but also by legal scholars and practitioners. An influential sixteenth-century English treatise, following Augustine's formula, described a three-tier hierarchy of laws—the law of God, natural law (the law of reason), and human law. In this treatise, known as "St. Germain, Doctor and Student," the doctrines of Augustine and Aquinas were applied to the emerging common law.[817] Constitutional scholar Guido Cappelletti reported similarly that the early

English judicial tradition had often tended to assign a subordinate role to the legislative function of King and Parliament, holding that law was not created by them but merely ascertained or declared. Common law was fundamental law, and although it could be complemented by the legislator, it could not be violated by him. Hence, law was largely withdrawn from arbitrary interventions of King and Parliament.[818]

By the beginning of the seventeenth century, the idea of applying natural law as a test for the validity of positive law (the law as it is found within a jurisdiction) had thus passed from the province of philosophy to the courts of law. In 1610, England's Lord Coke suggested in *Bonham's Case* that "when an act of Parliament is against common right or reason or repugnant or impossible to be performed, the common law will control it, and adjudge such act to be void."[819] Sir William Blackstone similarly saluted higher law as "the eternal, immutable laws of good and evil, to which the creator himself in all his dispensations conforms; and which he has enabled human reason to discover, so far as they are necessary for the conduct of human actions."[820]

As philosophers and jurists embraced the doctrines of natural law, so did a new generation of revolutionaries. Appeals to natural law furnished the doctrinal basis for the 1776 American Declaration of Independence, which speaks in terms of natural "truths" that are held to be "self-evident." Amongst these higher truths was man's endowment with certain "inalienable" rights, including life, liberty, and the pursuit of happiness. The French Declaration of the Rights of Man and Citizen, adopted in 1789 and embodied in the Constitution of 1793, similarly called upon the natural law guarantees of freedom of speech and press, and recognized mankind's inalienable rights to "liberty, property, security, and resistance to oppression."[821]

It is not surprising, therefore, that the concept of natural rights and natural law had great impact upon early constitutional theory and law in the United States. American constitutional scholar Edward S. Corwin succinctly noted:

> The attribution of supremacy to the Constitution on the ground solely of its rootage in popular will represent . . . a comparatively late outgrowth of American constitutional theory. Earlier the supremacy accorded to constitutions was ascribed less to their putative source than to their supposed content, to their embodiment of an essential and unchanging justice.[822]

Unwavering commitment to the supremacy of natural rights vested in the people is similarly voiced in several state constitutions. The Constitution of New Hampshire thus asserts:

> Whenever the ends of government are perverted and public liberty manifestly endangered and all other means of redress are ineffectual, the people may, and of right ought to, reform the old or establish a new government. The doctrine of non-resistance against arbitrary power and oppression is absurd, slavish, and destructive of the good and happiness of mankind.[823]

The U.S. Constitution (in its Bill of Rights in particular) spells out the initial parameters of a "higher law" to be applied by the courts and enforced by an alert citizenry. Over time, the doctrine of "judicial review" arose from these original affirmations of natural law, as a means of ensuring that the Constitution's higher values and principles would rule over conflicting legislative enactments and administrative practices. By analogizing constitutional law to natural law, the power of America's judiciary to review the activities of the other branches of the government for consistency with the Constitution was taken to include the power to declare such contradictory activities illegal and void.

American judicial statements during the early part of the nineteenth century went even further in support of natural law. Between 1814 and 1831 the judiciary often asserted its power to strike down statutes not only for violating explicit constitutional requirements but also for disregarding universal dictates and principles of justice. Elizabeth Mensch described this reliance placed upon natural law as a source of legitimacy for early American jurists:

> In a flowery vocabulary drawn largely from the natural law tradition, late-eighteenth and early-nineteenth century legal speakers made extravagant claims about the role of law and lawyers. Law was routinely described as reflecting here on earth the universal principles of divine justice, which in their purest form, reigned in the Celestial City.[824]

But the supremacy of natural law did not last long. Its decline had already been reflected in Western jurisprudence during the Enlightenment. Hobbes had already noted that "the Rights of Nature, that is, the naturall Liberty of man, may by the Civill Law be abridged, and restrained: nay, the end of making Lawes, is no other, but such Restraint; without which there cannot possibly be any peace."[825]

The rise of positive law soon overtook natural law in supplying guiding and legitimizing principles for government and its citizenry.[826] Several developments account for the contemporary decline of natural law in Western jurisprudence. The scientific temper of the Industrial Revolution led political and legal philosophers away from metaphysical thinking and into a new emphasis upon the pragmatic analysis of existing institutions and laws. Jeremy Bentham and John Austin, the English masters of analytical positivism, became compelling proponents of positivist jurisprudence. Concurrently, the emergence and consolidation of nationalism demanded a greater emphasis not upon divine and feudal relationships and duties but upon obedience to national laws.[827] Although the idea of establishing fun-

damental principles of human existence and civilization in jurisprudence was not totally lost, the tribunals of justice were increasingly
unwilling to use the standards of natural law as independent sources
of legal authority.

Natural law's decline did not drastically affect American jurisprudence. The grand phrases that were distilled from the jurisprudence
of natural law and deliberately embedded by the Founding Fathers
in the Constitution turned the latter into a consecrated substitute to
positive law. Instead of direct resort to natural law principles, the
courts subsumed some of these principles under such constitutionally articulated positive law safeguards as "due process," "equal
protection," "life, liberty, and property," and the like. As a consequence, in America's new legal world the combination of constitutionalism and judicial review served to lessen the possibility that an
unbridled legislature, given the power to mold positive laws, would
be left free to abuse its powers by issuing and enforcing oppressive
and unjust commandments.

On the European continent, by contrast, the rush toward positivism gave rise to great and unconscionable excesses. The horrors of
twentieth-century totalitarianism sadly illustrate the devastating outcome of a marriage between unprincipled positive law and doctrines
of absolute obedience. It was in response to the Nazi horror that liberal German legal philosopher Gustav Radbruch, onetime minister
of justice in the short-lived Weimar Republic, turned back to natural
law after having devoted his professional life to legal positivism. In
Radbruch's view, positivism, by declaring that "Gesetz is Gesetz"
(Law is Law), had inclined German lawyers and citizens to stand by
helplessly at the ostensively legal killing fields of Nazi barbarism.
Radbruch's ultimate embrace of natural law at the conclusion of
World War II was unavoidable: "Where justice is not even striven
for, where equality which is the core of justice is constantly denied in
the enactment of positive law, there the law is not only 'unjust law'
but lacks the nature of law altogether."[828] Only a handful of Radbruch's contemporaries, however, followed his return to natural law
as a protective shield against evil governance. Graham Hughes explained this voyage: "The barbarities of European dictatorships in
this century, and in particular the hideous brutalities of the Nazi
regime in Germany, left many jurists unhappy with the traditional
positivist insistence that an elucidation of the concept of law could
not properly include a reference to any element of morality.[829]

Yet the renewed post–World War II striving for a higher law produced more than a nostalgic return to the tenets of natural law. It further resulted in the deliberate creation, even before the war was over, of a dramatically evolving system of higher law, consisting mostly of human rights declarations, covenants, and other related international documents, to replace the natural law of old as a new beacon of hope against abuse of power. Radbruch and the other proponents of a return to natural law were thus vindicated, after a fashion, not so much by the revival of the natural law of old as by a new international legal order that began emerging after the Nazi defeat.

The New International "Higher Law"

The historical battle for primacy between the standards of national positive law and international natural law came to an unfortunate end during World War II. The failure of positive law to prevent and withstand the Nazi and Fascist terror inspired the world community, at the conclusion of hostilities, to set out in pursuit of a new global system of higher law. This task was carried out reasonably well through the articulation and adoption of a wide range of worldwide objectives and standards to protect the aspirations and rights of individuals and communities.

These new international standards, like the national constitutions that had come before them, were usually encapsulated in positively phrased and legally binding documents. Like America's Founding Fathers, post–World War II jurists and lawmakers sought to embody precepts and commands derived from natural law in formal and globally binding receptacles—the new body of international positive law. Henceforth, appeal to divine and natural laws no longer remained the sole avenue for reaching humanity's conscience and compassion. A new system of higher law, whose authority was derived from a worldwide social contract, began to emerge as a global guardian for human rights.

In 1948 the U.N. General Assembly adopted the Universal Declaration of Human Rights.[830] In the following quarter century, a host of other proclamations, declarations, conventions, and covenants emanated from the United Nations and its specialized agencies to deal with economic, social, and cultural rights, civil and political rights, slavery and genocide, racial discrimination and apartheid, collective bargaining for workers, children's rights, and the right of asylum.[831] Although the new international declarations were not always followed with legally binding enactments or with effective implementation procedures, they nevertheless left an indelible mark on world consciousness and public opinion. They also supplied new legitimacy to the causes, claims, and struggles of diverse categories of political protesters, resisters, and rebels.

The growing number of U.N. declarations, treaties, and conventions, and the instrumentalities established for their effectuation, have been only part of the postwar legal explosion of positive international higher law. The previously formulated and often unimplemented laws regarding the keeping of the peace and the conduct of war also received an enormous stimulus through the principles articulated by the Charter of the Nuremberg tribunal and similar courts, which were set up in 1945 and later by the Allies to try Axis offenders.[832] These principles drew their binding force both from existing treaties and from the long traditions of customary law. The treaties relied on by the Nuremberg court included the Hague Convention of 1907, the Geneva Convention of 1927, and the Kellogg-Briand Pact of 1928 (or Pact of Paris), agreements that regulated the conduct of all warfare and outlawed wars of aggression. These documents granted the Nuremberg tribunal the authority to try and mete out sanctions against the Nazi leadership, which was judged to have violated the rules of warfare ("war crimes") and to have engaged in aggressive warfare ("crimes against peace").

A second source of authority for the Nuremberg tribunal was provided by the customs of the civilized nations—those practices that had so grown in general acceptance as to make them legally binding upon all members of the community of nations. This customary source of law provided the foundation for a newly articulated class of offenses: "crimes against humanity." This additional category of crimes, unlike "crimes against peace" and "war crimes," was not limited to a state's misconduct against other nations and foreign populations. For the first time in international law, a nation and its leaders were held accountable for abuses of power against its own people.[833]

Some writers have criticized portions of the Nuremberg Charter as constituting *ex post facto* law, claiming that it punished behavior that had not been prohibited at the time of its commission. This complaint, that not all the Nuremberg offenses had been defined by preexisting positive law, has been answered by the telling assertion that "surely ... Hitler, Goering ... and the rest of the unholy alliance in supreme authority in Nazi Germany· knew full well that murder is murder."[834] Moreover, the Nuremberg principles and decisions were subsequently endorsed by an international convention. The Nuremberg outcome thus stands as firm evidence of new standards of higher international law to which both foreigners and citizens may look for relief from unjust and illegal practices ordained or tolerated by national law. The Nuremberg experience has thus greatly contributed to the building of a new system of higher law that, unlike its traditional natural law predecessors, claims no derivation from metaphysical or divine origins.

The principles extracted from the Nuremberg Charter and judgments, though at first challenged as expressing only the wishes and power of the victorious Allies, were swiftly reaffirmed through other treaties and agreements by the wider community of nations. The developing system of higher law, by which all nations were to be bound, included the Genocide Convention of 1948 and the twin conventions (on civil and political rights and on social and economic rights) formulated pursuant to the Universal Declaration of Human Rights.[835] Equally important transnational commitments to the cause of a higher law of human rights have come into being on a regional basis. The Inter-American Commission and Court[836] and the European Convention on Human Rights and its implementing agencies[837] are notable examples.

These new bodies of international law, created through treaties and conventions, have continued to expand dramatically in the second half of the twentieth century, extending the reach of the new international higher law to cover practically all aspects of life in the world community. It is to American political philosopher Leo Strauss that we are indebted for first pointing out, over forty years ago, that in contemporary thought and practice the old divinely or philosophically derived "natural law" was giving way to a new body of universally articulated and recognized "rights of man."[838]

Civilized nations have ostensibly accepted, at least in principle, the precepts of a higher international law of human rights. At the end of the twentieth century, the terminology and jurisprudence of human rights have become irrepressible components of the language and life of the international community. "Self-determination," "autonomy," "democracy," "free speech," "free elections," "genocide," and "abuse of power" are increasingly assuming a common international meaning. Unfortunately, however, the actual administrative and legal practices of many nations have not grown to meet either the expectations or the demands of this new higher law.

International Promises and Domestic Denials

The postwar explosion of international declarations, conventions, protocols, and judicial decisions designed to enhance the rights of individuals and groups and to punish their exploiters and tormentors has created an astonishing array of new expectations and claims. It has also raised an aegis of safeguards to shield those who were formerly unprotected against governmental abuses of power. One could reasonably argue that the new international standards do not merely create the right to demand justice but also recognize, by implication, the right to resist unjust government. Yet those protesting, resisting, or rebelling against alleged governmental abuses continue to be brought before domestic tribunals accountable to the very government they struggle against, rather than being granted a trial by independent international tribunals.

Faced with domestic judges, domestic laws, and domestic punishment, those charged with political offenses have tended to pursue two defense strategies in an effort either to challenge the very validity of the violated laws or to mitigate the penalties prescribed by the existing national laws. In the first place, the defense would seek to rely upon doctrines derived from international law, international human rights law, and humanitarian law (the "law of war") to protect political activists from domestic prosecution. This approach would urge that when internationally recognized rights are denied, rebellion, dissent, or disobedience may be protected, authorized, or even required by international law, and that national punishment would therefore offend against the law of nations. Second, the defense would rely upon the traditional domestic law defenses available to all those charged with criminal offenses. Such defense doctrines as necessity, self-defense, compulsion, good motive, and jury nullification, derived from customary common law and amplified by recent legislation, have thus been increasingly raised in cases involving political offenses.

Despite the grand phraseology and unqualified promises contained in such international pronouncements as the Nuremberg Charter, the Universal Declaration of Human Rights, the Human Rights Covenants, and the Helsinki Accords, these well-recognized documents generally have not been interpreted as binding upon governmental agencies and domestic courts in the United States and other nations. The refusal to accept the authority of the international documents contrasts sharply with the guarantee by America's Founding Fathers that the U.S. Constitution "and the laws of the United States . . . in pursuance thereof and all *treaties* . . . shall be the Supreme Law of the Land" (italics added).[839] As early as 1820 the nation's Supreme Court upheld this constitutional undertaking, thereby affirming that the law of nations was part of the country's common law.[840] But the road to an actual domestic implementation of new international standards has been rocky at best.

American jurisprudence admits, at least in principle, that international law is an integral part of the *ordre public:* a component of the general body of domestic law.[841] This axiomatic acknowledgment found renewed expression in the oft-quoted case *The Paquette Habana* (1900), in which Justice Gray of the U.S. Supreme Court proclaimed that "international law is part of our law."[842] Gray's words echoed Chief Justice Marshall's earlier declaration, in the case of *The Nereide* (1815), that "the Court is bound by the law of nations which is a part of the law of the land."[843]

Subsequent commentators and writings, including the 1986 Restatement of the Foreign Relations Law of the United States, have assumed, accordingly, that rights and duties embodied in international treaties and documents are part of America's law:

> The United Nations Charter and the Charter of the Organization of American States, both of which include human rights provisions, are treaties of the United States. The human rights conventions to which the United States is a party . . . are also treaties of the United States. Obligations assumed by the United States in these agreements are law of the land, either directly if the provisions are self-executing or upon implementation by Congress. . . . The customary law of human rights . . . is also law of the United States. Federal statutes refer to "internationally recognized human rights" and have legislated

national policy toward governments guilty of "consistent patterns of gross violations of such rights."[844]

But despite these assurances, American political offenders have not fared well when they sought to base their defenses on duties or rights derived from international law. In asserting provisions of international law before domestic courts, defense attorneys have constantly had to face a particularly difficult question: whether the international treaties, conventions, and declarations relied upon required further congressional enactment before they could be implemented or whether they could be considered "self-executing." The "self-execution question is perhaps one of the most confounding in treaty law," conceded one American court.[845] In 1829, Chief Justice Marshall explained the dilemma:

> Our Constitution declares a treaty to be the law of the land. It is, consequently, to be regarded in courts of justice as equivalent to an act of the Legislature, whenever it operates of itself, without the aid of any legislative provision. But when the terms of the stipulation import a contract . . . when . . . the treaty addresses itself to the political, not the judicial department . . . the Legislature must execute the contract, before it can become a rule for the court.[846]

In the United States, then, a self-executing treaty is one that does not require further congressional action to give it binding effect domestically. Non–self-executing treaties, on the other hand, must further be adopted by Congress in order to become enforceable as domestic law by the nation's legal system.

U.S. treaties are often presumed to be self-executing. Still, the human rights provisions of the United Nations Charter[847] were held, in *Sei Fujii v. State*,[848] a California case, not to fall within this category, despite the fact that other parts of the Charter, governing such subjects as diplomatic immunity, were determined to be self-executing.[849] Although much criticized and described as "ripe for overruling,"[850] the *Sei Fujii* decision has been upheld by other state and federal courts.[851] Some legal commentators have advanced the argument that the evolution of the Universal Declaration of Human Rights, an authoritative interpretation of the United Nations Charter, should be considered as making the Charter itself self-executing.[852] Though viewed favorably by human rights sympathizers, U.S. courts have been less than enthusiastic in their response to this argument.[853] In 1978, President Carter sent the United Nations Covenant on Civil and Political Rights, the United Nations Covenant on Economic, Social, and Cultural Rights, the International Convention on the Elimination of All Forms of Racial Discrimination, and the American Convention on Human Rights to the Senate for ratification.[854] These documents have yet to be acted upon,[855] and the nation's courts have accordingly rebuffed most attempts by civil rights activists to make the standards contained in these international documents applicable to domestic cases.

On top of the virtually unenforceable protections contained in these arguably non–self-executing conventions, other enactments, in the form of declarations and resolutions of the United Nations and other international bodies, have supplied additional sources of support for the claims of domestic offenders, but to little avail. Although these declarations may not compare to treaties in terms of stature and binding effect, the argument has frequently been made that they must be viewed as part of the traditional and evolving customary international law.[856] Even a mere declaration encompassing standards derived from "customary law" might therefore become part of the domestic "law of the land" without the need for congressional enactment. This binding power granted to nonlegislative pronouncements is derived from the universal recognition that the sources of international law include not only treaties and conventions but also judicial decisions, scholarly writings, and customary law.[857] The proposed Restatement of Foreign Relations Law of the United States accordingly reiterates: "The customary law of human rights [is] law of the United States.[858]

Yet despite the constant and growing efforts in the trial of political offenders, both in the United States and abroad, to advance defenses derived from international law standards (whether contained in declarations, conventions, customs, or scholarly writings), the impact of these attempts has been only marginal.[859] To the great and continuing disappointment of human rights activists, international human rights documents, despite their growing diversity and constantly increasing number, have not become an integral part of domestic law and enforcement in most countries. Even the widely known Nuremberg principles have had little impact on the consideration of defenses raised by political offenders in domestic courts.[860] In *United States v. Montgomery,* for example, American defendants sought to justify or excuse their destruction of missile components as "an effort to insulate themselves from personal responsibility for United States nuclear military policy," a policy they claimed was in violation of international law principles recognized at Nuremberg.[861] The defendants analogized their situation to that of the Nuremberg defendants, who had been convicted for their failure to defy Nazi Germany's laws that violated the law of nations.[862]

The *Montgomery* court conceded that the Nuremberg prosecutors had "argued that even individual private citizens have an obligation under international law which may require them to violate domestic law to prevent their government from committing war crimes in violation of international law."[863] Although the court agreed that the Nuremberg principles may impose a duty not to cooperate with an unjust domestic law ("a duty not to act"), the judge concluded that no affirmative duty was imposed upon individuals under Nuremberg to actively break the law, or to engage in a conflict with unjust authority.[864] Likewise, most similar attempts to rely on the Nuremberg principles, the Universal Declaration of Human Rights, and various other treaty or customary law rights, either as an excuse for taking militant action or as an excuse for disregarding the laws of abusive governments, have been consistently defeated in the United States and throughout the world.[865] Sometimes, however, those relying on new international standards in challenging the restrictive or abusive laws of their native countries have done much better in the regional courts of the European community or in the similar tribunals of the Americas.[866]

Domestic Defenses of Just Cause, Good Motive, and Necessity

American and most other courts generally have been inhospitable to defenses raised by political offenders, whether derived from international law or grounded in domestic legal principles. The failure of these courts to afford political offenders relief or even an opportunity to be effectively heard is not surprising, given the judiciary's historical practice of distancing itself from issues that are perceived as primarily "moral" or "political" rather than "legal."[867]

Judicial tribunals in America and elsewhere have insisted that in the discharge of their duties they may not unduly inquire into the "whys" behind a legislative enactment or the motives underlying an offender's deed. Accordingly, courts have described their primary functions as interpreting existing laws and determining whether they have been complied with or not. In the highly publicized conspiracy trial of Dr. Benjamin Spock, on charges of counseling draft evasion during the Vietnam War, the judge carefully instructed the jury that "we are not trying the legality, morality, or constitutionality of the war in Vietnam or the rights of a citizen to protest."[868] The courts in other cases have similarly rebuffed defense urgings to consider claims that the violated laws were unjust or contrary to "natural" or "higher" law, or claims that the offenders were motivated by moral considerations that negated the requisite *mens rea* and disproved the required criminal intent.

Nevertheless, American and most other criminal laws afford still other opportunities for the accused to challenge the validity of the law he or she is charged with violating. A criminal defendant may assert that a law in question is unduly vague and by being insufficient to warn a prospective violator of its prohibitions is "void for vagueness."[869] The accused may urge further that the law is void for imposing criminal penalties for conduct that amounts to nothing more than an involuntary illness (such as a drug or alcohol affliction) or an unblameworthy status (such as vagrancy or homelessness).[870] In America one may argue that a law, whether enacted by local, state, or federal authorities, is invalid for improperly proscribing conduct that is authorized and protected by the federal Constitution or state constitutions.[871]

When the law under which an offense is charged is closely interwoven with political issues, courts have often espoused a highly technical jurisprudential doctrine designed to narrow the judiciary's authority to consider the validity of contested laws. Characterized as the "political question" doctrine, its supposed purpose is to preserve the separation of powers decreed by the U.S. Constitution. The upholding of the doctrine often leads to the conclusion that the Constitution's grant of primary authority over political decisions to the legislative and executive branches precludes judicial interference with these politically charged issues. The U.S. Supreme Court defined the requisite conditions for determining the existence of a political question in the following manner:

> Prominent on the surface of any case held to involve a political question is found a textually demonstrable constitutional commitment of the issue to a

coordinate political department; or lack of judicially discoverable and manageable standards for resolving it . . . or the impossibility of a court's undertaking independent resolution without expressing lack of the respect due coordinate branches of government; or an unusual need for unquestioning adherence to a political decision already made; or the potentiality of embarrassment from multifarious pronouncements by various departments on one question.[872]

When America's David Mitchell III was prosecuted for willfully failing to report for induction into the armed forces during the Vietnam War, he made strenuous attempts to challenge the legality of required military service. He sought to advance the argument before the court that the Vietnam War was contrary to international law and contrary to American treaty obligations, and that military service in that context would have required him to commit war crimes. The court ruled the proposed evidence to be immaterial and inadmissible.[873] In this and similar cases, American courts concluded that the legality of the war was a political question and thus not subject to review and adjudication by the judicial branch.[874] Those refusing to obey induction laws on the ground that the draft was contrary to constitutional or international law, and therefore void, were thus denied the opportunity to be heard. The political question doctrine has acted to totally insulate the positive law relied upon by the legislative and executive branches from challenges by those urging adherence to the "higher" legal standards of constitutional or international law.

Neither have those charged with political offenses been successful in advancing their personal, moral, or legal motives as an appropriate defense. One of the fundamental principles of Anglo-American jurisprudence is its rejection of the defense of *good* or *worthy* motive.[875] How is it that an issue as logically relevant as an offender's motive merits so little attention in our contemporary system of jurisprudence? The U.S. Supreme Court has described criminal responsibility as a concurrence of "an evil-meaning mind with an evil-doing hand."[876] It is this linking of *mens rea* and *actus reus* that produces the crime. But these traditional articulations of criminal responsibility are deceiving. From them a layperson might conclude that the "evil-meaning mind," or *mens rea*, requires moral culpability or an evil motive. Yet it is merely intent, not motive, that is required to constitute the *mens rea* for criminal responsibility. It is sufficient under the law that the accused had an intention to commit the act proscribed by law. Whether such intention was derived from egoistic or altruistic motives is irrelevant. One who intentionally takes the life of another human being is responsible for murder, regardless of whether the death was the outcome of an attempted robbery or was committed to relieve a loved one from the intractable pains of a terminal illness.

"Intent and motive should never be confused," lawyers are usually warned.[877] Motive reflects the sum total of personal factors that prompt a person to act, while intent refers merely to the deliberate character of the offender's act. Motive encompasses such subjective elements as hate or love, jealousy or generosity, greed or selfishness. Intent, on the other hand, seeks to define a simpler and more objective reality: Was the actor aware of his or her deed and willful in its execution, or did he or she act while unconscious, as a consequence of a sudden seizure, or under external compulsion? Stated differently: "Motivation deals with ulterior reasons for acting and is largely a question of morality and psychology, while intention is concerned with the voluntariness of an act, which is the only relevant factor in determining whether a person can be held culpable for conduct proscribed by the criminal law."[878]

The inflexible Anglo-American legal doctrine that favors intent and disfavors motive is a doctrine designed mainly to make objective rather than subjective criteria the test for assessing human guilt or innocence. It thus prevents one charged with anti-abortion protests, euthanasia (mercy killing), or political crime from asserting his or her motive in negation or mitigation of the offense. But, despite the overall doctrinal rejection of defenses based on "good" motive, indirect attempts to introduce evidence of an offender's motive have nevertheless been attempted, and at times have even succeeded, in political trials.

Evidence of motive is often denied admission altogether on the ground that it lacks relevance. In *United States v. Cullen*, the court thus summarily rejected the defendant's attempt to offer his religious beliefs and moral opposition to the Vietnam War as a defense to a charge of destroying official selective service records. Said the court: "[I]f the proof discloses that the prohibited act was voluntary, and that the defendant actually knew, or reasonably should have known, that it was a public wrong, the burden of proving the requisite intent has been met; proof of motive, good or bad, has no relevance to that issue."[879]

Yet attorneys for political offenders have persisted in their innovative tactics to introduce motive-related evidence into courts of law. Sometimes, while a jury is being selected and sworn in, counsel may put prospective jurors on notice regarding the underlying issues involved in the forthcoming trial, thereby enhancing the jury's awareness despite the defense counsel's inability to enter formal evidence of motive. Prospective jurors in the trial of the "Oakland Seven" were thus advised during the initial jury selection: "The defendants believe the U.S. foreign policy is racist, colonialist, and genocidal. . . . Would it shock you to learn the defendants supported the Black Panthers? Could you be fair to a person who refused induction into the Armed Services?"[880]

Another technique that has often proved helpful in bringing an offender's political motives to the attention of the court and jury has been to have the defendant appear *pro se,* as his or her own counsel. One defense lawyer, in the trial of the "Gainesville Eight," described how the defendants, acting as their own counsel, succeeded in inserting political statements and defenses into the trial record.[881] When the judges ruled that the accused could not bring witnesses into court to testify on the issue of their motives, the defendants would take the stand themselves, primarily to testify concerning the facts, yet utilizing the opportunity to speak about their motives and states of mind in committing the prohibited acts. In some instances defense counsel would elaborately rely on the alleged offense's statutory definition, which might have specifically required the accused to have acted "willfully" or "maliciously," in order to address the issue of motive.

Most of these defense techniques have proven to be relatively ineffective.[882] When defendants seek to make jurors aware of their "good" motives, the courts usually hasten to warn the jury against giving undue consideration to allegations of altruism or righteousness. In *United States v. Malinowiski* the court gave the jury a typical instruction: "I charge you that you may not treat defendant's beliefs in respect to the war in Vietnam as a possible negation of criminal intent. Defendant's motivation in this case—the fact that he was engaged in a protest in the sincere belief that he was acting in a good cause—is not an acceptable legal defense or justification."[883]

A few departures from this judicial inflexibility have occurred from time to time. Judges have occasionally permitted defendants to introduce some evidence pertaining to their particular motivations. In the "Wounded Knee" trial, for example, Judge Nichol allowed the accused Native Americans to testify as to their reasons in taking over the Wounded Knee community in South Dakota.[884] "[O]nce admitted into evidence, it is almost certain that the political motivation of the defendants does influence the trier of fact," concluded an experienced observer.[885] At the conclusion of the Wounded Knee trial, an attorney for the defendants admitted publicly that "the judge's decision to allow the defense to develop the circumstances and the reasons for the 1973 Indian uprising had been essential to the [defense] victory."[886] The chief prosecutor, on the other hand, complained that the judge's decision to admit evidence of motives was "incredible."[887]

From a purely academic perspective one might sympathize with America's jurisprudential insistence upon such objective standards (or supposedly value-free abstractions) as "intent," the "reasonable man," "reasonable care," and "reasonable doubt" in its efforts to avoid the inequities inherent in the actual diversities of human heritage, education, intelligence, behavior, and motivation. One who does not comport oneself with the degree of care expected of a "reasonable" person is thus made liable for negligence. When provoked or acting in self-defense, one is justified in resorting to no more force or violence than a "reasonable" person would employ. When measuring one's "heat of passion" or the "cooling of blood" (elements essential for separating murder from manslaughter), it is not the offender's passion that is controlling, but that of a "reasonable" person.

Intent is less personal, less complex, less value-loaded, and at the same time more universally normative than the subjective standard of motive. Permitting courts and particularly juries to hear and be swayed by evidence of individual and subjective drives, emotions, and reactions is feared and rejected as a concession to individual and populist justice.

The Fear of Popular Conscience

Since earliest times, Anglo-American law has persistently sought to maintain a balance between formalism and flexibility, elitism and populism. This desire for an appropriate jurisprudential balance is evidenced in the original willingness to supplant the strict English common law with the more lenient principles of equity. Common law remained strictly attached to traditional principles and institutions. Equity became more responsive to change and to popular concepts of justice and fairness. To further enhance the quest for balance, common law subjected both the lawmaking powers of the majoritarian legislatures and the interpretive authority of the generally elitist judicial branch to the mediating influences of popular forces through reliance on grand and trial juries.

In earlier times, the trial jury possessed not only the power to determine the facts but also the power to construct the law. During some of the most repressive English regimes it was the lay jury that continued to guard against the erosion of the rights of citizens. When the English law of treason became increasingly oppressive to the rights of political activists and reformers, the jury was able to step in and, through exercising the power of nullification, preserve fundamental rights.[888]

The power of nullification was not unlike the modern practice of judicial review, which permits courts to invalidate legislative enactments on the grounds of incompatibility with constitutional values. But nullification was, at its core, an expression of the popular will, as contrasted with the more elitist present-day role of judicial review. "[T]he right of the jury to decide questions of law and fact," wrote historian Alan Sheflin, "prevailed in this country until the middle 1800s. By the end of the century, however, the power of the jury had been thoroughly decimated by a jealous judiciary eager to exercise tighter controls over lay participants in the administration of justice."[889]

With time, equity was merged back into law to create a new system of justice within which law predominates. Juries have been similarly stripped of their right to make decisions of law, and nullification has become a rarely tolerated practice. Some exceptions have continued to function here and there. One federal court noted emphatically in 1969:

> We recognize . . . the undisputed power of the jury to acquit even if its verdict is contrary to the law as given by the judge and contrary to the evidence. . . . If the jury feels that the law under which the defendant is accused is unjust, or that exigent circumstances justified the actions of the accused, or for any reason which appeals to their logic or passion, the jury has the power to acquit, and the courts must abide by that decision.[890]

Most contemporary scholars and courts, however, have either rejected outright or imposed severe restrictions on the doctrine of nullification. In *United States v. Dougherty*,[891] a typically suspicious federal court of appeals suggested that juries were more susceptible to sentiment than were judges, and that a jury might acquit on emotional grounds, ignoring the facts. In the court's opinion, the strong political overtones of the *Dougherty* trial, which involved an appeal by a group known as the "D.C. Nine" from a conviction for unlawful entry into the offices of Dow Chemical, presented just such an opportunity for emotional error. The *Dougherty* court grudgingly acknowledged that the jury possessed a "prerogative-in-fact" to acquit, but ruled that the law does not permit the jury to be informed of this choice.[892] The court further warned of the possibility of anarchy were the doctrine of nullification to be widely implemented.[893]

Chief Judge Bazelon of the appeals court, dissenting in *Dougherty*, insisted on the jury's right to be advised of its traditional powers. He pointed out that informing the jury of its right to acquit would remedy a "deliberate lack of candor" and would provide a mechanism for allowing the jury to serve as representatives of and spokespersons for community morality. Bazelon urged further:

> The Doctrine [of jury nullification] permits the jury to bring to bear on the criminal process a sense of fairness and particularized justice. The drafters of legal rules cannot anticipate and take account of every case where a defendant's conduct is unlawful but not blameworthy, any more than they can draw a bold line to mark the boundary between an accident and negligence. It is the jury—as spokesman for the community's sense of values—that must explore that subtle and elusive boundary.[894]

But Bazelon's view has not prevailed and jury nullification has not been generally admitted into the modern trials of American political offenders.[895] Nor has the principle of nullification gained broad adherence in other arenas of the law.[896]

One must also acknowledge that the oft-repeated textbook assertion that criminal law looks to intent and never to motive or individual belief is not totally accurate. Criminal law has always permitted the accused some individually defined defenses in order to escape responsibility. The accused may allege the absence of either the prohibited act *(actus reus)* or the requisite mental state *(mens rea)*. Similarly, the actions of one who engages in self-defense or in the defense of others against an aggressor do not constitute acts of criminality as long as they are proportionate to the threat posed. Neither can one be charged with the requisite criminal intent when his or her acts were produced by compulsion, such as an imminent threat by third parties to do grievous harm to the accused or the accused's family. One who commits nondeadly offenses (including larceny, forgery, and some forms of assault) in response to compulsion by his oppressors is thus exempted from guilt and punishment.[897]

An accused may similarly avoid responsibility and the penalties of the criminal process by establishing that his or her lawbreaking was prompted by necessity, meaning the desire of the actor to avoid a much greater social evil. The defense of necessity was illustrated long ago in Jesus' New Testament justification of the plucking of corn on the Sabbath by those who were hungry.[898] This entitlement of citizens to rely on their own judgment and discretion to violate the positive law in order to avoid greater social harm is codified to-day in the laws of many American states and foreign countries. For example, the laws of Illinois specify: "Conduct which would other-wise be an offense is justifiable by reason of necessity if the accused was without blame in occasioning or developing the situation and reasonably believed such conduct was necessary to avoid a public or private injury greater than the injury which might reasonably result from his own conduct."[899] Wisconsin's law similarly mitigates even the punishment for murder if the act is committed "[b]ecause the pressure of natural physical forces causes such person reasonably to believe that his act is the only means of preventing imminent public disaster or imminent death to himself or another."[900]

Political activists seeking to enhance their defense strategies have frequently combined the domestic defense of "necessity"[901] with a resort to the internationally derived "Nuremberg defense." Relying on the defense rule of necessity that citizens have the right to violate the law in order to avoid greater social harm, political offenders have occasionally sought to further justify their actions by arguing that the failure to act not only would have produced greater "social harms"[902] but also would have subjected them to punishment under the Nuremberg principles. Despite these innovative efforts, the ne-cessity defense has proven extremely difficult to apply and imple-ment. In the first place, the defendant must establish his or her standing, meaning a personal right or duty to respond to the per-ceived danger.

Those seeking to prove necessity have thus been required to demonstrate to the courts that: "(1) the defendant was faced with a clear and imminent danger, not one that is debatable or speculative; (2) the defendant can reasonably expect that his action will be effective [in] abating the danger; (3) there was no legal alternative which will be effective [for] abating the danger; and (4) that the Legislature has not acted to preclude the defense."[903] Because of these stringent criteria, and particularly due to the requirement of effectiveness, valiant efforts to assert the necessity defense have usually been rejected when the act of protest has been shown by the prosecution to constitute little more than a symbolic gesture. Even greater and often insurmountable hurdles have been erected by various courts to further curb the availability of the necessity defense. One commentator describes these difficult, judicially imposed playing grounds:

> The defendant must first introduce enough evidence so that a reasonable juror may conclude that the evidence satisfies each required element of the defense. If the defendant satisfies this burden, the judge must permit the defense and instruct the jury accordingly. Typically, in civil resistance or civil disobedience cases, courts refuse to present a necessity defense instruction to the jury. Nearly every reported state and federal appellate decision has rejected the application of the necessity defense under these circumstances because the defendants have been unable to satisfy the court's assessment of what constitutes "necessity."[904]

Recently, prosecutors have resorted yet to another procedural tool as a means for restricting a defendant's use of the necessity defense.[905] Known as a motion *in limine,* this procedure curtails the defense's use of specific items of evidence as the judge deems likely to prejudice or confuse the jury, or otherwise increase the complexity of a trial. Such a motion can be employed to ensure that the jury never sees critical evidence that might prove the necessity of the criminal's actions.

Due to these mounting impediments, the defense efforts of political offenders have not fared well in recent years.[906] For example, the necessity defense was rejected in *United States v. May,*[907] in which the defendants, who had destroyed missile parts, alleged that they were acting to prevent nuclear war. The few missile parts destroyed, the court ruled in rejecting the defense, would have had little effect on the army's ability to wage a nuclear war. Similar attempts to rely on the necessity defense have proven unsuccessful in other instances, including cases involving the bringing of the illegal drug laetrile into the United States for the treatment of cancer patients;[908] the burning of selective service records to protest U.S. military action;[909] engaging in anti-abortion protests;[910] protesting American involvement in El Salvador;[911] smuggling refugees from war-torn Central America in violation of immigration laws;[912] and protesting government policies regarding the treatment of the homeless.[913]

It is apparent that the defenses of good motive, compulsion, and necessity, and the concepts of jury nullification, generally have not been successful in protecting political offenders from prosecution or conviction under American and other domestic laws. International defenses, raised in justification of prohibited domestic acts and relying mainly on the Nuremberg principles, the Declaration of Human Rights, the United Nations Charter, and other instruments and principles of the law of nations, have not been well received either. Current trends in the handling of political offenders and their defenses by United States and most foreign courts suggest generally that Justice Fortas's perspectives on law and order have prevailed: The chains of positive criminal law continue to restrain those who resort to civil disobedience and rebellion in order to satisfy the demands of conscience or higher law. The denial of the political offender's prayers for a differential status has persisted despite the constantly widening panoply of defenses that have been accorded in America and elsewhere to common criminals charged with venal crimes. How long can this nation and the world community persist, in the face of the fierce winds of global change, in denying political offenders an opportunity to plead for special consideration? How long can we deny them the opportunity to proclaim their reliance upon natural law, international law, human rights law, constitutional law, and other internationally or nationally acclaimed principles of justice?

The Political Offender and the Law of War

Thus far, our examination of the political offender's legal status has focused on rights and defenses derived from the newly emerging international system of higher law, and on rights and defenses derived from the existing domestic jurisprudence. There is yet a third system of jurisprudence affecting the legal status of rebels and other political militants. This system is offered by "humanitarian law," the well-established yet still evolving body of international rules applicable to the conduct of international wars, a set of rules that sometimes affects domestic conflicts as well.

Although the seeds of the law of war, or *jus in bello*, were planted in antiquity and sprouted during the late Renaissance, the existing formulation of this law is relatively new, dating back to the latter part of the nineteenth century and the first half of the twentieth century. The prevailing rules of war, which have increasingly become known as "humanitarian law" since World War II, are said to represent an effort to (1) impose increasingly comprehensive restrictions upon the methods of warfare, (2) limit the effects of violence upon combatants and require humane treatment for disabled and surrendered belligerents, and (3) spare civilians and others not directly involved in the hostilities from the ravages of war.[914]

Most recently recodified by the Geneva Conventions of 1949 and by the subsequent Protocols I and II, the modern international law of war grants a protected status to those engaging in "lawful belligerency." Belligerents who conduct themselves according to the requirements of humanitarian law are viewed as warriors rather than criminals, despite their resort to arms, violence, and homicide. Theoretically, such warriors may at any time lay down their arms and be free from prosecution for warlike conduct.

In defining "belligerency," early U.S. rules of military conduct provided that "so soon as a man is armed by a sovereign government and taken the soldier's oath of fidelity, he is a belligerent; his killing, wounding, or other warlike acts are not individual crimes or offenses."[915] Upon surrender or capture the lawful belligerent, who becomes a prisoner of war, must be treated humanely and, upon the termination of hostilities, must be returned unharmed to his native country. Only the belligerent who fails to comply with the required standards of lawful warfare by acting deceitfully, by failing to safeguard innocent or neutral populations, or by committing other war crimes, is denied these protections of the humanitarian law. An unlawful belligerent becomes subject to punishment under both international and domestic law. Through most of recent history, these humanitarian protections, developed as part of the law of nations, have applied only to persons participating in or being affected by international conflicts. On the other hand, such domestic conflicts as rebellions, civil wars, protests, civil disobedience, and dissidence were seen exclusively as matters of local concern and therefore subject only to the domestic laws and policies of the sovereign governments involved.

Some early and very important exceptions to these limitations should be noted. During the American Civil War, the articles of war binding upon the Union forces (drafted by Columbia College's Professor Francis Lieber), while permitting the prosecution of Southern rebels as traitors, also offered Union military commanders the alternative of treating their Southern captives as prisoners of war.[916] With time, both Northern and Southern commanders took up this alternative option, which conceded in practice, if not in legal theory, that participants in the Civil War were not criminals and traitors but rather soldiers in a war between states. Throughout America's Civil War no treason trials were held and no criminal penalties were imposed upon surrendered or captured soldiers of either camp.[917] The rebellion's denomination as "the War Between the States" (a term favored to this day by Southern sympathizers) continues to reiterate a military, as opposed to criminal, designation for that terrible conflict.

In other times and countries, when a civil war had brought about a de facto division of territories, or where the rebelling party had established some form of stability or equality, members of the community of nations as well as the warring parties themselves have frequently accorded the status of "belligerency" to both contending armies.[918] Recent rebellions, insurgencies, and domestic wars in Africa, Asia, and South America reflect the growing readiness of both the world community and governing regimes to accord adversaries involved in popular and massive domestic conflicts the status of de facto belligerents.

Both the 1954–1962 Algerian struggle against French colonialism and the 1967–1970 Nigerian civil war aptly exemplify internal conflicts in which rebel forces, Algerian or Biafran, were granted virtual lawful combatant status by their French and Nigerian antagonists.[919] A similar mutuality of belligerency concessions (under which both those in authority and their adversaries were expected to comply with humanitarian law principles) was in evidence during the Nicaraguan conflict between the Sandinista government and the

Contras, as well as during several other smoldering African and Asian domestic conflicts.

The early post–World War II era witnessed a particularly aggressive international effort to expand, not only in informal practice but also in formal legal doctrine, the traditional provisions of the law of war in order to afford humanitarian safeguards to those engaging in domestic rather than international conflicts. Spurred by the increased incidence of wars of national liberation and by post-independence civil conflicts, the newly independent nations (which gained their own liberation through rebellion and civil war) particularly supported the extension of humanitarian law protections for the benefit of their still unliberated and struggling colonial brethren.

For most of the last half of the twentieth century, the support by Third World countries and by members of the Soviet camp for those professing to rebel against colonial and racist regimes seemed to be unabated. Yet this liberality toward the right of rebellion might undergo drastic changes in the face of the growing challenges posed by emerging separatist and centrifugal forces to the stability of the newly created governments of the Third World and of the former Soviet empire.

Article 3 of the four Geneva Conventions of 1949,[920] and the two 1977 Protocols expanding the Conventions,[921] are clear evidence of a concerted effort to extend the international law of war to domestic conflicts. Protocol I, which otherwise addresses only "international" conflicts,[922] specifies that those engaging in domestic conflicts "in which people are fighting against colonial domination and alien occupation and against racial regimes in the exercise of self-determination,"[923] are to be treated as international belligerents. Protocol I thereby elevates selected types of domestic conflicts (reminiscent of the classic category of "just" wars) to an international level.

Protocol I provides further that these elevated domestic combatants are to be treated as "prisoners of war" upon capture by those in authority. Such belligerency status is conditioned, however, upon the requirements that anti-colonial, anti-alien, and anti-racist militants (1) distinguish themselves from the civilian population by carrying their arms openly, (2) wear distinctive signs, (3) follow an organized command, and (4) adhere to the laws and customs of war.[924] Although Protocol I imposes stringent prerequisites upon those engaging in domestic conflicts before they are entitled to be treated as international belligerents,[925] the very fact that international standards were made applicable to domestic conflicts constitutes a major breakthrough for those engaging in domestic warfare. For the first time in the history of domestic conflicts, political rebels complying with specified standards of belligerency in their fight against colonial, alien, or racist regimes have been exempted by international law from domestic prosecution and punishment.

While Protocol I offers special protections only for those engaged in anti-colonial, anti-alien, and anti-racist wars of national liberation, participants in other domestic conflicts benefit from the lesser safeguards of Common Article 3 of the three 1949 Geneva Humanitarian Law Conventions and the provisions of Protocol II of 1977. It is generally agreed that Common Article 3, intended to articulate minimal humanitarian standards for all domestic armed conflicts, applies to all instances of domestic warfare and not merely to domestic conflicts that constitute "wars of national liberation."[926] But although Article 3 encompasses all domestic "armed conflicts," the latter term was left undefined.[927] The prevailing explanation for this omission is that the drafters of Article 3 intended to exclude from its coverage "situations of political unrest accompanied by nothing more than sporadic acts of violence."[928]

To better understand the definitional dilemma and its implications, one might benefit from consulting the language of Article 3 itself:

In the case of armed conflict not of an international . . . character each Party to the conflict shall be bound to apply, as a minimum, the following provisions:

1.   Persons taking no active part in the hostilities including members of armed forces who have laid down their arms . . . shall in all circumstances be treated humanely. . . .
     To this end, the following acts are and shall remain prohibited . . . with respect to the above-captioned persons:
     (a) violence to life of a person, in particular murder of all kinds, mutilation, cruel treatment and torture
     (b) taking of hostages
     (c) outrages upon personal dignity . . .
     (d) the passing of sentences and the carrying our of executions without previous judgement pronounced by a regularly constituted court . . .

2.   The wounded and sick shall be collected and cared for.

An impartial humanitarian body, such as the International Red Cross, may offer its services to the Parties of the conflict.

The Parties to the conflict should further endeavor to bring into force, by means of special agreements, all or part of the other provisions of the present Convention.

The application of the preceding provisions shall not affect the legal status of the Parties to the conflict.[929]

By so granting domestic political offenders whose actions reach the level of an "armed conflict" some forms of international protection (including safeguards against summary punishment for those who lay down their weapons), even if minimal, Article 3 has furthered the internationalization of many, if not all, of the activities of those engaged in domestic dissidence and rebellion. Parties to such armed conflicts who surrender, who are injured, who become ill, or who are captured must be accorded due process and must be treated humanely. Furthermore, though these combatants may be tried domestically and punished criminally for their rebellion, no penalties may be carried out against them without a prior judicial process.

Still broader potentials for extending international safeguards to domestic rebels are contained in Protocol II to the Geneva Conventions, designed to develop and supplement Common Article 3 of the three Humanitarian Law Conventions. Protocol II applies specifically to internal armed conflicts involving "dissident armed forces ... under responsible command, [who] exercise such control over a part of its territory as to enable them to carry out sustained and concerted military operations."[930] Protocol II's coverage, intended to apply to situations that resemble civil wars, specifically excludes lesser "situations of internal disturbances and tensions, such as riots [and] isolated and sporadic acts of violence."[931] For those coming within its coverage, including captured rebels, Protocol II seeks to develop and supplement the guarantees of humane treatment listed in Common Article 3. Whether and how these guarantees are to be enforced in the face of escalating and indiscriminate civil wars, such as those carried out in the recent past in Congo, Rwanda, Sudan, and former Yugoslavia, and before that in Nicaragua, remain matters of grave global concern.[932]

Significantly, during the drafting of Protocol II several voices were heard in support of conferring the traditional international prisoner-of-war status (thereby totally exempting them from responsibility for warlike activities) on those taking part in domestic, civil war–type, armed conflicts.[933] Few of the countries participating in the drafting conference were willing, however, to relinquish their right to punish criminally those engaged in domestic armed rebellion.[934] As a consequence, even though Protocol II establishes the duty of governments to accord humane treatment to civil war–type rebels in captivity, those in authority are not prohibited from trying such combatants as traitors or as common criminals.

The combined effect of the various provisions of the 1949 Geneva Conventions and the 1977 Protocols (although excluding major segments of the political offender community) is to manifest the drive to bring militant groups of domestic political offenders increasingly under the protection of international humanitarian law. Both in law and in practice, post–World War II developments have sought to endow those participating in wars of national liberation, in anti-alien and anti-racist conflicts, and even some of those engaged in other domestic armed conflicts, with a status and privileges previously accorded only to international belligerents.

Amnesties and Pardons

After their defenses of justification and necessity have been ignored, and the application of international declarations and human rights standards have been scoffed at, after their motives have been shunted into the shadows, and their claims to the status of lawful belligerent have been denied, political offenders most probably find themselves in prison or subject to other severe sanctions. At this point, their options become rather limited. Unless escape or the eventual victory of their camp present themselves, their last hopes are for an amnesty or a pardon. Considerations of mercy and conciliation provide the theoretical underpinnings for these remaining methods of relief. Yet, as the reader will see, political pragmatism rather than considerations of justice and compassion tends to be the driving force behind these remaining avenues for mitigating the political offender's fate.

The granting of amnesty or pardons to those previously taking part in anti-government protest or warfare, as well as to abusers of state power eventually turned out of office, has indeed become one of the most pressing issues facing national and international law- and policymakers today. As the incidence of domestic or intranational warfare continues to rise, the postconflict consequences—how offending participants in these conflicts are to be dealt with—pose intense dilemmas. Did Raoul Cedras, a leader of Haiti's former junta, deserve to have past offenses forgotten, or should he have been tried as a common criminal, as was suggested by Haiti's reinstalled president, Jean Bertrand Aristide? Should the supporters of the international offense of apartheid who have committed crimes in the name of that cause be treated the same under the law as those who have struggled to defeat apartheid? Should considerations of future political conciliation prevent or delay the prosecution and trial of the parties responsible for war crimes in former Yugoslavia? These questions continue to be unresolved, which often leads to the fostering of additional hostility, injustice, confusion, and communal unrest.

As amnesty plays a greater role in the arenas of national and international politics, there are growing calls for its application in a manner that is responsive, principled, and, most importantly, just. Yet Amnesty suffers from the lack of principled and systematic approaches that similarly plagues other questions relating to the political offender. The haphazard approach taken so far by the international community regarding amnesty has resulted in grave injustices and tragic consequences for the victims of some of the worst crimes visited upon humanity this century. To make matters worse, factors such as apathy, political compromise, and a tendency to eradicate national errors and abuses from the collective memory ("let bygones be bygones") contribute to make amnesty more a Machiavellian tool than a doctrine grounded in law, morality, and social conciliation.

Amnesty has been defined as a "sovereign act of oblivion" for past acts, granted to persons guilty of crimes against an existing regime, as well as a pardon by those newly assuming state power, extended to those who "composed, supported or obeyed the government which has been overthrown."[935] The amnesty may affect only those in specified (upper or lower) echelons of power, or it might be more extensive, encompassing broad groups or communities. Thus the central tenet and task of this book—to distinguish (through an implementation of existing norms and standards) between the altruistic political offender and the venal common criminal—could play a modest if not crucial role in the development of consistent principles and guidelines for a comprehensive doctrine and practice of amnesty.

This is not to suggest or advocate a talisman or panacea for the complex and wide-ranging current questions that have emerged in the amnesty arena. What is proposed, however, is that an overall framework developed for the classification of political offenders can and should be applied to amnesty as well, in order to more effectively and better differentiate between venal violators of human rights and those individuals or groups who truly deserve the benefits of amnesty. The power to extend mercy and forgiveness, the theoretical underpinnings of pardons and amnesties, is vested mostly in politically chosen leaders (whether in the legislative or executive branches), although social pragmatism and popular sentiment play direct roles in the exercise of these mitigating techniques.

After the overthrow of Salvador Allende's democratically elected rule in Chile, for example, General Augusto Pinochet's junta government carried out some of the worst human rights violations in the Western hemisphere. Then, five years into its imposed terror, the departing junta issued Decree Law Number 2192, which granted amnesty to all governmental agents for any crimes committed during the outgoing regime.[936] Clearly, high-minded altruism was not foremost in the generals' thoughts when this decree was promulgated. Instead, they merely wished to protect their own men, those who had been doing their dirty work and who might talk too much and incriminate their superiors. The Chilean amnesty totally obliterated the judicial power to punish some 2,115 murders.[937] Both the purpose and the effects of the amnesty were brutally revealed when, in October 1989, just before allowing free elections, General Pinochet told that press that "[n]o one touches anyone. The day they touch one of my men, the rule of law ends. This I say once and will not say again."[938]

Under U.S. law, amnesty is considered as only one of five differentiated types of exoneration, all grouped under the heading of "clemency." It has been recognized since the country's founding that the clemency power is vested in the executive branch of government, although there is nothing in the common law or in the Constitution to prevent the legislature or judiciary from exercising independent clemency functions. A number of Supreme Court decisions have asserted, however, that neither the legislature nor the judiciary may curtail the executive's power to grant clemency and reprieves. Clemency, and thus amnesty and pardon, have roots deep in the English common law. Historically, the king exercised various forms of clemency and shared the privilege with the clergy, the earls, and the feudal courts. It was Henry VIII who formally and authoritatively consolidated the clemency power solely in the Crown.[939] The executive nature of this exculpatory power carried over to the Thirteen Colonies, where typically the colony's royal governor was vested with the pardon power.[940] In the late seventeenth and early eighteenth centuries, the English Parliament sought to limit the king's clemency power through a variety of legislative enactments. But although the Crown's power to pardon impeachment was eventually blocked, the king's control over the clemency power remained largely unaffected.[941]

After the Revolutionary War and during the Constitutional Convention, the pardon power was one of the topics of discussion between the states' rights advocates and the federalists, but it did not play much of a role in the Convention's agenda.[942] In the end, the English approach to clemency was retained, with language inserted into the Constitution to reflect the English Act of Settlement of 1701, to the effect that the executive shall exercise the pardon power "except in Cases of Impeachment."[943] No guidelines were issued, however, nor were any standards propagated with which the executive was required to comply while exercising the clemency power.

In the United States an offender may submit a petition for clemency to either a state governor or to the president, depending on whether the conviction was for a state or federal offense. Frequently the grounds asserted for the conferral of clemency include: the modification of marginal convictions (when the factual evidence did not readily fall within the elements or intent of the law); the correction of unduly severe sentences; reviewing unresolved claims of innocence; the reconsideration of mitigating circumstances; the consideration of the offender's physical condition; the prevention of executing questionable death penalties; the consideration of compelling arguments for restoring the offender's civil rights; the prevention of an undeserved deportation of offenders; the consideration of changed political circumstances; and the consideration of other "reasons of state," including the offender's turning state's evidence or offering other valuable services to the state.[944]

Several U.S. Supreme Court and lower federal court decisions have enumerated other criteria for the exercise of clemency. Although these criteria do not seriously infringe upon the executive's authority to grant clemency, they do occasionally permit the judiciary to review and invalidate some pardons because of their overreaching effect. *Hoffa v. Saxbe*,[945] although only a Federal District Court and not a Supreme Court opinion, remains one of the clearest standards for reviewing presidential exercises of the clemency power. The basis of *Hoffa* was President Nixon's issuance of a conditional pardon to Jimmy Hoffa, the conditions of which were attacked by Hoffa on grounds that they not only were issued as a result of a conspiracy between Nixon and Teamster Union leaders, but furthermore that were designed to violate Hoffa's First Amendment rights.

Although the *Hoffa* court refused to examine the reasons for the issuance of the pardon, and declared that even corrupt use of presidential clemency power is insulated from judicial review, the decision did review the "effect" that the judiciary should accord to a clemency. The district court held that the law regarding pardons establishes "limits beyond which the President may not go in imposing and subsequently enforcing . . . conditions."[946] Thus while the president clearly may issue a pardon for any reason, he may not do so in a manner not "directly related to the public interest" or in a way that will "unreasonably infringe on the individual commutee's constitutional freedoms."[947]

Over the years, the Supreme Court has further listed several specific and technical standards regarding the granting of clemency, but only few of these relate to political offenders. *Burdick v. United States*,[948] for example, provided that an offender may refuse a conditional pardon granted on the condition that the offender waive his or her self-incrimination rights under the Fifth Amendment. *Schick v. Reed*[949] likewise held that the executive may condition a pardon on any grounds provided that such conditions do not infringe on the pardoned person's constitutional rights. The only relief against the abusive pardon-granting executive was articulated by Chief Justice Taft in *Ex parte Grossman*, which specified impeachment as the lone remedy.[950] Other than this sole and unlikely remedy, the president's clemency power remains largely unabridged and unassailable under American law.

Today all petitions for clemency are reviewed by the Office of the United States Pardon Attorney, which then makes nonbinding recommendations to the president. These recommendations are then reviewed and distilled by two officials at the Department of Justice and by two officials at the White House. After undergoing a screening process to select the most favorable candidates, the recommended petitions are sent back to the president, who makes the final clemency decision.[951] It is asserted, however, that inevitably and unfortunately, and despite the complexity of the process, political rather than legally driven motives and considerations dominate the clemency decisionmaking process.

As noted earlier, even though pardon is merely one of the five specific forms of clemency recognized under American law, amnesty has often been confused or lumped together with the granting of pardons in U.S. law. This interchange of the terminology by both the judiciary and law practitioners has added to the existing confusion, ambiguity, and potential for abuse. The Supreme Court, in a number of opinions dating to the late nineteenth and early twentieth centuries, has reflected the general disarray of the law of amnesty. Yet despite the great number of contradictions, overlapping principles, and "gray areas" in legal thought regarding this topic, a new attempt must be made to distill the doctrines that have been generally agreed upon.

In *Ex parte Garland*,[952] the petitioner's brief (not contested by the court) outlined some norms regarding amnesty. According to these norms, amnesties are usually extended to groups or communities, although they can also be granted to individuals, while pardons are generally applicable to individuals. Moreover, amnesties usually precede convictions while pardons operate afterwards. An amnesty's overall effect is to erase the past offense and theoretically place the offender in the position that he or she occupied before the offense took place. Thus, amnesty is viewed as the abolition and forgetting of the offense, while pardon is seen as the forgiving of the offense.[953]

According to the Supreme Court, however, these distinctions between pardon and amnesty remain mostly theoretical, without important "legal" or practical differences between the two.[954] Even the most expositive Supreme Court opinion concerning amnesty admits to the existence of only "incidental differences of importance" between pardon and amnesty.[955] As a result, amnesties have received less direct attention in judicial decisions and in legal scholarship than have pardons.[956]

The secondary place allocated to the doctrine and practice of amnesties has unfortunately deprived amnesty policy of clarity and specificity at a time of growing and urgent need for clear definitions and principled guidance. As a world leader in political affairs, the United States is in a position to offer direction to the pardon and amnesty processes worldwide. Yet America's limited development of amnesty laws, policies, and practices has greatly reduced the country's involvement in debating doctrine and setting standards in this internationally critical legal area.

The Benefits of Mercy and Conciliation

When amnesty law has been applied in American history, the exoneration generally took place after a particular armed or mass conflict had been concluded and the exculpatory grants consisted of both collective and individual relief. Drafting the surrender document for the Army of Northern Virginia at Appomattox Courthouse, General Ulysses S. Grant granted an amnesty to all Confederate soldiers who surrendered that day (arguably stepping far beyond his authority by doing so). The terms signed by Robert E. Lee read, in part: "[E]ach officer and man will be allowed to return to his home, not to be disturbed by the United States authorities so long as they observe their paroles and the laws in force where they may reside."[957] As Lee observed, "[t]his will have a very happy effect on my army . . . and will do much toward conciliating our people."[958] Grant, for his part, distilled even more effectively the true spirit behind the granting of amnesty: "The war is over. The rebels are our countrymen again."[959]

Before his assassination, President Lincoln tacitly accepted Grant's overreach when he extended amnesty to Confederate combatants on the condition that they take a loyalty oath to the Union.[960] Particularly illustrative of the mood of the time is an incident involving Confederate vice president Alexander Stephens' nephew, who at the time was a Union prisoner of war. President Lincoln had promised at a peace conference in February 1865 to amnesty the nephew, which he did immediately. Soon thereafter, Vice President Stephens himself was imprisoned. In response, his nephew framed his own letter of amnesty issued by Lincoln and hung it on the wall of Stephens' home.

The lenient amnesty policy did much to ease the reconciliation between the North and the South.[961] President Andrew Johnson continued to implement Lincoln's amnesty plan for several years following the Civil War, generally making it available more broadly. Although the Johnson policy did increase the number of applicant classes excepted from this relief from six to fourteen (including those who owned more than $20,000 worth of property and those who played a significant role in the uprising),[962] its overall effect was to increase the number of those amnestied after the Civil War and thereby enhance the "healing" and reconciliation spirit and action necessary after America's most traumatic internecine conflict.

The significance of clemency as a tool for combining mercy and reconciliation is testified to not only by its issuance to those actually facing or undergoing punishment, but also by its symbolic issuance for deeds or persons no longer sanctionable. The contemporary appeal of even a symbolic pardon and amnesty is exemplified by the August 5, 1975, action of the U.S. Congress with regard to the status of long-deceased Civil War leader Robert E. Lee. Citing section 3 of the Fourteenth Amendment of the U.S. Constitution in support of relieving General Lee of all legal disabilities placed upon him due to his service of the Southern cause, Congress justified the full restoration of his rights by declaring that "this entire Nation has long recognized the outstanding virtues of courage, patriotism, and self-less devotion to duty of General R. E. Lee, and has recognized the contribution of General Lee in healing the wounds of the war between the states."[963] Thus was the final settlement of the political accounts of the Civil War achieved more than a century after General Lee's surrender to General Grant at the Appomattox Courthouse in Virginia on April 9, 1865.

President Jimmy Carter's amnesty grant to draft resisters from the Vietnam War also stands as one of the more comprehensive conferments of clemency in recent years.[964] According to Executive Order 11967, all those facing possible indictments for violations of the Selective Service Act were to be amnestied, except those who committed "serious" acts of force or violence, as well as those serving as agents, employees, or officers of the Selective Service System who violated the Selective Service Act.[965] Although constituting one of the most recent and well-known examples of amnesty in the nation's history, President Carter's clemency order was not accompanied by any specified procedures, methods, or standards that could be used for future guidance in the granting of amnesties.

A noteworthy contemporary development related to the traditional doctrine of amnesty has been the resort to this jurisprudential concept in recent provisions of America's immigration law. In the

1986 congressional enactment of the Immigration Reform and Control Act,[966] limited amnesty was provided for selected classes of immigrants who had come to or stayed in the country illegally. Under the act, aliens who sought clemency had to prove that they had lived in the United States continuously since January 1, 1982.[967] For qualified illegal aliens, permanent legal residence status was assured at the conclusion of a required processing and probationary period.[968] Although the Immigration and Naturalization Service (INS) expected 2 to 4 million applicants for this exceptional relief, only 213,000 illegal immigrants had applied as of summer 1987. The low turnout has been attributed in part to the lack of clarity in INS amnesty provisions, and to the absence of "firm INS guidelines" concerning amnesty.[969]

America's historical experience, including the nation's Supreme Court amnesty dictates, its meager record of the doctrines enunciated by past grants of executive amnesty, and the 1986 Immigration Reform Act provide little understanding of U.S. amnesty theory and even less guidance for the amnesty-seeker. Although the largest segment of amnesty recipients in America appear to represent the political offender category, no particular emphasis has been placed on this class of beneficiaries in either official or scholarly documents. Political offenders are thus left, yet again, to be dealt with through a legal system unwilling to recognize their existence or distinctiveness.

Yet despite the legal system's unwillingness to confront the issue of the political offender directly, special public policy needs and considerations result in differential treatment of political offenders in both amnesty and pardon practices. When a government wants to differentiate and grant clemency to only a single person or a small select group, it will generally turn to the executive pardon rather than to amnesty. In the United States, one of the most noted exercises of the clemency power—albeit wielded to avoid potentially embarrassing criminal proceedings—was President Gerald Ford's granting of "a full, free and absolute pardon unto Richard Nixon for all offenses against the United States which he, Richard Nixon, ha[d] committed or may have committed or taken part in during the period from January 20, 1969 through August 9, 1974."[970]

Although it might be too partisan or at best unwise to speculate on President Ford's motives, it should be noted that the new president was Nixon's vice president and a member of the same political party. He was also facing reelection in two years and possibly sought through his grant to bring about a swift national conciliation. Considering the brief but intense firestorm that erupted after the pardon, that grant alone might have had great impact upon Ford's future as the next president. It is noteworthy also that when asked in later years for his reasons for not pardoning his loyal lieutenants, H. R. Haldeman and John Erlichman, Nixon noted that he had bowed to political reality and that although he "probably should have pardoned them . . . [he was not] sure that the country would have taken it at that time."[971]

Other clemencies in American legal history have been equally motivated by partisan and other suspect undercurrents. Some of these did not fully surface at the time. President George Bush pardoned some officials of the Reagan administration who had been accused of various illegal activities encompassed by the Iran-Contra Affair.[972] In doing so, he, like President Ford, was also exculpating himself from his actions while vice president in the former administration. As one seeks to take stock of the forces that continue to advocate the practices of amnesty and pardon, it becomes evident that clemency is grounded in two primary considerations: excusing the actions of the former opposing regime and its officials in the interest of communal conciliation, and helping to ensure that the future and successful regimes will exhibit the same consideration.

In the last decade of the twentieth century, international standards and practices have also begun to emerge to help supply the needed guidance for individual countries in the treatment of those seeking amnesty for domestic conduct. The Inter-American Commission on Human Rights was one of the first international entities to address this question, attempting to curb undeserved grants of amnesty to members of former abusive regimes in Central and South America. To help evaluate the propriety of amnesty grants the commission relied upon provisions of the American Declaration of the Rights and Duties of Man, the Genocide Convention, the Torture Convention, the American Convention on Human Rights, the International Covenant on Civil and Political Rights, and the European Convention for the Protection of Human Rights and Fundamental Freedoms.

The international principles that emerged from the desire to implement these global human rights treaties and standards, as well as from earlier customary international law, seem to mandate the prosecution of individuals whose offenses constitute not merely domestic offenses but amount to the commission of such international crimes as torture, extrajudicial killings, or forced disappearances. Although a regime may be free to pardon violators of domestic laws, it is not jurisdictionally capable of forgiving conduct that violates internationally "non-derogable rights"[973] as specified in the emerging Human Rights and Humanitarian law.

As new regimes came into power at the conclusion of civil wars in Latin America and Africa, some scholars and practitioners have resorted to the standards set forth in the Nuremberg prosecutions (which have gained growing respect and a high standing in international law) to support the proposition that "crimes against humanity" need to be prosecuted rather than pardoned or amnestied.[974] But despite the occasional and vehement criticisms by the world's human rights community, one can observe a growing failure to criminally prosecute former civil war enemies and a reliance instead on "Truth Commissions" as conciliatory tools at the conclusion of large-scale civil warfare.[975] The evolving status of amnesty within international as contrasted with domestic law thus appears to fluctuate between the old traditions of total domestic sovereignty and the newer urgings that violations of international as distinct from domestic crimes are not within the sole discretion of affected states but are the responsibility of the whole community of nations. Grave violations of human rights, it is therefore argued, must be prosecuted by successor regimes or by any countries obtaining jurisdiction and should not be amnestied or pardoned.

In South Africa, the transition from white minority rule to a black majority government similarly raised complicated amnesty questions. As escalating racial and political unrest threatened the very foundations of the nation, outgoing president F. W. de Klerk responded both to moral dictates and to the ever-pressing concern for national preservation by announcing that all persons imprisoned merely for being members of prohibited groups or parties would be released immediately, unless they had been convicted or charged with committing some other more dangerous or violent criminal offense.[976] Hailed by the international community as an important step toward mitigating the tragedy of apartheid, the actual results of de Klerk's compromise were disappointing: Only seventy-seven people walked out free of South African prisons in response to this limited amnesty.[977] The more serious political criminals, who offended against either the local apartheid regime or the standards of international human rights, remained in confinement to be dealt with at a later time.

The logic exhibited by South Africa's outgoing government toward an enemy on the verge of victory was both simple and sound: If those in power institute a policy of leniency and conciliation toward their enemies, indiscriminate and bloody retaliations are less likely to take place once the opponents come into office. Often, however, the long-term outcome of clemency policies is difficult to forecast. Consider, for example, the case of Azerbaijan. As domestic fighting raged in the outskirts of Baku after the collapse of the Soviet Union, Azerbaijan's government in power offered amnesty to all rebels who would lay down their arms.[978] The government's aims were clear: to undermine the support for the rebels as well as to foster a more conciliatory policy on the part of the rebels, should they prevail. Instituting such conciliatory domestic stances, those in power as well as those out of power exemplify their full, or at least partial, willingness to treat their adversaries as belligerents under the international humanitarian law rather than as common criminals under domestic penal provisions.

The practice of extending clemency to criminal offenders goes back far into history. Although the beneficiaries of clemency generally have tended to be political rather than common offenders, a clear policy of greater leniency toward political criminals has never been formulated in either literature or practice. Similarly unresolved remains the question of a state's right to extend an amnesty to offenders whose crimes constitute an offense against international as well as domestic law.

One further unresolved issue concerns determining which branch of government is most suitable, jurisprudentially and pragmatically, to be trusted with the clemency power. In post–Soviet Union Russia the conflict between the executive and the legislature over the pardon and amnesty power was highlighted in the planning and execution of a response against the leaders of the anti-Yeltsin coup attempt of 1993 as well as in the anti-Gorbachev coup attempt of 1991. In both instances the coup leaders were amnestied by the Russian Parliament in February 1994.[979] The Duma reasoned that the amnesty would promote national reconciliation. The former vice president of the Soviet Union, Gennady Yanayev, facing a military tribunal, said of the amnesty: "In August 1991 we tried, albeit clumsily, to rescue the fatherland, and I think that the [Duma] acted intelligently and made a profoundly moral decision."[980] By mid-May 1994, however, the Supreme Court of Russia interceded by overruling the amnesty for the anti-Gorbachev plotters but left unaffected the freed anti-Yeltsin offenders.[981]

Unique questions regarding pardons and amnesties were recently faced by reunited Germany as well. Of particular complexity was the question of the status to be accorded to former East German spies, intelligence officers, and other officials who committed offenses against West Germany while in the service of the East German regime. West Germany's initial theory was that legitimate national authority was vested only in West Germany, making East Germany merely a Communist puppet government. German nationals in either the West or the East therefore owed allegiance to the only legitimate authority and could be prosecuted for disloyalty in serving the causes of the Communist collaborators. Former East German intelligence officers had been charged accordingly with treason and related offenses against West Germany. Arguing in their defense that they could not be charged with treason against West Germany since they were not Western citizens at the time of the alleged criminal acts, the accuseds' defense was finally recognized and the verdicts were reversed. In early June 1995 the German constitutional court held that East Germans who spied against the West could not be prosecuted.[982] Amnesties for West German nationals who acted on behalf of the East German regime were also expected.[983] Once more the versatility of the amnesty and pardon powers helped demonstrate the ill-defined and fringe arenas of political criminality.

Pardon and amnesty powers serve as a double-edged sword in a world beset by internecine conflict. They offer powerful shields for the defense and protection of the political criminal. They accord nations and their leaders an opportunity to free more leniently their "honorable" opponents, to treat them with the dignity befitting the righteous and sometime lawful political belligerent. On the other hand, this leniency can be turned into a tool of iniquity to shield from punishment officers of a corrupt regime. In its latter role clemency turns from a shield that benefits the innocent and deserving into a shelter for the protection of the guilty and culpable.

Although the call for a new principled approach and well-defined standards regarding clemency—particularly with regard to its transnational implications—continues to be heard,[984] the approach that international law has taken thus far maintains, a narrow and monological perspective on this issue. Much like the legal doctrines that fail to address squarely the substantive questions of political criminality, international norms similarly skirt direct dealings with amnesty policies.

From sketchy early beginnings, the international community has managed in the past two centuries to develop a comprehensive code for the conduct of participants in international military contests. Even prior to the Hague and Geneva articulations, the United States managed in the midst of its own terrible civil war to adopt the Lieber Code as a reasoned means for downscaling its massive domestic military conflict. Indeed, it was the Lieber Code that gave substantive and procedural incentives to the international Hague and Geneva Codes that followed. It is not too ambitious an expectation, therefore, for American scholarly and practical minds to spearhead today a new effort to endow domestic conflicts with a conciliatory and pragmatic approach similar to that formerly extended to international warfare through the creating of the now well-established humanitarian law.

Because amnesty has developed international dimensions, and because it often affects the interests of the global community, standards are needed to guide its application in the international arena. It is a foregone conclusion that resort to or denial of amnesty will often produce conflicts between competing considerations of domestic and international law. The time has come therefore to explore the formulation of substantive and procedural amnesty standards for use throughout the world. In this enterprise America could play a leading role.

This volume's effort to address comprehensively the legal status of the political offender could be readily expanded also to deal with the amnesty arena. The many international issues involved in the exercise of clemency readily uplift this topic from its exclusive domesticity to place it within the international arena. Amnesties and pardons, when combined with the defenses of motive, necessity, and higher law, as well as with requested access to some of the privileges accorded to prisoners of war, greatly complicate both international and domestic questions pertaining to those rebelling against authority. The recent releases of convicted political offenders from the prisons of South Africa and Israel, India and Egypt, Russia and Yemen readily illustrate the growing sensitivity of nations toward political offenders.

There may indeed be a growing willingness at the end of this century to grant political offenders greater recognition for their role as committed and honorable combatants. Whether this trend to accord political offenders a differential status will expand or be curtailed in light of the escalating domestic violence worldwide (whether driven by ethnic, tribal, or religious conflicts), is too early to predict. Nevertheless, the concluding chapter of this volume remains committed to a thorough reassessment of political criminality, and the securing of the political offender's just and realistic place in both international and domestic law.[985]

Part Five

The Political Offender in Modernity

New Rules for Dissidence and Domestic Warfare

Laws are inoperative in war.
—Marcus Tullius Cicero,
Pro Milone

A soft answer turneth away wrath.
—Psalms 15:1

If one rebels, the cause for the rebellion must be just. If one resorts to violence, the violence must be within the parameters of justice. Terrorists differ from freedom fighters because they respect no such limitations.
—E. E. Rackman,
in *Terrorists or Freedom Fighters* (1986)

Martin Luther King Jr., his young son beside him, pulls up a four-foot cross, symbol of the Ku Klux Klan, that was burned on the front lawn of his home in Atlanta.

Chapter Eight

Rebels with a Cause

Toward a Jurisprudence of Domestic Conflict

*The surest way to prevent seditions . . . is
to take away the [cause] of them.*

—Francis Bacon,
Of Seditions and Troubles (1601)

*It is not power that corrupts but fear. Fear of losing
power corrupts those who wield it; and fear of the scourge
of power corrupts those who are subject to it.*

—Aung San Suu Kyi,
Burmese Nobel Peace Prize Laureate,
Freedom from Fear (1990)

*Means that do not befit the aim can pervert the
aim forever, and this being so, terror must be treated as
a drug, that while it can cure, it may also kill.*

—Grigori Gershuni,
Leader of Russian Revolution (1905)

Vote—Register, Malaquias Montoya, silkscreen (1973).

Lolita Lebrón, Puerto Rican nationalist convicted of attack on U.S. Congress, Linda Lucero, silkscreen (1975).

Political Rebellion and Criminality
in the Third Millennium

The history of the political offender's treatment by both governments and the public demonstrates a continuing vacillation between long periods of rejection and repression and short periods of affirmation and liberal permissiveness. During more than a hundred years (beginning in the 1830s and concluding with the end of the Cold War), the liberal democracies of the West have often been inclined toward leniency, while reactionary, totalitarian, and authoritarian regimes have viewed and treated the rebel and political dissident as a deadly enemy. Moreover, during the second half of the twentieth century no single or predominant pattern of response to political agitators and those engaging in political resistance and rebellion has been developed within the community of nations. Instead, a wide diversity of responses have emerged toward the increasingly troublesome phenomenon of political rebellion, protest, resistance, and criminality. This diversity can be correlated with ideological camps, prevailing political systems, geographic regions, and specific time periods. At least three major contemporary patterns or models of response to political opposition and resistance can be readily identified.

The Totalitarian Model

The most severely punitive responses to political dissidence have been offered by the twentieth century's totalitarian states, whether ideologically inclined toward the right or the left. The underlying foundations of recent totalitarianism have not necessarily been original—such as in the instance of Naziism and Stalinist Communism. Contemporary totalitarian regimes have often encompassed within themselves a resurgence of earlier religious and political fundamentalism, as seen in Iran, Libya, and the Sudan, or of outright classical tyranny, as evidenced in Iraq and Syria. Members of the totalitarian camp may seek and find their origins and justifications in both modern and ancient doctrine.

Totalitarianism can be uniformly described and explained. Yet, the records of Nazi Germany, of the pre–1991 Soviet Union, of Cambodia's Khmer Rouge regime, and of China's "Cultural Revolution" starkly illuminate the inevitability and tragic outcome of governmental abuse of power and reigns of terror wherever an absolutist and often millennial ideology combines with an absolutist and pathological leadership.[986] Although Nazi, Fascist, and Soviet-style absolutism appears to be rapidly falling out of favor around the world, our optimism must remain very guarded in an era that has witnessed the sacrifice of over 20 million human lives on the altar of Leninism-Stalinism (excluding millions of others who were uprooted and forcibly resettled),[987] the brutalization, enslavement, annihilation, and outright extermination of 25 million "undesirable" humans in the twelve brief years of the promised Thousand-Year Hitlerian Reich, and the more recent ethnic and religious massacres in Cambodia, former Yugoslavia, Rwanda, Burundi, and the Congo.

Within a relatively short span of time, this century's totalitarian regimes (Naziism-Fascism, Stalinism-Maoism, and others) turned the occasional elimination of political opponents into a precise and brutal science. Racial, ethnic, religious, ideological, economic, and other groups (e.g., Gypsies, homosexuals, Jehovah's Witnesses, Jews, non-Aryans, and Socialists under Naziism; Cosmopolitants, Crimean Tartars, and Kulaks under Stalinism; Hutus and Tutsis under tribal fanaticism) were irrevocably assigned to the status of disposable "state enemies." Through such classification, the state's hunt for real and imagined opponents and enemies shifted from an emphasis on individual actors, guilty of personal misdeeds, to a system of unrelenting collective sanctions arbitrarily imposed upon broad and diverse segments of the population making up the national or state communities.

Admittedly, unexpected changes in the status of the political offender have taken place during the past decade in the hitherto totalitarian countries of Eastern Europe. A highly successful and nearly bloodless "Velvet Revolution" (so denominated by poet Vaclav Havel, the first president of liberated Czechoslovakia) has swept through the six former nations of the Communist Eastern Bloc (Bulgaria, Czechoslovakia, East Germany, Hungary, Romania, and Poland). This revolution has further liberated the three former Soviet-ruled Baltic states (Estonia, Latvia, and Lithuania), and has shattered the centralized government of the remaining states of the former Soviet Union, turning it into a weak contemporary version of the old Holy Roman Empire—all with barely a gunshot. As oppressive totalitarian political structures precipitously withered away, the cadres of the former Stalinist-Marxist Party, police and military, stood relatively still in the face of the virtual dismantling of their old institutions of power. The transition from the old Communist authority to new, allegedly democratic institutions was also carried out with minimal changes in personnel and, generally, without the banishing or imposing severe penal sanctions upon the leading former abusers of governmental power.

One is reminded of Barton Ingraham's earlier portrayal of the liberal leniency toward political oppositions and offenders in the nineteenth and twentieth centuries as evidence of a tired bourgeoisie's death wish.[988] Could the new and inexplicable "chivalry" exhibited by Eastern Europe's totalitarian regimes in their final days be likewise attributed to a contemporary, and possibly only temporary, death wish on the part of an exhausted Marxism-Leninism-Stalinism? As political tolerance and economic liberty seem to be gradually replacing the stifling uniformity of totalitarianism throughout much of the world, an enthusiastic observer might be tempted to proclaim the arrival of the prophesied millennium. Indeed, although military, one-party, fanatically religious, or personality-cult regimes continue to prevail in much of Africa, Asia, and Latin America, only China, North Korea, and Cuba remain as reminders of the nearly extinct monolithic Communist state. Yet despite the self-congratulatory view that we are witnessing Western-style democracy's supposed final triumph over totalitarianism (a victory that began with democracy's World War II defeat of Nazi Germany and militarist Japan), we must not become overconfident that history's perpetual war between liberty and abuse of power has been permanently won.

It may be that we are merely seeing, in the lands of the former Communist camp and elsewhere, a transitional stage of readjustment and restructuring masquerading as a turn to democracy. Opportunistic leaders may be only proclaiming the slogans and symbols of democracy and pluralistic legitimacy to woo Western and other political and financial support. Although it seems certain that the major socioeconomic institutions of Marxism-Leninism are being buried, it is by no means clear that the tools of political repression will be interred alongside the corpse. Already there are indications that old repressive methods may again be advanced and instituted by those in power, who would justify their actions by referring to new emergencies and an urgent need to curb, albeit temporarily, escalating political, ethnic, social, and economic unrest.

The Democratic Model

The growing leniency exhibited toward nonviolent segments of the political dissenter and protestor community by the contemporary democratic governments of the West has been in stark contrast to the harsh treatment meted out to rebels and dissidents by the outgoing totalitarian regimes. Democracies have increasingly adopted a tolerant approach to the burgeoning ranks of political dissidents and to the outpourings of their dissent. This tolerance is reflected particularly in the growing permissiveness toward free speech and other forms of communications, and in the expansion of civil rights through both legislative and judicial reform.

The growth of political and civil liberties has greatly reduced the state's control over political activism. While a great number of traditional political offenses (particularly those involving acts of violence) continue to be treated as severe crimes, other prohibited forms of dissent and protest have been transformed into lawful conduct. Despite this lessened control, there has been little evidence of a general liberalization of attitudes toward political offenders as a collective group. The nineteenth century's call for overall leniency toward political offenders as a class of altruistic and nonvenal actors has therefore remained unheeded.

Admittedly, the growing recognition of the right to speak critically and provocatively of authority has meant, in the United States as well as in other democracies, that elements of such historical offenses as treason, sedition, and political conspiracy have withered away. The growing recognition of one's right to belong to unorthodox political organizations has greatly reduced the dread of the former offenses directed against "unlawful memberships." Other forms of political conduct once perceived as criminal now come within the safeguards offered under civil and political rights. Labor has won the right to organize and to engage in collective action. Women have obtained and have been increasingly and effectively exercising the right to political franchise and economic equality. Demands for social, economic, and political justice by people of color, immigrants, homosexuals, and other minorities are being received with increased understanding and even sympathy.

Yet against the background of this growing liberalization, questionable exceptions persist. Throughout the democratic world, lawmakers as well as the judiciary have continued to turn a deaf ear toward pleas for leniency from selectively disfavored political dissenters. Some Western European nations, not yet fully recovered from their Nazi or Fascist experiences, consider the advocacy of totalitarian, racist, and other unorthodox doctrines unacceptable. The West German Constitution, seeking to redeem its nation from its past, specifically outlaws Naziism as an ideology and as a political party.[989] Similarly, the Communist Party, as well as its members and sympathizers, were long singled out for indiscriminate persecution in the United States, including judicial prosecutions and the rabid inquisitions of Senator Joseph McCarthy's era.[990] Similar selectivity toward political liberty has been demonstrated with regard to adherents of the Palestine Liberation Organization and subsequently toward Hamas members in Israel, toward Bosnians in former Yugoslavia, and toward fundamentalist Moslem organizations and their memberships in many westernized Arab countries. The Provisional Irish Republican army remained outlawed until recently in Great Britain, and for a long time organizations agitating for racial justice in South Africa or for ethnic and indigenous equality in Latin America were portrayed as terroristic while their members were subjected to particularly harsh and collective penalties.[991]

Other than in these selected cases, the relative political stability that characterized the domestic affairs of the well-established democratic nations during the last third of the twentieth century has acted to enhance these countries' lenient attitudes toward political dissenters and activists. This relative political calm, which has been both the product of and the cause for the expansion of political and civil rights, acted constantly not only to narrow the types and classes of political activity prohibited by the state, but also to produce a leniency in sentencing practices and a willingness to offer broad amnesties to convicted political offenders.

The liberalization of state policies toward political offenders, including deposed leaders of former abusive regimes, has also been manifested recently in such newly democratically transformed countries as Haiti, Nicaragua, Romania, Poland, and South Africa. Most of these transitions from totalitarianism to sprouting democracy have been accompanied by general amnesties to the offending members of the former abusive governments.

The Authoritarian Model

Between the two hitherto described extremes of totalitarianism and democracy lie the zealous, intolerant, and frequently inconsistent policies carried out by the authoritarian regimes of the Third World toward their real and imagined political opponents. Although these regimes (unlike their totalitarian cousins in the Fascist and Marxist camps) have not sought total control over all facets of their peoples' political, economic, cultural, and social life, they have been and continue to be set apart from the democracies of the West due to their nonelective and often military-based forms of governance.[992]

The authoritarian model offers yet a third perspective on the contemporary worldwide treatment of political opponents, rebels, and dissidents. These regimes, inherently unstable, feel compelled to resist the divisive and centrifugal forces emanating from ethnic and clan rivalries, interregional hostilities, colonially perpetuated class structures, and emerging political diversities. The leaders of these nations often rise to power from tribal, military, or proletarian origins. They tend to assume authority through extralegal means and have little interest or faith in legitimizing their authority through electoral politics. After dealing harshly with their own predecessors, many of these leaders and ruling cliques severely restrict access to power for all but their own handpicked successors.

Many of the authoritarian regimes in Africa, Latin America, and Asia have managed to combine the worst features of Stalinist Marxism (apathy, crushing bureaucracy, and institutionalized terror) with the flaws of capitalism (personal greed, socioeconomic injustice, and corporate corruption). Political conflict and constant unrest become inevitable when these Third World and often economically emerging regimes attempt to solve their many problems through a single absolutist doctrine (such as religious fundamentalism or modified forms of Marxism or Maoism), a centralized "command" economy, one-party rule, favoritism for certain tribes, clans, or ruling classes, and, finally, the creation of personality cults (whether Idi Aminism, Duvalierism, Marcosism, Kaddafism, Peronism, or Saddamism).

Some commentators may suggest that the authoritarian regimes of Latin America and of postcolonial Africa and Asia, despite their resort to death squads, kidnappings, disappearances, secret tribunals,[993] and other methods for the brutal liquidation of their political opponents, have retained some of the nineteenth century's chivalry toward political opponents. Although authoritarian governments have inappropriately resorted to "states of emergency,"[994] "states of siege," and "martial law"[995] to tighten their grip over unruly or restless populations, they have also often shown inexplicable gallantry toward their opponents.

At the conclusion of successful coups d'état in such places as the Dominican Republic, Uganda, Ethiopia, and Sierra Leone, deposed heads of states have frequently been allowed to depart discreetly without retribution. In other places, deposed heads of state have been ceremoniously delivered to the nation's airport with one-way travel arrangements. Former political luminaries in countries such as Syria, Yemen, or Haiti, finding themselves out of favor with their former ruling allies, have often been given extended appointments to their country's diplomatic posts in remote capitals. Even heads of military juntas and commanders of failed military rebellions have occasionally been allowed to temporarily continue in office or to depart in peace. Evidently, newly established regimes may prefer for their challengers a curtailed presence or a departure overseas rather than an unexplained death or a politically sensitive prosecution at home.

◊　◊　◊

As the twentieth century draws to an end, one must recognize the rich diversity of the prevailing worldwide responses to the threats posed by rebellion and political dissidence. Political rebels inevitably bring forth unique responses from the regimes they set out to sensitize, reform, or overthrow. While totalitarian regimes have indiscriminately expanded the reaches of political criminality in an effort to stifle even the least-threatening expressions of popular opposition, the Western democracies have traveled an opposite road by liberalizing and decriminalizing much of the formerly proscribed political activity. The third approach, exemplified by unstable Third World regimes, combines brutal suppression of dissent with occasional displays of generosity—however self-serving—toward their opponents in the defeated and outgoing regime.

Global Standards for Political Offenses

Keeping in mind the three major contemporary models for the political offender's treatment by diverse systems of government, we must revisit conventional wisdom's oft-repeated cliché that "one person's freedom fighter is another's terrorist." Particularly dissatisfying is the implication that the difference between freedom fighter and terrorist is merely a matter of individual or collective perspective and bias, and that philosophy, science, and law are incapable of distinguishing the worthy rebel from the venal and indiscriminate criminal. Having labeled this maxim simplistic, nihilistic, sterilely relativistic, and devoid of scholarly or practical merit, we must now replace it with an objective and value-consistent system for the classification of the diverse community of political offenders.

Upon the foundations laid in the intervening chapters, an ambitious framework can now be advanced to comprehensively classify all those who take part in what is described as political dissent, rebellion, and resistance. The proposed framework seeks to accommodate all political activists engaging in nonparliamentary conduct, be their activities peaceful or violent, individual or collective, civilian or military, altruistic or venal. Equally addressed are those activists whose defiance is directed against tyrants and abusers of power as well as those who seek to overthrow professedly just or democratic governance.

To endow the proposed classification with credibility and to avoid its dismissal on grounds of ideological, ethnic, or cultural bias, its criteria must be universal rather than parochial. To make the classification broadly acceptable, it must be encompassing rather than particular. To enhance its utility, it must be concrete instead of abstract. To give it validity, it must be derived empirically rather than theoretically. To maintain its viability, the framework must seek an appropriate balance between the conscience and strivings of individuals and the needs and values of collectives (be they small or big, local, national or international). Finally, such a framework must reconcile the greater society's needs for the maintenance of legitimacy, authority, and public order with the equally compelling and growing individual and smaller collectives' quest for liberty, autonomy, and self-governance.

The currently escalating political strife worldwide urgently calls for the construction of such a classification scheme. Indeed, despite the optimistic calls for a "new world order" in the aftermath of communism's collapse, the end of bipolar international politics has intensified rather than diminished history's perpetual struggle between authority and autonomy. The advancing forces of tribalism, fundamentalism, and xenophobia are now threatening to wholly consume all extant institutions of law and order. To assess the present status and forecast the future of the eternal conflict between those in power and those who consider themselves politically, socially, economically, or otherwise disenfranchised, one must take notice not only of corrupt and tyrannical regimes and their reigns of terror but also of the worldwide prevalence of governments resorting to milder forms of illegality, exploitation, and abuses of power. To accurately survey existing and potential arenas of political strife, one must also take notice of the zeal and excessive means resorted to by those who resist authority.

The proposed framework for the classification of political criminality must therefore include not only diverse types of governmental abuses of power but also the wide spectrum of means resorted to by political resisters, ranging from civil disobedience to indiscriminate terrorism. No comprehensive mapping of the battlefields of political compliance and defiance is indeed possible without constructing a scale on which one can weigh the manifest evils produced by those in authority (whether through reigns of terror, abuse of power, or misgovernance) and contrast them with the harm unleashed by their resisters (who resort to various forms of sieges of terrorism, civil disobedience, and political crime).

In constructing such a scale for the weighing and balancing of political rebellion and activism, it is incumbent upon us to revisit and redefine the historical and legal foundations upon which the columns of this proposed new classification system are to rise. Who precisely are the main subjects of this volume and the objects of the proposed classification system, the so-called rebels and political offenders? This inquiry should commence with an examination of the unusually broad category of men and women wearing such diverse labels as political offenders, political refugees, asylum-seekers, dissenters, dissidents, civil disobedients, protesters, resisters, guerrillas, rebels, belligerents, terrorists, and international criminals. What all these labels point to is the complex and entangled relationship between the rebel or defier of authority on the one hand, and politics, crime, and warfare on the other hand.

In large measure, the effort to define political dissidents and rebels must commence with an acknowledgment of three unorthodoxies— unorthodox politics, unorthodox crime, and unorthodox warfare. In the annals of the social and behavioral sciences, the arenas of politics and crime appear to be only marginally related. At first glance the two indeed seem to reflect opposite social functions and behavior. Politics is generally described as a set of theories and practices concerned with the marshaling of individual and group resources for the attainment of common goals. Politics therefore embraces efforts to channel both individualism and egoism into the service of the public good. Criminality, on the other hand, represents departures from agreed-upon communal norms and laws. Although criminality is thus portrayed as a pursuit of selfish goals and as a rejection of altruism (thereby turning criminality into a psychosocial pathology), this book's analysis of political criminality has put in question this dualistic view of politics and crime, and suggests hitherto ignored connections.

The political offender is, above all else, political. He or she shares, even claims exclusively, the highest goals of politics. Professing the good of the people, the political offender cloaks his or her criminal conduct in an aura of morality and conscience, claiming that his or her acts are inspired by the same noble motives that drive the conventional politician. At the same time, the political offender is clearly a political deviant. He or she does not play by the rules decreed by those in authority, but eschews evolutionary and "reformist" politics, collective deliberation, and collegial compromise. In an electoral political system the political offender transcends parliamentary rules, preferring measures of individual brinkmanship and risk-taking. He or she does not shrink from the methods and tools of the criminal.

But just as the political offender differs from the common politician, he or she is different also from the common criminal. The political offender's motives often are communal and even broadly humane rather than self-indulgent or antisocial. Willing to take personal risks and undergo privations, the political offender claims readiness to sacrifice him- or herself in order to secure for others what is perceived to be a better community and world. Thus, just as the political offender cannot be viewed as equal to the conventional politician, he or she cannot be simply relegated to the status of common criminal.

Finally, the disorder and violence wrought by the modern political offender do not readily compare with the battles fought by the orthodox warrior. Unlike the lawful belligerent, the political offender often functions surreptitiously, without a uniform or military insignia. While the political offender is often subject to the commands of some superiors, he or she is not in the service of a sovereign and internationally recognized state. Moreover, the conflicts in which the political offender is engaged are usually domestic rather than international. Traditional standards and laws of warfare were not initially designed with domestic dissent, rebellion, and insurgency in mind. The political offender's status is a composite of several fundamental unorthodoxies, reflecting the diversity of roles he or she plays. Yet by synthesizing the moral and legal principles applicable to the three main arenas of the political offender (politics, crime, and warfare), a classification system can be established for mapping the broad and previously ill-charted borders of the lands of political criminality.

To address the enormously wide spectrum of questions raised by political criminality, we must continue to view the term "political" quite liberally, including in our definition not only actors in pursuit of purely political or ideological objectives but also those committed to religious, ethnic, economic, social, linguistic, and other professedly communal and altruistic goals. We need to consider political offenses not merely as direct and violent assaults against the state, its agencies, and functionaries (e.g., the assassination of a head of state or the bombing a government facility) but also as consisting of peaceful challenges to authority (e.g., resistance to the military draft or pregnancy without governmental approval), and at times merely as prohibited communications (e.g., questioning the infallibility of government or religion, or preaching prohibited political, religious, or social doctrines). Recent history has further demonstrated that mere status (e.g., being a Socialist in Nazi Germany, a "social parasite" in Stalin's Soviet Union, a Japanese American in World War II California, or a "counter-revolutionary" in the People's Republic of China) can qualify one as a political offender.

Political criminality can thus consist of such diverse elements as prohibited action, prohibited communications, and unfavored status. Considering the term "political offender" liberally, we must beware also of the particular problems posed by the pseudo-political offender, the one who falsely claims altruistic motives but in fact pursues his or her selfish psychological and pathological objectives. Both Stephen Schafer, in *The Political Criminal: The Problem of Morality and Crime*,[996] and Brian Crozier, in *The Rebels: A Study in Post-War Insurrections*,[997] dwell on this class of actors for whom political agendas serve as mere masks for common criminality or as covers for their own particular psychopathologies.

The history of religion, politics, law, and warfare offers a variety of foundations upon which the building blocks of this new and comprehensive classification system for political criminality can be erected. From the earliest biblical, Greek, and Roman confrontations between divinely appointed prophets and profane temporal rulers, one may first derive the principle that divine laws reign supreme over secular commandments. Even in the most ancient of times the representatives of Heaven and its deities always viewed themselves as justified in speaking out and even rebelling against the base and unjust rules imposed by earthly kings. "There is no duty to obey sinful commands," professes the creed of Islam.[998]

Yet biblical accounts, which similarly favored prophetic reiterations of divine commands over kingly commands, failed to specify the precise types of inequity or degrees of secular evil sufficient to justify disobedience and rebellion, just as they failed to specify "appropriate" means of protest and resistance. An untimely death for the unrighteous ruler, the burning and pillage of his city, the enslavement of his family, and the dispersement of his people were typical punishments ordained by an angry Jeremiah for the kings of Judah who offended against Jehovah's commandments.[999] Daniel similarly detailed to mighty Nebuchadnezzar, the king of Babylon, the Lord's unleashing of the ruler's enemies as punishment for his defiance of divine rules: "[T]hey shall drive thee from men, and thy dwelling shall be with the beasts of the field, and they shall make thee to eat grass as oxen."[1000]

Not only were these divinely decreed penalties extreme and unremitting, but the ordained commandments whose violation led to such cruel sanctions often lacked, and seem to be lacking even more in historical perspective, proper precision, and universality. Although such all-pervading offenses as "iniquity towards widows and orphans" and "denial of justice" dominate the prophets' charges of abuse against those holding the reins of power, other complaints lodged against impious kings and their profane rule might be viewed as vague, ethnocentric, and anachronistic. Moreover, the biblical cures for abuse of political power relied on direct divine intervention, often through such heavenly appointed agents as plagues or invasion by foreign empires and their rulers. The Bible fails to specify a system or standards for human resistance against abuses.

Other important building blocks for constructing a general theory and classification scheme regarding those engaged in political resistance can be found in ancient and medieval European efforts to stem tyranny, dictatorship, and abuse of power.[1001] Tyranny, an appellation stemming from the Lydian designation for king, initially referred to governance through monocracy ("one-man rule"), as contrasted with the more prevailing collective or oligarchical ruling systems. During the sixth and seventh centuries B.C., the Greek city-states, both in Sicily and on the Greek mainland, often turned to "tyrannies" in response to the exigencies of communal survival:

> The stress of class warfare and the imminence of barbarian invasion gave rise during this period to recurrent crises which demonstrated the incompetence of the reigning oligarchies, thus placing a premium on the efficiency of one-man rule. Various talented individuals, usually supported by the lower classes, forcibly seized power and established a personal absolutism which dealt effectively with the problems of the moment.[1002]

Roman history added to this Hellenic legacy the concept and institution of "dictatorship." The dictator, usually a man of outstanding merit, was appointed by the Roman Senate to deal with an imminent and temporary threat, and was vested with unlimited political power. The dictator's term, originally, was never to exceed six months. Julius Caesar's lifetime appointment became the death knell of republican governance and the model for turning the Roman dictatorships into "tyrannies of the first magnitude."[1003]

Despite the initially apparent merits of one-man rule, in terms of both charismatic appeal and efficiency, and the strong support for monocratic governance voiced by the ancient Spartans, the labels "tyranny" and "dictatorship" soon degenerated into pejorative rather than descriptive terms. Aristotle defined tyranny as "a government by a single person directed to the interest of that person." More precisely, he saw in tyranny "the perversion of kingship."[1004] Aristotle distinguished, moreover, between three categories of monocracy. The first, kingship, tended to be hereditary. The second, tyranny, came about through the unlawful seizure of power. And the third, dictatorship, "may roughly be described as an elective form of tyranny."[1005]

Debates about the competing merits of collective rule as contrasted with monocracy abound in classic literature. In their opposition to monocracy, the classic advocates of collective rule laid great emphasis on the fact that tyrants, as distinguished from oligarchs and even dictators, usurped power rather then being vested with legitimate authority. "From this point it was but a step to assert that capricious lawlessness was characteristic of the exercise as well as of the origins of tyrannical power."[1006]

Favoring collective over monocratic rule and seeking to go beyond the narrow confines of traditional aristocracy, Greek civilization eventually witnessed the resurgence and survival of oligarchical and democratic governance among its city-states.[1007] It is to Athens (the most noted of the Hellenic cities) that the modern world remains indebted for the institution of democratic governance, beginning with Solon's constitution around 594 B.C. and continuing intermittently through antiquity's fifth and fourth centuries.[1008] Although tyrannical and dictatorial rule had thus met transitory historical needs in the Hellenic and Roman worlds, the record of classical history serves mostly as a reminder of the potentials for abuses of power inherent in monocratic governance.[1009]

As Greek and Roman societies intensified their quest for broader-based oligarchical or democratic rule, they also began increasingly to view dictatorship and tyranny as particularly unsuitable for the social character and organizational needs of humankind. A special remedy, tyrannicide, began to emerge as a cure for the ills brought about by usurpers and abusers of legitimate power. Concurrently, those engaging in tyrannicide were being elevated to the ranks of civic virtue and heroism. In ancient Greece and Rome there was no word corresponding to the term "assassination," noted political scientist David C. Rapoport. "A killing was simply a means to an end; its moral significance depended entirely on the *nature* of the person killed."[1010] In Rome, even those advocating or suspected of aspiring to tyranny were subject to severe public sanctions.[1011] One regarded as a tyrant in Republican Rome was thus beyond the protection of the law. Despite these early manifestations of the social acceptance

of tyrannicide, it was not until much later that the various types of
tyranny, governmental abuse, and their accompanying iniquities
came under careful scrutiny, and an articulation of the specific forms
of resistance appropriate against particular evils did emerge.[1012]
That eventual development had to await the emergence and blos-
soming of the doctrines of natural law.

Contributions from the Natural Law and Just War Doctrines

It was from earlier formulations of natural law that the Platonic and
Aristotelian standards for distinguishing good government from evil
(or perverse) rule derived their criteria.[1013] Moreover, only a few
short steps, as we have already seen, led from these early formulations of good and perverse governance to the justification of tyrannicide, which was perceived as a proper remedy against an evil rule or
ruler. Later Christian concepts of natural law[1014] contributed significantly to the emergence of political resistance theories. Christian adherents of natural law posited the existence of certain immutable
and rationally discoverable principles of justice and governance.
"Ethical science," it was pointed out, "is already forever completed,
so far as her general outline and main principles are concerned, and
has been, as it were, waiting for physical science to come up with
her."[1015] Any deliberate denial or negation of natural law principles
by those in power were therefore considered as tyranny.

During the Middle Ages, in particular, the Greek and Roman classical principles regarding tyranny and tyrannicide were being constantly supplemented by newly refined doctrines of Christian natural
law. Together they joined in producing a new and often comprehensive body of theory regarding one's rightful opposition to evil authority. These new and celebrated principles of tyrannicide created
strict and precise criteria both for determining the goodness or per-
versity of a ruler's conduct and for prescribing appropriate means
for a tyrant's removal.[1016]

In medieval Christian philosophy tyranny consisted primarily of
violations of the law of God (as interpreted by various religious authorities), or of the traditions and customary laws of the realm.[1017] It
was generally agreed that a tyrant might be resisted by all appropriate public means and, if necessary, might even be put to death. An

extreme position, represented by John of Salisbury, advocated even private assassinations in unavoidable cases.[1018] St. Thomas Aquinas, representing a more moderate view, insisted that any individual had the right to kill a usurper of power, but that tyrannical practices by legitimately derived rulers should be dealt with only through public action.[1019] However, medieval writers preferred and advocated resort to peaceful means initially. These included appeals to available tribunals and institutions (ecclesiastic and others) as a means for reforming or terminating the misconduct of those in power, be they feudal lords or kings.[1020]

The development of natural law doctrines defining tyranny and specifying proper forms of domestic popular resistance was eventually supplemented by the emergence of parallel doctrines relating to the conduct of internationally "just wars." Admittedly, the just war doctrines applied not to resistance to domestic tyrants or dictators but instead to the use of force against foreign enemies. Yet the impact of just war theories was soon felt also in the domestic arenas of resistance to abuse of power.

Just war principles, like the doctrines justifying tyrannicide and resistance to temporal impiety, can be traced back to antiquity. The biblical prescriptions applicable to the Israelites' conquest of the land of Canaan are widely known. The Bible mandates not only prior resort to conciliatory measures toward one's enemies, but also subsequent standards of warfare to protect the natural environment against abuse by the warring armies.[1021] Reflecting his concern for the deleterious effect of unrestricted warfare on the life of Greece, Plato likewise articulated "rules of war" in *The Republic*.[1022] The Japanese traditional code of Bushido, similarly honored for centuries by that nation's military, also placed emphasis upon the correct treatment of honorable prisoners of war.[1023]

Most early attempts to restrict resort to war, as well as to curb the destructiveness of the means utilized during hostilities, tended to be parochial. The restrictive efforts often were binding only internally upon members of related communities, such as the Greek city-states, the Hebrew tribes, or members of the Moslem faith. In its 1139 proscription of the use of the crossbow, the Christian Church thus limited the use of that weapon among church members on the ground that the knight-felling weapon was "hateful to God and unfit for Christians."[1024]

In time, however, the early and more parochial efforts to civilize and regulate combat were reinforced and broadened in scope throughout the broader communities of warriors. The advance of technology turned warfare increasingly into the province of a small class of professionals, usually nobles bound by a set of strict moral and religious precepts. Military historians have pointed out that for nearly a thousand years, "[f]rom the Battle of Adrianopole (378) to the Battle of Laupen (1339) the primary mode of warfare was heavy cavalry. . . . Of necessity, then, the art of war came to be practiced mainly by the nobility sworn to a code of honor denoted by the church."[1025] With the constant expansion of the Christian Church, the restraining principles of warfare, developed in the Middle Ages under the influence of St. Augustine, St. Thomas Aquinas, and other scholastics, were being incorporated into the military conduct of non-Christian armies as well. The quest for reciprocity and the wish to be considered civilized meant that Christian just war principles were eventually to become part of an emerging customary wartime law of nations.[1026]

The effective development of just war doctrines first had to overcome early Christianity's leanings toward pacifism as well as its initial opposition to the legitimacy of war. St. Augustine was the main figure in supplying Christianity with the doctrinal justification for its departure from total pacifism. He drew the noted distinction between the Two Cities—the divine city that was to rise after the Second Coming, and the civil city functioning under a worldly Rome.[1027] Not only did St. Augustine advocate a departure from early Christianity's exclusive reliance upon pacifism in matters pertaining to nondivine and civil governance, but he attributed to the scriptures an implied permission for Christians to employ selected force in the pursuit of just causes.[1028]

The Puritans, the next major proponents of limited warfare, were not reluctant to borrow from the earlier Christian just war principles. They applied these doctrines in times of war to foster their concept of a modern soldier—well-disciplined, somber and, businesslike in his approach to combat. Moreover, the Puritans applied the just war standards not only in warfare abroad but also domestically, making them applicable to instances of civil war as well. In their quest to justify the propriety of their rebellious actions (to institute legitimate authority and to establish the "Kingdom of God" here on

Earth),[1029] the Puritans gave new forms and scopes to the modern just war theory.

To be considered a just war *(bellum justum)* under the Christian doctrine, a conflict had to comply with two distinct requirements: The cause *(jus ad bellum)* had to be just and the means employed *(jus in bello)* had equally to be just.[1030] A just cause had to be supported by certain specified objectives. These included: (1) self-defense against aggression, (2) correcting an injustice imposed by a foreign authority, (3) the reestablishment of a just order, and (4) the bringing about of peace.[1031] A just war also had to be declared by a legitimate authority, thus excluding private warfare or acts of individual revenge.[1032] Finally, a just war was to serve as a last resort, taking place only after other means of dispute resolution had proven inadequate.[1033]

Not only had the cause for war to comply with stringent standards, but the means employed in combat also were equally strictly prescribed. Moreover, *jus in bello* required that the force employed be proportionate to the rights protected and to the pursued ends. And force could not be deliberately applied against noncombatants or other innocent persons.[1034]

It is abundantly clear that the just war doctrine was intended not only to dampen the state's resort to violence but also to narrow the adverse consequences of warfare upon nonwarring parties. Restricted to defense against aggression, and permissible only to advance the ends of justice, the just war doctrine virtually outlawed aggressive, exploitative, and indiscriminate warfare. Moreover, making war an act of last resort and insisting that it be exclusively a tool of sovereign authority reduced popular resort to military means, and the protection extended to noncombatants served as one more step in the effort to regulate as well as to restrict the destructive forces unleashed by warfare.

The growth of just war doctrines, which were later to be incorporated in a newly emerging international humanitarian law,[1035] thus functioned mainly as a delimiting force upon emperors', kings', and princes' resort to arms. Cognizant of the fundamental breach between early Christianity's pacifism (which denied war altogether) on the one hand, and the subsequent primacy of national sovereignty (which granted nations free rein in matters of war and peace) on the other hand, one can readily appreciate the observation that "it is the intent of just-war theory to occupy an intermediate position between the extremes of pacifism and realpolitik."[1036]

Derived from natural law precepts, the just war doctrines served to reconcile the deep chasm between humanity's emerging aspirations for morality and peace and the prevailing Hobbesian realities of a "state of nature" full of cruel and unremitting conflict. In the modern era, many of the early just war principles (defining both the justifications for and the means to be utilized in warfare) became permanently enshrined in the law of nations.[1037] Initially, the principles governing the means of conflict *(jus in bello)* garnered greater attention and acceptance than standards for delineating between just and unjust causes of war *(jus ad bellum)*. But contemporary international law addresses both means and causes in its global campaign against the ravages of warfare. Some fierce advocates of the modern nation-state continue to resist any diminution of a sovereign country's prerogative to wage war. Yet the United Nations Charter, signed at the conclusion of World War II, imposed a drastic limitation upon the traditional right of nations to wage war by specifying self-defense as the lone internationally permissible cause for resort to armed conflict.[1038]

Piercing the Sanctity of National Sovereignty

The just war doctrine, regenerated and substantially vindicated in modern international law, supplies an important building block for our undertaking—the building of a classification system for the appraisal of the political offender's assertion of "just causes" and "just means" in justification of his or her dissent, disobedience, and violent deeds. Throughout modern history, various proponents and supporters of just war doctrines (whether attributing them to religious or classical natural law sources or basing them upon contemporary doctrines, treaties, and conventions) have attempted to combine the standards applicable to both the causes and the means of international warfare under a unified jurisprudential umbrella.[1039] From Hugo Grotius's ambitious seventeenth-century classification to post–World War II international conventions and protocols, this effort to create a comprehensive legal guide for international warfare has not ceased.

We now turn to the proposal of a similar classification scheme to identify just causes and means not for international warfare, but for domestic rebellion and conflict. Such a scheme must, in the first place, draw definite lines of demarcation between what constitutes just causes and unjust causes, just means and unjust means, in the arenas of domestic warfare. "Since war is not a condition of anarchy and lawlessness, International Law requires that belligerents shall comply with its rules in carrying on their military . . . operations," wrote Lassa Oppenheim with regard to humanitarian law standards in his treatise on international law.[1040] It is the objective of the proposed classification scheme to similarly take domestic dissidence and warfare out of the realms of anarchy and lawlessness.

Several key principles contained in contemporary international humanitarian law can be utilized and expanded upon for application to domestic conflicts. A foundation for such expansion can be unearthed in previous legal history. The drafting of the Nuremberg Charter after World War II must be viewed as an example not merely of a contemporary crystallization of international just war principles, but also as a dramatic expansion of humanitarian law to cover not only foreign conflicts but also instances of domestic tyranny and abuse of power. The Charter[1041] accomplished both tasks by reiterating first the historically acknowledged "war crimes" (relating to the protection of civilians and lawful belligerents and the enforcement of other humane standards of *jus in bello*), as well as identifying the more recently recognized "crimes against peace" (constituting violations of *jus ad bellum*)—the dual components of the traditional just war doctrine. The Charter went on to criminalize tyrannical regimes' abusive treatment of their own populations. For the first time in human history, these new "crimes against humanity" (which include a regime's murder, extermination, enslavement, and deportation of domestic populations) were made subject to international regulation and punishment. The Nuremberg Charter thus made each country accountable to the community of nations not only for aggressive and inhumane foreign warfare but also for war-connected tyranny and abuse of power against the country's own people.

Crimes against peace, and particularly war crimes, had long been recognized in international law. "The prosecution of these acts by the IMT [International Military Tribunal] at Nuremberg did not, therefore, constitute an innovation in international law," wrote historian Robert Woetzel.[1042] However, the third class of offenses, the "crimes against humanity" tried at Nuremberg, was novel. "[A] completely different legal situation exists with the so-called crimes against humanity perpetrated by the German government against its own citizens, e.g., political, racial, and religious groups such as Jews, German Jehovah's Witnesses, Freemasons, and political opponents of the Nazi regime."[1043] The novelty was in the fact that before Nuremberg, those "[a]cts of state which affect only the state's own citizens in an area under its legitimate control [were] generally considered the exclusive sovereign concern of the authorities of the state."[1044]

The Nuremberg trial, by pursuing the charges contained in the Charter, demonstrated that international standards of conduct could from then on be applicable to domestic as well as foreign conduct of nations and their leaders. By so imposing a duty upon those in authority to observe the international standards regarding peace, war, and domestic humanity, the Nuremberg Charter (as reinforced by the Nuremberg tribunal's subsequent convictions)[1045] seemed to place upon those in positions of power the further duty not only to refrain from doing evil, but also to resist the evil deeds ordered or carried out by those higher up.[1046]

The standards articulated by Nuremberg have had an increasing impact not only upon other international tribunals but also on domestic courts.[1047] By pointing out that violations of international law are carried out by individuals in positions of power rather than by elusive and faceless governmental entities, the Nuremberg principles have firmly placed the responsibility for the observance of the growing body of the international law of peace, war, and humanity not upon governments alone but upon individuals as well. Professor Woetzel, in his definitive work on Nuremberg, reiterates the importance of bringing to an end the previous immunity of individuals to international law violations: "Crimes against international law are committed by men, not by abstract entities, and only by punishing individuals who commit such crimes can the provisions of international law be enforced."[1048]

The Nuremberg rules further attenuated the standing and sanctity of the principle of national sovereignty in international law by decreeing domestic conduct to be subject to the law of nations. Soon thereafter, the newly drafted Genocide Convention served to further curtail the former immunity of abusive nations and regimes from scrutiny by the international community. The 1948 Genocide Convention served notice on the world community that a regime's abuse of its own ethnic, religious, or cultural minorities and communities would be subject to scrutiny, condemnation, adjudication, and, ultimately, punishment.[1049]

The contemporaneous formulation in 1948 of the Universal Declaration of Human Rights (followed by the political, social, and economic covenants developed pursuant to it)[1050] has vested new rights in the people of the world that go far beyond the proscriptive standards imposed upon governments by the Nuremberg and Genocide obligations. These newly proclaimed rights set out to grant individuals and groups throughout the world direct legal entitlements as well as standing to challenge the violations of their rights by those holding positions of domestic authority. Individuals thus are no longer unprotected pawns in the hands of their states and their rulers. Not only new transnational standards of human rights but also enforcement agencies (regional and global, fact-finding and adjudicatory)[1051] have come forth to help guard individuals and groups against domestic abuse and torment.

International legal developments during the second half of the twentieth century have been extraordinary. The world community has articulated not only a wide-ranging list of "inalienable rights" for individuals and communities but has, at least in principle, established tentative criteria to aid in the definition of "evil governments." The universal support accorded to the cause of self-determination, and the sympathy extended to those struggling against colonialism and racism, are indeed contemporary elaborations and codifications of some of the ancient principles of justice and humanity manifested in the historic doctrines of tyrannicide and just war. The community of nations, through contemporary declarations, resolutions, enactments, adjudications, and missions of humanitarian intervention, has explicitly granted its approval to a variety of "just causes." By offering legal, diplomatic, and material support (economic as well as military) to peoples and minorities struggling for relief from colonial, foreign, racist, ethnic, and other oppression,[1052] the United Nations and other organizations have helped differentiate just causes from unjust causes.

The Geneva Conventions and Protocols on humanitarian law[1053] have acted to further supplement and strengthen not only the traditional concern for just means of warfare, but also to solidify the emerging international consensus regarding just causes. By according the domestic warrior against colonialism or racism (who complies with specified standards of belligerency) the opportunity for a quasi-legitimate status under international law, the cause of that domestic protagonist has been favorably singled out. Rebels and resistance fighters, struggling against internationally defined evil regimes, are increasingly advancing their claim to be placed on an equal footing with the military forces of the belligerent governments. Both the de jure and de facto efforts to treat as legitimate international belligerents those who might otherwise be described as domestic "political criminals" have irretrievably undone some of the traditions that have long propped up the antiquated and obsolete notions of state sovereignty.

Safeguarding the Values and Institutions of Humanity

The international community's granting of guarded legitimacy to those engaging in militant struggles for such internationally approved objectives as anti-colonialism, self-determination, racial justice, and basic human rights is not the sole development to dramatically affect the political rebel's standing in the post–World War II era. The new leniency exhibited toward these internationally favored resisters to evil has been countervailed by an opposite international movement to delegitimize political activists who pursue proscribed political causes or resort to indiscriminate militance. The latter development, which deprives a great many asserters of political claims of a lawful belligerency standing, has been the result of a growing worldwide antipathy toward political militants who resort to extreme means (often described as terrorist violence) in the pursuit of their causes, however just they might be.

Beginning in the second half of the nineteenth century, an ever growing number of methods of political resistance began to be internationally proscribed due to their particularly deleterious effect upon the values and institutions of the world community. We previously noted that in the 1860s assassinations or assaults upon heads of state and their families had been internationally condemned through the formulation of the *clause d'attentat*.[1054] A generation later, in the 1890s, anarchists were declared enemies of all humanity and were consequently denied the protections afforded to other political offenders.[1055] Four decades later, the League of Nations, in its failed 1938 anti-terrorism convention, made a further international attempt to strip political dissidents of legitimacy or other benefits if they resorted to violence or incitement across national boundaries.[1056]

Various other categories of indiscriminate violence (often grouped under the informal and ill-defined umbrella of "terrorism") were similarly proscribed in the post–World War II era because of a widespread recognition of their universal danger. Aircraft hijacking, which jeopardized the world's instrumentalities of civil aviation, was banned in the interest of safeguarding international commerce and travel.[1057] Assaults against diplomatic personnel were prohibited in the name of the sanctity of international political intercourse.[1058] Letter bombs[1059] and hostage-taking[1060] were similarly proscribed in the interest of protecting the innocent. Most of these emerging international prohibitions of specified means of political resistance and rebellion can be viewed as an effort to apply the mitigating and humanizing standards of nexus and proportionality (concepts introduced and discussed in earlier chapters in connection with the categorizing of political offenses and with regard to extradition policies) to the arenas of domestic conflict and warfare.[1061]

Since political offenders were first exempted from international extradition in the middle of the nineteenth century, the growing imposition of absolute prohibitions against some specified means of political warfare (e.g., assassinations and assaults upon heads of state and their families, anarchistic violence, aircraft hijacking, letter bombs), and the condemnation of such other means as fail to conform with the requirements of nexus and proportionality (differentiating, for example, between an assault against an innocent civilian and an assault against an occupying soldier) had served to limit the political offender's protection against unreasonable extensions. Similar limitations can continue to provide effective tools for protecting the world community against those measures of political rebellion and resistance that are considered unduly detrimental to international well-being.

One can similarly explore and articulate other legal principles in order to develop guidelines for the definition of objectionable or illegitimate causes. Such proscribed causes will undoubtedly include the waging of aggressive wars (as in the Iraqi invasion of Kuwait); the preservation or furtherance of slavery, colonialism, and racism; the perpetration of genocide; and the deliberate deprivation of human rights. In so condemning certain despicable causes or ends, even if carried out for alleged political objectives, the world community can contribute to the construction of a new world order, one free of today's most egregious forms of racial, ethnic, and political exploitation and abuse.

There would seem to be evidence of an emerging consensus regarding what is to constitute internationally prohibited causes or ends, as well as what might qualify for the category of proscribed means. For the first time in history a growing understanding between the globe's different countries and different sociopolitical, religious, and legal blocs is forming as to what should constitute just causes for domestic rebellion and warfare, as well as to what might be considered the appropriate and just means for their attainment.

When one takes stock of the growing attempts to clarify and implement international standards defining the requisites of good governance and responsible citizenship, it becomes clear that the second half of the twentieth century, a century known for its earlier tolerance of Fascist, Nazi, and Soviet totalitarianism and their resulting unparalleled holocausts, might be also remembered in history for its dramatic downsizing of the myth of national sovereignty. The conclusion of the twentieth century might therefore hopefully be equally remembered for its contributions to the worldwide repulsion against tyranny and reigns of terror and to the growth of international humanitarian intervention on behalf of the victims of such regimes.

The newly emerging international principles regarding just and unjust causes and means, when taken together, readily suggest a reclassification of most instances of political militance and criminality, new and old, into three discernable classes. The first consists of those causes and/or means of conduct that have been generally condemned and made punishable by the international community. The second encompasses those activities where the causes and/or means have generally been met with international tolerance or even approval. The third class of political militance, which consists generally of activities that might be described as civil wars or related internecine domestic belligerency, has been met by the community of nations with a more neutral, though evidently concerned and increasingly protective, stance.

Included in the first and negative category of political activism one might include conduct resembling piracy (the most ancient of all international crimes), slavery, and slave labor, as well as war crimes and crimes against peace, all of which have long been defined as international offenses. Since the conclusion of World War II, either the causes or means manifested in crimes against humanity, genocide, colonialism, racism, aircraft hijacking, assaults against diplomatic personnel, hostage-taking, and other abuses of innocents have been condemned by international law.[1062] Even when militants assert and advocate a political cause or objective that is internationally endorsed or tolerated, the perpetrators' resort to internationally proscribed means will suffice to condemn their conduct as universal criminality.

The second category of political activism has been met, on the other hand, with considerable international understanding, tolerance, and even support. Those persecuted or in danger of persecution for their opposition to racism and colonialism, for their exercise of such recognized human rights as religious or political freedom, familial autonomy, freedom of speech, and other forms of communication, have been increasingly accorded many of the benefits available under the international laws and practices relating to extradition and asylum. Prisoners of conscience, convicted or otherwise confined for nonviolent conduct in pursuit of internationally recognized human rights, are being granted relief, often due to the interventions of organizations such as Amnesty International and the International Committee of the Red Cross. Even political militants resorting to violence, so long as they do not violate internationally proscribed standards, are likely to receive protection from extradition when they seek refuge abroad. As the pursuit of anti-colonialism, anti-racism, self-determination, and human rights has become internationally approved or even mandated, honest and reasonable pursuers of these causes have earned the respect, the moral support, and, at times, the legal protection of the world community.

The third discernable category of political activism encompasses those rebels, such as guerrillas, participants in civil wars, separatists, and members of resistance movements, who, due to the quasi-military nature of their organization and operations, claim for themselves the status usually accorded to "belligerents" in international wars. In those instances where the size and militancy of the rebellious movement have risen to the level of a domestic "armed conflict," the claims of participants to a prisoner-of-war status and other international law protections have been increasingly granted in practice and even in law.

The conduct of America's warring parties in the Civil War, as well as more recent practices in the Nigerian, Nicaraguan, Yugoslav, Yemeni, and other civil wars testify to this emerging trend. Combatants seem to be increasingly attempting to apply to domestic conflicts the civilizing standards made applicable to international wars by humanitarian law. The expansion of humanitarian law from its restricted traditional role in the regulation of international warfare to its new and growing application to intranational conflicts indeed represents one of the most significant developments in the modern international law and in the jurisprudence of political conformity and defiance.

Epilogue

Clarifying the Rules of Just Governance and Just Resistance

[E]ven irregular . . . domestic . . . warfare can be kept somewhat cleaner, avoiding the slaughter of innocents.

—Yuval Ne'eman,
in *Terrorists or Freedom Fighters* (1986)

There is but one law for all, namely, that law which governs all law . . . the law of humanity, justice, equity—the law of nature, and of nations.

—Edmund Burke,
Impeachment of Warren Hastings (1794)

The verdict of the world is conclusive.

—St. Augustine,
Contra Epistolam Parmeniani (400)

The Last Moments of John Brown, Thomas Hovenden, etching (1884).

From Historical Fragments
to a New Blueprint

The preceding analysis of both historical and recent developments pertaining to the treatment of political offenders demonstrates the growing emergence of an international consensus regarding the criteria that separate just causes and means from unjust causes and means. This analysis also points to new jurisprudentially sound approaches to the difficult legal and moral questions posed by domestic rebellion and political criminality. It would seem that, through confrontations with these complex and painful realities, the diverse and highly divided community of nations is increasingly coming to recognize the intellectual dishonesty, as well as pragmatic disutility, of the oft-quoted assertion that "one person's freedom fighter is another's terrorist," a cliché that apparently identifies the freedom fighter and the terrorist as moral equivalents.

We have seen how three divisions of politically related activism and militance have come to be identified in international law and practice. The first consists of conduct in the pursuit of internationally proscribed causes, usually carried out through internationally prohibited means. The second category encompasses conduct in the pursuit of internationally endorsed causes, usually carried out through internationally approved means. The third comprises massive incarnations of domestic rebellion and warfare, which tend to resemble traditional forms of belligerency among nations but with regard to which few firm international standards have emerged. These three categories of political activism can serve as foundational pillars in our proposed comprehensive typology of political criminality. The framework of this typology can be further assembled through a critical review of both the causes advocated by political actors in the course of their political resistance, and the means they resort to in the pursuit of their causes.

Causes might be divided generally into three classes. "Just causes" would encompass those that have been internationally approved, including the defeat of colonialism and racism and the attainment of self-determination and human rights. "Unjust causes" would be those that have been internationally condemned, including the promotion of slavery and the pursuit of genocide, racism, or other ob-

331

jectives that transgress upon world peace and humanity. The third class of causes would be those toward which the international community might maintain a more neutral posture, meaning that they are neither favored nor disfavored by the laws or customs of the community of nations. Such internationally neutral causes would encompass most domestic conflicts with regard to issues of local autonomy, conflicts connected with political secession, struggles over ideological or party preferences, contests involving succession or relating to the transfer of the reins of power, and other intranational conflicts that have thus far been left outside the evolving standards and objectives of the world community.

The means resorted to by rebels, dissidents, and other political militants might be similarly divided into three classes. "Just" means would be those that have been internationally approved or upheld, including appropriate militant resistance to colonialism and racism, as well as the direct and nonviolent exercise of such internationally acknowledged human rights as freedom of speech, religion, and peaceful political activity. "Unjust" means would be those that have been internationally proscribed, including hijacking, hostage-taking, and the victimization of internationally protected persons. Finally, the third and generally neutral class of means would include such activities as the prevailing international law has failed to address. This class generally encompasses such means as have historically come under the "mixed" or "connected" categories of political offenses (discussed in Chapter 6). It is this class of means that accounts for most of the offenses currently predominating in controversies regarding extradition requests throughout the world.

Superimposing this framework of causes and means upon the three previously identified divisions of political activism and militance—(1) conduct in the pursuit of internationally proscribed causes (or political offenses as crimes), (2) conduct in the pursuit of internationally endorsed causes (or political offenses as politics), and (3) conduct consisting of larger incarnations of domestic rebellion and warfare that resemble international war (or political offenses as belligerency)—and then applying to these distinct divisions appropriate tests of nexus and proportionality (see Chapter 6), results in our proposed "Typology of Political Offenses: From Terrorism to Human Rights Struggles" (see Appendix). This typology surveys the political crime arena more thoroughly than has been done before.

The three divisions of political activism—political offenses as crimes, politics, and belligerency—are correspondingly colored dark grey, white, and light grey. Moreover, the typology creates two categories for each division: (1) conduct toward which international law has clearly declared its position, for which a solid is used, and (2) conduct toward which international law (sometimes in contrast with domestic law) remains uncertain or neutral, for which stripes are used. The typology also supplies descriptions of both the conduct necessary to qualify for a given category and the appropriate domestic and international reactions usually applicable to that category. In sum, the six categories to which all political offenses are assigned consist of: (1) international crimes, (2) domestic crimes, (3) domestic armed conflicts, (4) anti-colonial and anti-racist conflicts (5) political offenses, and (6) international rights conflicts.

The intricacies of the typology are not too difficult to fathom. For a political offense to constitute an international crime (dark grey), which turns the actor into an international offender or what is often popularly referred to as a "terrorist," the conduct in question must either serve a cause or resort to means that are internationally condemned by treaty, convention, or international custom. Condemned causes, as we have seen, include the unsavory enforcement of racism, colonialism, and genocide, the instigation of aggressive wars, and the gross abuse of other internationally acknowledged human rights. Condemned means are types of conduct specifically prohibited by international agreements or custom, such as piracy, skyjacking, hostage-taking, letter-bomb campaigns, the abuse of diplomatic personnel, the commission of war crimes, and the mistreatment of civilians, whether native or enemy-affiliated, in warfare.

As one reexamines the twelve "visions" or historical vignettes detailed in the Prologue, which were intended to introduce the reader to the diverse activities and actors that make up the community of political offenders and offenses, it becomes readily apparent that several of the portrayed instances fall within the category of international crime. Under the criteria advanced in the typology, the international offenders in Vision One were not Mary Dyer, who preached a prohibited version of the Gospel amongst the Massachusetts Bay Pilgrims, and the Cheyenne, who gave up their arms in exchange for a promise of protection, but rather the intolerant Pilgrims and the zealous Colorado Militia under the command of J. M. Chivington.

Likewise, the designation of international criminality can be readily attached to the actions of the Soviet governmental functionaries, in Vision Three, who deprived the citizenry of their internationally protected rights. The indiscriminate violence and the endangering of aircraft dealt with in Vision Seven are international crimes as well.

A domestic or common crime (with dark grey stripes) involves causes or means that are proscribed domestically and that tend to be disfavored, but not proscribed, internationally. Common offenses usually lack an appropriate nexus to a claimed political grievance and tend to utilize means that are disproportionate to the asserted grievance or to the relief sought. Any assertedly political conduct that exceeds the bounds of nexus and proportionality, such as bank robbery or indiscriminate bombing in pursuit of allegedly political causes, is thus likely to be viewed as a common crime. Offenders falling within this category are not entitled to the defenses available under international law, nor are they entitled, upon their flight, to protection from extradition to the offended state. Indeed, if the conduct of the common offender transgresses international law as well, the resultant offense might constitute an international crime.

Reviewing again the twelve historical vignettes detailed in the Prologue, we find that some of the reported events fall within the category of common crime. Shalom Schwarzbard's assassination of Simon Petlyura, described in Vision Nine, constituted a common crime. John Wilkes Booth's assassination of Abraham Lincoln, most likely carried out in quest for historical notoriety, and John W. Hinckley Jr.'s similarly motivated assault on Ronald Reagan, both described in Vision Eleven, were nothing more than common crimes.

Political offenses as belligerency, or warfare-type conflict, begin with the category of domestic armed conflicts (with light grey stripes). Since these intranational conflicts are not carried out in the pursuit of universally recognized causes, affected countries are at liberty to respond to and punish all participants in these struggles in compliance with their own domestic criminal law. Nevertheless, all standards of humane treatment and the due process requirements made applicable by Geneva Conventions to such domestic armed conflicts are to be observed by the affected countries (see "The Political Offender and the Law of War" in Chapter 7).

Vision One comes close to presenting a situation of domestic armed conflict. The conflict between the Cheyenne and the Colorado

Militia was perceived at the time as a domestic or intranational confrontation, and therefore exempt from international regulation. Yet under the contemporary Geneva Conventions (specifically Common Article 3 and the attached Protocols), this class of conflict is subject to humanitarian requirements. Several of the recent domestic conflicts, rebellions, and coups d'état in countries such as Afghanistan, Cambodia, Liberia, Sierra Leone, and Zaire similarly come within the humanitarian standards applicable to this category of political criminality.

Anti-colonial and anti-racist conflicts (light grey), a category generally known as freedom fighting, refers to forms of political militancy and resistance that are generally favored by the international community. Where the aim of a conflict or rebellion is to implement internationally approved causes, the domestic participants are entitled, under the Protocols to the Geneva Conventions on humanitarian law, to the same protections that are afforded to lawful international combatants by the existing laws of war, including exemption from punishment. Of course, rebels seeking these protections (which include prisoner-of-war status upon capture or surrender) must themselves conform to the requirements imposed by the applicable humanitarian law.

Among the historical vignettes are two instances that might fall into the category of freedom fighting. Vision Two, which describes the 1859 military raid of John Brown and his "Army of Liberation" against the U.S. Federal Arsenal in Harper's Ferry, presents a likely instance of domestic warfare supported and protected by international standards. Similarly, the Cheyenne in Vision One would benefit from the contemporary safeguards available to international belligerents under the Geneva Conventions and its accompanying Protocols. Many instances of contemporary domestic warfare supply similar examples of rebels entitled to treatment as international belligerents, as is the case when the resisters seek the defeat and removal of foreign, colonial, and racist regimes.

We come next to political offenses (white with stripes). The benefits of international law are extended to political offenders in this category mostly through their traditional entitlement to exemption from extradition or pursuant to the expanding laws of asylum. The political offender may also be accorded more lenient intranational treatment than the common criminal through the operations of the domestic sentencing and corrections systems. For the conduct in question to be excepted as a political offense under extradition law, its motives as well as its means must not be among those condemned by international law. Political offenders may at times seek to further characterize their conduct as internationally mandated or protected, above the mere fact that it is not condemned, thereby seeking for themselves the benefits of the sixth and most favored category of political activists, those accorded the status of international heroes in the pursuit of human rights. However, since members of this category usually pursue internationally neutral rather than internationally mandated causes, and since their means are usually violent, they are likely to attain only the lesser protections or benefits available to political offenders, consisting mainly of an exemption from extradition, the right to asylum, and the occasional benefits of a more lenient sentence.

Because political offenders often resort to violence and occasionally overlook the standards of nexus and proportionality, their conduct is frequently placed within the "mixed" or "connected" categories of political crime. The specific characteristics of their activities thus become the key to determining which actors are to be extradited, which are to be accorded refuge, and which might be granted more lenient sentences. Their motives likewise serve as a critical test for determining international dispositions, regarding both extradition and asylum, as well as domestic treatment, regarding the imposition of sanctions and the granting of amnesties.

Visions Two, Six, Eight, and Ten serve as fitting illustrations for the variable and changing status of the political offender. John Brown, who rebelled against slavery in an era preceding the international abolition of slavery, falls into the political offender category. So does Philip Berrigan, who set out to burn selective service records in protest of the Vietnam War. Martin Luther King Jr., who refused to abide by an invalid court injunction against his proposed civil rights march, is another suitable candidate for this category, as are the twenty-three assassins of Gaius Julius Caesar, whom they suspected of aspiring to become a lifetime tyrant. Those who attempted the assassination of Adolf Hitler, one of history's most murderous rulers, could readily be classified as political offenders, and so could thousands, if not millions, of Americans who have engaged in lesser but prohibited acts of civil disobedience. Whether engaging in militant warfare against institutions and individuals of authority, or merely taking part in proscribed nonviolent protests, the earmarks of the political offender are a refrainment from indiscriminate violence and an adherence to forms of resistance that do not violate international standards.

International rights conflicts in the typology (white) constitute the most protected category of political crime. Only a limited, but dramatically increasing, segment of so-called political dissidents qualify under it. This category encompasses those politically motivated actors who pursue internationally approved causes by resorting to means that transgress neither international law nor the standards of nexus and proportionality. Generally, political actors within this category (whether those who speak out against abusive authority, those who print critical tracts that evade government licensure, or those who resist foreign or racist regimes) are to be afforded the right of international asylum in case of flight, granted the domestic opportunity to raise all available legal defenses, and accorded the general sympathy and protections of the world community.

Revisiting once more the diverse historical vignettes presented in the Prologue, one finds in Visions Three, Four, and Five ample examples of political activists entitled to the world community's sympathy as well as to active support. The Soviet civil activists who protested the abuses of their religious, familial, and other civil rights, Chinese asylum-seekers Wang Saizhen and Li Jinlin, who fled to Canada and then the United States in fear of criminal penalties for giving birth to their prohibited second child, and Swiss naturalist Bruno Manser, who struggled for environmental protections, are all fitting examples of political activists who should be classified as international heroes in the pursuit of human rights.

Based on the classification in the proposed typology, some political protestors, resisters, and rebels might find themselves condemned as international criminals. Others might qualify as lawful belligerents or even international heroes. For still others the typology offers no absolute categorizations, leaving each instance of dissidence and rebellion to be judged on a case-by-case basis and subjected to evolving international and domestic laws. But despite this and other obvious shortcomings of the typology, its very presence should make it more difficult for both those in power and those contesting authority to continue relying on simplistic and indiscriminate accusations of their opponents. The typology should make it impossible for parties to a political conflict to indiscriminately describe their opponents as adherents to "venal" means and causes, or to falsely assert their own compliance with acknowledged "higher" causes and means. No longer would the protagonists and antagonists, the media, and the world community be comfortable in labeling political activists as either terrorists or freedom fighters merely on the basis of the labelers' own unchallenged preferences or biases.

The proposed typology is a synthesis and restatement of principles derived from existing comparative and international laws, customs, and scholarly writings. Gathered from diverse arenas of theory and practice, these principles are distilled from the fields of human rights, humanitarian law, and international criminal law, and seek greater interaction between such institutions and doctrines as motive, necessity, asylum, extradition, nexus, and proportionality. Each of these principles and strains of legal thought and practice deals in part with the same thorny problem—the unorthodox nature of the political offender. Not readily fitting into the established legal categories of either domestic or international law, the political offender has hitherto resisted definition and systematic treatment. Bringing these diverse laws, customs, and doctrines together can produce a consistent system of jurisprudential classifications for political criminality. Hopefully, this undertaking will help advance the creation of a broader consensus regarding international and national responses to the growing worldwide eruption of political dissent, activism, criminality, and violence.

From a Typology to a Bill of Rights

In the eight preceding chapters, we have examined the eternal conflict between the forces of authority and their antagonists, the proponents of greater autonomy. The tools of the conflict have been many and diverse: abuses of power and reigns of terror on the part of those in authority, and dissent, civil disobedience, rebellion, belligerency, and even terrorism on the part of their opponents.

Part One of the book identified the unique dilemmas posed by political criminality and its perpetrators. Characterizing the primary actors involved in the conflict and examining both the abusers of power and their political adversaries, Chapter 1 reviewed the historical and contemporary responses, political as well as legal, to this perpetual war. It reviewed also the long, colorful, and often bloody history of this conflict, detailing progress as well as regression in the treatment of political offenses. Chapter 2 further detailed the historical efforts to identify and classify the political offender, introducing such concepts as "just" and "unjust" causes and such criteria as nexus and proportionality.

Part Two presented a social and psychological profile of the political offender. Chapter 3 warned against the deification of the political offender and the demonization of authority, concluding that political opposition and rebellion can arise in any context and in response to a wide range of real or perceived political, economic, and social ills and grievances.

Part Three concentrated on the political offender's standing under domestic laws, in the United States and abroad. Chapter 4 examined the history of the American struggle with political offenders. After surveying the harsh sanctions imposed upon political offenders throughout history, Chapter 5 proceeded to document the subsequently lenient treatment accorded to "honorable offenders" under Western European laws in the nineteenth and twentieth centuries.

Part Four examined, in Chapter 6, the fluctuating yet important international position accorded to political dissidents and rebels historically and under contemporary extradition and asylum laws. Chapter 7 further undertook to enumerate and analyze the defenses and justifications advanced on behalf of the political offender in both international and domestic laws. It particularly traced the post–World War II rise of domestic-law justifications and defenses of rebellion derived from the newly emerging international laws governing human rights and international crime, and humanitarian standards.

Part Five began with an exploration of the likelihood that mounting ethnic, clannish, cultural, linguistic, and religious centrifugal forces will make political crime and domestic warfare the preeminent problem of the coming century. Chapter 8 then commenced with a daring and groundbreaking endeavor—attempting to bring together and integrate the diverse historical, political, legal, and practical strands of knowledge pertaining to political criminality and its treatment. Finally, it sought to demonstrate that appropriate jurisprudential principles and doctrines already exist for addressing many of the problems raised by the conflict between authority and autonomy. This brings us to the proposed typology, which seeks to show that potentially every confrontation between political resisters and those who mete out domestic and international justice can be judged by prescriptive standards that are both domestically and universally sound and acceptable.

The proposed typology is primarily an exercise to validate two of this volume's earlier and central claims. First, that the community of civilized nations is in the process of arriving at a common core of universal principles regarding both proper governance and proper response to political resistance and rebellion. Second, that these principles can be concretely and objectively applied to virtually all categories of actors taking part in political conflicts—whether they are the wielders of power or those striving to attain it, whether their conduct is active or passive, violent or peaceful, military or civilian, individual or collective, discriminate or indiscriminate, just or unjust. That the typology hopefully succeeds in validating these two claims serves as a further rejection of the tired cliché granting terrorists and freedom fighters some claim to moral equivalence.

The remaining task is to identify the principles that might be derived from the proposed typology of political crime and criminals—an instrument that, by supplementing the vague arena of political criminality with a set of prescriptive principles, might hopefully bear upon the treatment of the varied classes of political militants in the halls of justice and in the media, as well as in the parade of civilization. These principles could be applicable not only to those who challenge authority but also to those who possess and abuse it. Most if not all of these principles, as previously noted, have been carefully extracted from the world community's historical record of cultural, political, and jurisprudential developments, particularly those emerging in recent decades.

Helpful for expressing these principles in prescriptive terms is a "Bill of Rights"—a formulation befitting this study, whose main vehicle has been the discipline of law. The principles to be advanced indeed address primarily the legal status, domestic and international, of the political offender. One might wish to address here other historically and contemporarily compelling, but nonlegal, issues raised by the perpetual war between authority and autonomy. One might wish as well to address the overall social, economic, and political utility of dissent and rebellion. And one might wish to discuss the question of the individual's and the collective's choice or duty to take part in militant opposition to evil governance. But many of these issues have already been addressed in the fist two volumes of this trilogy, as well as in works by other authors.

This trilogy began over a quarter century ago, in an effort to examine political criminality from a broad, comprehensive, and multidisciplinary vantage point. The initial mission was accomplished through *The Tree of Liberty: A Documentary History of Rebellion and Political Crime in America* and *The War Against Authority: From the Crisis of Legitimacy to a New Social Contract.* These volumes dealt with resistance and rebellion from the perspectives of history and culture, economics and politics, sociology and psychology. Now, to successfully conclude this initial endeavor in the complex arena of political criminality, some critical jurisprudential and quasi-legal principles must be put forth. Deeper questions regarding the transcendental role of rebellion in the making and remaking of politics, governance, and human rights and values must be left for future treatment.

The jurisprudential principles advanced here will hopefully convey a greater clarity and a more balanced understanding, as well as a greater spirit of conciliation, upon those empowered to judge the participants in the eternal struggle between authority and autonomy. In guiding this mediation between the commands of authority and the rule of law, on one hand, and the demands of individual or collective conscience and well-being, on the other, these principles could also illuminate and inform public opinion on this critical subject, permitting both the media and the citizenry to more correctly distinguish between the noble freedom fighter and the vile terrorist. Hopefully, these principles will not merely reiterate the emerging international law but will serve also as a guide for domestic courts faced with the unique claims of political offenders. Though not perfect, these principles could be called upon by both the protagonists and the antagonists in this struggle, wherever and whenever their actions run afoul of domestic as well as international law. Though not absolute, these principles could serve as a resource whenever national and international tribunals are called upon to respond to an offender's assertion of obedience to positive, natural, higher, divine, domestic, or international law.

These principles, in the hands of national and international readers and scholars, legal tribunals and political agencies, and other guardians of world peace, could also serve as tools for assessing the justice and wisdom of the world community's decisions to resort to neutrality or to intervention in the face of the ever mounting domestic conflicts throughout the countries of this globe. Finally, the principles could serve as rules of conduct for both the protagonists and the antagonists in domestic conflicts throughout the world. Combatants, whether struggling for the cause of rebellion or defending existing authority, should be on notice that universal principles and standards apply to both sides in these conflicts. They should know further that these standards (and, implicitly, such sanctions as might be arrived at under these standards) are likely to be upheld and enforced by the world community.

However, the immediate tasks of the proposed "Bill of Rights" (below) remain modest—to shed light on a unique offender, who usually admits to no wrongdoing in his or her struggle against those in power. The principles embodied therein, the reader should be reminded, are merely restatements of traditional and emerging international and domestic law. The important contribution here is that, for the first time, these principles are applied in a comprehensive and systematic way.

A Bill of Rights for Just Governance and Just Resistance

1. All rights and protections accorded to individuals, groups, and communities by international law, human rights law, and humanitarian law (as manifested by international treaties, conventions, and customary international law) shall be designated "international rights."

2. No persons shall suffer criminal penalties under either international or domestic law for reasonably carrying out activities or exercising rights authorized by or recognized as international rights.

3. Persons subject to persecution for seeking or exercising such international rights shall be accorded the privilege of asylum and freedom from extradition by all civilized nations.

4. The governments and officials of all nations are bound to respect these international rights in the treatment of citizens and all others under their jurisdiction. The failure to observe international rights shall constitute Abuse of Power.

5. Willful and grievous Abuse of Power shall constitute an international crime.

6. Persons who engage in resistance, protest, or rebellion in the pursuit of internationally proscribed causes or through resort to internationally proscribed means shall be considered offenders against international criminal law.

7. Persons who commit international crimes shall be subject to prosecution and punishment by all civilized nations.

8. No citizens or residents shall be obligated to obey national laws or superior orders if such obeyance would constitute an international crime.

9. Citizens shall not be punished for reasonable and proportionate resistance, protest, or rebellion against governmental policies or measures constituting Abuse of Power.

10. Citizens and residents who resist, protest, or rebel against Abuse of Power must at all times offer maximum possible protection to the life, liberty, and property of innocent and uninvolved parties, must not be in violation of internationally proscribed means, and must reasonably conform to standards of nexus and proportionality.

11. Domestic belligerents who engage in armed rebellion against colonialism, racism, or Abuse of Power, and who comply with the requirements of humanitarian law, shall be considered international belligerents and shall be treated as such, wherever applicable, under domestic law.

12. All other domestic belligerents shall be treated humanely and accorded due process of law, both internationally and domestically, after they have laid down their weapons.

13. Persons who engage in resistance, protest, or rebellion against existing authority, yet who do not pursue rights or use means upheld by international law, may be tried as common criminals under domestic law. Such persons need not be accorded any unique protections and benefits other than those generally available to all criminals. However, they may raise any and all defenses stemming from domestic, international, human rights, and humanitarian law. When appropriate, they shall be granted differential and more lenient domestic treatment.

14. Persons who engage in resistance, protest, or rebellion against existing authority, as long as their means are not internationally proscribed (but whether or not in pursuit of rights upheld by international law), shall be accorded poli-

tical offender status upon finding shelter abroad, to prevent their extradition to the country in which their offenses were committed.

15. Any individuals, groups, or communities whose rights and privileges under this Bill of Rights are denied or violated shall be given all opportunities to seek redress from existing legal and human rights agencies and tribunals—national, regional, and international.

To Advance Justice, Moderation, and Conciliation

That the proposed jurisprudential principles for governance and resistance are put forth under such an immodest and provocative label, Bill of Rights on Just Governance and Resistance, may be of question to some. Why a "Bill of Rights"? Is this not too fanciful and controversial a moniker for a modest effort to instill greater humanity and a spirit of reconciliation into the arena of domestic conflict and warfare? Some brief comments on our motives and expectations are in order.

First, it is no longer a mere theoretical exercise to ask whether international and national law should consider, tolerate, or even uphold a reasonable and responsible pursuit of universally recognized rights by individuals, groups, or communities considering themselves abused. When an accused, brought before a domestic court of law, argues in self-defense that his or her alleged "criminality" constitutes the pursuit of a universally endorsed cause by means that are reasonable and proportional, we can no longer prevent this claim from being heard and echoed on the stages of public opinion and in the halls of justice worldwide. If obediance to a higher law is be given hearing as excuse or defense, how should involved governments and the community of nations respond? Past responses have been based on parochial concerns and on the naked assertion that positive (existing) law—right or wrong—must always be observed. This book seeks to demonstrate that new jurisprudential standards, in accordance with universally articulated values and criteria, are evolving to govern the political activist's rights as well as his or her responsibilities.

Second, defining a "just cause" as the pursuit of internationally recognized rights, or as resistance to those who deny such rights, provides a common denominator that intellectuals, moralists, policymakers, criminal justice agencies, and military institutions in any country can feel comfortable with. By permitting evidence of internationally recognized causes to mitigate the "criminality" of those who transgress domestic laws, we will be moving to increasingly imbue domestic laws with universal values. By allowing evidence of evolving international standards, as well as evidence of such traditional domestic standards as necessity and self-defense, to modify the harshness of positive law, we will permit a greater injection of popular justice and compassion into its operation. Furthermore, by requiring militant offenders to adhere to standards of nexus and proportionality, not only will greater protection be afforded to the innocent citizen, but general safeguards will be provided against grave public disorder and the ravages of anarchy. With the introduction of these requisite limitations, greater safety would be ensured in permitting individuals to follow the demands of their individual consciences and the commands of higher law and transcendental justice. Permitting limited departures from the prevalent and inflexible rules that currently govern political activism would help strike a new balance between the demands of positive law and the needs of domestic public order, on the one hand, and individual conscience and international rights, on the other.

Third, as previously noted, this age of social fragmentation and separatism has spawned a culture of multiple and diverse rights and entitlements. Thus, despite the worldwide trend toward interdependence, ours is proving to be not an era of communitarianism but one of fierce individualism, tribalism, and sectarianism. Increasingly, we see individuals and groups proclaiming their distinctive interests and asserting their particular claims. One increasingly hears new enumerations of the rights of employees and employers, of prisoners and keepers, of patients and healers, of pro-choicers and pro-lifers, of heterosexuals, homosexuals, and bisexuals, of women and men, of children and the elderly, of those who advocate self-realization and those who plead for "family values," of taxpayers and welfare recipients.

Each distinct clan, caste, and segment of society has recently and aggressively sought to enhance its standing—locally, nationally, and internationally. The militant claims of these distinct groups can be expected to give rise to an even more extraordinary proliferation of both accusations of abuse of power and expressions of rebellion and political resistance. The articulation of a distinct and comprehensive "Bill of Rights" for all those who claim to heed the demands of individual conscience and higher law is an appropriate way to control greater conflagrations. At the same time, it helps preserve justice for individuals and communities seeking broader recognition for their inherent and natural right to resist abuses of authority by evil or merely inattentive governments. Thus the citizen's and the community's rights to corrective action must be defined. National governments are no more entitled to stifle a people's quest for internationally recognized rights than county, state, or provincial governments are entitled to prevent citizens from asserting their federal entitlements.

Fourth, developing a comprehensive international code for the regulation of internal conflicts will hopefully help restrain, control, and even co-opt rebels as well as potential abusers of governmental power. To both compliers and violators, the proposed code offers positive incentives as well as negative sanctions. The international legitimation and support offered to the code's adherents, combined with the threat of international outlawry for its violators, should help stimulate greater compliance with the newly emerging rules of domestic conflict, by both those asserting authority and those rebelling against it. The "Bill of Rights" thus offers to replace the current climate of unrestrained domestic warfare, anarchy, and indiscriminate violence with moderation and conciliation.

By addressing governmental abuse of power and identifying causes that justify popular protest and resistance, the proposed code will hopefully foster better standards of governance as well as more humane rules of law enforcement and warfare. The desire for world approbation, and the fear of growing international support for domestic rebels, may well act to discourage governments from resorting to state terrorism, tyranny, and abuse of power. At the same time, the proposed standards should help moderate the conduct of those in opposition to authority. Rebels who consider resort to such heinous measures as hostage-taking, skyjacking, or other hostilities against innocent or uninvolved bystanders will be on notice. They will learn that resort to unjust causes and means, as violations of international standards, subjects them to extradition and punishment by all nations.

Fifth, the creation of a comprehensive international code for the regulation of internal conflicts should help harmonize international and national responses to problems posed by the worldwide growth of domestic unrest and rebellion. The proposed code should help guarantee consistency between national and international policies and procedures. The Contra rebellion against Nicaragua's Sandinista government, the Mujahideen rebellion against Afghanistan's Communist regime, the Kurd rebellion against Iraq's Saddam Hussein, the Baltic rebellion against Soviet colonialism, and the bloody dismemberment of the former Yugoslavia all dramatically illustrate the need for such harmonization of domestic and international rules and responses.

Other global benefits resulting from the proposed "Bill of Rights" are self-evident. The rules advocated for internal conflicts will hopefully advance the realization that such doctrines as the sovereignty of states, the immutability of self-determination, the sanctity of government (whether evil or good), and the social compact as license for abusive majority rule, are, much like the archaic myths regarding the "divine right of kings," fallible dogmas whose time has long since passed.[1063] Not only do these dogmas disregard the legitimate claims of the diverse populations that inhabit the globe, but they frequently overlook the historical and contemporary evidence of the fact that those seeking to impose and preserve their authority often fail themselves to comply with minimal standards of good and just governance.

Finally, among scholars and practitioners alike, there seems to persist the impression that although the formulation and acceptance of an international body of rules of warfare has greatly advanced the humanity of international conflicts, no similar benefits can be attained in the arena of domestic conflicts. The prospects for arriving at a set of binding rules for domestic warfare are often assumed to be poor if not totally hopeless. Yet this is precisely the stance that was taken toward international warfare before the contributions of Hugo Grotius, now acknowledged as the father of international law, including the law of international warfare. Following in the footsteps of Grotius, the proposed "Bill of Rights" attempts an immodest mission: to demonstrate that existing doctrinal principles, derived from both domestic and international law, make possible the introduction and implementation of legal and humanitarian rules applicable to domestic conflicts.

Thus the "Bill of Rights for Just Governance and Just Resistance" is placed before the readership—public officials, citizens, scholars, practitioners, and the world community. It is hoped that this code will stimulate a new quest for worldwide solutions to what many perceive as the twenty-first century's greatest hazard—the increasing incidence of domestic divisiveness and bloodshed. And it is hoped that the principles advanced here will help effect the next century's greatest promise: the creation of a new world order based upon institutions of governance and a jurisprudence of dissent that will permit a more pluralistic, just, and creative societal coexistence.

The articulation of this "Bill of Rights" represents a modest yet optimistic step toward regulating relations and enhancing conciliation between the contesting domestic forces of authority and autonomy. The prospects for domestic disorder and violence in the century to come are terrifying, and demand our undivided and immediate attention. Formulating a system of rules for the management of internal political rebellion and criminality, like the much older efforts of Hugo Grotius to humanize the conduct of international warfare, will be a difficult task, but the task is at hand.

Appendix

Sketch for Peace, Pablo Picasso (1952).

A Typology of Political Offenses: From Terrorism to Human Rights Struggles

Division	Category	General Typology of Conduct	Causes and Means Qualifying for Category	International Posture of Actors	Domestic Posture of Actors
Political Offenses as Crimes	International Crimes (i.e., Terrorism)	Conduct internationally proscribed and, accordingly, domestically prohibited	Conduct whose underlying causes or means are internationally proscribed (i.e., war crimes; crimes against peace; crimes against humanity; piracy; genocide; etc.)	Actors are subject to "universal jurisdiction" of all states and may be apprehended and prosecuted wherever found. If not prosecuted actors are subjected to extradition	Actors are subject to domestic prosecution unless extradited to requesting state
		A1	A2	A3	A4	A5
	Domestic Crimes	Conduct domestically proscribed, internationally disfavored, and having only marginal political connection	Conduct whose underlying causes and means are not internationally approved, tolerated, or protected (conduct not falling within D2, E2, F2)	Actors are subject to extradition by haven state to requesting state	Actors are subject to punishment as common offenders
		B1	B2	B3	B4	B5
Political Offenses as Belligerency	Non-International Armed Conflicts	Conduct domestically proscribed but internationally regulated by humanitarian law (more commonly known as the law of war)	Non-international armed conflict whose underlying causes are not internationally approved	Actors are guaranteed humane treatment and due process by Common Article 3 and Protocol II of the Geneva Conventions	Actors are subject to punishment as common offenders
		C1	C2	C3	C4	C5
	Anti-Colonial and Anti-Racist Conflicts (i.e., Freedom Fighting)	Conduct domestically proscribed, but internationally favored and regulated by humanitarian law	Non-international armed conflict in which underlying causes are internationally approved	Actors entitled to belligerent rights under Protocol I of the Geneva Conventions	Actors treated as prisoners of war and may not be prosecuted as common criminals
		D1	D2	D3	D4	D5
Political Offenses as Politics	Political Offenses	Conduct domestically condemned but internationally tolerated	Domestic criminal conduct in pursuit of political causes and by means that are internationally tolerated (actors comply with standards of nexus and proportionality)	Actors not subject to extradition by haven state to offended state	Actors may be punished domestically; international and domestic defenses should be permitted in mitigation
		E1	E2	E3	E4	E5
	International Rights Conflicts (i.e., Human Rights Struggles)	Conduct domestically proscribed but internationally favored by treaty, convention, or custom	Conduct whose underlying causes and means are internationally approved (including status offenses and nonviolent exercise of guaranteed human rights)	Actors not subject to extradition; actors entitled to asylum abroad and other international support	Actors—if subjected to domestic prosecution—should be permitted domestic and international defenses to negate criminality
		F1	F2	F3	F4	F5

Notes

Preface

1. Christopher S. Wren, "Terrorist or Freedom Fighter? Pretoria Debates Whom to Amnesty," *New York Times,* 3 June 1990, 18. "South Africa Proposes Amnesty for Political Criminals Who Confess," *Washington Post,* 8 June 1994, A25.

2. Bill Keller, "A Bomber Lives with His Guilt in a Land of Scant Innocence," *New York Times,* 18 October 1992, sec. 4, p. 7.

3. *Ha'aretz,* 7 July 1994, 10A.

4. The first two of these terms are frequently reserved for offenders charged with exclusively nonviolent conduct, such as speech, press, and membership violations or mild manifestations of civil disobedience.

5. Lois Romano, "A Man of Independent Means; Attorney Michael Tigar Is Putting His Leftist Leanings to Work for Terry Nichols," *Washington Post,* 29 September 1997, D1, 6.

6. See James Adams, *Secret Wars* (London: Hutchinson, 1987), 1; Editorial, "Carnage Unseen," *New York Times,* 12 April 1993, E12.

7. For further discussion of the escalating struggle between authority and autonomy, see Nicholas N. Kittrie, *The War Against Authority: From the Crisis of Legitimacy to a New Social Contract* (Baltimore: The Johns Hopkins University Press, 1995).

8. Stephen S. Rosenfeld, "Sovereignty and Suffering," *Washington Post,* 2 October 1992, A29.

9. Pranay Gupte, "Why the Center May Not Hold," *Newsweek,* 29 June 1987, 3.

10. Nicholas N. Kittrie and Eldon D. Wedlock Jr., *The Tree of Liberty: A Documentary History of Rebellion and Political Crime in America* (Baltimore: The Johns Hopkins University Press, 1986; 2nd. ed., 1998).

11. Nicholas N. Kittrie, *The War Against Authority: From the Crisis of Legitimacy to a New Social Contract* (Baltimore: The Johns Hopkins University Press, 1995).

Prologue

12. Peter Weiss, *The Persecution and Assassination of Jean-Paul Marat as Performed by the Inmates of the Asylum of Charendon Under the Direction of the Marquis de Sade* (New York: Atheneum, 1965), 11.

13. George Rude, *Paris and London in the Eighteenth Century: Studies in Popular Protest* (New York: Viking Press, 1952), 93.

14. James Trager, *The People's Chronology* (New York: Holt, Rinehart & Winston, 1979), 349.

15. Ibid., 351.

16. Barrington Moore Jr., *Social Origins of Dictatorship and Democracy* (Boston: Beacon Press, 1967), 103–104. See also R. R. Palmer, *Twelve Who Ruled: The Year of the Terror in the French Revolution* (Princeton: Princeton University Press, 1971), 220–224.

17. Simon Schama, *Citizens: A Chronicle of the French Revolution* (New York: Alfred A. Knopf, 1989).

18. U.N. Charter, art. 2, ¶4.

19. See for example Geneva Convention Relative to the Protection of Civilian Persons in Time of War, 6 U.S.T. 3516, T.I.A.S. No. 3365, 75 U.N.T.S. 287 (12 August 1949); Geneva Convention Relative to the Treatment of Prisoners of War, 6 U.S.T. 3316, T.I.A.S. No. 3364, 75 U.N.T.S. 135 (12 August 1949).

20. In 1997 just over 60 percent of the world's population were living within "free" or "partly free" nations. See *Freedom in the World, 1996–1997* (New York: Freedom House, 1997). In 1988 Amnesty International reported that more than half of the member countries of the United Nations held "prisoners of conscience." Associated Press, "U.N. Members Challenged on Rights Abuses; Majority Hold Political Prisoners, Amnesty International Says," *Washington Post,* 14 December 1988, A9.

21. Henry Grunwald, "Liberté, Oui. Égalité? Fraternité?" *New York Times,* 30 January 1989, 29.

22. See William V. O'Brien, *The Conduct of Just and Limited War* (New York: Praeger Publishers, 1981); Robert L. Phillips, *War and Justice* (Norman: University of Oklahoma Press, 1984); and Paul Ramsey, *The Just War: Force and Political Responsibility* (New York: Charles Scribner's Sons, 1968).

23. For the contemporary autobiography of this political activist, who preferred to be known as a *"physicist,* not a dissident," see Andrei Sakharov, *Memoirs* (New York: Alfred A. Knopf, 1990).

24. Richard Bernstein, "The New Tribalism, Letters" (in response to "The Arts Catch Up with Society in Disarray"), *New York Times,* 23 September 1990, 4.

25. John Stuart Mill, *On Liberty, Representative Government, and the Subjugation of Women* (London: Oxford University Press, 1971), 5.

26. *The Oxford Dictionary of Quotations* (London: Oxford University Press, 1955), 1.

27. Daniel J. Boorstin, *The Americans: The Colonial Experience* (New York: Vintage Books, 1958), 35–40.

28. Richard Hofstadter and Michael Wallace, eds., *American Violence: A Documentary History* (New York: Alfred A. Knopf, 1970), 273–274.

29. Kittrie, *War Against Authority,* 56–57.

30. Kittrie and Wedlock, *Tree of Liberty,* 134.

31. See generally S. P. de Boer, E. J. Driessen, and H. L. Verhaar, *Biographical Dictionary of Dissidents in the Soviet Union, 1956–1975* (Boston: Martinus Nijhoff Publishers, 1982).

32. Ibid., 2.

33. A. M. Rosenthal, "Shatter the Silence," *New York Times,* 21 October 1997, A33.

34. *Criminal Justice with Chinese Characteristics* (New York: Lawyers Committee for Human Rights, 1993), 79.

35. Ibid., 50.

36. Seth Faison, "Prisoner Release," *New York Times,* 21 October 1997, A6.

37. *New York Times,* 22 October 1997, A9.

38. *Washington Post,* 21 October 1997, A4.

39. *New York Times,* 13 May 1990, 28.

40. *New York Times,* 28 July 1991, 6.

41. *The Nation (Bangkok),* 9 July 1991, A10.

42. Herbert Mitgang, "How Would Lincoln Have Used TV?" *New York Times,* 10 February 1981.

43. Daniel Berrigan, *The Trial of the Catonsville Nine* (Boston: Beacon Press, 1970), 27–28.

44. Ibid., 69.

45. Kittrie and Wedlock, *Tree of Liberty,* 487–490.

46. Abe Fortas, *Concerning Dissent and Civil Disobedience* (New York: New American Library, 1968), 59–64.

47. *Jerusalem Post,* 22 July 1988, 2.

48. *Life Magazine,* June 1989.

49. Edward Hyams, *Killing No Murder* (London: Panther Modern Society, 1970), 73.

50. David C. Rapoport, *Assassination and Terrorism* (Toronto: Canadian Broadcasting Corporation, 1971), 7.

51. *New York Times,* 26 May 1926, 1.

52. *New York Times,* 30 May 1926, 10.

53. *Encyclopedia Judaica,* vol. 14 (Jerusalem: Encyclopedia Judaica, 1972), 1027.

54. *New York Times,* 30 October 1927, 8.

55. Rapoport, *Assassination and Terrorism,* 2.

56. Stanley Kimmel, *The Mad Booths of Maryland* (New York: Dover Publications, 1969), back cover.

57. *Washington Post,* 18 October 1984, C1.

58. Stephen Schafer, *The Political Criminal: The Problem of Morality and Crime* (New York: The Free Press, 1974), 154–155.

59. See Schama, *Citizens,* 442–444.

60. See *USSR: Sixty Years of the Union, 1922–1982* (Moscow: Progress Publishers, 1982), 69. This Constitution, prepared by Lenin himself, was the "fundamental law" of the Russian Socialist Federative Soviet Republic, the entity that continues today as Boris Yeltsin's Russian Republic.

61. Ibid., 299. The 1977 ("Brezhnev") Constitution applied to the entire Soviet Union.

62. "Conference on Security and Co-operation in Europe, Final Act," *Department of State Bulletin,* August 1975, 8826; reprinted in 14 I.L.M. 1292 (1975).

354 **Notes**

63. See Mill, *On Liberty*, 5.
64. Robert Paul Wolff, *In Defense of Anarchism* (New York: Harper Torchbooks, 1970), 12, 18–19.

Chapter 1

65. Bronislaw Malinowski, *Crime and Custom in Savage Society* (London: Routledge and Kegan Paul, 1926).
66. E. Sidney Hartland, *Primitive Law* (New York: Kennikat Press, 1970), 138.
67. Malinowski, *Savage Society*, 46.
68. Adamson Hoebel, *Law of Primitive Man* (Cambridge: Harvard University Press, 1961), 196–197, 240, 319.
69. 1 Samuel 10:1. All quotations from the Bible are from the King James Version.
70. Exodus 22:28.
71. 2 Samuel 1:14.
72. Gaetano Mosca, *The Ruling Class* (New York: McGraw-Hill, 1939), 70.
73. Ibid., 74.
74. Ibid., 70.
75. Barton L. Ingraham, *Political Crime in France, Germany and England in Modern Time* (Berkeley: University of California Press, 1979), 136.
76. Ibid., 145.
77. Rapoport, *Assassination and Terrorism*, 7.
78. Pierre A. Papadatos, *Le délit politique: Contribution à l'étude des crimes contre l'état* (Theses No. 507) (Geneva: Librarie E. Droz, 1954), 8, 10, 12.
79. Rapoport, *Assassination and Terrorism*, 7.
80. Cicero, "No Fellowship with Tyrants," in Walter Laqueur and Yonah Alexander, eds., *The Terrorism Reader* (New York: NAL Penguin, 1987), 16.
81. Rapoport, *Assassination and Terrorism*, 8.
82. Ibid., 10.
83. John of Salisbury, "On Slaying of Public Tyrants," in Laqueur and Alexander, *Terrorism Reader*, 12–24.
84. Rapoport, *Assassination and Terrorism*, 10.
85. Ibid., 5.
86. Nicolo Machiavelli, *The Prince*, trans. H. Mansfield (Chicago: University of Chicago Press, 1985).
87. Rapoport, *Assassination and Terrorism*, 10.
88. See Kittrie and Wedlock, *Tree of Liberty*, 11.
89. See generally John Locke, "On Civil Government," chap. 8 in *Introduction to Contemporary Civilization in the West: A Source Book*, 3d ed. (New York: Columbia University Press, 1960), 1030. See also, the Mayflower Compact, Kittrie and Wedlock, *Tree of Liberty*, 8.
90. Manuel R. García-Mora, *International Law and Asylum as a Human Right* (Washington, D.C.: Public Affairs Press, 1956), 74–75.
91. Hyams, *Killing No Murder*, 29.

92. Barton L. Ingraham and Kazuhiko Tokoro, "Political Crime in the United States and Japan: A Comparative Study," in *Issues in Criminology*, vol. 4 (Berkeley: University of California Press, 1969), 145.

93. Georges Vidal, *Cours de droit criminel et de science penitentiaire*, 5th ed. (Paris: Rousseau, 1916), 111–112, quoted in Robert Ferrari, "Political Crime," 20 *Columbia Law Review* 308 (1920).

94. Aleksandr I. Solzhenitsyn, *The Gulag Archipelago, 1918–1956: An Experiment in Literary Investigation*, vol. 1, trans. T. P. Whitney (New York: Harper & Row, 1973), 499–500.

95. Ibid., 500.

96. See Ingraham and Tokoro, "Political Crime," 150.

97. Ibid., 146–147.

98. See Ivan A. Shearer, *Extradition in International Law* (Manchester: Manchester University Press, 1971), 166–193.

99. G.A. Res. U.N. 128, U.N. GAOR, 44th sess., U.N. Doc. A/RES/44/128 (1989), reprinted in 29 I.L.M. 1464 (1990).

100. "Polish Church Urges Papal Visit Amnesty," *Washington Post*, 31 January 1983, A16.

101. Solzhenitsyn, *Gulag Archipelago*, 500.

102. Cesare Lombroso, with R. Laschi, *Il delitto politico e le rivoluzioni* (Turin, Italy: Bocca, 1890).

103. Wilfred G. C. Hall, *Political Crime: A Critical Essay on the Law and Its Administration in Cases of a Certain Type* (London: Geo. Allen & Unwin, 1923).

104. Pierre A. Papadatos, *Le délit politique* (Geneva: Librarie E. Droz, 1954).

105. Stephen Schafer, *The Political Criminal: The Problem of Morality and Crime* (New York: The Free Press, 1974).

106. Francis A. Allen, *The Crimes of Politics: Political Dimensions of Criminal Justice* (Cambridge: Harvard University Press, 1974).

107. George Breitman, *Malcolm X Speaks* (New York: Grove Press, 1965).

108. Eldridge Cleaver, *Soul on Ice* (New York: Dell Publishing, 1968).

109. George Jackson, *Blood in My Eye* (New York: Random House, 1972).

110. Michael V. Miller and Susan Gilmore, *Revolution at Berkeley: The Crisis in American Education* (New York: Dell Publishing, 1965).

111. Jessica Mitford, *The Trial of Dr. Spock* (New York: Vintage Books, 1970).

112. Daniel Berrigan, *The Trial of the Catonsville Nine* (Boston: Beacon Press, 1970).

113. Harold Jacobs, ed., *Weatherman* (New York: Ramparts Press, 1970).

114. Les Payne and Tim Findley, *The Life and Death of the SLA* (New York: Ballantine Books, 1976).

115. Ellen Frankfort, *Kathy Boudin and the Dance of Death* (New York: Stein & Day, 1983).

116. See for example H. D. Graham and T. R. Gurr, eds., *Violence in America: Historical and Comparative Perspectives* (New York: Praeger, 1969).

117. National Advisory Committee on Criminal Justice Standards and Goals, *Disorders and Terrorism: Report of the Task Force on Disorders and Terrorism* (Washington, D.C.: U.S. Government Printing Office, 1976), 40–41.

118. *Public Report of the Vice President's Task Force on Combating Terrorism* (Washington, D.C.: U.S. Government Printing Office, 1986).

119. Julian Roebuck and Stanley C. Weeber, *Political Crime in the United States: Analyzing Crime By and Against Government* (New York: Praeger, 1978).

120. Austin Turk, *Political Criminality: The Defiance and Defense of Authority* (Beverly Hills: Sage Publications, 1982).

121. Nicholas N. Kittrie and Eldon D. Wedlock Jr., *The Tree of Liberty: A Documentary History of Rebellion and Political Crime in America* (Baltimore: The Johns Hopkins University Press, 1986; rev. ed., 1998).

122. Nicholas N. Kittrie, *The War Against Authority: From the Crisis of Legitimacy to a New Social Contract* (Baltimore: The Johns Hopkins University Press, 1995).

123. Barton L. Ingraham, *Political Crime in France, Germany and England in Modern Time* (Berkeley: University of California, 1979).

124. John Laffin, *Fedayeen: The Arab-Israeli Dilemma* (New York: The Free Press, 1973).

125. Sean Edwards, *The Gun, the Law, and the Irish People* (Tralee, Rep. of Ireland: Anvil Books, 1971).

126. J. Bowyer Bell, *The Irish Troubles: A Generation of Political Violence, 1967–1992* (New York: St. Martin's Press, 1993).

127. Ludmilla Alexeyeva, *Soviet Dissent: Contemporary Movements for National, Religious, and Human Rights* (Middletown, Conn.: Wesleyan University Press, 1985).

128. Henry David Thoreau, *On the Duty of Civil Disobedience* (Springfield, Va.: Lancer Books, 1968), 413–414.

129. William Butler Yeats, "The Second Coming" from *Michael Robartes and the Dancer* (1922).

130. See generally Nicholas N. Kittrie, *The Right to Be Different: Deviance and Enforced Therapy* (Baltimore: The Johns Hopkins University Press, 1971).

131. See Edwin Sutherland, "Is 'White Collar Crime' Crime?" 10 *American Sociological Review* 132 (1945).

132. See for example Francis A. J. Ianni, with Elizabeth Reuss-Ianni, *A Family Business: Kinship and Social Control in Organized Crime* (New York: Russell Sage Foundation, 1972).

133. See Freda Adler, *Sisters in Crime: The Rise of the New Female Criminal* (New York: McGraw-Hill, 1975).

Chapter 2

134. Exodus 5–11.

135. Elaine Pagels, *The Gnostic Gospels* (New York: Vintage Books, 1989), 76–81.

136. G.A. Res. 86, U.N. GAOR, 46th sess., 74th mtg., U.N. Doc. A/RES/46/86 (1991).

137. See Kittrie, *War Against Authority,* for further elucidation of these important concepts.

138. Francis A. Allen, *The Crimes of Politics: Political Dimensions of Criminal Justice* (Cambridge: Harvard University Press, 1974), 49.

139. Edwin R. A. Seligman, ed., *Encyclopedia of the Social Sciences* (New York: Macmillan, 1933), 199.

140. *Webster's New Collegiate Dictionary* (Springfield, Mass.: Merriam Webster, Inc., 1979).

141. Kate Millett, *The Politics of Cruelty: An Essay on the Literature of Political Imprisonment* (New York: Norton, 1994).

142. Kittrie and Wedlock, 626–628.

143. Francesco Carrara, *Programma,* 6th ed. (Torino, Italy, 1886), ¶3916–3939.

144. Jeremiah 22:2–3.

145. Daniel 5:25–26.

146. Kittrie and Wedlock, 34.

147. Ibid., 488.

148. Ibid.

149. Ibid.

150. Abe Fortas, *Concerning Dissent and Civil Disobedience* (New York: New American Library, 1968), 59–64.

151. Philip Haillie, "Justification and Rebellion," in *Sanctions for Evil,* eds. Nevitt Sanford and Craig Comstock (San Francisco: Jossey-Bass, 1971), 247.

152. Richard M. Brown, "Historical Patterns of Violence in America", in *Violence in America,* vol. 1, eds. Hugh D. Graham and Ted R. Gurr (New York: Praeger, 1969), 35–64.

153. Ibid., 35.

154. Ibid.

155. In a later and expanded volume Brown appears to have abandoned this classification altogether. See Richard M. Brown, *Strain of Violence: Historical Studies of American Violence and Vigilantism* (New York: Oxford University Press, 1975).

156. Ibid., 156.

157. Nachman Ben-Yehuda, *Political Assassination by Jews: A Rhetorical Device for Justice* (Albany: State University of New York Press, 1993), 57–58.

158. Brown, 39.

159. Herbert Aptheker, *American Negro Slave Revolts* (New York: Columbia University Press, 1943), 313.

160. Eric J. Hobsbawn, *Primitive Rebels: Studies in Archaic Forms of Social Movement in the 19th and 20th Centuries* (Manchester: Manchester University Press, 1959).

161. William A. Settle Jr., *Jesse James Was His Name, or Facts and Fiction Concerning the Careers of the Notorious James Brothers of Missouri* (Columbia: University of Missouri Press, 1966).

162. Margaret B. Boni, *The Fireside Book of Favorite American Songs* (New York: Simon & Schuster, 1952), 224–226.

163. Jerome C. Smiley, *History of Denver* (Denver: Denver Times Publishing, 1901), 349.

164. T. M. Tomlinson, "The Development of a Riot Ideology Among Urban Negroes," in Brown, 185.

165. See for example the 1843 extradition provisions between the United States and France. Kittrie and Wedlock, 144.

166. See generally Ivan A. Shearer, *Extradition in International Law* (Manchester: Manchester University Press, 1971).

167. Barton L. Ingraham and Kazuhiko Tokoro, "Political Crime in the United States and Japan: A Comparative Study," in 4 *Issues in Criminology* (Berkeley: University of California Press, 1969), 4:145.

168. Sarah R. Blanshei, "Crime and Law Enforcement in Medieval Bologna," 1 *Journal of Social History* 121 (1982); Sarah R. Blanshei, "Criminal Law and Politics in Medieval Bologna," 2 *Criminal Justice History: An International Review* 5 (1981).

169. Marshall B. Clinard and Richard Quinney, *Criminal Behavior Systems: A Typology* (New York: Holt, Rinehart & Winston, 1967), 177.

170. Stephen Schafer, *The Political Criminal: The Problem of Morality and Crime* (New York: The Free Press, 1974), 20.

171. Richard Quinney, *The Social Reality of Crime* (Boston: Little, Brown 1970), 15.

172. Ibid., 19.

173. Clinard and Quinney, 178.

174. See generally David Abrahamson, *Who Are the Guilty: A Story of Education and Crime* (Westport, Conn.: Greenwood Press, 1972).

175. Statute of Amnesty International, Art. 1(a) (1991).

176. See "Text of Hinckley Letter," *Washington Post,* 18 October 1984, C1.

177. Barton L. Ingraham, *Political Crime in Europe: A Comparative Study of France, Germany, and England* (Berkeley: University of California Press, 1979), 20–21, 115–126.

178. Edwin H. Sutherland, *White Collar Crime* (New York: Holt, Rinehart & Winston, 1961). See also E. Sutherland, "Is 'White Collar Crime' Crime?" 10 *American Sociological Review* 132 (1945).

179. Schafer, 145–150.

180. Austin T. Turk, *Political Criminality: The Defiance and Defense of Authority* (Beverly Hills, Calif.: Sage Publications, 1982), 99–108.

181. Thomas H. Greene, *Comparative Revolutionary Movements* (Englewood Cliffs, N.J.: Prentice-Hall, 1974), 74–93.

182. See Nathaniel Weyl, *Treason: The Story of Disloyalty and Betrayal in American History* (Washington, D.C.: Public Affairs Press, 1950).

183. Fred R. von der Mehden, *Comparative Political Violence* (Englewood Cliffs, N.J.: Prentice-Hall, 1973), 7–17.

184. *Washington Post,* 13 October 1984, C8.

185. Clinard and Quinney, 179.

Chapter 3

186. Richard B. Morris, *Seven Who Shaped Our Destiny: The Founding Fathers as Revolutionaries* (New York: Harper and Row, 1973), 2.

187. Ibid., 259–265.

188. William A. Bonger, *Criminality and Economic Conditions* (New York: Agathon Press, 1967). (Original English translation published in 1916.)

189. Ibid., 648.

190. See Stephen Schafer, *The Political Criminal: The Problem of Morality and Crime* (New York: The Free Press, 1974), 156.

191. Bonger, 649.

192. Zeev Ivianski, *Individual Terror: Revolutionary Violence in the Late 19th and the Beginning of the 20th Centuries* (Ph.D. diss., Hebrew University, 1973), 57, n.30. Ivianski's data are based on B. S. Itenberg, *Dvizhenie revoliutsiyanovo narod-nichestva* (Moscow: izd. Nauka, 1965).

193. Ibid.

194. Ibid., 58.

195. Martin Malia, *Alexander Herzen and the Birth of Russian Socialism: 1812–1855* (Cambridge: Harvard University Press, 1961), 5.

196. Staff of Senate Committee on the Judiciary, 97th Cong., 1st sess., *Report on Domestic and International Terrorism* (Washington, D.C.: Committee Print, 1981), 26.

197. C. A. Krause, "Colombian Guerrillas: Alienated and Threatened," *Washington Post,* 2 March 1980, A22.

198. Karl M. Schmitt and Carl Leiden, eds., *The Politics of Violence: Revolution in the Modern World* (Englewood Cliffs, N.J.: Prentice-Hall, 1968), 86–88.

199. Matthew Ross Lippman, *Through Their Eyes: A Glance at the Personality of the Political Offender in America* (Washington, D.C.: American University Law Library, 1976), 2. Lippman is due credit for many of the portrayals of American offenders cited in this chapter.

200. J. Kirkpatrick Sale, "Ted Gold: Education for Violence," *The Nation,* 13 April 1970, 424.

201. Thomas Powers, *Diana: The Making of a Terrorist* (Boston: Houghton Mifflin, 1971), 76.

202. Marshall B. Clinard and Richard Quinney, *Criminal Behavior Systems: A Typology* (New York: Holt, Rinehart & Winston, 1967), 180.

203. Bayard Rustin, "Towards Integration as a Goal," in *AFL-CIO American Federationist,* January 1969, 6.

204. *Senate Report on Terrorism,* 28–29.

205. James F. Kirkham, Sheldon G. Levy, and William J. Crotty, *Assassination and Political Violence: A Report to the National Commission on the Causes and Prevention of Violence* (Washington, D.C.: U.S. Government Printing Office, 1969), 62.

206. Ibid., 62–67.

207. Ibid., 66.

208. Ibid.

209. Ibid., 49–61.

210. Ibid., 66

211. David G. Hubbard, *The Skyjacker: His Flights of Fantasy* (New York: Collier Books, 1971).

212. David G. Hubbard, "A Glimmer of Hope: A Psychiatric Perspective," in *International Terrorism and Political Crime*, M. Cherif Bassiouni, ed. (Springfield, Ill.: Charles C. Thomas, 1975), 31.

213. Hubbard, 178–179.

214. U.S. Department of Justice, *Sourcebook of Criminal Justice Statistics—1980* (Washington, D.C.: U.S. Government Printing Office, 1981), 328.

215. See Sidney Monas, *The Third Section: Police and Society in Russia Under Nicholas I* (Cambridge: Harvard University Press, 1961).

216. Ivianski, 254.

217. Ibid., citing *Die Welt* (Vienna), 12 June 1903.

218. Anatoly Scharansky, *Fear No Evil* (New York: Random House, 1988).

219. Judith 4:1–21.

220. *Apocrypha* (New York: Nelson, 1957).

221. Sergei Nachaeyeff, "Revolutionary Catechism," in *Assassination and Terrorism*, David C. Rapoport, ed. (Toronto: Canadian Broadcasting Corporation, 1971), 29–84.

222. Ibid., 83.

223. Freda Adler, *Sisters in Crime: The Rise of the New Female Criminal* (New York: McGraw-Hill, 1975), 101.

224. H. H. A. Cooper, "Woman as Terrorist," in *The Criminology of Deviant Women*, Freda Adler and R. J. Simon, eds. (Boston: Houghton Mifflin, 1979), 151, n.43.

225. *Senate Report on Terrorism*, 19.

226. Alice Cook and Gwyn Kirk, *Greenham Women Everywhere: Dreams, Ideas and Actions from the Women's Peace Movement* (London: Pluto Press, 1983), 50–54.

227. See for example *United States v. Aguilar*, 883 F.2d 662 (9th Cir. 1989).

228. Schafer, 134.

229. Gina Lombroso-Ferrero, *Criminal Man According to the Classification of Cesare Lombroso* (Montclair, N.J.: Patterson Smith, 1972). See also Cesare Lombroso, *L'Uomo Delinquente* (Milan, 1876), and Cesare Lombroso, *Crime: Its Causes and Remedies*, P. Horton trans. (Boston: Little, Brown, 1918).

230. *Criminal Man*, 102.

231. Ibid., 119.

232. Ibid.

233. Ibid., 297–298.

234. Ibid., 294–298, *citing Il Delitto Politico e le Rivoluzioni* (with R. Laschi) (Turin: Bocca, 1890).

235. Ibid., 305–307, *citing Gli Anarchici* (Turin: Bocca, 1894).

236. Ibid., 305.

237. Robert K. Merton, "Social Problems and Sociological Theory," in *Contemporary Social Problems* (New York: Harcourt, Brace & World, 1966), 775–822.

238. Ibid., 810.

239. See Robert K. Merton, *Social Theory and Social Structure* (New York: The Free Press, 1968), 194–197.

240. J. Anthony Lukas, *Don't Shoot—We Are Your Children!* (New York: Random House, 1971), 123.

241. Powers, 13.

242. See Lippman, 5, citing *Washington Star*, 6 June 1968, 3.

243. David Dellinger, *Revolutionary Non-Violence* (Indianapolis: Bobbs-Merril, 1970), 14.

244. "Conspiracy of Compassion," *Sojourners*, March 1985, 17.

245. J. Guadelupe Carney, *To Be a Revolutionary: An Autobiography* (San Francisco: Harper & Row, 1985), 429.

246. Lippman, 14, *citing* Rowland, "Against the System," in Alice Lynd Collector, *We Won't Go* (Boston: Beacon Press, 1968), 45–46.

247. Lippman, 14, *citing The Diary of Che Guevara* (New York: Bantam Books, 1968).

248. Dietrich Bonhoeffer, *Letters and Papers from Prison* (New York: Macmillan, 1953), 19.

249. See Lippman, 7, *citing* Daniel Ellsberg, *Servants of the State* (an interview with Studs Terkel).

250. Lippman, 3.

251. Lukas, 323.

252. Kenneth Keniston, *Young Radicals: Notes on Committed Youth* (New York: Harcourt, Brace & World, 1968), 123.

253. J. Cohen, *Introduction: Samuel Melville, Letters from Attica* (New York: Morrow, 1972), 77–78.

254. Nachman Ben-Yehuda, *Political Assassination by Jews: A Rhetorical Device for Justice* (Albany: State University of New York Press, 1993).

255. Ibid., 416–419

256. Jane Alpert, "I Bombed the Federal Building," *Rolling Stone*, 23 July 1981, 21.w

257. Kirkham, Levy, and Crotty, 64.

258. Ibid., 69.

259. "The Unabomber's Manifesto: Industrial Society and Its Future," *Washington Post*, 2 August 1995, A16.

260. *Sojourners*, January 1985, 32.

261. J. Wallis, "A Pledge of Resistance: A Contingency Plan," *Sojourners*, August 1984, 10.

262. "Civil Disobedience Pledge," *Sojourners*, January 1985, 8.

263. P. Finch, "Renegade Justice," *New Republic*, 25 April 1983, 10.

264. Francie du Plessix Gray, "Profiles," *The New Yorker*, 14 March 1970, 115.

265. Clinard and Quinney, 182.

266. Daniel Berrigan, *No Bars to Manhood* (New York: Doubleday, 1970), 26.

267. *United States v. McVeigh*, Criminal Complaint No. M–95–98-H, U.S. Dist. Court, West. Dist. of Oklahoma (1995).

268. Powers, 38.

269. Jessica Mitford, *The Trial of Dr. Spock* (New York: Vintage Books, 1970), 11.

270. H. Schipper, "A Trapped Generation on Trial," *The Progressive,* January 1974, 48.

271. Cook and Kirk, 27–28 (statement of Susan Labb).

272. Berrigan, 49.

273. Dave Foreman, "No Compromise in Defense of Mother Earth," *The Mother Earth News,* January/February 1985, 17–18.

274. *Washington Post,* 26 June 1976, C8.

275. Eugene L. Meyer, "Slayer 'Did It with Honor,'" *Washington Post,* 26 October 1975, A1, A24.

276. Ibid.

277. Ibid.

278. Ibid.

279. "Duty to Disobey: One GI's Haiti Crusade," *Washington Post,* 5 February 1995, C1.

280. Ibid.

281. Ibid.

282. "Army Finds Captain Guilty of Leaving Post to Inspect Haitian Prison," *Washington Post,* 14 May 1995, A17.

283. Ibid.

284. Maurice Parmalee, *Criminology* (New York: Macmillan, 1918), 462.

285. Ibid., 462–465.

286. Kirkham, Levy, and Crotty, 62.

287. Ibid., 1–2 (emphasis added).

288. Ibid., 2.

289. Ibid., 62.

290. Ibid., 63–64.

291. Schafer, 137.

292. Brian McConnell, *The History of Assassination* (Nashville, Tenn.: Aurora, 1970), 79.

293. Kirkham, Levy, and Crotty, 60.

294. Kittrie, *The Right to Be Different: Deviance and Enforced Therapy.*

295. *Manchester Guardian Weekly,* 3 April 1971, 5.

296. *Le Monde,* no. 143, 15 January 1972.

297. See S. P. de Boer, E. S. Driesser, and H. L. Verhaar, eds., *Biographical Dictionary of Dissidents in the Soviet Union, 1956–1973* (Boston: Martinus Nijhoff Publishers, 1982), 450.

298. George Orwell, *The Road to Wigan Pier* (London: Victor Gollancz, 1937), 64.

299. James C. Coleman, *Community Conflict* (New York: The Free Press, 1957), 24.

300. See Richard Hofstadter and Michael Wallace, *American Violence: A Documentary History* (New York: Alfred A. Knopf, 1970), 180–181.

301. R. F. Farnen, *Terrorism and the Mass Media,* 13 Terrorism 2, 112 (1990), quoted in Anzovin, *Terrorism,* 97.

302. Fred Ferretti, "What Do You Do with a Man Who Says He Has the Right to Steal," *Washington Post Book World,* 27 February 1972, 8.

303. Eldridge Cleaver, *Soul on Ice* (New York: Dell Publishing, 1968), 26.

304. Philip Berrigan, *Prison Journals of a Priest Revolutionary* (New York: Holt, Rinehart & Winston, 1970), 35.

305. Vincent Bugliosi and Curt Gentry, *Helter Skelter: The True Story of the Manson Murders* (New York: W. W. Norton, 1974), 245–245, 297, 312, 389.

306. Ibid., 220–221.

307. The following account is largely based upon Les Payne, Tim Findley, and Carolyn Craven, *The Life and Death of the SLA* (New York: Ballantine Books, 1976), 332–354. See also Kittrie and Wedlock, 562–564.

308. Robert B. Kaiser, *R.F.K. Must Die! A History of the Robert Kennedy Assassination and Its Aftermath* (New York: E. P. Dutton, 1970), 270.

309. Ibid., 273, 276.

310. Schafer, 156.

311. "Condemned to Silence," *Washington Post*, 18 May 1995, C1.

312. "Pennsylvania Death Row Prisoner Captivates Europeans," *Washington Post*, 4 August 1995, A1.

313. Ibid., 138–140.

314. Lawrence Kohlberg and Elliot Turiel, "Moral Development and Moral Education," in *Psychology and Educational Practice*, Gerald S. Lesser, ed. (Glenview, Ill.: Scott, Foresman, 1971).

315. Ronald Duska and Mariellen Whelan, *Moral Development: A Guide to Piaget and Kohlberg* (New York: Paulist Press, 1975), 79.

316. Lawrence Kohlberg, "Stages of Moral Development as a Basis for Moral Education," in *Moral Education: Inter-Disciplinary Approaches*, C. M. Beck, B. S. Crittendon, and E. V. Sullivan, eds. (Toronto: University of Toronto Press, 1971), 86–88.

317. See accompanying text.

318. Parmalee, 465.

319. Kittrie and Wedlock, 634.

320. Rollo May, *Power and Innocence: A Search for the Sources of Violence* (New York: W. W. Norton, 1972), 219–239.

321. Ibid., 220. Original quote at 223.

322. Ibid., 221.

323. Ibid., 4.

324. Dante Alighieri, *The Divine Comedy*, trans. John Ciardi (New York: W. W. Norton., 1954), 177.

325. Schafer, 156.

326. May, 220.

Chapter 4

327. Charles Tilly, "Collective Violence in European Perspective," in *Violence in America: Historical and Comparative Perspectives*, eds. Hugh Graham and Ted R. Gurr (New York: Praeger, 1969), 1:62.

328. Ibid., 792.

329. Isaiah 65:25.

330. Rollo May, *Power and Innocence* (New York: W. W. Norton, 1972), 51.

331. Richard E. Rubenstein, *Rebels in Eden: Mass Political Violence in the United States* (Boston: Little, Brown, 1970), 2–3.

332. Ibid., 5.

333. Edward C. Smith, ed., *The Constitution of the United States* (New York: Barnes & Noble Books, 1979), 27.

334. J. Walter Coleman, *The Molly Maguire Riots: Industrial Conflict in the Pennsylvania Coal Region* (New York: Arno & The New York Times, 1969), 22, n.6.

335. Rubenstein, 7.

336. Nathaniel Weyl, *Treason: The Story of Disloyalty and Betrayal in American History* (Washington: Public Affairs Press, 1950), 205.

337. Benjamin Schwarz, "The Diversity Myth: America's Leading Export," *The Atlantic Monthly,* May 1995, 57.

338. Rubenstein, 7.

339. Richard M. Brown, "Historical Patterns of Violence in America," in Graham and Gurr, 1:35.

340. Ramsey Clark, *Crime in America: Observations on Its Nature, Causes, Prevention and Control* (New York: Simon & Schuster, 1970), 164.

341. Brown, 35.

342. Graeme Newman, *Understanding Violence* (New York: J. B. Lippincott Co., 1979), 58–59.

343. Adam B. Ulam, *The Unfinished Revolution: An Essay on the Sources and Influence of Marxism and Communism* (New York: Random House, 1960), 282.

344. See CAL. PENAL CODE 422.6 (West 1991); 1990 FLA. LAWS, chap. 89–133 (1990); IDAHO CODE § 18–7901–7908 (1991); WASH. REV. CODE ANN. § 9A.36.080 (West 1990) To date, thirty-two states have enacted hate crime legislation.

345. James Morsch, "The Problem of Motive in Hate Crime: The Argument Against Presumptions of Racial Motivation," 82 *Journal of Criminal Law* 659 (1991).

346. Brendan Behan, *Borstal Boy* (New York: Alfred A. Knopf, 1959), 287.

347. For a general discussion of this principle, see Abe Fortas, *Concerning Dissent and Civil Disobedience* (New York: New American Library, 1968), 59–64. See also Eugene V. Rostow, "The Rightful Limits of Freedom in a Liberal Democratic State: Of Civil Disobedience," in *Is Law Dead?* ed. Eugene Rostow (New York: Simon & Schuster, 1971), 39–93.

348. H. M. Dougherty, "Respect for Law," *The Report of the Forty-fourth Annual Meeting of the American Bar Association* (Baltimore: The Lord Baltimore Press, 1921), 198.

349. *United States v. Moylan,* 417 F.2d 1002, 1009 (4th Cir. 1969), *cert. denied,* 397 U.S. 910 (1970).

350. Matthew 22:21.

351. *In re Ezeta,* 62 F. 972, 995 (N.D. Cal. 1894).

352. Maria Koklanaris, "CIA Suspect's Home Country to Assist Police," *Washington Times,* 11 February 1993, 1.

353. Ralph Blumental, "F.B.I. Inquiry Failed to Detect Any Sign of Attack," *New York Times,* 6 March 1993, 1.

354. U.S. Department of Justice, *Sourcebook of Criminal Justice Statistics,* available at <http://www.Albany.edu/sourcebook/table 1.68> (visited 20 September 1998).

355. Ibid., 502.

356. Ibid., 18.

357. Ibid.

358. *1997 Statistical Abstract of the United States* (U.S. Department of Commerce, Bureau of the Census), 215.

359. Ibid., 201.

360. W. Hinckle, "An Editorial Preface," *Scanlan's,* January 1971, 11–12.

361. U.S. Bureau of the Census, *Statistical Abstract of the United States: 1978* (99th ed.) (Washington, D. C.: U.S. Government Printing Office, 1978), 183.

362. U.S. Department of Justice, *Sourcebook of Criminal Justice Statistics,* available at <http://www.Albany.edu/sourcebook/table 3.176> (visited 20 September 1998).

363. United States Department of State, *Patterns of Global Terrorism: 1991* (Washington, D.C.: Department of State, 1992), 1. After the war the number of incidents fell precipitously, with the postwar level actually dropping below the 1990 level of 456 incidents.

364. U.S. Department of Justice, *Sourcebook of Criminal Justice Statistics: 1993* (Washington, D.C.: U.S. Government Printing Office, 1993), 405. The *Sourcebook* dropped the "skyjacking" classification after 1994.

365. U.S. Department of Justice, *Sourcebook of Criminal Justice Statistics: 1991* (Washington, D.C.: U.S. Government Printing Office, 1991), 428.

366. Ibid. Significantly, 69 deaths and 326 personal injuries were caused by these explosions. For the 582 bombing attacks on private residences and the 585 assaults on commercial operations, no breakdown of motives was given.

367. U.S. Department of Justice, *Sourcebook of Criminal Justice Statistics: 1996* (Washington, D.C.: U.S. Government Printing Office, 1996), 394.

368. Ibid., 427.

369. "Fires That Chill the Soul," *Life,* July 1996, 10.

370. U.S. Department of Justice, *Sourcebook of Criminal Justice Statistics: 1995* (Washington, D.C.: U.S. Government Printing Office, 1995), 381.

371. Ted Robert Gurr, "A Comparative Study of Civil Strife," in Graham and Gurr, 445.

372. Ibid.

373. Ibid., 448.

374. Sheldon G. Levy, "A 150-Year Study of Political Violence in the United States," in Graham and Gurr, 66.

375. Ibid., 77.

376. United States Constitution, Art. III, Sec. 3.

377. Nathaniel Weyl, *The Battle Against Disloyalty* (New York: Thomas Crowell, 1951), 38.

378. An Act Concerning Aliens, 1 Stat. 570 (1798), and An Act Respecting Alien Enemies, 1 Stat. 577 (1798), in Kittrie and Wedlock, 85–86.

379. 18 U.S.S.G. Appx. 3A1.1 (1996).

380. *Commonwealth v. Barrett*, 36 Va. 233 (19 Leigh 655) (1839), in Kittrie and Wedlock, 141.

381. *United States v. Anthony*, 24 F. Cas. 829 (C.C.D.N.Y. 1875) (No. 14,459).

382. The Espionage Act, 40 Stat. 217 (1917); The Espionage Act (Amended), 40 Stat. 555 (1918).

383. Elizabeth Drew, "The Files Fiasco," *Washington Post*, 30 June 1996, C1.

384. *United Press International*, 15 December 1984, Regional News Section.

385. *Washington Post*, 17 June 1977, D8.

386. *USA Today*, 19 January 1994, A8.

387. *City of Chicago v. Gregory*, 39 Ill.2d 47, 233 N.E.2d 422 (1968); *Gregory v. City of Chicago*, 394 U.S. 111 (1969).

388. Donald A. Downs, *Nazis in Skokie: Freedom, Community and the First Amendment* (New York: Harper & Row, 1985); *The Chicago Tribune*, 29 May 1992, C1.

389. *Washington Post*, 12 February 1981, A7.

390. *New York Times*, 22 October 1985, B3.

391. Philip Berrigan, *Prison Journals of a Priest Revolutionary* (New York: Holt, Rinehart & Winston, 1970), 111.

392. Ibid., 103.

393. William Forsyth, *History of Trial by Jury* (London: Parker & Son, 1852), 164–165.

394. Ammon Hennacy, *Autobiography of a Catholic Anarchist* (New York: The Catholic Workers, 1954).

395. William Moses Kunstler, "Back to Attica," *The Nation*, 25 March 1991, 364.

396. US Const, Art. II, § 2, cl. 1.

397. South Africa's Law No. 34 (1995), Promotion of National Unity and Reconciliation Act (Preamble). See generally Michael Scharf, "The Case of a Permanent International Truth Commission," 7 *Duke Journal of Comparative and International Law* 375 (Spring 1997).

398. See generally Enrico Ferri, *Criminal Sociology*, Joseph I. Kelly and John Lisle, trans., William L. Smithers, ed. (Boston: Little, Brown, 1917).

399. T. E. Arnold, "Is the U.S. Becoming a Terrorist Haven?" *Washington Post*, 23 October 1985, A23.

400. Kittrie and Wedlock, 666.

401. *United States v. Artukovic*, 170 F. Supp. 383 (S.D. Cal., Cent. Div'n, 1959); *Karadzole v. Artukovic*, 247 F.2d 198 (9th Cir. 1957); *Karadzole v. Artukovic*, 355 U.S. 393 (1958).

402. *Artukovic*, 170 F. Supp. at 393, 401.

403. *In the Matter of the Extradition of Andrija Artukovic*, CV84–8743 (C. D. Cal., March 5, 1985).

404. Immigration Act of 1903, 32 Stat. 1213, § 2 (1913).

405. *Washington Post*, 22 April 1983, A13.
406. "Asylum Cases Filed with INS District Directors: Approved and Denied by Select Nationalities," *Refugee Reports*, 30 December 1991, 12.
407. See for example *Haitian Refugee Center v. Smith*, 676 F.2d 1023 (5th Cir. 1982).
408. *Washington Times*, 24 January 1989, B8.

Chapter 5

409. Pitirim Sorokin, *Social and Cultural Dynamics,* vol. 2 (New York: American Book, 1937), 530–533.
410. Pierre A. Papadatos, *Le délit politique: Contribution à l'étude des crimes contre l'état* (Thesis No. 507) (Geneva: Librarie E. Droz, 1954), 1.
411. Ibid., 11.
412. *Black's Law Dictionary,* 6th ed.(St. Paul: West, 1990), 902.
413. Theodore Momsen, *Le droit penal romain,* trans. J. Duquesne (Paris: A. Fontemoing, 1907), 232.
414. Barton L. Ingraham, *Political Crime in France, Germany and England in Modern Time* (Berkeley: University of California, 1979), 136.
415. Ibid., 46 n.13.
416. Papadatos, 412.
417. Christian Baltzer, *Die Geschichtlichen Grundlagen der Privilegierten Behandlung Politischer Straftäter im Reichsstrafgesetzbuch von 1871* (Bonn: Ludwig Rohrscheid Verlag, 1966), 34–36.
418. Ibid., 35.
419. Ingraham, 424.
420. Ibid., 49.
421. Papadatos, 36.
422. Baltzer, 36–37, 55–64, 148.
423. First Treason Act, 25 Edward III, Stat. 5, chap. 2 (1352).
424. Ingraham, 50.
425. Ibid., 53–55.
426. *Case of Seven Bishops,* 4 James II, 12 *State Trials* 183 (1688).
427. Sir James F. Stephen, *Digest of Criminal Law* (London: Macmillan, 1877), art. 93, 56.
428. Sir James F. Stephen, II *A History of the Criminal Law of England* (London: Macmillan, 1883), 348.
429. Ingraham, 659.
430. Papadatos.
431. Ingraham, 56.
432. Ibid., 673.
433. Ibid., 46.
434. Ibid.
435. André Maurois, *A History of France* (New York: Farrar, Straus & Cudahy, 1956), 257–287.
436. Adhemar Esmein, *Historie de la procedure criminelle en France* (Paris: L. Larose et Forcel, 1882), 410–469.

437. Jean Batists Sirey, I Lois Annotées 4 (1789) [hereinafter Lois Ann.]. See also Ingraham, 414.

438. R. R. Palmer, *Twelve Who Ruled: The Year of Terror in the French Revolution* (Princeton: Princeton University Press, 1971), 21.

439. I Lois Ann., 227 (1793).

440. I Lois Ann., 221–222, 248, 271 (1793).

441. I Lois Ann., 221 (1793).

442. I Lois Ann., 265 (1793).

443. I Lois Ann., 259 (1793).

444. Palmer, 365.

445. Ibid., 362.

446. Ibid., 384.

447. See Ingraham, 245. See also E. J. Hobsbawm, *The Age of Revolution* (New York: Mentor Books, 1962), 96.

448. I & II Code pénal de 1810, *reprinted in* Ingraham, 68–70.

449. Ingraham, 23–24.

450. Ibid., 27.

451. Amnesty Law, I Lois Ann., 933 (1816).

452. CONST. CHARTER art. 7, I Lois Ann., 1235.

453. CONST. CHARTER art. 29, ¶ 1, I Lois Ann., 1237, 1242 (1830).

454. This last provision was held over from Article 10 of the law of 25 March 1822. I Lois Ann., 1073 (1822).

455. II Lois Ann., 125 (1832).

456. Ibid., art. 7, ¶5.

457. Ibid., art. 20.

458. Ibid., art. 17.

459. II Lois Ann., 179 (1833).

460. Ibid.

461. Ibid.

462. Ingraham, 259–260.

463. Papadatos, 44.

464. François Guisot, *Memoirs,* vol. 3, trans. J. W. Cole (London: Getly, 1869), 180.

465. Maurois, 396–398.

466. III Lois Ann., 8, 11 (1848).

467. Robert J. Foster, *Oxford Illustrated History of Ireland* (New York: Oxford University Press, 1989).

468. Ibid., 109 (map).

469. 1 Wm. & Mary, 2d sess, ch. 9. These laws were modeled on the English penal laws with which Elizabeth I sought to combat Roman Catholic sentiments and pretensions to the Crown. See Supremacy Act, 1 Eliz., chap. 1, and its successors, 5 Eliz., chap. 1; 13 Eliz., chap. 2; 23 Eliz., chap. 1; 27 Eliz, chap. 12; and 35 Eliz., chap. 1.

470. Foster, 274.

471. David H. Wilson, *A History of England* (New York: Holt, Rinehart & Winston, 1967), 606.

472. Aliens Act, 33 Geo. III, chap. 4 (1793).

473. Habeas Corpus Act, 34 Geo. III, chap. 54 (1794).

474. Seditious Assemblies Act, 36 Geo. III, chap. 8 (1795).

475. Foster, 276.

476. Ibid., 278–279.

477. See Unlawful Societies Act, 39 Geo. III, chap. 79 (1799).

478. Treason Act, 39 and 40 Geo. III, chap. 93 (1800).

479. Henry Cockburn, *Examination of Trials for Sedition in Scotland,* vol. 2 (Edinburgh: David Douglas, 1888), 204.

480. Unlawful Drilling Act, 60 Geo. III and I Geo. IV, chap. 1 (1819).

481. Attainder of Treason and Felony Act, 54 Geo. III, chap. 145 (1814).

482. Treason Act, 54 Geo. III, chap. 146 (1814).

483. Ingraham, 713.

484. Jeremy Bentham, *Treatise on Legislation,* vol. 2, trans. C. M. Atkinson (London: Oxford University Press, 1914).

485. Ibid., 123–124.

486. Ibid., 124–125.

487. *Dictionary of National Biography,* 10th ed. (London: London University Press, 1921–1922), 268.

488. Baltzer, 34–36.

489. Ibid., 35–36.

490. Ibid.

491. Ingraham, 92, 93–95.

492. Ibid., 171.

493. J. F. H. Abegg, *Lehrbuch der Strafrechts-Wissenschaft* (Neustadt a.d.: Orla, 1836).

494. See for example Georges Vidal, *Cours de droit criminel et de science peniteniaire,* 5th ed. (Paris: Rousseau, 1916), 111–112, quoted in Ferrari, "Political Crime," 20 *Columbia Law Review* 308 (1920).

495. Baltzer, 78–121.

496. Ingraham, 90–91.

497. Ibid., 142.

498. Penal Code of 1871, 1871 Reichsgesetzblatt 127, art. 20 (hereinafter RGBI). *The Imperial German Code,* trans. R. H. Gage and A. J. Waters (Johannesburg: W. G. Horton, 1917).

499. 1871 RGBI 127, arts. 31–37.

500. Ibid., art. 80.

501. Ibid., arts. 128–130.

502. Ibid., art. 130a.

503. Ibid., arts. 128–130.

504. Ibid., art. 130a.

505. Vidal, 111–112.

506. Patrick Moynihan, *Pandaemonium* (New York: Oxford University Press, 1993), 140.

507. Otto Kirchheimer, *Political Justice: The Use of Legal Procedure for Political Ends* (Princeton: Princeton University Press, 1961), 62–76.

508. V (n.s.) Lois Ann., 289 (1918).

509. VI (n.s.) Lois Ann., 1179 (1934).

510. Ibid., 1180.

511. See V. A. D. Dalloz, *Recuil périodique et critique,* vol. 4 (1936), 169.

512. VIII (n.s.) Lois Ann., 1153 (1939).

513. Ibid., sec. 1, chap. 1, title I.

514. VIII (n.s.) Lois Ann., 1395, arts. 75–77 (1939).

515. Ibid., art. 83.

516. Ibid., art. 84, sec. 4.

517. VIII Lois Ann., 1629 (1944).

518. Marc Ancel, "Le crime politique et le droit pénal du XXe Siècle," *Revue d'historie politique et constitutionelle,* 2 January–March 1938, 103.

519. V. A. D. Dalloz, XXXVIII *Le Bulletin Législatif* 366 (1955).

520. XL Dalloz BL 452 (1957); XLI Dalloz BL 673 (1958).

521. Article 38 of the 1958 Constitution granted the government special powers for a one-year period subject to legislative ratifications. These powers may be exercised for the "maintenance of the public order" and the "safekeeping of the state." CONST. (1958) art. 38.

522. XLI Dalloz BL 676 (1958).

523. Ibid.

524. XLIV Dalloz BL 148 (1961).

525. Code de Procédure Pénale, XLIII Dalloz BL 432 (1960).

526. C. PR. PÉN. arts. 697–698.

527. See Zvi Hadar, "Administrative Detentions Employed by Israel," 1 *Israel Yearbook on Human Rights* 283 (1971); Alan Dershowitz, "Preventive Detention of Citizens During a National Emergency–A Comparison Between Israel and the United States," 1 *Israel Yearbook on Human Rights* 295 (1971).

528. See for example 21 and 22 Eliz. II, chap. 53 (1973); 22 and 23 Eliz. II, chap. 56 (1974); 24 and 25 Eliz. II, chap. 8 (1976); 32 and 33 Eliz II, chap. 8 (1984).

529. I Reichsgesetzblatt 585 (1922).

530. Karl D. Bracher, *The German Dictatorship: The Origin, Structure, and Effect of National Socialism* (New York: Praeger, 1970), 185.

531. Harold L. Poor, *Kurt Tucholsky and the Order of Germany, 1914–1935* (New York: Charles Scribner's Sons, 1968), 247.

532. Bracher, 173–174.

533. I RGBI 296 (1923).

534. William W. Fearnside, *National Socialist Ideology in German Criminal Law* (Ph.D. diss., University of California–Berkeley, 1949), 224.

535. Bracher, 205.

536. I RGBI 35 (1933).

537. Hannah Arendt, *The Origins of Totalitarianism* (New York: Harcourt, Brace & World, 1966), 423–425.

538. I RGBI 83 (1933).

539. Bracher, 197.

540. Opposition Political Parties, I RGBI 479 (1933).

541. I RGBI 341 (1934).

542. *Reprinted in* Roper and Leiser, *Skeleton of Justice* (New York: E. P. Dutton, Inc., 1941), 93.

543. Ibid., 94.

544. Bracher, 213.

545. Ibid., 239.

546. Ibid., 240.

547. Ingraham, 248–256.

548. Grundgesetz, in U.S. Department of State Publication 3526, *The Basic Law for the Federal Republic of Germany* (Washington, D.C.: U.S. Government Printing Office, 1949).

549. Ibid., art. IX.

550. Ibid., art. XVII.

551. Ibid., art. XXI.

552. Ingraham, 610.

553. V *Entscheidengen des Bundesverfassungsgerichts* 85, 139 (1959).

554. See Merle Fainsod, *How Russia Is Ruled* (Cambridge: Harvard University Press, 1963), 5–62.

555. George Leggett, *The Cheka: Lenin's Political Police* (Oxford: Clarendon Press, 1981), xxiv. See generally, Peter Standsfield Squire, *The Third Department: The Political Police Under Nicolas I* (Cambridge: Harvard University Press, 1968).

556. Ivo Lapenna, *Soviet Penal Policy* (Westport, Conn.: Greenwood Press, 1980); Leggett, 13.

557. Leggett, 14.

558. Lapenna, 44.

559. This proclamation is from the minutes of the Sovnarkom meeting that authorized the CHEKA's formation. See Leggett, 17.

560. Leggett, xxxv.

561. Ibid., 59 (mentions the May 23, 1918, resolution condemning the Kadets and a June 14, 1918, resolution expelling other political factions).

562. Ibid., xxxiv.

563. *Krasnaya Gazeta,* 1 September 1918, cited in Leggett, 109.

564. Leggett, 55.

565. Robert Conquest, *The Great Terror: A Reassessment* (New York: Oxford University Press, 1990), 486.

566. Solzhenitsyn, *Gulag Archipelago.*

567. See Decree of the Central Executive Committee of the Council of People's Commissars, December 27, 1932, from *Izvestia,* 28 December 1932, no. 358, translated in *Slavonic [and East European] Review* 1(11)–3:695, *reprinted in* Mervyn Matthews, *Party, State and Citizen in the Soviet Union: A Collection of Documents* (London: M. E. Sharpe, 1989), 164–166. The passport system is governed by Articles 1, 7, 12–15, 22, 25, 37, and 38 of the Grazhdanskii Kodeks RSFSR (Civil Code); see Thomas B. Smith, *The Other Establishment* (Chicago: Regnery Gateway, 1984), 48–49.

568. Leggett, 81; Zigmas A. Butkus, *Major Crimes Against the Soviet State* (Ph.D. diss., Washington, D.C.: Law Library, Library of Congress), 4.

569. Butkus, 87; Matthews, 87.

570. Butkus, 12, 26.

571. Ibid., 34.

572. Sidney Block and Peter Reddaway, *Soviet Psychiatric Abuse: The Shadow over World Psychiatry* (Boulder: Westview Press, 1985), 16, 30. See also Block and Reddaway, *Psychiatric Terror* (New York: Basic Books, 1977).

Chapter 6

573. Jonah 1:1–4, 3:2–4.

574. Shearer, *Extradition in International Law,* 5.

575. Frederic Coudert, "Address on the Nature and Definition of Political Offense in International Extradition," 3 *American Society of International Law Proceedings* 127 (1909).

576. Sir Edward Clarke, *A Treatise upon the Law of Extradition,* 4th ed. (London: Stevens and Hayes, 1903), 18–22.

577. Shearer, *Extradition in International Law,* 8.

578. Numbers 35:11–25.

579. S. Prakash Sinha, *Asylum and International Law* (The Hague: Martinus Nijhoff, 1971), 5–15.

580. Ibid., 6–7.

581. Ibid., 10–11.

582. Ibid., 15–17.

583. Atle Grahl-Madsen, *Territorial Asylum* (New York: Oceana Publications, 1980), 32.

584. Kittrie and Wedlock, *Tree of Liberty,* 636.

585. Hugo Grotius, *De jure belli et pacis, libritres,* trans. F. W. Kelsey (n.p.: 1925), book 3, chap. 20, sec. 41(2).

586. Ibid., book 2, chap. 5, sec. 24.

587. Ibid., book 1, chap. 4, sec. 2(1).

588. Ibid., book 2, chap. 21, sec. 5(1).

589. Ibid., book 2, chap. 2, sec. 26.

590. Christian Wolff, *Jus gentium methodo scientifica pertractum,* trans. J. H. Drake (New York: Oceana Publications, 1964), sec. 150.

591. Emmerich de Vattel, *Les droit des gens,* trans. J. Chitty (Philadelphia: T. & J. W. Johnson, 1863), book 1, chap. 19, sec. 228.

592. Ibid., book 1, chap. 19, sec. 230.

593. Manuel R. García-Mora, *International Law and Asylum as a Human Right* (Washington, D.C.: Public Affairs Press, 1956), 152.

594. Grahl-Madsen, *Territorial Asylum,* 5. See also Convention Relating to the Status of Refugees, Final Act of the United Nations Conference of Plenipotentiaries on the Status of Refugees and Stateless Persons, 606 U.N.T.S. 267, 19 U.S.T. 6223, T.I.A.S. No. 6577 (28 July 1951); Declaration on Territorial Asylum, G.A. Res. 2312 (XXIII) (1968).

595. Amos J. Peaslee, *Constitutions of Nations,* vol. 2 (Concord, N.H.: The Rumford Press, 1950), 8.

596. Ibid., 280.

597. Ibid., 608.

598. R. H. Fitzgibbon, *The Constitutions of the Americas* (Chicago: University of Chicago Press, 1948), 233.

599. Grahl-Madsen, *Territorial Asylum,* 33.

600. Ibid.

601. Convention on Asylum, Final Act, Sixth International Conference of American States, Havana, 16 January–20 February 1928.

602. Sinha, *Asylum and International Law,* 28.

603. Ibid., 28–29.

604. Ibid., 61.

605. See Julius Stone, *International Guarantees of Minority Rights: Procedure of the Council of the League of Nations in Theory and Practice* (London: Oxford University Press, 1932).

606. U.N. Doc. E/CN4/Sub.2/6, Report by the Secretary-General on the International Protection of Minorities Under the League of Nations; L.N. Doc. C.8 M.5. 1931, I, 2d ed., 7ff.

607. International Covenant on Economics, Social and Cultural Rights, and International Covenant on Civil and Political Rights, U.N. General Assembly Resolution 2200 A (XXI), in *Human Rights: A Complication of International Instruments* (New York: United Nations, 1966).

608. Universal Declaration of Human Rights, Art. 14, G.A. Res. 217, U.N. GAOR, 3d sess., U.N. Doc. A/810 (1948) (states that "everyone has the right to seek and enjoy in other countries asylum from persecution").

609. United Nations Commission on Human Rights, Report of the Fifteenth Session, U.N. Doc. E/CN.4/789, 9. See also García-Mora, *Asylum as a Human Right,* 7–19.

610. U.N. Doc. E/CN.4/L.191.

611. Convention Relating to the Status of Refugees, Final Act of the United Nations Conference of Plenipotentiaries on the Status of Refugees and Stateless Persons, 606 U.N.T.S. 267, 19 U.S.T. 6223, T.I.A.S. No. 6577 (28 July 1951).

612. See Patricia Hyndman, "Refugees Under International Law with a Reference to the Concept of Asylum," 60 *Australian Law Journal* 148, 149 (1986).

613. Convention Relating to the Status of Refugees, Final Act of the United Nations Conference of Plenipotentiaries on the Status of Refugees and Stateless Persons, 189 U.N.T.S. 137 (28 July 1951).

614. Article 33 of the 1951 Convention states, "No Contracting State shall expel or return *(refouler)* a refugee in any manner whatsoever to the frontiers of territories where his life or freedom would be threatened on account of his race, religion, nationality, membership of a particular social group or political opinion."

615. Paul Taylor, "A Country in Search of a Population," *Washington Post,* 5 August 1994, 1.

616. "22 Million Refugees," *Washington Post,* 7 August 1994, C8.

617. Pierre Bertrand, "An Operational Approach to International Refugee Protection," 26 *Cornell International Law Journal* 495 (1993).

618. Pub. L. No. 96–212, 94 Stat. 102 (codified in various sections of 8 U.S.C.).

619. 19 U.S.T. 6223, T.I.A.S. No. 6577, 606 U.N.T.S. 267 (31 January 1967).

620. Davalene Cooper, "Promised Land or Land of Broken Promises? Political Asylum in the United States," 76 *Kentucky Law Journal* 923, 927–930 (1988).

621. Pub. L. No. 82–414, 66 Stat. 163 (1952) (codified as amended in 8 U.S.C. §§ 1101–1525 [1988]).

622. 8 C.F.R. § 207.1(a) (1993).

623. 8 U.S.C. § 1101(a)(42) (1988).

624. 8 U.S.C. § 1157(a)(3–4) (1988).

625. 8 U.S.C. § 1253(h)(1) (1988).

626. *INS v. Stevic,* 467 U.S. 407 (1984); Robert Suro, "U.S. to Ease Strict Chinese Asylum Policy," *Washington Post,* 5 August 1994, A16.

627. *Diaz-Escobar v. INS,* 782 F.2d 1488 (9th Cir. 1986).

628. 8 U.S.C. § 1158(a) (1988).

629. 8 U.S.C. § 1101(a)(42) (1988).

630. 8 C.F.R. § 208.13(b)(2) (1993); *INS v. Cardoza-Fonseca,* 480 U.S. 421 (1987).

631. 8 C.F.R. § 208.8(f)(2) (1993).

632. 8 U.S.C. § 1159(b) (1988).

633. *Reno v. Flores,* 113 S. Ct. 1439 (1993).

634. Joseph F. Sullivan, "Immigration Service Shifts Its Policy on Stowaways," *New York Times,* 5 August 1994, B5.

635. Marian Nash, "Privileges and Immunities," 75 *American Journal of International Law* 142 (1981).

636. "Asylum Cases Filed with INS District Directors: Approved and Denied by Select Nationalities," *Refugee Reports,* 30 December 1991, 12.

637. 55 Fed. Reg. 30, 674 (published 27 July 1990; effective 1 October 1990; codified at 8 C.F.R. § 208 (1993).

638. Sarah Ignatius, "Recent Development: Restricting the Rights of Asylum Seekers: The New Legislative and Administrative Proposals," 7 *Harvard Human Rights Journal* 225, 228 (1994).

639. *Refugee Reports,* 12.

640. Stephen H. Legomsky, "Political Asylum and the Theory of Judicial Review," 73 *Minnesota Law Review* 1205 (1989).

641. Ignatius, "Restricting the Rights of Asylum Seekers," 225.

642. Constitution of Germany, Art. 16(2).

643. Sam Blay and Andreas Zimmerman, "Current Development: Recent Changes in German Refugee Law: A Critical Assessment," 88 *American Journal of International Law* 361 (1994).

644. Ibid.

645. Gesetz zur Anderung asylverfahrenscrechtlicher-, auslander- und staatsangehorigkeitsrechtlicher Vorschriften, 1993 BGBI. I 1062.

646. Ibid.

647. James C. Hathaway, "Harmonizing for Whom? The Devaluation of Refugee Protection in the Era of European Economic Integration," 26 *Cornell International Law Journal* 719 (1993).

648. Arthur Helton, "Toward Harmonized Asylum Procedures in North America," 26 *Cornell International Law Journal* 737, 738–739 (1993).

649. European Union Treaty, 1 February 1992, 31 *I.L.M.* 247 (1992).

650. Tamas Foldesi, "The Right to Move and Its Achilles' Heel, the Right to Asylum," 8 *Conn. J. Int'l L.* 289, 301 (1993).

651. Bertrand, "International Refugee Protection," 497.

652. F. Von Martens, II *Volkerrecht,* vol. 2, ed. Bergbohm (1884), 394, in Shearer, *Extradition in International Law,* 6–7.

653. Shearer, *Extradition in International Law,* 11–12.

654. Cesare de Baccaria, *Dei delitti dele pene* (1764), in James Anson Farrer, *Crimes and Punishments* (London, 1880), 193–194.

655. William M. Malloy, S. Doc. No. 357, *Treaties, Conventions, International Acts, Protocols and Agreements,* 61st Cong., 2d sess. (Washington, D.C.: U.S. Government Printing Office, 1910), 590.

656. Act of Congress, 12 August 1848, chap. 167, 9 Stat. 302 (1848).

657. Extradition Act of 1870, 17 *Halsbury's Statutes of England and Wales* 478 (1986) [hereinafter *Halsbury*].

658. Art. X, 1 Malloy, *Treaties, Conventions, International Acts, Protocols and Agreements,* 650, 655.

659. Convention for the Surrender of Criminals Between France and the United States, 9 November 1843; IV *Treaties and Other International Acts of the United States 515*, in 95 *The Consolidated Treaty Series,* ed. Clive Parry (Dobbs Ferry, N.Y.: Oceana Publications, 1969), 393 [hereinafter *CTS*].

660. Extradition Convention Between Denmark and Great Britain, 15 April 1862, LII *British and Foreign State Papers* 27, 125 *CTS* 465; Extradition Convention Between Great Britain and Prussia, 5 March 1864, LIV *British and Foreign State Papers* 16, 129 *CTS* 65.

661. 17 *Halsbury* 478.

662. Shearer, *Extradition in International Law,* 15.

663. Clarke, *Law of Extradition,* 28–29.

664. Shearer, *Extradition in International Law,* 40.

665. Ibid.

666. Ibid., 17.

667. Extradition Convention Between France and New Grenada, 9 April 1850, VI *Recueil des traités de la France* 2, 104 *CTS* 19. Extradition Convention Between France and Venezuela, 23 March 1853, LXVIII *British and Foreign State Papers* 854, 109 *CTS* 487.

668. 95 *CTS* 393.

669. Convention for the Suppression of the White Slave Trade, CIII *British and Foreign State Papers* 245 (1914); International Convention for the Suppression of Counterfeiting Currency, 20 April 1929, 112 L.N.T.S. 371, T.I.A.S. No. 2623; Convention of 1936 for the Suppression of the Illicit Traffic in Dangerous Drugs, 26 June 1936, 198 L.N.T.S. 299, T.I.A.S. No. 4648; 1971 Montreal Convention, T.I.A.S. No. 7570; 1970 Hague Convention, T.I.A.S. No. 7192.

670. Lassa Oppenheim, I *International Law: A Treatise* (New York: Longmans, Green, 1955), 696, 704.

671. Thomas Hobbes, *Leviathan* (1947), ed. M. Oakeshott, 236.

672. M. Cherif Bassiouni, *International Extradition and World Public Order* (Dobbs Ferry, N.Y.: Oceana Publications, 1974), 4, 53.

673. F. F. Martens, "Nouveau receuil des traitès 44," in Bassiouni, *International Extradition*, n.6. A similar chronology is advanced in Latrè, "L'Extradition St. Les Delits Politiques" (1911), in Africa, *Political Offenses in Extradition* 4, n.1 (1927).

674. Bassiouni, *International Extradition*, 371.

675. See Jacques Godechot, *Les constitutions de la France* (Paris: Garnier-Flammarion, 1970).

676. Satya D. Bedi, *Extradition in International Law and Practice* (Buffalo, N.Y.: Dennis & Co., 1968), 181.

677. Ingraham, *Political Crime*, 180. See also Kittrie, *War Against Authority*.

678. Christine van den Wijngaert, *The Political Offense Exception to Extradition: The Delicate Problem of Balancing the Rights of the Individual and the International Public Order* (Boston: Kluwer, Deventer, 1980), 9–10.

679. Ibid., 10–11, n.51.

680. Ibid., 13–14.

681. Ibid., 11–12, citing H. Lammasch, *Auslieferungspflicht und Asylrecht* (Leipzig: Verlag von Duncker & Humbolt, 1987), 206–207. See also E. Reale, "Droit d'asile," in *Recueil des cours* (The Hague: Académie des droit international de la haye, 1938), 549–550; H. Schultz, *Das Schweizerische Auslieferungsrecht*, in van den Wijngaert, *Political Offense Exception to Extradition*, 411.

682. Art. 5, 22 *British Foreign State Papers* 223.

683. Art. 10, I Malloy, *Treaties, Conventions, International Acts, Protocols and Agreements*, 650, 655.

684. Art. 5, I Malloy, *Treaties, Conventions, International Acts, Protocols and Agreements*, 527.

685. George Lewis, *On Foreign Jurisdiction and the Extradition of Criminals* (London: John W. Parket & Son, 1859), 44–45.

686. 9 *Herslet's Commercial Treaties* 281.

687. van den Wijngaert, *Political Offense Exception to Extradition*, 11, citing Papadatos, *Le délit politique*, 63.

688. Clarke, *Law of Extradition*, 99–101, citing Ann. Reg. 520 (1961).

689. Ibid., 67–101.

690. Clarke, *Law of Extradition*, 128–129.

691. *Report of the Select Committee on Extradition of the House of Commons*, Cmnd. 393, 6 *British Digest* 804 (1868).

692. 17 *Halsbury* 478.

693. Shearer, *Extradition in International Law*, 167.

694. Ibid.

695. 17 *Halsbury* 478.

696. García-Mora, *Asylum as a Human Right*, 76.

697. Bassiouni, *International Extradition*, 388.

698. *In re Castioni*, 1 Q.B. 149, 152 (1891).

699. 782 W.B. 415 (1894).

700. 1 Q.B. 540 (1955).

701. Shearer, *Extradition in International Law,* 173.

702. 833 All E.R. 529 (1962).

703. 62 F. 972, 978 (N.D. Cal. 1894).

704. *In re Gonzalez,* 217 F. Supp. 717 (S.D.N.Y. 1963). See also *Ornelas v. Ruiz,* 161 U.S. 502, 689 (1896).

705. Bassiouni, *International Extradition,* 395.

706. 4 Hackworth, *Digest,* 316, 49–50 (1942).

707. *Ramos v. Diaz,* 179 F. Supp. 459, 462 (S.D. Fla. 1959).

708. *United States v. Artukovic,* 170 F. Supp. 383 (S.D. Cal. 1959).

709. Memorandum for the United States, *Karadzole v. Artukovic,* 247 F.2d 198 (1957).

710. *United States v. Artukovic,* 170 F. Supp. 392–393 (1959).

711. *In the Matter of the Extradition of Andrija Artukovic,* CV84–8743 (D.C. Cal., 5 March 1985). Warren Richey, "Methods Questioned in War Crimes Extradition," *Christian Science Monitor,* 25 February 1986, 3.

712. Don Schanche, "Artukovic Convicted in Zagreb," *Washington Post,* 15 May 1986, A23.

713. Shearer, *Extradition in International Law,* 180.

714. *Jimenez v. Aristeguieta,* 311 F.2d 547 (5th Cir. 1962), *cert. denied,* 275 U.S. 48 (1963).

715. Ibid., 560.

716. *In re McMullen,* No. 3–78–1099 MG (N.D. Cal. 11 May 1979).

717. *Matter of Macklin,* 80 Misc. 2d 1 (S.D.N.Y. 13 August 1981), *aff'd,* 668 F.2d 122 (2d Cir. 1981).

718. *Quinn v. Robinson,* No. C–82–6688 RPA (N.D. Cal. 1983).

719. *United States v. Doherty,* 599 F. Supp. 270 (S.D.N.Y. 1984).

720. James O'Connor, "International Extradition and the Political Offense Exception: The Granting of Political Offender Status to Terrorists by United States Courts," 4 *New York Law School Journal of International and Comparative Law* 613 (1983).

721. 24 I.L.M. 1104, *UK-US: Extradition Treaty Supplement Limiting the Scope of Political Offenses to Exclude Acts of Terrorism,* 1985.

722. *Washington Star,* 12 December 1979, A19.

723. Reuters, 29 January 1987, Thursday, A.M.

724. *In the Matter of Extradition of Hecort Jose Campora and Others,* 58 *American Journal of International Law* 690–695 (1957).

725. *U.S. Foreign Relations, 1909* (Dept. of State), 520–521.

726. *In re Pavan,* 1923 Ann. Dig. 347 (No. 239).

727. *In re Ockert,* 1933–1934 Ann. Dig. 369 (No. 157).

728. *In re Kavic,* 19 I.L.R. 371 (Tribunal Fédéral 1952).

729. Ibid., 372.

730. *Ktir v. Ministère Public Fédéral,* 34 I.L.R. 143 (Tribunal Fédéral 1961).

731. Ibid., 143–144.

732. Extradition Law of 10 March 1927, unofficial trans., in American Society of International Law, *Research in International Law* (Concord, N.H.: The Rumford Press, 1935), 380.

733. Shearer, *Extradition in International Law,* 184.

734. 1957 European Convention on Extradition, Art. 3, in Shearer, *Extradition in International Law,* 181.

735. Ibid.

736. Bassiouni, *International Extradition.*

737. *In re Giovanni Gatti,* 1945–1947 Ann. Dig. 145 (No. 70).

738. Shearer, *Extradition in International Law,* 185.

739. Ibid.

740. Ibid.

741. 782 W.B. 419 (1894).

742. Pan American Convention, 1902, Art. 2.

743. For more recent materials on piracy, see Convention on the High Seas, 29 April 1958, 450 U.N.T.S. 82, T.I.A.S. No. 6465.

744. International Convention for the Suppression of Counterfeiting Currency, 20 April 1929, 112 L.N.T.S. 371, T.I.A.S. No. 2623.

745. Convention for the Suppression of the White Slave Traffic, CIII *British and Foreign State Papers* 245 (1914).

746. Convention of 1936 for the Suppression of the Illicit Traffic in Dangerous Drugs, 26 June 1936, 198 L.N.T.S. 299, T.I.A.S. No. 4648.

747. Hague Convention for the Suppression of Unlawful Seizure of Aircraft (1970), 860 U.N.T.S. 105; 22 U.S.T. 1641. Montreal Convention for the Suppression of Unlawful Acts Against the Safety of Civil Aviation (1971), 974 U.N.T.S. 177; 24 U.S.T. 564; T.I.A.S. 7570.

748. International Convention Against the Taking of Hostages (1979), 1316 U.N.T.S. 205.

749. European Convention on the Suppression of Terrorism (1976), 15 I.L.M. 1272 (Art. 1).

750. Extradition Law of 10 March 1927, unofficial trans., in American Society of International Law, *Research in International Law* (Concord, N.H.: The Rumford Press, 1935), 380.

751. Hudson, vii. 862, Annex G.

752. Convention Relative to the Protection of Civilian Persons in Time of War, 12 August 1949, 6 U.S.T. 3516, 75 U.N.T.S. 287.

753. Convention Relating to the Status of Refugees, Final Act of the United Nations Conference of Plenipotentiaries on the Status of Refugees and Stateless Persons, 606 U.N.T.S. 267, 19 U.S.T. 6223, T.I.A.S. No. 6577 (22 April 1954).

754. G.A. Res. 2923, 27 U.N. GAOR Supp. 30, at 25, U.N. Doc. A/8730 (1972).

755. García-Mora, *Asylum as a Human Right,* 33, 91.

756. Convention on the Prevention and Punishment of the Crime of Genocide, 78 U.N.T.S. 277, T.I.A.S. No. 1021 (9 December 1948).

757. Ibid.

758. The U.S. ratification is subject to a reservation that makes the treaty's mandatory extradition unenforceable in American courts. Genocide Convention Implementation Act of 1987, P.L. 100–606, 102 Stat. 3045 (1988).

759. *In re Kaphengst* (7 October 1930), cited in *In re Ockert,* 1933–1934 Ann. Dig. 369–370 (1940).

760. *Re Bohme* (Supreme Court of Argentina), 62 *American Journal of International Law* 784–785 (1968).

761. Bassiouni, *International Extradition,* 410.

762. 159 *British Foreign State Papers* 606.

763. Ibid., 4.

764. The Department of State defines "terrorism" as "premeditated, politically motivated violence perpetrated against noncombatant targets by subnational groups or clandestine agents, usually intended to influence an audience." *Department of State Report, Patterns of Global Terrorism: 1997,* available at <http:thesouth.com/USInternational/reports/dos/terror97/1997index.html> (visited 25 September 1998).

765. Convention to Prevent and Punish the Acts of Terrorism Taking the Form of Crimes Against Persons and Related Extortion That Are of International Significance, OAS/Off.Rec./Ser.P/English, 3d Special Sess., General Assembly, AG Doc. 88 rev. 1 corr. 1, 2 February 1971. See also Convention on the Prevention and Punishment of Crimes Against Internationally Protected Persons, Including Diplomatic Agents, G.A. Res. A/3166 (XXVIII) (1974).

766. See 1971 Montreal Convention, T.I.A.S. No. 7570 (outlawing the sabotage of aircraft); 1970 Hague Convention, T.I.A.S. No. 7192 (proscribing hijacking); 1963 Tokyo Convention, T.I.A.S. No. 6768 (addressing offenses committed aboard aircraft).

767. See Universal Postal Union, 16 U.S.T. 1291 (1964).

768. See *United States of America v. Fawaz Yunis,* 681 F. Supp. 896 (D.C. 1988).

769. de Vattel, *Les droit des gens,* book 1, chap. 19, 233.

770. Convention on the Prevention and Punishment of Crimes Against Internationally Protected Persons, Including Diplomatic Agents, G.A. Res. A/3166 (XXVIII) (1974); Convention on Offenses and Certain Other Acts Committed On Board Aircraft, 704 U.N.T.S. 219, 20 U.S.T. 2941, T.I.A.S. No. 6768 (14 September 1963); Convention on the High Seas, 450 U.N.T.S. 82, 13 U.S.T. 2312, T.I.A.S. No. 6465 (29 April 1958).

771. *Los Angeles Times,* 24 December 1988.

Chapter 7

772. See generally Mortimer R. Kadish and Sanford H. Kadish, *Discretion to Disobey: A Study of Lawful Departures from Legal Rules* (San Francisco: Stanford University Press, 1973); and K. C. Wheare, *Modern Constitutions* (London: Oxford University Press, 1952), 87–94. For discussion on the morality of rebellion in those situations where all elements of democracy are absent, see Hyams, *Killing No Murder;* and Kittrie, *War Against Authority,* specifically chap. 2.

773. Herbert C. Kelman and V. Lee Hamilton, *Crimes of Obedience: Toward a Social Psychology of Authority and Responsibility* (New Haven: Yale University Press, 1989), 53–76.

774. See for example Peter Singer, *Democracy and Disobedience* (Oxford: Clarendon Press, 1973), 1.

775. T. H. Green, *Lectures on the Principles of Political Obligation* (London: Longmans, 1907), § 100, 111.

776. "A Speech by the Rt. Hon. J. G. Gorton," *The Australian*, 27 August 1970, 1.

777. See for example Michael Walzer, *Obligations: Essays on Disobedience, War and Citizenship* (Cambridge, Mass.: Harvard University Press, 1970).

778. Abe Fortas, *Concerning Dissent and Civil Disobedience* (New York: Signet Books, 1968), 62.

779. Ibid., 120.

780. Ibid., 125.

781. Ibid., 63.

782. Ibid., 35.

783. Howard Zinn, *Disobedience and Democracy: Nine Fallacies on Law and Order* (New York: Random House, 1968), 29.

784. Kelman and Hamilton, *Crimes of Obedience*, 53–76.

785. Zinn, *Disobedience and Democracy*, 65.

786. Ibid., 29.

787. Wheare, *Modern Constitutions*, 93.

788. Quoted in Hannah Arendt, *On Revolution* (New York: Viking, 1965), 307.

789. Matthias N. Forney, *Political Reform by the Representation of Minorities* (New York: Published by the author, 1894), 29.

790. Simon Sterne, *Representative Government and Personal Representative* (Philadelphia: Lippincott & Co., 1871), quoted in Forney, *Political Reform*, 35–36.

791. Leonard Courtney, *Nineteenth Century*, July 1897, quoted in Forney, *Political Reform*, 33–34.

792. *Scott v. Sandford*, 60 U.S. 393 (1856).

793. Kittrie and Wedlock, *Tree of Liberty*, 13, 28–31.

794. Ibid., 177–182.

795. *Debs v. U.S.*, 249 U.S. 211, 214 (1919).

796. *Schenk v. United States*, 249 U.S. 47, 39 S.Ct. 247, 63 L.Ed. 470 (1919). See also *Abrams v. United States*, 250 U.S. 616 (1919); and *United States v. Steene*, 263 F. 130 (D.C.N.Y. 1920).

797. See for example *Hirabayashi v. United States*, 320 U.S. 21 (1943); *Korematsu v. United States*, 323 U.S. 214 (1944); and *Ex Parte Endo*, 323 U.S. 283 (1944).

798. *Dennis v. United States*, 341 U.S. 491 (1951).

799. *Schenk v. United States*, 249 U.S. 47, 39 S.Ct. 247, 63 L.Ed. 470 (1919).

800. US Const, Art. I, § 9.

801. Jeremiah 1:9.

802. Jeremiah 21:7.

803. Rollo May, *Power and Innocence* (New York: W. W. Norton, 1972), 224.

804. Koran, N. J. Duwood, trans. (New York: Penguin Books, 1993).

805. May, *Power and Innocence*, 225.

806. *International Encyclopedia of the Social Sciences*, vol. 11 (New York: Macmillan, The Free Press, 1968), 80.

807. "Cicero, On the Nature of the Gods," in *International Encyclopedia of the Social Sciences,* vol. 11 (New York: Macmillan Co., The Free Press, 1968), 82.

808. David G. Ritchie, *Natural Rights: A Criticism of Some Political and Ethical Conceptions* (London: Sonnenschein, 1895), 30.

809. *Institutes,* cited in Edward S. Corwin, *The "Higher Law" Background of American Constitutional Law* (Ithaca: Cornell University Press, 1957), 17.

810. Brenda Brown, *The Natural Law Reader* (New York: Oceana Publications, 1960), 63–64.

811. "Thomas Aquinas, Summa Theologica," in *International Encyclopedia of the Social Sciences,* vol. 11 (New York: Macmillan Co., The Free Press, 1968), 83.

812. Edward Dumbauld, *The Life and Legal Writings of Hugo Grotius* (Norman: University of Oklahoma Press, 1969), 80–81.

813. Hobbes, *Leviathan,* 314–315.

814. See A. P. d'Entrèves, *Natural Law* (London: Hutchinson, 1972).

815. John Locke, *Two Treatises of Government,* book 2, sec. 12 (New York: Cambridge University Press, 1963), 374–377.

816. John Finnis, *Natural Law and Natural Rights* (Oxford: Clarendon Press, 1980), 371–388.

817. Brown, *Natural Law Reader,* 91–94.

818. Guido Cappelletti, *The Judicial Process in Comparative Perspective* (Kansas City: The Bobbs-Merril, 1971), 36–37.

819. 8 Co. 108a (1610), 2 Brown 1.225 (1610).

820. Clinton Rossiter, Prefatory Note, in Corwin, *"Higher Law" Background,* vi.

821. Simon Schama, *Citizens: A Chronicle of the French Revolution* (New York: Alfred A. Knopf, 1989), 592.

822. Corwin, *"Higher Law" Background,* 4.

823. New Hampshire Const, Art. 10.

824. Elizabeth Mensch, "The History of Mainstream Legal Thought," in *The Politics of Law,* ed. David Kairys (New York: Pantheon, 1982), 19.

825. Hobbes, *Leviathan,* 314–315.

826. John Merryman, *The Civil Law Tradition* (Stanford: Stanford University Press, 1969), 20–24.

827. See A. Heinrich Rommen, *The Natural Law: A Study in Legal and Social History and Philosophy* (St. Louis: Herder, 1974); Hans Kelsen, "Natural Law Doctrine and Legal Positivism," in *A General Theory of Law and State* (New York: Russell, 1961), 389–446; and Leo Strauss, *Natural Right and History* (Chicago: University of Chicago Press, 1953).

828. For an introduction to and review of Radbruch's philosophical development, see generally Gustav Radbruch, *Die Natur der Sache A's Juristische Denkform* (Darmstadt: Wissenschaftliche Buchgesellschaft, 1960); Norman Bentwich, A. S. De Bustamonte, Donald A. MacLean, Gustav Radbruch, and H. A. Smith, *Justice and Equity in the International Sphere* (London: Constable, 1936); and *Legal Philosophies of Lask, Radbruch and Dubin,* trans. K. Wilk (Cambridge: Harvard University Press, 1950), xxxi–xxxv.

829. Graham Hughes, "The Concept of Law," in *Dictionary of Pivotal Ideas* (New York: Macmillan, 1979), 1–6.

830. *Universal Declaration of Human Rights,* G.A. Res. 217 (III), U.N. Doc. A/810 (1948).

831. See generally *Human Rights: A Compilation of International Instruments of the United Nations* (1973), No. E. 73, XIV, 2.

832. *Charter of the International Tribunal* (London, 1–8 August 1945).

833. *Opinion of the International Tribunal at Nuremberg,* 6 F.R.D. 69.

834. Sheldon Glueck, *59 Harvard Law Review* 396 (1946).

835. *Convention on the Prevention and Punishment of the Crime of Genocide,* G.A. Res. 2670 (III), U.N. Doc. A/810, 78 U.N.T.S. 277, T.I.A.S. No. 1021 (1948). See also *Universal Declaration of Human Rights, General Assembly Resolution,* G.A. Res. 217 (III), U.N. Doc. A/810 (1948); *International Covenant on Civil and Political Rights,* G.A. Res. 2200 (XXI), U.N. Doc. A/6316, 999 U.N.T.S. 171, 6 I.L.M. 383 (1966); *Basic Principles for Protection of Civilian Populations in Armed Conflicts,* G.A. Res. 2675 (XXV) (1970); *Hague Conventions of 1899 (II) and 1907 (IV) Respecting the Laws and Customs of Wars on Land in the Hague Conventions and Declarations of 1899 and 1907,* 2d ed., ed. James Brown Scott (1915); *the Geneva Convention Relative to the Treatment of Prisoners of War* (August 12, 1949); *the American Convention of Human Rights,* OAS Treaty Series No. 36 (November 22, 1969).

836. See *American Convention on Human Rights,* OAS T.S. No. 36, OAS Off.Rec. OEA/Series K/XVI/1.1 (1978), Art. 33.

837. See generally A. H. Robertson, "The United Nations Covenant on Civil and Political Rights and the European Convention on Human Rights," XLIII *British Yearbook of International Law* 21 (1968–1969); O'Hanlon, "The Brussels Colloquy on the European Convention on Human Rights," 5 *Irish Jurist* 252 (1970); Comte, "The Application of the European Convention on Human Rights in Municipal Law," 4 *Journal of International Committee of Jurists* 94 (1962–1963).

838. Leo Strauss, "Natural Law," in *International Encyclopedia of the Social Sciences,* vol. 11 (New York: Macmillan, The Free Press, 1968), 84.

839. US Const, Art. 6, cl. 2.

840. *United States v. Smith,* 18 U.S. (5 Wheat.) 152 (1820).

841. Henri Capitant gives a more precise definition of this useful concept: "that body of institutions and rules designed to ensure, in a given country, the satisfactory functioning of the public services, security, and morality of transactions between individuals, who may not exclude their applications in private agreements." *Vocabulaire Juridique,* quoted in Van Der Meersch, "Does the Convention Have the Force of 'Ordre Public' in Municipal Law?" in *Human Rights in National and International Law,* ed. A. H. Robertson (Dobbs Ferry: Oceana Publications, 1968), 97.

842. *The Paquette Habana,* 175 U.S. 677 (1900).

843. 9 Cranch 388 (U.S. 1815). See also *Filartiga v. Pena-Irala,* 630 F.2d 876, 886 (2d Cir. 1980) ("The law of nations forms an integral part of the common law, and a review of the history surrounding the adoption of the Constitution demonstrates that it became a part of the common law of the United States upon the adoption of the Constitution").

844. *Restatement of the Foreign Relations Law of the United States (Revised)*, introductory note to Part VII (1986).

845. *United States v. Postal*, 589 F.2d 862, 876 (5th Cir. 1979), *cert. denied*, 444 U.S. 832 (1979), cited in Bert Lockwood, "The United States Charter and Civil Rights Litigation: 1946–1955," 69 *Iowa Law Review* 901, 905 (1984). See also Richard B. Lillich, "Invoking International Human Rights Law in Domestic Courts," 54 *University of Cincinnati Law Review* 367, 372 (1985) (discussing a 1948 State Department memo concluding that "it seems quite possible that a precise definition of a self-executing treaty is not possible").

846. *Foster v. Nielson*, 2 Pet. 253, 314, n.3 (U.S. 1829).

847. 59 Stat. 1033 (1945). The particular sections of the Charter concerned were Article 55, which declares that the United Nations "shall promote . . . universal respect for, and observance of, human rights and fundamental freedoms for all without distinction as to race, sex, language, or religion," and Article 56, in which the members "pledge themselves to take joint and separate action in cooperation with the Organization for the achievement of the purposes set forth in Article 55." *Sei Fujii v. State*, 242 P.2d 617, 621 (1952).

848. 38 Cal.2d 718, 242 P.2d 617 (1952), *aff'g*, 217 P.2d 617 (1950). Although the lower court's opinion struck down a discriminatory ordinance based on both the U.N. Charter and the Fourteenth Amendment, the California Supreme Court affirmed only on constitutional grounds, explicitly rejecting the domestic applicability of Articles 55 and 56. This despite a prior Supreme Court pronouncement that "[t]reaties are to be construed in a broad and liberal spirit, and, when two constructions are possible, one restrictive of rights which may be claimed under it, and the other favorable to them, the latter is preferred." *Asakura v. Seattle*, 265 U.S. 332, 342 (1924).

849. See for example *Curran v. City of New York*, 191 Misc. 229, 77 N.Y.S.2d 206 (Sup.Ct. 1947), *aff'd mem.*, 275 A.D. 784, 88 N.Y.S.2d 924 (App.Div. 1949).

850. Note, "Individual Enforcement of Obligations Arising Under the United Nations Charter," 19 *Santa Clara Law Review* 195, 209 (1979).

851. See for example *Camacho v. Rogers*, 199 F. Supp. 155, 158 (S.D.N.Y. 1961); *Diggs v. Richardson*, 555 F.2d 848 (D.C. Cir. 1976) (holding that the charter "does not confer rights on the citizens of the United States that are enforceable in court in the absence of implementing legislation"); *Sipes v. McGhee*, 316 Mich. 614, 25 N.W.2d 638 (1947), *rev'd*, 334 U.S. 1 (1948); *Frolova v. Union of Soviet Socialist Republics*, 761 F.2d 370 (7th Cir. 1985); and *Pauling v. McElroy*, 164 F.Supp. 390 (D.D.C. 1958), *aff'd*, 278 F.2d 252 (D.C. Cir.), *cert. denied*, 364 U.S. 835 (1960).

852. See for example *People of Saipan ex. rel. Guerrero v. United States Department of Interior*, 502 F.2d 90 (9th Cir. 1974), *cert. denied*, 420 U.S. 1003 (1975) (determining whether parts of the U.N. Trusteeship Agreement for Micronesia were self-executing). The extent to which an international agreement establishes affirmative and judicially enforceable obligations without implementing legislation must be determined in each case by reference to many contextual factors: (1) the purpose of the treaty and the objectives of its creators, (2) the existence of domestic procedures and institutions appropriate for direct implementation, (3) the availability and feasi-

bility of alternative enforcement methods, and (4) the immediate and long-range social consequences of self- or non–self-execution. Ibid. This view applies a later and
less stringent *Foster v. Nielson* standard to treaties. It requires in part that self-executing agreements have a judicial character and ascertainable standards for courts
to apply. See note and accompanying text.

853. But see *United States v. Toscanino,* 500 F.2d 267 (2d Cir. 1974).

854. See *Message from the President Transmitting Four Treaties Pertaining to
Human Rights,* S. Exec. Docs. C, D, E, and F, 95th Cong., 2d sess., III (1978).

855. See Philip Alston, "U.S. Ratification of the Covenant on Economic, Social
and Cultural Rights: The Need for an Entirely New Strategy," 84 *American Journal
of International Law* 365 (1990); *International Human Rights Treaties: Hearings
Before the Senate Committee on Foreign Relations,* 96th Cong., 1st sess., 35
(1979). The Covenant on Civil and Political Rights was signed 31 December 1979,
and the Covenant on Economic, Social, and Cultural Rights was signed 31 December 1979.

856. The General Assembly has declared that the articles of the Universal Declaration "constitute basic principles of international law." See G.A. Res. 2625 (XXV)
(24 October 1970).

857. It is correct that the body of international law is not determined merely by
examining the obligations of the United States. The law of nations "may be ascertained by consulting the works of jurists, writing professedly on public law; or by
the general usage and practice of nations; or by judicial decisions recognizing and
enforcing that law." *Tel-Oren v. Libyan Arab Republic,* 517 F. Supp. 542, 546, 547
(1981), citing *United States v. Smith,* 18 U.S. (5 Wheat.) 153, 160–161 (1820).

858. *Restatement of the Foreign Relations Law of the United States (Revised),* introductory note to part VII (1986).

859. Francis Anthony Boyle, *Defending Civil Resistance Under International
Law* (Dobbs Ferry, N.Y.: Transnational Publishers, 1987).

860. See for example *United States v. Lowe,* 654 F.2d 652, 656–667 (9th Cir.
1981); *United States v. May,* 622 F.2d 1000 (9th Cir. 1980); *United States v. Shiel,*
611 F.2d 526 (4th Cir. 1979); and *United States v. Kabat,* 797 F.2d 580 (8th Cir.
1986).

861. 772 F.2d 733 (11th Cir. 1985).

862. Ibid., 738, citing *The Justice Case,* 3 *Trials of War Criminals Before the
Nuremberg Military Tribunals Under Control Council Law No. 10* (1951), and *The
Flick Case,* 6 *Trials of War Criminals Before the Nuremberg Military Tribunals Un-
der Control Council Law No. 10* (1952).

863. 772 F.2d, 738.

864. Ibid., 739.

865. *In re Alien Children Litigation,* 501 F.Supp. 544 (S.D.Tex. 1980), *aff'd un-
reported mem.* (5th Cir. 1981), *aff'd sub nom., Plyler v. Doe,* 457 U.S. 202 (1982).
The Declaration of Human Rights' guarantee of the right to education (in § 26[1])
was not held to be a part of customary international law. However, there are some
cases in which customary international law has been applied in domestic courts. A
landmark case is *Filartiga v. Pena-Irala,* 557 F.Supp. 860 (E.D.N.Y. 1984), which
held that Article 5 of the Universal Declaration of Human Rights had indeed be-

come a part of customary international law. The court used the Declaration to demonstrate a violation of the "law of nations"—the necessary prerequisite for a suit under the Alien Tort Claims Act. See also *Fernandez v. Wilkinson,* 505 F.Supp. 787 (D.Kan. 1980) (applying the Universal Declaration as a statement of customary law), *aff'd sub nom. on other grounds, Rodriguez-Fernandez v. Wilkinson,* 654 F.2d 1382 (10th Cir. 1981). Even where international law can be seen as "customary," there are significant limitations on its use. Subsequent federal enactments can prevent a treaty or agreement from having domestic effect, even though this means that the United States will violate the treaty.

866. *Lawless v. Ireland,* 1 EHRR 15; *Welch v. United Kingdom,* 20 EHRR 247.

867. *Goldwater v. Carter,* 449 U.S. 996, 998 (1979); *Baker v. Carr,* 369 U.S. 186, 217 (1962).

868. *New York Times,* 15 June 1968, 2.

869. Note "The Void for Vagueness Doctrine in the Supreme Court," 109 *University of Pennsylvania Law Review* 67 (1968); *Smith v. Goguen,* 415 U.S. 566 (1974).

870. *U.S. v. Moore,* 486 F.2d 1139 (D.C. Cir. 1973); *Fenster v. Leary,* 20 N.Y.2d 309 (1967); *Robinson v. California,* 370 U.S. 660 (1962); *Powell v. Texas,* 392 U.S. 514 (1964).

871. *Haitian Refugee Center v. Smith,* 676 F.2d 1023, 1038 (5th Cir. 1992) (regarding the right to petition for asylum).

872. *Baker v. Carr,* 369 U.S. 186, 217 (1962).

873. *United States v. Mitchell,* 354 F.2d 767, 769 (2d Cir. 1966); *United States v. Mitchell,* 369 F.2d 323, 324 (2d Cir. 1966).

874. See for example *United States v. Sisson,* 294 F. Supp. 511 (D. Mass. 1968); *United States v. Eberhardt,* 417 F.2d 1009, 1012 (4th Cir. 1969), *cert. denied,* 397 U.S. 909 (1970).

875. Rollin Perkins, *Criminal Law,* 2d ed. (Mineola, N.Y.: Foundation Press, 1969), 829–830.

876. *Morisette v. United States,* 342 U.S. 246, 252 (1952).

877. E. Devitt and C. Blackman, *Federal Jury Practice & Instruction* (St. Paul, Minn.: West Publishing, 1970), § 13.05.

878. Martin J. Freedman, "Criminal Responsibility and the Political Offender," 24 *American University Law Review* 797, 809 (1975).

879. 454 F.2d 386, 392 (7th Cir. 1971).

880. Langer, "The Oakland 7," *The Atlantic* 76 (October 1969), 76, 80.

881. Cunningham, "The Trial of the Gainesville Eight: The Legal Lessons of a Political Trial," 10 *Criminal Law Bulletin* 215 (1974). See also Bertier, "Evidence: Did Angela Davis Testify?" 37 *Albany Law Review* 1 (1972).

882. See for example *United States v. Boardman,* 419 F.2d 110 (1st Cir. 1969) (demonstrating defendant's unsuccessful attempt to use the statutory language for a discourse on motivation).

883. See for example *United States v. Malinowiski,* 472 F.2d 850 (3d Cir. 1972), *cert. denied,* 411 U.S. 970 (1973).

884. *New York Times,* 18 September 1974, 40.

885. Freedman, "Criminal Responsibility," 805.

886. *New York Times*, 18 September 1974, 44.

887. Ibid.

888. Thomas Green, *Verdict According to Conscience* (Chicago: University of Chicago Press, 1985).

889. Alan Scheflin, "Jury Nullification," 45 *California Law Review* 168 (1972); Alan Scheflin and Jon Van Dyke, "Jury Nullification: The Contours of a Controversy," 43 *Law and Contemporary Problems* 51 (1980).

890. *United States v. Moylan*, 417 F.2d 1002, 1006 (4th Cir. 1969).

891. *United States v. Dougherty*, 473 F.2d 1113, 1130–1137 (1972).

892. Ibid., 1133, citing *Sparf v. United States*, 156 U.S. 51, 102 (1895).

893. 473 F.2d, 1137.

894. Ibid., 1142.

895. See for example *United States v. Moylan*, 417 F.2d 1002, 1006–1008 (4th Cir. 1969). In the appeal of the "Catonsville Nine," the court rejected the defendants' claim that the jury should be informed of its absolute power to acquit. Ibid. See also *United States v. Boardman*, 419 F.2d 110, 116 (1st Cir. 1969); and *United States v. Sisson*, 294 F. Supp. 520, 523–524 (D. Mass. 1968), *appeal dismissed*, 399 U.S. 267 (1970).

896. See *The People of the State of Colorado vs. Laura Kriho*, Case #96CR91, 1996; and Thomas A. Green, *Verdict According to Conscience* (Chicago: University of Chicago Press, 1985).

897. *State v. Hunter*, 241 Kan. 629 (1987); *State v. Toscano*, 74 N.J. 421 (1977); *U.S. v. Bailey*, 444 U.S. 394 (1980).

898. Matthew 12:3–4.

899. Illinois Ann. Stat., chap. 38, ¶ 7–13 (Smith-Hurd 1989).

900. Wisconsin Stat. Ann., § 940.05 (West 1982).

901. Frank Lawrence, "The Nuremberg Principles: A Defense for Political Protesters," 40 *Hastings Law Journal* 397 (1989).

902. Ibid.

903. *Commonwealth v. Brugmann*, 13 Mass. App. Ct. 373, 379, 433 N.E.2d 457, 461 (1982), cited in Matthew Lippman, "Reflections on Non-Violent Resistance and the Necessity Defense," 11 *American Journal of International Law* 277, 294 (1989). See also *United States v. Contento-Pachon*, 723 F.2d 691, 695 (1984); *United States v. Bailey*, 444 U.S. 394, 410 (1980); and *United States v. Gant*, 691 F.2d 1159 (5th Cir. 1982).

904. Kyle Bettigols, "Comment: Defending Against Defense: Necessity and the United States Military's Toxic Legacy," 21 *Boston College Environmental Affairs Law Review* 667, 671 (1994).

905. Douglas Colbert, "The Motion in Limine in Politically Sensitive Cases: Silencing the Defendant to Trial," 39 *Stanford Law Review* 1271 (1987).

906. Matthew Lippman, "Liberating the Law: The Jurisprudence of Civil Disobedience and Resistance," 2 *San Diego Law Journal* 299 (1994).

907. 622 F.2d 1000 (1980).

908. *United States v. Richardson*, 588 F.2d 1235, 1239 (9th Cir. 1978), *cert. denied*, 441 U.S. 931, *cert. denied*, 440 U.S. 947 (1979).

909. *United States v. Simpson*, 460 F.2d 515, 517 (9th Cir. 1972).

910. *Hoover v. State*, 402 S.E.2d 92 (Ga. Ct. App. 1991).

911. *United States v. Schoon*, 971 F.2d 193 (9th Cir.), *cert. denied*, 112 S. Ct. 2980 (1992).

912. *United States v. Aguilar*, 883 F.2d 662 (9th Cir. 1989), *cert. denied*, 111 S. Ct. 751 (1991).

913. *Shiel v. United States*, 515 A.2d 405 (D.C. 1986), *cert. denied*, 485 U.S. 1010 (1988). See also *State v. Warshow*, 138 Vt. 22, 410 A.2d 1000 (1979); *State v. Dorsey*, 118 N.H. 844, 395 A.2d 855 (1978); Lippman, "Liberating the Law"; *United States v. Dorrell*, 758 F.2d 427 (9th Cir. 1985); and *Commonwealth v. Averill*, 12 Mass. App. Ct. 260, 262, 423 N.E.2d 6, 7–8 (1981) ("publicity designed to marshal public opinion could not extinguish an immediate peril, if there was one").

914. See generally *Hague Convention 1907, Geneva Conventions 1864, 1906, 1929, 1949*. See also Geva Herczegh, *Development of International Humanitarian Law* (Budapest: Akademiai Kiado, 1984); and Michel Veuthney, *Non-International Armed Conflict and Guerrilla Warfare*, in *International Criminal Law*, vol. 1, ed. M. Cherif Bassiouni (Dobbs Ferry, N.Y.: Transnational Publishers, Inc., 1986), 243.

915. General Order, No. 100, 24 April 1953. Article 37 of Lieber Instructions.

916. Ibid., Arts. 152–153.

917. Kittrie and Wedlock, *Tree of Liberty*, 191–193.

918. "Manila, Communists in War of Words over Belligerent Status," *Agence France Presse*, 30 June 1996; "Mexico Pledges to Maintain Cease-Fire," *United Press International*, 13 June 1994; "Leaders Make Decisive Peace Breakthrough," *Agence France Presse*, 1 September 1993; Jim Lobs, "Nicaragua: U.S. Acknowledges 'Contra' Infiltration," *Inter Press Service*, 2 November 1989.

919. See generally Dan Jacobs, *The Brutality of Nations* (New York: Knopf, 1987). See also, Veuthney, *Non-International Armed Conflict*, n.921.

920. *Common Article Three to the Geneva Conventions of 1949*, 6 U.S.T. 3114, T.I.A.S. No. 3362, 75 U.N.T.S. 3217, 3364, 75 U.N.T.S. 135; 6 T.I.A.S. No. 3365, 75 U.N.T.S. 287.

921. *Protocol Additional to the Geneva Conventions of 1949* (Protocol I), opened for signature 12 December 1977, reprinted in 16 I.L.M. 1442 (1977) [hereinafter *Protocol I*]; *Protocol Additional to the Geneva Conventions of 1949* (Protocol II), opened for signature 12 December 1977, reprinted in 16 I.L.M. 1442 (1977) [hereinafter *Protocol II*].

922. M. Both, K. Partsch, and W. Solf, *New Rules for Victims of Armed Conflicts: Commentary on the Two 1977 Protocols Additional to the Geneva Conventions of 1949* (1982), 47.

923. *Protocol I*, 157, Art. 1(4).

924. Ibid., Art. 44. This article provides, however, that "while all combatants are obligated to comply with the rules of international law applicable to armed conflict, violations of these rules shall not deprive a combatant of his right to be a combatant or . . . if he falls into the power of an adversary, of his right to be a prisoner of war."

925. Frits Kalshoven, 8 *New York International Law Review* 122 (1977).

926. Sylvie Junod, "Additional Protocol II: History and Scope," 33 *American University Law Review* 29, 30 (1983).

927. Even though the superpowers have been reluctant to classify their military activities as more than "police actions," the United States treated the Viet Cong insurgents in Southeast Asia as combatants. Charles Lysaght, "The Scope of Protocol II and Its Relations to Common Article 3 of the Geneva Conventions of 1949 and Other Human Rights Instruments," 33 *American University Law Review* 9, 11, 13 (1983).

928. Ibid., 39.

929. *Common Article Three, 925.*

930. *Protocol II,* Art. 1(1).

931. Ibid., Art. 1(2).

932. See Security Council Resolution 808, S/RES/808, 22 February 1993; and Security Council Resolution 827, S/RES/827, 25 May 1993.

933. Lysaght, "Scope of Protocol II," 21.

934. Ibid., 22.

935. *Black's Law Dictionary,* 3d ed. (St. Paul: West Publishing, 1933), 105–106.

936. Decree Law No. 2191 (18 April 1978), published in Diario Oficial, No. 30,042 (19 April 1978).

937. *Report of the National Commission on Truth and Reconciliation,* trans. Phillip E. Berryman (South Bend, Ind.: University of Notre Dame Press, 1993), 899. In American terms, this is the equivalent of 108,000 lives lost through government murder.

938. Quoted in Tina Rosenberg, "Overcoming the Legacies of Dictatorships," *Foreign Affairs,* Spring 1995, 134.

939. An Acte for Recontynuyng of ctayne libties and franchness heretofore taken from the Crowne, 1535–1536, 27 Hen. 8, chap. 24, § I.

940. Daniel T. Kobil, "The Quality of Mercy Strained," 69 *Texas Law Review* 569, 589 (1991).

941. Habeas Corpus Act, 1679, 31 Car. 2, chap. 2, § 11; Bill of Rights, 1689, W. & M., chap. 2, § 2; 16 H.L. Jour. 737 (1701).

942. 1 *The Records of the Federal Convention of 1787,* ed. M. Ferrand (1911).

943. US Const, Art. 2, § 2.

944. Samuel Stafford, *Clemency* (Williamsburg, Va.: Research and Information Center, 1977), xvi.

945. 378 F. Supp. 1221 (D.D.C. 1974).

946. *Hoffa,* 378 F. Supp., 1234–1235.

947. Ibid., 1236.

948. 236 U.S. 79 (1915).

949. 419 U.S. 256 (1974).

950. 267 U.S. 87 (1925).

951. Kobil, "Quality of Mercy Strained," 601.

952. 71 U.S. 333 (1866).

953. *Knote,* 95 U.S., 152–153.

954. Ibid., 153.

955. *Burdick,* 236 U.S. 79, 94–95 (1915).

956. *United States v. Klein,* 80 U.S. 128, 147 (1871); *Knote,* 95 U.S. 149, 152–153 (1877); *Brown v. Walker,* 161 U.S. 591, 601–602 (1896).

957. Emory Thomas, *Robert E. Lee* (New York: W. W. Norton, 1995), 365.

958. Shelby Foote, *The Civil War: Red River to Appomattox* (New York: Vintage Books, 1974), 948.

959. Ibid., 951.

960. 12 Stat. at Large, 592, 17 July 1862; Jonathan Dorris, *Pardon and Amnesty Under Lincoln and Johnson* (Westport, Conn.: Greenwood Press, 1977), 34–35.

961. Ibid., 74–75.

962. 13 Stat. at Large, 758, 29 May 1865.

963. Kittrie and Wedlock, *Tree of Liberty,* 568

964. 3 C.F.R. 91 (1978).

965. Ibid.

966. Pub. L. No. 99–603, 100 Stat. 3359 (codified at 8 U.S.C. §§ 1150–24 [Supp. 1987]) (signed into law 6 November 1986).

967. 8 U.S.C. § 1255a(a)(1)(C).

968. 8 U.S.C. § 1255a(b)(1)(A).

969. Pamela Nichols, "The United States Immigration Reform and Control Act of 1986," 8 *Northwestern Journal of International Law and Business* 503, 508–509 (1987).

970. Pres. Proc. 4311, 39 Fed. Reg. 32,601 (1974).

971. Richard M. Nixon, responding, NBC, "Meet the Press," 10 April 1988.

972. Proclamation 6518, Public Papers of the Presidents, 24 December 1992, 28 *Weekly Compilation of Presidential Documents* 2382.

973. Robert K. Goldman, "Amnesty Laws, International Law and the American Convention on Human Rights," *The Law Group Docket,* Summer 1989, 1.

974. Diane Orentlicher, "Settling Accounts: The Duty to Prosecute Human Rights Violations of a Prior Regime," 100 *Yale Law Journal* 2537, 2586–2595 (1991).

975. See *Interim Report of the Truth and Reconciliation Commission* (Cape Town: 1996).

976. F. W. de Klerk, D.M.S., "Address at the Opening of the Second Session of the Ninth Parliament of the Republic of South Africa," Cape Town (2 February 1990).

977. 4 *Temple International and Comparative Law Journal* 1.

978. James Meeks, "Army Besieges Rebel Azeri Police Barracks," *The Guardian,* 17 March 1995, p. 12.

979. Fred Hiatt, "Yeltsin Warns His Freed Foes," *Washington Post,* 2 March 1994, p. A19.

980. Ibid.

981. Margaret Shapiro, "Coup Trial Ordered in Russia," *Washington Post,* 12 March 1994, p. A16.

982. Tina Rosenberg, "Where's the Crime," *New York Times,* 2 June 1995, p. A2.

983. Ibid.

984. Orentlicher, "Settling Accounts," 2550.

985. Virginia Morris and M. C. Bourloyannis-Vrailas, "The Work of the Sixth Committee at the Forty-Eighth Session of the U.N. General Assembly," 88 *Ameri-*

can Journal of International Law 343 (1994); Mark Hutchinson, "Restoring Hope: U.N. Security Council Resolutions for Somalia and the Expanded Doctrine of Humanitarian Intervention," 34 *Harvard International Law Journal* 624 (1993); John E. Paperson Jr., "United States Compliance with Humanitarian Law Respecting Civilians During Operation Just Cause," 133 *Military Law Journal* 31 (1991); *Draft Charter of the International Tribunal for Violations of International Humanitarian Law in the Former Yugoslavia*, Article 10(a) (grounding jurisdiction of international tribunal and application of international law); "Yemen Frees 4,000 Southern P.O.W.'s," *New York Times*, 27 July 1994, p. A8 (Yemeni government considers civil war combatants as prisoners of war).

Chapter 8

986. Jerrold M. Post and Robert S. Robins, *When Illness Strikes the Leader* (New Haven: Yale University Press, 1993).

987. *Washington Times*, 6 February 1989, A11.

988. Ingraham, *Political Crime*.

989. Ibid., 267.

990. See Internal Security Act of 1950 (the McCarran Act), 64 Stat. 987 (1950); and Communist Control Act of 1954, 68 Stat. 775 (1954). See also Kittrie and Wedlock, *Tree of Liberty*, 393–480.

991. South Africa's apartheid laws provided that a person writing letters to Africans likely "to encourage feelings of hostility between the white and other inhabitants will be presumed to have done so with intent to endanger the maintenance of law and order." Convicted as terrorists, such letter writers were subject to the death penalty. Terrorism: Nr. 83 of 1967, § 2. L. Rubin, *Apartheid in Practice*, UN Publication OPI/533 (1976), 40.

992. Jeanne Kirkpatrick, *Dictatorships and Double Standards* (New York: Simon & Schuster, 1982).

993. In Liberia, for example, a supreme military tribunal consisting of five army officers, sitting *in camera*, was given exclusive power over the trial of treason cases. Bill Berkeley, *Liberia, A Promise Betrayed: A Report on Human Rights* (New York: Lawyers Committee for Human Rights, 1986), 15.

994. International Commission of Jurists, *States of Emergency: Their Impact on Human Rights* (1983). Under Poland's Constitution, a state of emergency permitted the prohibition of strikes and public protests, the establishment of internment camps for political suspects, restrictions on the freedom of travel, and the institutions of wiretapping and state interception of correspondence.

995. Despite the absence of explicit martial law provisions in Poland's Communist-era's law (Art. 33 of the Constitution authorized the imposition of a "state of war" only in instances of external threat to the state security), Poland's Communist government, on December 13, 1981, declared a state of war, thereby imposing martial law in response to Solidarity's domestic threat. Lawyers' Committee for International Human Rights, *Poland: Three Years After* (1984), 13.

996. Stephen Schafer, *The Political Criminal: The Problem of Morality and Crime* (New York: The Free Press, 1974).

997. Brian Crozier, *The Rebels: A Study in Post-War Insurrections* (London: Chatto and Windus, 1960).

998. See the Koran.

999. Jeremiah 4:6–29; 5:15–17; 9:11.

1000. Daniel 4:25.

1001. George W. F. Hallgarten, *Devils or Saviours: A History of Dictatorship Since 600 B.C.* (London: Oswald Wolff Publishers, 1960).

1002. Frederick Mundell Walkings, "Tyranny," in *Encyclopedia of the Social Sciences*, vol. 15 (New York: The Macmillan Company, 1934), 135. See also P. N. Ure, *The Origins of Tyranny* (Cambridge: Harvard University Press, 1922).

1003. Hallgarten, *Devils or Saviours,* 1.

1004. Aristotle, *Politics*, 1279 b 6, in *The Politics of Aristotle,* trans. E. Baker (Oxford: 1946).

1005. Ibid., 1285 a 30.

1006. Ibid., 135.

1007. Robert J. Hopper, *The Early Greeks* (London: Weidenfeld and Nicholson, 1976), 202.

1008. A. H. M. Jones, *Athenian Democracy* (Baltimore: The Johns Hopkins University Press, 1986), 5, 75.

1009. Hopper, *Early Greeks,* 109–155.

1010. Rapoport, *Assassination and Terrorism,* 7.

1011. Cicero, "No Fellowship in Tyrants," in *The Terrorism Reader: A Historical Reader,* ed. Walter Laqueur and Yonah Alexander (New York: Meridian Books, NAL Penguin, 1987), 16.

1012. For a contemporary classification, see generally Hallgarten, *Devils or Saviours.*

1013. Leo Strauss, *Natural Right and History* (Chicago: University of Chicago Press, 1953), 85–101.

1014. H. A. Rommen, "The Natural Law," in *The Natural Law Reader*, ed. Brendan Brown (New York: Oceana, 1960), 61–73.

1015. "Paradoxical Philosophy," in Henry Drummon, *Natural Law in the Spiritual World* (New York: John B. Alden, 1889), 21.

1016. George W. F. Hallgarten, *Why Dictators?* (New York: Macmillan, 1954); Hallgarten, *Devils or Saviours.*

1017. Jean Dunbabin, "Government," in *Medieval Political Thought,* ed. J. H. Burns (Cambridge: Cambridge University Press, 1991), 493–498.

1018. John of Salisbury, *Policraticus* III. 15 (Turnholti: Typographi Brepols Editores Pontificii, 1993).

1019. Thomas Aquinas, *Summa Theologiae,* ed. R. Spiazzi (Taurini: Marietti, 1951), 247.

1020. Dunbabin, "Government," 493–498.

1021. Deuteronomy 20:10–15; 20:19

1022. Robert L. Phillips, *War and Justice* (Norman: University of Oklahoma Press, 1984), ix.

1023. J. Toland, *The Rising Sun* (New York: Random House, 1971), 218.

1024. Ibid., x.

1025. Ibid., 10.

1026. L. Oppenheim, *International Law* (London: Longmans, Green, 1952), 226.

1027. Phillips, *War and Justice,* 7–9.

1028. Ibid., 9.

1029. Michael Waltzer, *The Revolution of the Saints* (Cambridge: Harvard University Press, 1965), 268–299.

1030. Ibid., 268–270.

1031. Ibid. Compare this articulation with the Marxist-Leninist doctrine of "just cause" for war: "[A]ny class struggle leading to war makes that war just; and specifically, a just war is a non-predatory, liberatory war." Paul Ramsey, *The Just War: Force and Political Responsibility* (New York: Charles Scribner's Sons, 1968), 189. See also Y. A. Korovin et al., *International Law* (Moscow: Foreign Language Publishing House), 402.

1032. *Faustum* (XXII, 73); St. Thomas Aquinas, *Summa Theologica, secunda secundae,* No. 15, Q40 (art. 1), in *Aquinas: Selected Political Writings,* ed. A. P. D'Entreves, trans. J. G. Dawson (Oxford: Blackwell, 1948), 159.

1033. William V. O'Brien, *The Conduct of Just and Limited War* (New York: Praeger, 1981), 17.

1034. Phillips, *War and Justice,* 13, 19.

1035. Convention for the Amelioration of the Condition of the Wounded and Sick in Armed Forces in the Field, 12 August 1949, 6 U.S.T. 3114, 75 U.N.T.S. 31; Convention for the Amelioration of the Condition of Wounded, Sick and Shipwrecked Members of Armed Forces at Sea, 12 August 1949, 6 U.S.T. 3217, 75 U.N.T.S. 85; Convention Relative to the Treatment of Prisoners of War, 12 August 1949, 6 U.S.T. 3316, 75 U.N.T.S. 135; Convention Relative to the Protection of Civilian Persons in Time of War, 12 August 1949, 6 U.S.T. 3516, 75 U.N.T.S. 287.

1036. Phillips, *War and Justice,* 27.

1037. R. Tucker, *The Just War: Exposition of the American Concept* (Baltimore: The Johns Hopkins University Press, 1960); I. M. Walzer, *Just and Unjust War* (New York: Basic Books, 1973).

1038. UN Charter, Art. 2(3–4).

1039. Tucker, *Just War;* Walzer, *Just and Unjust War;* Ramsey, *Just War;* O'Brien, *Just and Limited War.*

1040. Oppenheim, *International Law,* 557.

1041. *Charter of the International Tribunal,* 8 August 1945), Art. 6(a–c).

1042. Robert K. Woetzel, *The Nuremberg Trials in International Law* (London: Stevens & Sons, 1962), 177–178.

1043. Ibid.

1044. Ibid.

1045. Ibid.

1046. Ibid., 108–121.

1047. *U.S. v. Thaxter,* 437 F.2d 417 (9th Cir. 1971); *U.S. v. Garrity,* 433 F.2d 649 (8th Cir. 1970); *Al-Adsani v. Govt. of Kuqait,* Court of Appeals (Civil Division), 21 January 1994; *Limbo v. Little,* 65 N.T.R. 19 (1988).

1048. Woetzel, *The Nuremburg Trials,* 96.

1049. *Convention on the Prevention and Punishment of the Crime of Genocide,* 9 December 1948, 78 U.N.T.S. 278, T.I.A.S. No. 1021.

1050. Universal Declaration of Human Rights, 10 December 1948, U.N.G.A. Res. 217 A (III).

1051. Statute of the International Court of Justice, 26 June 1945, 50 Stat. 1055; American Convention on Human Rights, Sections VII and VIII, 22 November 1969, 9 I.L.M. 673 (1970); European Convention for the Protection of Human Rights and Fundamental Freedoms, Art. 19(b), 4 November 1950, 312 U.N.T.S. 221.

1052. International Convention on the Suppression and Punishment of Apartheid, 30 November 1973, 13 I.L.M. 51 (1974); United Nations Security Council Resolution 717, 16 October 1991 (Cambodia); United Nations Security Council Resolution 841, 16 June 1993 (Haiti).

1053. Convention for the Amelioration of the Condition of the Wounded and Sick in Armed Forces in the Field, 12 August 1949, 6 U.S.T. 3114, 75 U.N.T.S. 31; Convention for the Amelioration of the Condition of Wounded, Sick and Shipwrecked Members of Armed Forces at Sea, 12 August 1949, 6 U.S.T. 3217, 75 U.N.T.S. 85; Convention Relative to the Treatment of Prisoners of War, 12 August 1949, 6 U.S.T. 3316, 75 U.N.T.S. 135; Convention Relative to the Protection of Civilian Persons in Time of War, 12 August 1949, 6 U.S.T. 3516, 75 U.N.T.S. 287.

1054. Shearer, *Extradition in International Law,* 185.

1055. *In re Meunier,* 782 W.B. 415 (1894).

1056. Manley O. Hudson, ed., *International Legislation* (Washington, D.C.: Carnegie Endowment for International Peace, 1941), 7:862–878.

1057. 1971 Montreal Convention, T.I.A.S. No. 7570; 1970 Hague Convention, T.I.A.S. No. 7192; 1963 Tokyo Convention, T.I.A.S. No. 6768.

1058. Convention on the Prevention and Punishment of Crimes Against Internationally Protected Persons, including Diplomatic Agents, G.A. Res. A/3166 (XXVIII) (1974).

1059. 1906 Postal Convention, 35 Stat. 1639 (1906).

1060. International Convention Against the Taking of Hostages, 17 December 1979, U.N.G.A. Res. 34/14b (XXXIV).

1061. See Chapters 2 and 6. See also Michael Lillenberg, "The Political Offender Exception: An Historical Analysis and Model for the Future," 64 *Tulane Law Review* 1196 (1990).

1062. M. Sassoli, "International Humanitarian Law and Terrorism," in P. Wilkinson and A. M. Stewart, *Contemporary Research on Terrorism* (Aberdeen, Scotland: Aberdeen University Press, 1988), 466. Douglas J. Feith, "Law in the Service of Terror," *The National Interest,* no. 1, 1985, 47.

Epilogue

1063. See Nicholas Kittrie, *The War Against Authority: From the Crisis of Legitimacy to a New Social Contract* (Baltimore: The Johns Hopkins University Press, 1995).

Selected Bibliography

Abels, Jules. 1971. *Man on Fire: John Brown and the Cause of Liberty*. New York: Macmillan.

Adams, James. 1987. *Secret Wars*. London: Hutchinson.

Adler, Freda. 1975. *Sisters in Crime: The Rise of the New Female Criminal*. New York: McGraw-Hill.

Ali, Tariq, ed. 1969. *The New Revolutionaries: A Handbook of the International Radical Left*. New York: Morrow.

Allen, Francis A. 1974. *The Crimes of Politics: Political Dimensions of Criminal Justice*. Cambridge, Mass.: Harvard University Press.

Aptheker, Herbert. 1978. *American Negro Slave Revolts*. New York: International Publishers.

Arendt, Hannah. 1970. *On Revolution*. New York: Viking Press.

Bailyn, Bernard. 1967. *The Ideological Origins of the American Revolution*. Cambridge, Mass.: Harvard University Press.

Barak, Gregg, ed. 1991. *Crimes by the Capitalist State: An Introduction to State Criminality*, Albany, N.Y.: State University of New York Press.

Bassiouni, M. Cherif. 1974. *International Extradition and World Public Order*. Dobbs Ferry, N.Y.: Oceana Publications.

Becker, Theodore L., ed. 1971. *Political Trials*. Indianapolis: Bobbs-Merrill.

Bedau, Hugo Adam, ed. 1969. *Civil Disobedience: Theory and Practice*. New York: Pegasus.

Behan, Brendan. 1959. *Borstal Boy*. New York: Alfred A. Knopf.

Belknap, Michal R. 1977. *Cold War Political Justice: The Smith Act, the Communist Party and American Civil Liberties*. Westport, Conn.: Greenwood Press.

Bell, J. Bowyer. 1993. *The Irish Troubles: A Generation of Political Violence, 1967–1992*. New York: St. Martin's Press.

Ben-Dak, Joseph D., ed. 1974. *The Future of Collective Violence: Societal and International Perspectives*. Lund: Student Litteratur.

Berrigan, Philip. 1970. *Prison Journals of a Priest Revolutionary*. New York: Holt, Rinehart & Winston.

Black, Bob, and Parfrey, Adam. 1989. *Rants and Incendiary Tracts: Voices of Desperate Illumination, 1558 to Present*. New York: Amok Press.

Blaustein, Albert P., and Zangrando, Robert L., eds. 1968. *Civil Rights and the American Negro: A Documentary History*. New York: Trident Press.

Block, Sidney, and Reddaway, Peter. 1985. *Soviet Psychiatric Abuse: The Shadow over World Psychiatry*. Boulder, Colo.: Westview Press.

Bonger, William A. 1967. *Criminality and Economic Conditions*. New York: Agathon Press.

Bozeman, Adda B. 1971. *The Future of Law in a Multicultural World*. Princeton, N.J.: Princeton University Press.

Bracher, Karl Dietrich. 1970. *The German Dictatorship: The Origins, Structure and Effects of National Socialism*. New York: Praeger Publishers.

Breitman, G., ed. 1965. *Malcolm X Speaks*. New York: Grove Press.

Brinton, Crane. 1952. *The Anatomy of Revolution*. New York: Random House.

Brown, Richard M. 1975. *Strain of Violence*. New York: Oxford University Press.

Brownlie, Ian. 1968. *The Law Relating to Public Order*. London: Butterworth.

Burton, Anthony. 1978. *Revolutionary Violence*. New York: Crane, Russak.

Camus, Albert. 1991. *The Rebel; an Essay on Man in Revolt*. New York: Vintage Books.

Cappelletti, Guido. 1971. *Judicial Review in the Contemporary World*. Kansas City: Bobbs-Merrill.

Chafee, Zechariah. 1952. *How Human Rights Got into the Constitution*. Boston: Boston University Press.

Chapin, Bradley. 1964. *The American Law of Treason*. Seattle: University of Washington Press.

Chomsky, Noam, et al. 1970. *Trials of the Resistance*. New York: Vintage Books.

Cleaver, Eldridge. 1968. *Soul on Ice*. New York: Dell Publishing.

Clinard, Marshall B., and Quinney, Richard. 1967. *Criminal Behavior Systems: A Typology*. New York: Holt, Rinehart, and Winston.

Commager, H. S., ed. 1973. *Documents of American History*. New York: Meredith.

Conquest, Robert. 1990. *The Great Terror: A Reassessment*. New York: Oxford University Press.

Cook, Alice, and Kirk, Gwyn. 1983. *Greenham Women Everywhere: Dreams, Ideas and Actions from the Women's Peace Movement*. London: Pluto Press.

Corwin, Edward. 1957. *The "Higher Law" Background of American Constitutional Law*. Ithaca: Cornell University Press.

Crozier, Brian. 1960. *The Rebels*. London: Chatto & Windus.

Dahl, Robert A. 1982. *Dilemmas of Pluralistic Democracy: Autonomy v. Control*. New Haven, Conn.: Yale University Press.

Davies, James C., ed. 1971. *When Men Revolt and Why*. New York: The Free Press.

de Boer, S. P., Driesser, E. S., and Verhaar, H. L., eds. 1982. *Biographical Dictionary of Dissidents in the Soviet Union, 1956–1973*. Boston: Martinus Nijhoff Publishers.

Dellinger, Dave. 1971. *Revolutionary Nonviolence*. New York: Doubleday.

Desind, Philip. 1990. *Jewish and Russian Revolutionaries Exiled to Siberia, 1901–1917*. Lewiston, N.Y.: Edwin Mellen Press.

Dubois, W. E. B. 1962. *John Brown*. New York: International Publishers.

Dumbauld, Edward. 1969. *The Life and Legal Writings of Hugo Grotius*. Norman, Okla.: University of Oklahoma Press.

Duska, Ronald, and Whelan, Mariellen. 1975. *Moral Development: A Guide to Piaget and Kohlberg*. New York: Paulist Press.

Ekstein, Harry, ed. 1964. *Internal War: Problems and Approaches*. New York: The Free Press of Glencoe.

Ferri, Enrico. 1917. *Criminal Sociology*. Boston: Little, Brown.

Finnis, John. 1980. *Natural Law and Natural Rights*. Oxford: Clarendon Press.

Ford, W. J. 1968. "Resistance Movements and International Law." 8 *International Review of Red Cross*, p. 43.

Fortas, Abe. 1968. *Concerning Dissent and Civil Disobedience*. New York: New American Library.

Foucault, Michel. 1979. *Discipline and Punish*. New York: Vintage Books.

Freud, Sigmund. 1961. *Civilization and its Discontents*. New York: W.W. Norton.

Garcia-Mora, Manuel R. 1956. *International Law and Asylum as a Human Right*. Washington, D.C.: Public Affairs Press.

Gaylin, Willard. 1970. *In the Service of Their Country: War Resisters in Prison*. New York: Grosset & Dunlap.

Goodell, Charles E. 1973. *Political Prisoners in America*. New York: Random House.

Goodspeed, D. J. 1962. *The Conspirators: A Study of the Coup d'Etat*. New York: Viking Press.

Graham, Hugh Davis, and Gurr, Ted Robert. 1969. *Violence in America: Historical and Comparative Perspectives*. Washington, D.C.: U.S. Government Printing Office.

Grahl-Madsen, Atle. 1980. *Territorial Asylum*. New York: Oceana Publications.

Green, Thomas. 1985. *Verdict According to Conscience*. Chicago: University of Chicago Press.

Greene, T. H. 1974. *Comparative Revolutionary Movements*. Englewood Cliffs, N.J.: Prentice-Hall.

Gurr, Ted Robert. 1971. *Why Men Rebel*. Princeton: Princeton University Press.

Hagan, Frank E. 1997. *Political Crime: Ideology and Criminality*. Boston: Allyn and Bacon.

Hall, Wilfred G. C. 1923. *Political Crimes: A Critical Essay on the Law and Its Administration in Cases of a Certain Type*. London: G. Allen & Unwin.

Hallgarten, George W. F. 1960. *Devils or Saviours: A History of Dictatorship Since 600 B.C.* London: Oswald Wolff Publishers.

Havens, Murray Clark, Leiden, Carl, and Schmitt, Karl M. 1970. *The Politics of Assassination.* Englewood Cliffs, N.J.: Prentice-Hall.

Hendrick, Burton J. 1939. *Statesmen of the Lost Cause: Jefferson Davis and His Cabinet.* Boston: Little, Brown.

Herczegh, Geva. 1984. *Development of International Humanitarian Law.* Budapest: Akademia, Kiado.

Hobsbawn, Eric J. 1973. *Revolutionaries.* New York: Pantheon Books.

Hofstadter, Richard, and Wallace, Michael, eds. 1970. *American Violence: A Documentary History.* New York: Knopf.

Honderich, Ted. 1976. *Three Essays on Political Violence.* Oxford: Basil Blackwell.

Hurst, James Willard. 1971. *The Law of Treason in the United States: Collected Essays.* Westport, Conn.: Greenwood Publishing.

Hyams, Edward. 1975. *Terrorists and Terrorism.* New York: St. Martin's Press.

Ingraham, Barton L. 1979. *Political Crime in France, Germany and England in Modern Time.* Berkeley: University of California.

Kadish, Mortimer R., and Kadish, Sanford H. 1973. *Discretion to Disobey: A Study of Lawful Departures from Legal Rules.* San Francisco: Stanford University Press.

Kelman, Herbert C., and V. Lee Hamilton. 1989. *Crimes of Obedience: Toward a Social Psychology of Authority and Responsibility.* New Haven, Conn.: Yale University Press.

Keniston, Kenneth. 1968. *Young Radicals: Notes on Committed Youth.* New York: Harcourt, Brace & World.

Kircheimer, Otto. 1961. *Political Justice: The Use of Legal Procedure for Political Ends.* Princeton, N.J.: Princeton University Press.

Kirkham, James F., Levy, Sheldon G., and Crotty, William J. 1969. *Assassination and Political Violence: A Report to the National Commission on the Causes and Prevention of Violence.* Washington, D.C.: U.S. Government Printing Office.

Kittrie, Nicholas N., and Wedlock, Eldon D., Jr. 1996; 1998 (2nd Ed.). *The Tree of Liberty: A Documentary History of Rebellion and Political Crime in America.* Baltimore: The Johns Hopkins University Press.

Kittrie, Nicholas N. 1995. *The War Against Authority: From the Crisis of Legitimacy to a New Social Order.* Baltimore: The Johns Hopkins University Press.

Kohlberg, Lawrence. 1971. "Stages of Moral Development as a Basis for Moral Education." In C. M. Beck, B. S. Crittendon, and E. V. Sullivan, eds., *Moral Education: Inter-disciplinary Approaches.* Toronto: University of Toronto Press.

Kohn, Hans. 1955. *Nationalism: Its Meaning and History.* New York: D. Van Nostrand Company.

Laquer, Walter, and Alexander, Yonah. 1987. *The Terrorism Reader.* New York: Meridian Books.

Lipset, Seymour Martin. 1988. *Revolution and Counterrevolution: Change and Persistence in Social Structures*. New Brunswick: Transaction Books.

Lombroso-Ferrero, Gina. 1972. *Criminal Man According to the Classification of Cesare Lombroso*. Montclair, N.J.: Patterson Smith.

Lukacs, John. 1971. *Don't Shoot—We Are Your Children!* New York: Random House.

Lynd, S., ed. 1966. *Nonviolence in America: A Documentary History*. New York: Bobbs-Merril.

Macknight, Gerald. 1974. *The Terrorist Mind*. Indianapolis: Bobbs-Merrill.

Malcolm X, and Haley, Alex. 1969. *The Autobiography of Malcolm X*. New York: Grove Press.

Malinowski, Bronislaw. 1926. *Crime and Custom in Savage Society*. London: Routledge and Kegan Paul.

May, Rollo. 1972. *Power and Innocence: A Search for the Sources of Violence*. New York: W.W. Norton.

Merton, Robert K. 1968. *Social Theory and Social Structure*. New York: The Free Press.

Mill, John Stuart. 1971. *On Liberty, Representative Government, and the Subjugation of Women*. London: Oxford University Press.

Moore, Barrington, Jr. 1969. *Social Origins of Dictatorship and Democracy*. Boston: Beacon Press.

Morison, Samuel Eliot, Merk, Frederick, and Freidel, Frank. 1970. *Dissent in Three American Wars*. Cambridge, Mass.: Harvard University Press.

Morris, Richard B. 1973. *Seven Who Shaped Our Destiny: The Founding Fathers as Revolutionaries*. New York: Harper & Row.

Mosca, Gaetano. 1939. *The Ruling Class*. New York: McGraw-Hill.

Moynihan, Patrick. 1993. *Pandaemonium*. New York: Oxford University Press.

Mullins, W. C. 1988. *Terrorist Organizations in the United States: An Analysis of Issues, Organizations, Tactics and Responses*. Springfield, Ill.: Charles C. Thomas.

Newman, Graeme. 1979. *Understanding Violence*. New York: J. B. Lippincott Co.

Nozick, Robert. 1974. *Anarchy, State, and Utopia*. New York: Basic Books.

O'Brien, William V. 1981. *The Conduct of Just and Limited War*. New York: Prager Publishers.

Palmer, R. R. 1971. *Twelve Who Ruled: The Year of the Terror in the French Revolution*. Princeton: Princeton University Press.

Parmalee, Maurice. 1918. *Criminology*. New York: MacMillan.

Poor, Harold L. 1968. *Kurt Tucholsky, the Ordeal of Germany (1914–1935)*. New York: Charles Scribner's Sons.

Post, Jerrold M., and Robins, Robert S. 1993. *When Illness Strikes the Leader*. New Haven: Yale University Press.

Ra'anan, Uri, et al. 1991. *State and Nation in Multi-Ethnic Societies: The Breakup of Multinational States*. New York: Manchester University Press.

Ramsey, Paul. 1968. *The Just War: Force and Political Responsibility*. New York: Charles Scribner's Sons.

Rapoport, Anatol. 1989. *The Origins of Violence: Approaches to the Study of Conflict*. New York: Paragon House.

Rapoport, David C., ed. 1971. *Assassination and Terrorism*. Toronto: Canadian Broadcasting Corporation.

Raschhofer, Hermann. 1964. *Political Assassination*. Tübingen: Fritz Schlichtenmayer.

Reich, Walter, ed. 1990. *Origins of Terrorism*. Cambridge: Cambridge University Press.

Roebuck, Julian and Weeber, Stanley C. 1978. *Political Crime in the United States: Analyzing Crime by and Against Government*. New York: Praeger.

Rommen, A. Heinrich. 1974. *The Natural Law: A Study in Legal and Social History and Philosophy*. St. Louis, Mo.: Herder.

Rosenau, James M., ed. 1964. *International Aspects of Civil Strife*. Princeton: Princeton University Press.

Rostow, Eugene V., ed. 1971. *Is Law Dead?* New York: Simon & Schuster.

Rubenstein, Richard E. 1970. *Rebels in Eden: Mass Political Violence in the United States*. Boston: Little, Brown.

Said, Abdul A., and Collier, Daniel M. 1971. *Revolutionism*. Boston: Allyen & Bacon.

Schafer, Stephen. 1974. *The Political Criminal: The Problem of Morality and Crime*. New York: The Free Press.

Schlissel, Lillian, ed. 1968. *Conscience in America: A Documentary History of Conscientious Objection in America, 1757–1967*. New York: Dutton.

Schmidt, Karl M., and Lieden, Carl, eds. 1968. *The Politics of Violence: Revolution in the Modern World*. Englewood Cliffs, N.J.: Prentice-Hall.

Shearer, Ivan A. 1971. *Extradition in International Law*. Manchester: Manchester University Press.

Shoham, Shlomo. 1966. *Crime and Social Deviation*. Chicago: Henry Regnery.

Shuman, Samuel I., ed. 1971. *Law and Disorder: The Legitimation of Direct Action as an Instrument of Social Policy*. Detroit: Wayne State University Press.

Singer, Peter. 1973. *Democracy and Disobedience*. Oxford: Clarendon Press.

Sinha, S. Prakash. 1971. *Asylum and International Law*. The Hague: Maratinus Nijhoff.

Sink, John M. 1974. *Political Criminal Trials: How to Defend Them*. New York: Clark Boardman.

Skolnick, Jerome H. 1970. *The Politics of Protest*. New York: Ballantine Books.

Sorokin, Pitirim. 1937. *Social and Cultural Dynamics: Fluctuations of Social Relationships and Revolutions*. New York: American Book.

Taylor, Telford. 1961. *Grand Inquest*. New York: Ballantine Books.

Thibaut, John, and Walker, Laurens. 1975. *Procedural Justice*. New York: Lawrence Erlbaum.

Thoreau, Henry David. 1968. *"Walden" and the "Essay on Civil Disobedience."* New York: Lancer Books.

Tunnell, Kenneth D., ed. 1993. *Political Crime in Contemporary America*, N.Y.: Garland Publishing.

Turk, Austin T. 1982. *Political Criminality*. Beverly Hills, Calif.: Sage.

Ulam, Adam B. 1960. *The Unfinished Revolution*. New York: Random House.

van den Wijngaert, Christine. 1980. *The Political Offense Exception to Extradition: The Delicate Problem of Balancing the Rights of the Individual and the International Public Order*. Boston: Kluwer, Deventer.

Von der Mehden, Fred R. 1973. *Comparative Political Violence*. Englewood Cliffs, N.J.: Prentice-Hall.

Walzer, Michael. 1973. *Just and Unjust War*. New York: Basic Books.

_____. 1970. *Obligations: Essays on Disobedience, War and Citizenship*. New York: Clarion Book, Simon Schuster.

Weber, Max. 1947. *Max Weber, The Theory of Social and Economic Organization*. New York: Oxford University Press.

Weyl, Nathaniel. 1951. *The Battle Against Disloyalty*. New York: Thomas Y. Cromwell.

_____. 1950. *Treason: The Story of Disloyalty and Betrayal in American History*. Washington, D.C.: Public Affairs Press.

Wilkinson, P. 1988. *Contemporary Research on Terrorism*. Aberdeen: Aberdeen University Press.

Woetzel, Robert K. 1962. *The Nuremberg Trials in International Law*. London: Stevens & Sons.

Wolff, Robert Paul. 1970. *In Defense of Anarchism*. New York: Harper Torchbooks.

Zinn, Howard. 1968. *Disobedience and Democracy*. New York: Random House.

Index